THE DAILY STUDY BIBLE

THE GOSPEL OF MARK

D1335375

THE GOSPEL OF MARK

The Rev. WILLIAM BARCLAY, D.D.

*Professor of Divinity and Biblical Criticism at the
University of Glasgow.*

THE SAINT ANDREW PRESS
EDINBURGH

Published by The Saint Andrew Press
121 George Street, Edinburgh
and printed in Scotland by
Robert MacLehose & Company Limited
The University Press, Glasgow

First Edition - September, 1954
Second Edition - January, 1956
Reprinted September 1957, October 1958, May
1960, April 1961, November 1962, November
1964, March 1965, September 1966, May 1969,
February 1971, December 1971, May 1973,
April 1974

ISBN 0 7152 0081 X

GENERAL INTRODUCTION

IT may truly be said that this series of Daily Bible Studies began almost accidentally. A series which the Church of Scotland was using came to an end, and another series was immediately required. I was asked to write a volume on *Acts*, and, at the moment, had no intention beyond that. But one volume followed another, until the demand for one volume became a plan to write on the whole New Testament.

The translation which is given in each volume claims no special merit. It was included in order that the reader might be able to carry both the text of the New Testament and the comments on it wherever he went, and that he might be able to read it anywhere. While I was making the translation, the translations of Moffatt, Weymouth, and Knox were ever beside me. *The American Revised Standard Version*, *The Twentieth Century New Testament*, and *The New Testament in Plain English*, by Charles Kingsley Williams, have been in constant use. Since its publication, I have consistently consulted *The Authentic New Testament*, translated by Hugh J. Schonfield.

I cannot see another edition of these books going out to the public without expressing my very deep and sincere gratitude to the Church of Scotland Publications Committee for allowing me the privilege of first beginning, and then continuing, this series. And in particular I wish to express my very great gratitude to the convener, Rev. R. G. Macdonald, O.B.E., M.A., D.D., and to the committee's secretary and manager, Rev. Andrew McCosh, M.A., S.T.M., for constant encouragement and never-failing sympathy and help.

As these volumes went on, the idea of the whole series developed. The aim is to make the results of modern scholarship available to the non-technical reader in a form that it does not require a theological education to understand; and then to seek to make the teaching of the New Testament books relevant to life and work to-day. The whole aim of these books is summed up in Richard of Chichester's famous prayer; they are meant to enable men and women to know Jesus Christ more clearly, to love Him more dearly, and to follow Him more nearly. It is my prayer that they may do something to make that possible.

FOREWORD

THERE are many debts which I must acknowledge. It so happens that the *Gospel according to St. Mark* has been most fortunate in its commentators, and the material to draw upon is immense and valuable. For once the International Critical Commentary fails us, for the volume on *Mark* in that series by Ezra P. Gould is long out of date, and was in any event a sadly inadequate work. Of commentaries which require little or no Greek, the volume on *Mark* in the Clarendon Bible is characteristically excellent. That by A. E. J. Rawlinson in the Westminster Commentary is one of the best commentaries in the English language. The volume in the Moffatt Commentary by B. Harvie Branscomb is not quite so helpful for the general reader as most of the volumes in that invaluable series are. Two of the newest works on *Mark*, *The Gospel according to St. Mark*, by R. H. Lightfoot, and *A Study in Mark*, by Austin Farrer, are works for the scholar rather than for the general reader. On the Greek text there are two of the greatest of all commentaries. That by H. B. Swete in the Macmillan Commentary was published as long ago as 1898, but is still indispensable. Lastly there is that monument of scholarship, the commentary on *Mark*, published in 1952 by Dr. Vincent Taylor, which is fit to rank with the great commentaries of all time.

For myself I have rediscovered how great a work Mark's Gospel is. " Art," said the Roman critic, " lies in concealing art," and it is only when one lives with Mark and studies him for months at a time that one realizes how consummate an artist he was.

It is my hope and prayer that this book will not only enable its readers to know Mark's Gospel a little better, but that it may bring them a little closer to that Lord and Saviour whose life Mark sought to write.

TRINITY COLLEGE, GLASGOW.
November, 1955.   WILLIAM BARCLAY.

THE GOSPEL OF MARK

CONTENTS

THE GOSPEL OF MARK

CONTENTS

THE GOSPEL OF MARK

CONTENTS

xi

THE GOSPEL OF MARK

CONTENTS

INTRODUCTION
TO THE GOSPEL ACCORDING TO SAINT MARK

The Synoptic Gospels

The first three gospels, Matthew, Mark and Luke, are always known as the Synoptic Gospels. The word *synoptic* comes from two Greek words which mean *to see together* ; and these three gospels are called the Synoptic Gospels because they can be set down in parallel columns, and their common matter can be looked at together. It would be possible to argue that of them all Mark's gospel is the most important. It would indeed be possible to go further and to argue that Mark's gospel is the most important book in the world, because it is agreed by nearly everyone that Mark is the earliest of all the gospels, and is therefore the first life of Jesus that has come down to us. Mark may not have been the first man to write the life of Jesus. Doubtless there were simple attempts to set down the story of Jesus' life ; but his gospel is certainly the earliest life of Jesus which has come down to us.

The Pedigree of the Gospels

When we think how the gospels came to be written we must try to think ourselves back to a time when there was no such thing as a printed book in all the world. The gospels were written long before printing had been invented; they were written when every book had to be carefully and laboriously written out by hand. It is clear that so long as that was the case only a very limited number of copies of any book could exist. How do we know, or, how can we deduce, that Mark was the first of all the gospels? When we read the gospels even in English we see that there are remarkable similarities between them. They contain the same incidents often told in the same words ; and they contain accounts of the teaching of Jesus which are often almost identical. If we compare the story of the Feeding of the Five Thousand in the three gospels (Mark 6 : 30-44 ; Matthew 14 : 12-21 ; Luke 9 : 10-17) we see that it is told in almost exactly the same words and in exactly the same way. A very clear instance of this is the story of the healing of the man who was sick of the palsy (Mark 2 : 1-12 ; Matthew 9 : 1-8 ; Luke 5 : 17-26). These three accounts are so very similar that even a little parenthesis—" then saith he to the sick of the palsy "—occurs in all three in exactly the same place. The correspondences between the three gospels are so close that we are forced to one of two conclusions. Either, all three are taking their material from some common source, or, two of the three are based on the third.

When we come to study the matter closely we find that Mark can be divided into 105 sections. Of these 105 sections 93 occur in Matthew and 81 in Luke. Only four are not included either in Mark or in Luke. What is even more compelling is this. Mark has 661 verses ; Matthew has 1,068 verses ; Luke has 1,149 verses. Of Mark's 661 verses Matthew reproduces no fewer than 606. Sometimes he alters the wording slightly but he even reproduces 51 per cent. of Mark's actual words. Of Mark's 661 verses Luke reproduces 320, and he actually uses 53 per cent. of Mark's actual words. Of the 55 verses of Mark which Matthew does not reproduce 31 are found in Luke. So the result is that there are only 24 verses in Mark which do not occur somewhere in Matthew and Luke. This makes it look very like as if Matthew and Luke were using Mark as the basis of their gospels. What makes the matter still more certain is this. Both Matthew and Luke very largely follow Mark's order of events. Sometimes Matthew alters Mark's order and sometimes Luke does. But when there is a change in the order Matthew and Luke *never* agree together as against Mark. Always one of them retains Mark's order of events. A close examination of the three gospels makes it clear that Matthew and Luke had Mark

before them as they wrote ; and they used his gospel as
the basis into which they fitted the extra material which
they wished to include.

It is a thrilling thing to remember that when we read
Mark's gospel we are reading the first life of Jesus, the life
of Jesus on which all succeeding lives ever since have
necessarily been based.

Mark, the Writer of the Gospel

Who then was this Mark who wrote the gospel? The
New Testament tells us a good deal about him. He was
the son of a well-to-do lady of Jerusalem whose name was
Mary, and whose house was a rallying-point and meeting
place of the Early Church (Acts 12 : 12). From the very
beginning Mark was brought up in the very centre of the
Christian fellowship. Mark was also the nephew of
Barnabas, and when Paul and Barnabas set out on their
first missionary journey they took Mark with them to be
their secretary and attendant (Acts 12 : 25). This journey
was a most unfortunate one for Mark. When they reached
Perga Paul proposed to strike inland up to the central
plateau ; and for some reason Mark left the expedition and
went home (Acts 13 : 13). He may have gone home because
he was scared to face the dangers of what was notoriously
one of the most difficult and dangerous roads in the world,
a road hard to travel, and haunted by brigands and bandits.
He may have gone home because it was increasingly clear
that the leadership of the expedition was being assumed
by Paul, and Mark may have felt with disapproval that
his uncle was being pushed into the background. He may
have gone home because he did not approve of the work
which Paul was doing. Chrysostom—perhaps with a flash
of imaginative insight—says that Mark went home because
he wanted his mother ! Paul and Barnabas completed
their first missionary journey and then proposed to set out
upon their second. Barnabas was anxious to take Mark
with them again. But Paul refused to have anything to

do with the man " who had played the quitter on them at Pamphylia." (Acts 15 : 37-40.) So serious was the difference between them that Paul and Barnabas split company, and, so far as we know, never worked together again. For some years Mark vanishes from history. Tradition has it that he went down to Egypt and founded the Church of Alexandria there. Whether or not that is true we do not know, but we do know that when Mark re-emerges it is in the most surprising way. We learn to our surprise that when Paul wrote the letter to the Colossians from prison in Rome Mark is there with him (Colossians 4 : 10). In another prison letter, Philemon, Paul numbers Mark among his fellow-labourers (verse 24). And, when Paul was waiting for death and very near the end, he wrote to Timothy, his right-hand man, and said, " Take Mark and bring him with you ; for he is a most useful servant to me." (2 Timothy 4 : 11.) It is a far cry from the time when Paul contemptuously dismissed Mark as the quitter. Whatever had happened Mark had earned the title of " the man who had redeemed himself." The one man Paul wanted at the end was Mark.

Mark's Sources of Information

The value of any man's story will depend on the sources of his information. So, we must ask, where did Mark get his information about the life and work of Jesus? We have seen that Mark's home was from the beginning a Christian centre of Jerusalem. Many a time he must have heard people tell of their personal memories of Jesus. But it is most likely that Mark had a source of information than which none could be better. Towards the end of the second century there was a man called Papias who liked to obtain and transmit such information as he could glean about the early days of the Church. Papias tells us that Mark's gospel is nothing other than a record of the preaching material of Peter, the greatest of the apostles. Certainly Mark stood so close to Peter, and so near to his heart, that

Peter could call him " Mark, my son." (I Peter 5 : 13.)
Here is what Papias says :

> " Mark, who was Peter's interpreter, wrote down
> accurately, though not in order, all that he recollected
> of what Christ had said or done. For he was not a
> hearer of the Lord or a follower of His. He followed
> Peter, as I have said, at a later date, and Peter
> adapted his instruction to practical needs, without
> any attempt to give the Lord's words systematically.
> So that Mark was not wrong in writing down some
> things in this way from memory, for his one concern
> was neither to omit nor to falsify anything that he
> had heard."

We may then take it that in Mark's gospel we have what
Mark remembered of the preaching material of Peter
himself.

So, when, we have two great reasons why Mark is a book
of supreme importance. First, it is the earliest of all the
gospels. If it was written just shortly after Peter died its
date will be about A.D. 65 ; and, second, it embodies
nothing less than the record of what Peter preached and
taught about Jesus. We may put it this way—Mark is
the nearest approach we will ever possess to an eye-witness
account of the life of Jesus.

The Lost Ending

There is one very interesting thing about Mark's gospel.
In its original form the gospel stops at Mark 16 : 8. We
know that for two reasons. First, the verses which
follow (Mark 16 : 9-20) are not in any of the great early
manuscripts. It is only later and inferior manuscripts
which contain them. Second, the style of the Greek is
quite different, so different that they cannot have been
written by the same person who wrote the gospel. But the
gospel cannot have been *meant* to stop at Mark 16 : 8.
What then happened? It may be that Mark died, perhaps

he even suffered martyrdom, before he could complete his gospel. Perhaps, more likely, it may be that at one time only one copy of the gospel remained, and that, a copy in which the last part of the roll on which it was written had got torn off. There was a time when the Church did not much use Mark. They preferred Matthew and Luke and neglected Mark. And it may well be that Mark's gospel was so neglected that all the copies but one mutilated one were lost. If that is so we were within an ace of losing the gospel which in many ways is the most important gospel of all.

The Characteristics of Mark's Gospel

Now let us look at the characteristics of Mark's gospel so that we may watch for them as we read and study it.

(i) Mark's gospel is the nearest thing we will ever get to a report of Jesus' life. His aim was to give a picture of Jesus as He was. Westcott called it " a transcript from life." A. B. Bruce said that it was written " from the viewpoint of loving, vivid recollection," and that its great characteristic was *realism*. If ever we are to get anything approaching a biography of Jesus, it must be based on Mark, for it is the delight of Mark to tell the facts of Jesus' life in the simplest and the most dramatic way.

(ii) Mark never forgot the divine side of Jesus. He begins his gospel with the declaration of faith, " The beginning of the gospel of Jesus Christ, the Son of God." He leaves us in no doubt about what he believed Jesus to be. Again and again Mark speaks of the impact that Jesus made on the mind and heart of those who heard Him. The awe and astonishment which He evoked are always before Mark's mind. " They were astonished at His doctrine." (1 : 22.) " They were all amazed." (1 : 27.) Such phrases occur again and again. Not only was this astonishment in the minds of the crowds who listened to Jesus ; it was still more in the minds of the inner circle of the disciples. " They feared exceedingly and said one to another, ' What manner

xviii

of man is this? ' " (4 : 41). " They were sore amazed in themselves beyond measure and wondered." (6 : 51.) " The disciples were astonished at His words." (10 : 24, 26.) To Mark Jesus was not simply a man among men ; He was God among men, ever moving men's minds to a wondering amazement with His words and deeds.

(iii) At the same time, there is no gospel which gives such a human picture of Jesus. In fact sometimes Mark's picture is so human that the later gospel writers alter it a little because they were almost afraid to say what Mark said. To Mark Jesus is simply " the carpenter." (6 : 3.) Later Matthew alters that to " the carpenter's son " (Matthew 13 : 55), as if to call Jesus a village tradesman is too daring a thing. When Mark is telling of the temptations of Jesus, he writes, " The Spirit *driveth* Him into the wilderness." (1 : 12.) Matthew and Luke do not like this word *drive* used of Jesus, so they soften it down and they say, " Jesus was *led* of the Spirit into the wilderness." (Matthew 4 : 1 ; Luke 4 : 1.) No one tells us so much about the emotions of Jesus as Mark does. Jesus sighed deeply in His spirit (7 : 34 ; 8 : 12). He was moved with compassion (6 : 34). He marvelled at their unbelief (6 : 6). He was moved with righteous anger (3 : 5 ; 8 : 33 ; 10 : 14). Only Mark tells us that when Jesus looked at the rich, young ruler He loved him (10 : 21). Jesus could feel the pangs of hunger (11 : 12). He could be tired and want to rest (6 : 31). It is in Mark's gospel, above all, that we get a picture of a Jesus who was of like passions with us. The sheer humanity of Jesus in Mark's picture of Him brings Him very near to us.

(iv) One of the great characteristics of Mark is that over and over again he inserts little vivid details into the narrative which are the hall-mark of an eye witness. Both Matthew and Mark tell of Jesus taking the little child and setting him in the midst. Matthew (18 : 2) says, "And Jesus called a little child unto Him and set him in the midst of them." Mark adds something which lights up the whole picture (9 : 36). "And He took a child and set him in the midst of them ; and, *when He had taken him up in His arms,* He said unto them . . ." In the lovely picture of Jesus and the children, when Jesus rebuked the disciples for keeping the children from Him, only Mark finishes, "*and He took them up in His arms and put His hands on them and blessed them.*" (Mark 10 : 13-16 ; cp. Matthew 19: 13-15 ; Luke 18 : 15-17.) All the tenderness of Jesus is in these little vivid additions. When Mark is telling of the Feeding of the Five Thousand he alone tells how they sat down *in hundreds and in fifties,* and how they looked like vegetable beds in a garden (6 : 40) and immediately the whole scene rises before us. When Jesus and His disciples were on the last journey to Jerusalem, only Mark tells us, "*and Jesus went before them.*" (10 : 32 ; cp. Matthew 20 : 17 ; Luke 18 : 31) ; and in that one vivid little phrase all the loneliness of Jesus stands out. When Mark is telling the story of the stilling of the storm he has one little sentence that none of the other gospel-writers have. "And He was in the hinder part of the ship *asleep on a pillow*" (4 : 38). And that one touch makes the picture vivid before our eyes. There can be little doubt that all these details are due to the fact that Peter was an eye-witness, and he was seeing these things again with the eye of memory.

(v) Mark's realism and his simplicity come out in his Greek style. (*a*) His style is not carefully wrought and polished. He tells the story as a child might tell it. He adds statement to statement connecting them simply with the word " and." In the third chapter of the gospel, in the Greek, there are 34 clauses or sentences one after another introduced by " and " after one principal verb. It is the way in which an eager child would tell the story. (*b*) Mark is very fond of the words " and straightway," " and immediately." They occur in the gospel almost 30 times. It is sometimes said of a story that " it marches." But Mark's story does not so much march ; it rushes on in a kind of breathless attempt to make the story as vivid to others as it was to himself. (c) Mark is very fond of the historic present. That is to say, he talks of events in the present tense instead of in the past. "And when Jesus heard it, He *says* to them, ' Those who are strong do not need a doctor, but those who are ill '." (2 : 17.) "And when they *come* near to Jerusalem, to Bethphage and to Bethany, to the Mount of Olives, He *sends* two of His disciples, and *says* to them, ' Go into the village opposite you . . .'." (11 : 1, 2.) "And immediately, while He was still speaking, Judas, one of The Twelve, *comes*." (14 : 43.) We know well that that is the way in which many a simple person tells a story. Generally speaking we do not keep these historic presents in translation because in English they do not sound well ; but they show how vivid and real the thing was to Mark's mind, as if it was happening before his very eyes. (d) Mark quite often gives us the very Aramaic words which Jesus spoke. To Jairus' daughter, Jesus said, " *Talitha cumi.*" (5 : 41.) To the deaf man with the impediment in his speech Jesus said, " *Ephphatha.*" (7 : 34.) The dedicated gift is " *Korban.*" (7 : 11.) In the Garden Jesus says, "*Abba*, Father." (14 : 36.) On the Cross He cries, " *Eloi Eloi lama sabachthani?* " (15 : 34.) There were times when Peter could hear again the very sound of Jesus' voice speaking, and could not help giving the thing in the very words that Jesus spoke.

The Essential Gospel

It would not be unfair to call Mark *the essential gospel*. We will do well to study with loving care the earliest gospel we possess, the gospel where we hear again the preaching of Peter himself.

MARK

THE BEGINNING OF THE STORY

Mark I: I-4

> This is the beginning of the story of how Jesus Christ, the Son of God, brought the good news to men. There is a passage in Isaiah the prophet like this—" Lo! I send my messenger before you and he will prepare your road for you." " He will be like a voice crying in the wilderness, ' Get ready the road of the Lord. Make straight the path by which he will come '." This came true when John the Baptizer emerged in the wilderness, announcing a baptism which was the sign of a repentance through which a man might find forgiveness for his sins.

MARK starts the story of Jesus a long way back. The story of Jesus did not begin with His own birth upon earth ; it did not even begin with the emergence of John the Baptizer in the wilderness; it began with the dreams of the prophets long ago; that is to say that it began long, long ago in the mind of God. The Stoics were strong believers in the ordered plan of God. " The things of God," said Marcus Aurelius, " are full of foresight. All things flow from heaven." There are things we may well learn here.

(i) It has been said that " the thoughts of youth are long, long thoughts," and so are the thoughts of God. God is characteristically a God who is working His purposes out. History is not a random kaleidoscope of disconnected events; it is a process directed by the God who seas the end in the beginning.

(ii) We are within that process, and because of that we can either help or hinder it. In one sense it is as great an honour to help in some great process as it is a privilege to see the ultimate goal. Life would be very different if instead of yearning for some distant and at present unattainable goal, we did all that we could to bring that goal nearer every day.

I

" In youth, because I could not be a singer,
I did not even try to write a song;
I set no little trees along the roadside,
Because I knew their growth would take so long.

But now from wisdom that the years have brought
me,
I know that it may be a blessed thing
To plant a tree for someone else to water,
Or make a song for someone else to sing."

The goal will never be reached unless there are those who labour to make it possible.

The prophetic quotation which Mark uses is suggestive.

I send my messenger before you and he will prepare your road for you. This is from Malachi 3: 1. In its original context it is a threat. In Malachi's day the priests were failing in their duty. The offerings were blemished and shoddy second-bests; the service of the temple was to them a weariness. The messenger was to come *to cleanse and purify* the worship of the temple before The Anointed One of God emerged upon the earth. So then the coming of Christ is a *purification of life.* And the world needed that purification. Seneca called Rome " a cesspool of iniquity." Juvenal spoke of her " as the filthy sewer into which flowed the abominable dregs of every Syrian and Achaean stream." Wherever Christianity comes it brings purification.

That happens to be a fact capable of factual demonstration. Bruce Barton tells how the first important journalistic assignment that fell to him was to write a series of articles designed to expose Billy Sunday, the evangelist. Three towns were chosen. " I talked to the merchants," Bruce Barton writes, " and they told me that during the meetings and afterward people walked up to the counter and paid bills which were so old that they had long since been written off the books." He went to visit the president of the chamber of commerce of a town that Billy Sunday had visited three years before. " I am not a member of any church," he said. " I never attend but

I'll tell you one thing. If it was proposed now to bring Billy Sunday to this town, and if we knew as much about the results of his work in advance as we do now, and if the churches would not raise the necessary funds to bring him, I could raise the money in half a day from men who never go to church. He took eleven thousand dollars out of here, but a circus comes here and takes out that amount in one day and leaves nothing. He left a different moral atmosphere." The exposure that Bruce Barton meant to write became a tribute to the cleansing power of the Christian message. When Billy Graham preached in Shreveport, Louisiana, liquor sales dropped by 40 per cent. and the sale of Bibles increased 300 per cent. During a mission in Seattle, amongst the results there is stated quite simply, " Several impending divorce actions were cancelled." In Greensboro, North Carolina, the report was that " the entire social structure of the city was affected." One of the great stories of what Christianity can do comes from the history of the mutiny of the *Bounty*. The mutineers from that ship were put ashore on Pitcairn Island. There were nine mutineers, six native men, ten native women and a girl, fifteen years old. One of them succeeded in making crude alcohol. A terrible situation ensued. They all died except Alexander Smith. Smith chanced upon a Bible. He read it and he made up his mind to build up a state with the natives of that island based directly on the Bible; whatever it said, they would do. It was twenty years before an American sloop called at the island. They found a completely Christian community. There was no gaol because there was no crime. There was no hospital because there was no disease. There was no asylum because there was no insanity. There was no illiteracy; and nowhere in the world was human life and property so safe. Christianity had cleansed that society. Where Christ is allowed to come the antiseptic of the Christian faith cleanses the moral poison of society and leaves it pure and clean.

John came announcing *a baptism of repentance*. The Jew was familiar with ritual washings. Leviticus 11—15 details them. " The Jew," said Tertullian, " washes himself every day because every day he is defiled." Symbolic washing and purifying was woven into the very fabric of Jewish ritual. Now a Gentile was necessarily unclean for the Gentile had never kept any part of the Jewish law. Therefore, when a Gentile became a *proselyte*, that is a convert to the Jewish faith, he had to undergo three things. First, he had to undergo *circumsion*, for that was the mark of the covenant people ; second, *sacrifice* had to be made for him, for a Gentile, as such, stood in need of atonement and only blood could atone for sin ; third, he had to undergo *baptism*, which symbolized his cleansing from all the pollution of his past life. Very naturally therefore the baptism was not a mere sprinkling with water, but a bath in which his whole body was bathed. The Jew knew baptism ; but the amazing thing about John's baptism was that he, a Jew, was asking Jews to submit to that which only a Gentile was supposed to submit to. John had made the tremendous discovery that to be a Jew in the racial sense was not to be a member of God's chosen people ; a Jew might be in exactly the same position as a Gentile ; not the Jewish life, but the cleansed life belonged to God.

The baptism was accompanied by *confession*. In any act of return to God confession must be made to three different people.

(i) A man must make confession to *himself*. It is a part of human nature that we shut our eyes to what we do not wish to see, and above all for that very reason we shut our eyes to our own sins. Someone tells of a man's first step to grace. As he was shaving one morning he looked at his own face in the mirror, and suddenly said, " You dirty, little rat ! " And from that day he began to be a changed man. No doubt when the prodigal son left home he thought himself a fine and adventurous character. Before he took his first step home he had to take a good look at himself and say, " I will get up and go home and say that I am an utter rotter." (Luke 15 : 17, 18.) There is no one in all the world harder to face than ourselves ; and the first step to repentance and to a right relationship to God is to admit our own sin to ourselves.

(ii) A man must make confession *to those whom he has wronged*. It will not be much use saying to God that we are sorry until we say we are sorry to those whom we have hurt and injured and grieved. The human barriers have to be removed before the divine barriers can be removed. In the revival in the East African Church, confession of sin has been a characteristic emergence. A husband and wife were members of one group. One of them came and at confession confessed that there was a quarrel at home. The native minister at once said, " You should not have come and confessed that quarrel at all just now ; you should have made it up and *then* come and confessed it." It can often be the case that confession to God is easier than confession to men. But there can be no forgiveness without humiliation.

(iii) A man must make confession to *God*. The end of pride is the beginning of forgiveness. It is when a man says, " I have sinned," that God gets the chance to say, " I forgive." It is not the man who desires to meet God on equal terms who will discover forgiveness, but the man who kneels in humble contrition and whispers through his shame, " God be merciful to me a sinner."

THE HERALD OF THE KING.

Mark 1 : 5-8

And the whole country of Judea went out to him, and so did all the people of Jerusalem, and they were baptized by him in the River Jordan, while they confessed their sins. John was clad in a garment of camel's hair, and he had a leather girdle round his waist, and it was his custom to eat locusts and wild honey. The burden of his proclamation was, "The one who is stronger than I is coming after me. I am not fit to stoop down and to loosen the strap of his sandals. I have baptized you with water, but He will baptize you with the Holy Spirit."

IT is clear that the ministry of John was mightily effective, for they flocked out to listen to him and to submit to his baptism. Why was it that John made an impact such as this upon his nation ?

(i) John was a man who lived his message. Not only his words, but also his whole life was a protest. Three things about him marked the reality of his protest against contemporary life. (a) There was the place in which he stayed. He stayed in the wilderness. Between the centre of Judaea and the Dead Sea there lies one of the most terrible deserts in the world. It is a limestone desert ; it looks warped and twisted. It shimmers in the haze of the heat ; the limestone rock is hot and blistering and sounds hollow to the feet as if there was some vast furnace underneath. It moves out to the Dead Sea and then descends in dreadful and unscalable precipices down to the level of the sea. In the Old Testament it is sometimes called *Jeshimmon*, which means *The Devastation*. John was no city-dweller. He was a man from the desert and from its solitudes and its desolations. Clearly he was a man who had given himself a chance to hear the voice of God. (b) There were the clothes he wore. He wore a garment woven of camel's hair and a leather belt about his waist. So did Elijah (2 Kings I : 8). To look at the man was to be reminded, not of the fashionable orators of the day, but of the ancient prophets who lived close to the great simplicities and avoided the soft and effeminate luxuries which kill the soul. (c) There was the food he ate. Locusts and wild honey were his food. It so happens that both words are capable of two interpretations. The locusts can be the animals for the law allowed them to be eaten (Leviticus

II : 22, 23) ; but they can also be a kind of bean or nut, the *carob*, which was the food of the poorest of the poor. The honey can be the honey the wild bees made in some hollow tree ; or it can be a kind of sweet sap that distilled from the bark of certain trees. It does not matter what the words precisely mean. They mean that in any event John's diet was of the simplest fare. So John emerged. People had to listen to a man like that. It was said of Carlyle that " he preached the gospel of silence in twenty volumes." There is many a man who comes with a message which he himself denies. There has been many a man with a very comfortable bank account who preached about not laying up treasures upon earth ; and many a man who extolled the blessings of poverty from a very comfortable home. But in the case of John, the man was the message, and because of that people listened.

(ii) His message was effective because he told people what in their heart of hearts they knew, and he brought them what in the depths of their souls they were waiting for. (a) The Jews had a saying that " if Israel would only keep the law of God perfectly for one day the Kingdom of God would come." When John summoned men to repentance he was confronting them with a choice and a decision that they knew in their heart of hearts they ought to make. Long ago Plato said that education did not consist in telling people new things ; it consisted in extracting from their memories that which they already knew. No message is so effective as that which speaks to a man's own conscience, and that message becomes well-nigh irresistible when it is spoken by a man who obviously has the right to speak. (b) The people of Israel were well aware that for three hundred years the voice of prophecy had been silent. They were waiting for some authentic word from God. And in John they heard it. In every walk of life the expert is recognizable. A famous violinist tells us that no sooner has Toscanini mounted the rostrum than the orchestra feels the authority of this man flowing over them. We recognize at once a doctor who has real skill. We recognize at once a speaker who knows his subject. John had come from God and to hear him was to know it.

(iii) His message was effective because he was completely humble. His own verdict on himself was that he was not fit for the duty of a slave. The sandals were composed simply of leather soles fastened to the foot by straps which passed through the toes. The roads were quite unsurfaced. In dry weather they were dust heaps ; in wet weather rivers of mud. To remove the sandals was the work and office of a slave. John asked for nothing for himself but for everything for the Christ whom he proclaimed. The man's obvious self-forgottenness, his obvious yieldedness, his complete self-effacement, his utter lostness in his message compelled people to listen to him.

(iv) Another way to put the same thing is to say that John's message was effective because he pointed to something and someone beyond himself. He told men that his baptism drenched them in water ; but one was coming who would drench them in the Holy Spirit ; and while water could cleanse a man's body, the Holy Spirit could cleanse a man's life and self and heart. Dr. G. J. Jeffrey often uses a favourite illustration. When we make a telephone call and there is some delay, the operator will often say, " I'm trying to connect you." When the connection has been effected the operator fades out and leaves us in direct contact with the person to whom we wish to speak. John's one aim was not to occupy the centre of the stage himself, but to try to connect men with the one who was greater and stronger than he ; and men listened to him because he pointed, not to himself, but to the one whom all men need.

THE DAY OF DECISION

Mark 1 : 9-11

In those days Jesus came from Nazareth in Galilee and was baptized by John in the Jordan ; and as soon as

He came up out of the water He saw the heavens being riven asunder and the Spirit coming down upon Him, as a dove might come down ; and there came a voice from heaven, " You are my beloved Son ; I am well pleased with you."

To any thinking person the baptism of Jesus presents a problem. John's baptism was a baptism of repentance. It was meant for those who were sorry for their sins and who wished to express their determination to leave them and to have done with them. What had such a baptism to do with Jesus ? Was He not the sinless one, and was not such a baptism quite unnecessary and quite irrelevant as far as He was concerned ? For Jesus the baptism was four things.

(i) It was for Him the moment of *decision*. For thirty years He had stayed in Nazareth. Faithfully He had done the day's work and had discharged His duties to His home. For long He must have been conscious that the time for Him to go out had to come. He must have waited for a sign. For Him the emergence of John was that sign. This, He saw, was the moment when He had to launch out upon His task. In every life there come moments of decision which can be accepted or rejected. To accept them is to succeed in life ; to reject them, or to shirk them, is to fail. As Lowell had it :

" Once to every man and nation comes the moment
    to decide
In the strife of Truth with falsehood, for the good
    or evil side ;
Some great cause, God's new Messiah, offering each
    the bloom or blight,
And the choice goes by for ever 'twixt that darkness
    and that light."

To every man there comes the unreturning decisive moment. As Shakespeare saw it :

" There is a tide in the affairs of men,
Which, taken at the flood, leads on to fortune ;
Omitted, all the voyage of their lives
Is bound in shallows and in miseries."

9

The wasted life, the frustrated life, the discontented life, and often the tragic life is the undecided life. As John Oxenham saw it :

> " To every man there openeth
> A way and ways and a way;
> The high soul treads the high way,
> And the low soul gropes the low,
> And in between on the misty flats,
> The rest drift to and fro."

The drifting life can never be the happy life. Jesus knew when John emerged that the moment of decision had come. Nazareth was peaceful and home was sweet, but He answered the summons and the challenge of God.

(ii) It was for Him the moment of *identification*. It is quite true that Jesus did not need to repent from sin ; but here was a movement of the people back to God ; and with that Godward movement He was determined to identify Himself. A man night himself possess ease and comfort and wealth, but, if he saw the emergence of a movement which was going to bring better things to the downtrodden and the poor and the ill-housed and the over-worked and the under-paid, that is no reason why he should fail to identify himself with it. The really great identification is when a man identifies himself with a movement, not for his own sake, but for the sake of others. In John Bunyan's dream, Christian came in his journeying with Interpreter to the Palace which was heavily guarded and into which it was a battle to seek an entry. At the door there sat the man with the inkhorn taking the names of those who would dare the assault. All were hanging back, then Christian saw " a man of a very stout coun-tenance come up to the man that sat there to write, saying, ' Set down my name, sir '." When great things are afoot the Christian is bound to say, " Set down my name, sir," for that is what Jesus did when He came to be baptized.

(iii) It was for Him the moment of *approval*. No man

lightly leaves his home and sets out on an unknown way.
He must be very sure that he is right. Jesus had decided
on His course of action, and now He was looking for the
seal of the approval of God. In the time of Jesus the Jews
spoke of what they called the *Bath Qol*, which means, *the
daughter of a voice*. By this time they believed in a series of
heavens, in the highest of which God sat in the light to
which no man could approach. There were rare times
when the heavens opened and God spoke ; but, to them,
God was so distant that it was only the far away echo of
the voice of God that they heard. To Jesus the voice of
God came completely directly. As Mark tells the story,
this was a personal experience which Jesus had, and not
in any sense a demonstration to the crowd. The voice did
not say, " This is my beloved Son," as Matthew has it
(Matthew 3 : 17). It said, " You are my beloved Son,"
speaking direct to Jesus. At the baptism Jesus submitted
His decision to God and that decision was unmistakably
approved.

(iv) It was for Him the moment of *equipment*. At that
time the Holy Spirit descended upon Him. Now there is
a certain symbolism here. The Spirit descended as a dove
might descend. The simile is not chosen by accident.
The dove is the symbol of *gentleness*. Both Matthew and
Luke tell us of the preaching of John. (Matthew 3 : 7-12 ;
Luke 3 : 7-13.) John's message was a message of the axe
laid to the root of the tree, of the terrible sifting, of the
consuming fire. It was a message of doom and not a message
of good news. But from the very beginning the picture of
the Spirit likened to a dove is a picture of gentleness. He
will conquer, but the conquest will be the conquest of love.

THE TESTING TIME

Mark 1 : 12, 13

And immediately the Spirit thrust Him into the
wilderness. He was in the wilderness forty days, and

all the time He was being tested by Satan. The wild beasts were His companions, and the angels were helping Him.

No sooner was the glory of the hour of the Baptism over than there came the battle of the temptations. One thing stands out here in such a vivid way that we cannot miss it. It was the *Spirit* who thrust Jesus out into the wilderness for the testing time. That very Spirit which came upon Him at His baptism now drove Him out for His test. In this life it is impossible that we should escape the assault of temptation ; but one thing is sure—temptations are not sent to us to make us fall ; they are sent to us to strengthen the nerve and the sinew of our minds and hearts and souls. They are not meant for our ruin, but for our good. They are meant to be tests from which we emerge better warriors and athletes of God. Suppose a lad is a football player ; suppose he is doing well in the second team and shows real signs of promise, what then will his trainer do ? He certainly will not send him out to play for the third team in which he could walk through the game and never break sweat ; he will send him out to play for the first team where he will be tested as he never was tested before ; he will give him the chance to prove himself in the greater test. That is what temptation is meant to do. It is the test which is given us to prove our manhood and to emerge the stronger for the fight.

Forty days is a phrase which is not to be taken literally It is the regular Hebrew phrase for a considerable time. So Moses was said to be on the mountain with God for forty days (Exodus 24 : 18) ; it was for forty days that Elijah went in the strength of the meal the angel gave him (I Kings 19 : 8). Just as we use the phrase *ten days or so*, so the Hebrews used the phrase *forty days*, not literally, but simply to mean a fair length of time.

It was Satan who tempted and tested Jesus. The development of the conception of Satan is very interesting. The word *Satan* in Hebrew simply means an *adversary* ;

and in the Old Testament it is so used of ordinary human adversaries and opponents again and again. The angel of the Lord is the *satan* who stands in Balaam's way (Numbers 22 : 22) ; the Philistines fear that David may turn out to be their *satan* (I Samuel 29 : 4) ; David regards Abishai as his *satan* (2 Samuel 19 : 22) ; Solomon declares that God has given him such peace and prosperity that he has no *satan* left to oppose him (I Kings 5 : 4). The word began by meaning *an adversary* in the widest sense of the term. But the word takes another step on its downward path ; it begins to mean *one who pleads a case against a person*. It is in this sense that it is used in the first chapter of Job. It is to be noted that in that chapter Satan is no less than one of the sons of God (Job I : 6); but the particular task of Satan was to consider men (Job I : 7) and to search for some case that could be pleaded against them in the presence of God. Satan was the accuser of men before God. The word is so used in Job 2 : 2 and Zechariah 3 : 2. The task of Satan was to say everything that could be said against a man. The other title of Satan is the *Devil* ; the word *devil* comes from the Greek *diabolos*, which literally means *a slanderer*. It is a small step from the thought of one who searches for everything that can be said against a man to the thought of one who deliberately and maliciously slanders man in the presence of God. But in the Old Testament Satan is still an emissary of God and not yet the malignant, supreme enemy of God. He is the *adversary of man*.

But now the word takes the last step on its downward course. Through their captivity the Jews learned something of Persian thought. Persian thought is based on the conception that in this universe there are two powers, a power of the light and a power of the dark, Ormuzd and Ahriman, a power of good and a power of evil ; the whole universe is a battle-ground between them and man must choose his aide in that cosmic conflict. In point of fact that is precisely what life looks like and feels like. To put it in a word, in this world there is God and *God's Adversary*. It was almost inevitable that Satan should come to be regarded as *The Adversary par excellence*. That is what his name means ; that is what he always was to man ; Satan becomes the essence of everything that is against God.

When we turn to the New Testament we find that it is the Devil or Satan who is behind human disease and suffering (Luke 13 : 16) ; it is the Satan who seduces Judas (Luke 22 : 3) ; it is the devil whom we must fight (I Peter 5 : 8, 9 ; James 4 : 7) ; it is the devil whose power is being broken by the work of Christ (Luke 10 : 1-19) ; it is the devil who is destined for final destruction (Matthew 25 : 41). Satan is the power which is against God.

Now here exactly we have the whole essence of the Temptation story. Jesus had to decide how He was to do His work. He was conscious of a tremendous task and He was also conscious of tremendous powers. God was saying to Him, " Take my love to men ; love them till you die for them ; conquer them by this unconquerable love even if you finish up upon a cross." Satan was saying to Jesus, " Use your power to blast men ; obliterate your enemies ; win the world by might and power and bloodshed." God said to Jesus, " Set up a reign of love." Satan said to Jesus, " Set up a dictatorship of force." Jesus had to choose that day between the way of God and the way of the Adversary of God.

Mark's brief story of the Temptations finishes with two vivid touches. (i) *The beasts were His companions.* In the desert there roamed the leopard, the bear, the wild boar and the jackal. This is usually taken to be a vivid detail that adds to the grim terror of the scene. But perhaps it is not so. Perhaps this is a lovely thing, for perhaps it means that the beasts were Jesus' friends. Amidst the dreams of the golden age when the Messiah would come, the Jews dreamed of a day when the enmity between man and the beasts would no longer exist. " In that day I will make a covenant for them with the beasts of the field, and with the fowls of heaven, and with the creeping things of the ground." (Hosea I : 18.) " The wolf shall lie down with the lamb and the leopard shall lie down with the kid. . . . The suckling child shall play on the hole of the asp, the weaned child shall put his hand on the cockatrice' den ; they shall not hurt nor destroy in all my holy mountain." (Isaiah II : 6-9.) In later days St. Francis preached to the beasts ; and it may be that here we have a first foretaste of the loveliness when man and the beasts shall be at peace. It may be that here we see a picture in which the beasts recognized, before men did, their friend and their king. (ii) *The angels were helping Him.* There are ever the divine reinforcements in the hour of trial. When Elisha and his servant were shut up in Dothan with their enemies pressing in upon them and no apparent way of escape, Elisha opened the young man's eyes and all around them were the horses and the chariots of fire which belonged to God. (2 Kings 6 : 17.) Jesus was not left to fight his battle alone—and neither are we.

THE MESSAGE OF THE GOOD NEWS

Mark I : 14, 15

> After John had been committed to prison, Jesus came into Galilee, announcing the good news about God, and saying, " The time that was appointed has come ; and the Kingdom of God is here. Repent and believe the good news."

THERE are in this summary of the message of Jesus three great, dominant words of the Christian faith.

(i) There is *the good news.* It was pre-eminently good news that Jesus came to bring to men. If we follow the word *euaggelion, good news, gospel* through the new Testament we can see at least something of its content. (*a*) It is good news of *truth* (Galatians 2 : 5 ; Colossians I : 5).

Until Jesus came, men could only guess and grope after God. " O that I knew where I might find Him," cried Job (Job 23 : 3). Marcus Aurelius said that the soul can see but dimly, and the word he uses is the Greek word for seeing things through water. But with the coming of Jesus men see clearly what God is like. No longer do they need to guess and grope ; they know. (b) It is good news of *hope* (Colossians 1 : 23). The ancient world was a pessimistic world. Seneca talked of " our helplessness in necessary things." In their struggle for goodness men were defeated. The coming of Jesus brings hope to the hopeless heart. (c) It is good news of *peace* (Ephesians 6 : 15). The penalty of being a man is to have a split personality. In human nature the beast and the angel are strangely intermingled. It is told that once Schopenhauer, the gloomy philosopher, was found wandering. He was asked, " Who are you ? " " I wish you could tell me," he answered. Robert Burns said of himself, " My life reminded me of a ruined temple. What strength, what proportion in some parts ! What unsightly gaps, what prostrate ruins in others ! " Man's trouble has always been that he is haunted both by sin and goodness. The coming of Jesus unifies that disintegrated personality into one. He finds victory over his warring self by being conquered by Jesus Christ. (d) It is good news of God's *promise* (Ephesians 3 : 6). It is true to say that men had always thought rather of a God of threats than a God of promises. All non-Christian religions think of a demanding God ; only Christianity tells of a God who is more ready to give than we are to ask. (e) It is good news of *immortality* (2 Timothy 1 : 10). To the pagan, life was the road to death ; man was characteristically a dying man ; but Jesus came with the good news that we are on the way to life and not to death. (f) It is good news of *salvation* (Ephesians 1 : 13). And that salvation is not merely a negative thing ; it is also a positive thing. It is not simply liberation from penalty and escape from past sin ; it is the power to live life victoriously and to conquer sin. The message of Jesus is good news indeed.

(ii) There is the word *repent*. Now repentance is not so easy as sometimes we think. The Greek word *metanoia* literally means *a change of mind*. We are very apt to confuse two things—sorrow for the consequences of sin, and sorrow for sin. There is many a man who is desperately sorry because of the mess that sin has got him into, but that man very well knows that, if he could be reasonably sure that he could escape the consequences, he would do the same thing again. It is not the sin that he hates ; it is the consequences of the sin. But real repentance means that a man has come, not only to be sorry for the consequences of his sin, but to hate sin itself. Long ago that wise, old writer, Montaigne, wrote in his autobiography, " Children should be taught to hate vice for its own texture, so that they will not only avoid it in action, but abominate it in their hearts—that the very thought of it may disgust them whatever form it takes." Repentance means that the man who was in love with sin comes to hate sin because of its exceeding sinfulness.

(iii) There is the word *believe*. " Believe," says Jesus, in the good news." To believe in the good news simply means to take Jesus at His word, to believe that God is the kind of God that Jesus told us about, to believe that God so loves the world that He will make any sacrifice to bring us back to Himself, to believe that what sounds too good to be true is really true.

JESUS CHOOSES HIS FRIENDS

Mark I : 16-20

> While He was walking beside the Sea of Galilee, He saw Simon and Andrew, Simon's brother, casting their nets into the sea, for they were fishermen. So Jesus said to them, " Follow me ! and I will make you fishers of men." And immediately they left their nets

and followed Him. He went a little farther and He saw James, the son of Zebedee, and John, his brother, who were in their boat, mending their nets. Immediately He called them ; and they left their father Zebedee in the boat, with the hired servants, and went away after Him.

No sooner had Jesus taken His decision and decided His method than he proceeded to build up His staff. A leader must begin somewhere. He must get to himself a little band of kindred souls to whom he can unburden his own heart and on whose hearts he may write his message. So Mark here shows us Jesus literally laying the foundations of His Kingdom, and calling His first followers.

There were many fishermen in Galilee. Josephus, who, for a time, was governor of Galilee, and who is the great historian of the Jews, tells us that in his days three hundred and thirty fishing boats sailed the waters of the lake. Ordinary people in Palestine seldom ate meat ; usually they ate it not more than once a week. Fish was their staple diet (Luke 11 : 11 ; Matthew 7 : 10 ; Mark 6 : 30-44 ; Luke 24 : 42). Usually the fish was salt fish because there was no means of transporting fresh fish. Fresh fish was one of the greatest of all delicacies in the great cities like Rome. The very names of the towns on the lakeside show how important the fishing business was. *Bethsaida* means *House of Fish* ; *Tarichaea*, another of the lake-side towns, means *The Place of Salt Fish*, and it was there that the fish were preserved for export to Jerusalem and even to Rome itself. The salt fish industry was big business in Galilee.

The fishermen used two kinds of nets, both of which are mentioned or implied in the gospels. They used the net called the *sagēnē*. This was a kind of seine—or trawl-net. It was let out from the end of the boat. It was so weighted that it stood, as it were, upright in the water. The boat then moved forward, and, as it moved, the four corners of the net were drawn together, so that the net became like a great bag which was drawn through the water, thus enclosing the fish. The other kind of net, the net which Peter and Andrew were using here, was called the *amphiblēstron*. It was a much smaller net. It was skilfully cast into the water by hand. It was shaped rather like an umbrella, and as it was drawn through the water it caught and enclosed the fish.

It is very naturally of the greatest interest to study the men whom Jesus picked out as His first followers.

(i) We must notice *what they were*. They were simple folk. They did not come from the schools and the colleges ; they were not drawn from the ecclesiastics or the aristocracy ; they were neither learned nor wealthy. They were fishermen. That is to say, they were ordinary people. No one ever believed in the ordinary man as Jesus did. Once George Bernard Shaw said, " I have never had any feeling for the working-classes, except a desire to abolish them, and replace them by sensible people." In *The Patrician* John Galsworthy makes Miltoun, one of the characters, say, " The mob ! How I loathe it ! I hate its mean stupidity, I hate the sound of its voice, and the look on its face—it's so ugly, so little ! " Once in a fit of temper Carlyle declared that there were twenty-seven millions of people in England—mostly fools ! Jesus did not feel like that. Lincoln said, " God must love the common people— He made so many of them." It was as if Jesus said, " Give me twelve ordinary men and with them, if they will give themselves to me, I will change the world." A man should never think so much of what he is as of what Jesus Christ can make him. A man should never think so much of what he thinks of someone else as of what Jesus thinks of him.

(ii) We must notice *what they were doing* when Jesus called them. They were doing their day's work. They were catching the fish and mending the nets when Jesus called them. It was so with many a prophet. " I was no prophet," said Amos, " neither was I a prophet's son ; but I was an herdman and a gatherer of sycomore fruit ;

and *the Lord took me as I followed the flock*, and said unto me, ' Go, prophesy unto my people Israel '." (Amos 7 : 14, 15.) The call of God can come to a man, not only in the house of God, not only in the secret place, but in the middle of the day's work. As Macandrew, Kipling's Scots engineer, had it :

> " From coupler flange to spindle guide
>   I see Thy hand, O God ;
> Predestination in the stride
>   Of yon connecting rod."

The man who lives in a world that is full of God cannot ever escape God.

(iii) We must notice *how He called them.* Jesus summons was, " Follow me ! " It is not to be thought that on this day for the first time He stood before them. No doubt they had stood in the crowd and listened ; no doubt they had stayed to talk long after the rest of the crowd had drifted away. No doubt they already had felt the magic of His presence and the magnetism of His eyes. But Jesus did not say to them, " I have a theological system which I would like you to investigate ; I have certain theories that I would like you to think over ; I have an ethical system I would like to discuss with you." He said, " Follow me ! " It all began with a personal reaction to Himself ; it all began in that tug on the heart which begets the unshakable loyalty. This is not to say that there are none who think themselves into Christianity ; but it is to say that for most of us following Christ is like falling in love. It has been said that " we admire people for reasons ; we love them without reasons." The thing happens just because they are they and we are we. " I," said Jesus, " if I be lifted up from the earth will draw all men unto me." (John 12 : 32.) In by far the greatest number of cases a man follows Jesus Christ, not because of anything that Jesus said but because of everything that Jesus is.

(iv) Lastly we must note *what Jesus offered them.* He

offered them a task. He called them not to ease but to service. Someone has said that what every man needs is " something in which he can invest his life." So Jesus called His men, not to a comfortable ease and not to a passive and lethargic inactivity ; He called them to a task in which they would have to spend themselves and burn themselves up, and, in the end, die for His sake and for the sake of their fellow men. He called them to a task wherein they could only win something for themselves by giving their all to Him and to others.

JESUS BEGINS HIS CAMPAIGN

Mark I : 21, 22

So they came into Capernaum ; and immediately on the Sabbath day Jesus went into the Synagogue and began to teach ; and they were completely astonished at the way He taught, for He taught them like one who had personal authority, and not as the experts in the law did.

MARK'S story unfolds in a series of logical and natural steps. Jesus recognized in the emergence of John God's call to action. Jesus was baptized and received God's seal of approval and God's equipment for His task. Jesus was tested by the devil and chose the method He would use and the way He would take. Jesus chose His men that He might have a little circle of kindred spirits and that He might write His message upon them. And now Jesus had to make a deliberate launching of His campaign. If a man had a message from God to give, the natural place to which he would turn would be the Church where God's people meet together. That is precisely what Jesus did. He began His campaign in the Synagogue.

There are certain basic differences between the Synagogue and the Church as we know it to-day. (*a*) The Synagogue was primarily *a teaching institution*. The Synagogue service consisted of only three things—prayer, the reading of God's word, and the exposition of it. There was no music, no singing and no sacrifice. It may be said that the *Temple* was the place of *worship and sacrifice* ; the Synagogue was the place of *teaching and instruction*. The Synagogue was by far the more influential, for there was only one Temple— the Temple in Jerusalem. But the law laid it down that wherever there were ten Jewish families there must be a Synagogue, and, therefore, wherever there was a colony of Jews, there was a Synagogue. If a man had a new message to preach the Synagogue was the obvious place in which to preach it. (*b*) Further, the Synagogue did in fact provide an opportunity to deliver such a message. The Synagogue had certain officials. There was *the Ruler of the Synagogue*. He was responsible for the administration of the affairs of the Synagogue and for the arrangements for its services. There were *the distributors of alms*. Daily a collection was taken in cash and in kind from those who could afford to give. It was then distributed to the poor ; the very poorest were given food for fourteen meals per week. There was *the Chazzan*. He is the man whom the Authorised Version describes as *the minister*. He was responsible for the taking out and storing away of the sacred rolls on which scripture was written ; for the cleaning of the Synagogue ; for the blowing of the blasts on the silver trumpet which told people that the Sabbath had come ; for the elementary education of the children of the community. But one thing the Synagogue had not got, and that was a permanent preacher or teacher. When the people met at the Synagogue service it was open to the Ruler of the Synagogue to call on any competent person to give the address, and the exposition. There was no professional ministry whatsoever. That is why Jesus was able to open His campaign in the Synagogues. The opposition had not yet stiffened into hostility. He was known to be a man with a message ; and for that very reason the Synagogue of every community provided Him with a pulpit from which to instruct and to appeal to men.

But when Jesus did teach in the Synagogue the whole method and atmosphere of His teaching was like a new revelation. He did not teach like the scribes, the experts in the law. Who were these scribes ? To the Jews the most sacred thing in the world was *The Torah*, The Law. The core of the law is The Ten Commandments, but the Law was taken to mean the first five books of the Old Testament, The Pentateuch, as they are called. To the Jews this Law was completely divine. It had, so they believed, been given direct by God to Moses. It was absolutely holy and absolutely binding. They said, " He who says that *The Torah* is not from God has not part in the future world." " He who says that Moses wrote even one verse of his own knowledge is a denier and despiser of the word of God." Now, if *The Torah* is so divine two things emerge. First, it must be the supreme rule of faith and life ; and second, it must contain everything necessary to guide and to direct life. If that be so *The Torah* demands two things. First, it must obviously be given the most careful and meticulous study. Second, *The Torah* is expressed in great, wide principles ; but, if *The Torah* contains direction and guidance for *all* life, what is in it implicitly, if not explicitly, must be brought out. The great laws must become rules and regulations—so their argument ran. To give this study and to supply this development a class of scholars arose. These scholars are the *Scribes*, the experts in the law. The title of the greatest of them is the title *Rabbi*. These scribes had three duties. (i) They set themselves out of the great moral principles of *The Torah* to extract rules and regulations for every possible situation in life. They reduced principles to rules and regulations. Obviously this was a task that was literally endless. Jewish religion began with the great moral laws ; it ended with an infinity of rules and regulations. It began as religion ; it ended as legalism. (ii) It was the task of the scribes to transmit and to teach this law and its developments. These deduced and extracted rules and regulations were never

23

written down ; they are known as *The Oral Law*. Although never written down they were considered to be even *more* binding than the written law. From generation to generation of scribes they were taught and committed to memory. A good student had a memory which was like " a well lined with lime which loses not one drop." The Scribes were men who entangled themselves and others in a labyrinth of rules and regulations. Religion became a matter of obeying regulations. (iii) Lastly, the Scribes had the duty of giving judgment in individual cases ; and, in the nature of things, practically every individual case must have produced a new law.

Wherein did Jesus' teaching differ so much from the teaching of the Scribes ? He taught with *personal authority*. No Scribe ever gave a decision on his own. He would always begin, " There is a teaching that . . ." and would then quote all his authorities. If he made a statement he would buttress it with this, that and the next citation or quotation from the great legal masters of the past. The last thing he ever gave was an independent judgment. How different was Jesus ! When Jesus spoke, He spoke as if He needed no authority beyond Himself. He spoke with utter independence. He cited no authorities and quoted no experts. He spoke with the finality of the voice of God. To the people it was like a breeze from heaven to hear someone speak like that. The terrific, positive certainty of Jesus was the very antithesis of the careful quotations of the Scribes. The note of personal authority rang out—and that is a note which captures the ear of every man.

THE FIRST VICTORY OVER THE POWERS OF EVIL

Mark 1 : 23-28

There was in the Synagogue a man in the grip of an unclean spirit. Immediately he broke into a shout. " What have we to do with you, Jesus of Nazareth ? "

he said. "Have you come to destroy us ? I know
who you are—you are The Holy One of God." Jesus
spoke sternly to him. "Be silent," He said, "and
come out of him." When the unclean spirit had convulsed the man and had cried with a great cry it came
out of him. They were all so astonished that they
kept asking each other, "What is this ? This is a
new kind of teaching. He gives His orders with
authority even to unclean spirits and they obey Him."
And immediately the report about Jesus went out
everywhere over the whole surrounding district of
Galilee.

IF Jesus' words had amazed the people in the Synagogue,
His deeds left them thunderstruck and astonished. In the
Synagogue there was a man in the grip of an unclean spirit.
The man created a disturbance and Jesus healed him.
Now all through the gospels we keep meeting these people
who had unclean spirits and who were possessed by demons
or devils. What lies behind this ? The Jews, and indeed
the whole ancient world, believed strongly in demons and
devils. As Harnack put it, "The whole world and the
circumambient atmosphere were filled with devils ; not
merely idolatry, but every phase and form of life was ruled
by them. They sat on thrones, they hovered around
cradles. The earth was literally a hell." Dr. A. Rendle
Short cites a fact which shows the intensity with which the
ancient world believed in demons. In many ancient cemeteries
skulls are found which have been trepanned. That is to say,
a hole has been bored in the skull. In one cemetery out of
one hundred and twenty skulls six had been trepanned.
With the limited surgical technique available that was no
small operation. Further, it was clear from the bone
growth that the trepanning had been done during life.
It was also clear that the hole in the skull was too small
to be of any physical or surgical value ; and it is known
that the removed disc of bone was often worn as an
amulet round the neck. The reason for the trepanning was
to allow the demon to escape from the body of the man.
Now if primitive surgeons were prepared to undertake that

operation, and if men were prepared to undergo it, the belief in demon-possession must have been intensely real.

Where then did these demons come from ? There were three answers to that question. (i) Some believed that they were as old as creation itself. (ii) Some believed that they were the spirits of wicked men who had died and were still carrying on their malignant work. (iii) Most people connected the demons with the old story in Genesis 6 : 1-8 (cp. 2 Peter 2 : 4, 5). The Jews elaborated the story in this way. There were two angels who forsook God and came to this earth because they were attracted by a lust for the beauty of mortal women. Their names were Assael and Shemachsai. One of them returned to God ; one remained on earth and gratified his lust ; and the demons are the children that he begat and their children. The collective word for demons is *mazzikin*, which means *one who does harm*. So the demons were malignant beings intermediate between God and man who were out to work men harm.

The demons, according to Jewish belief, could eat and drink and beget children. They were terrifyingly numerous. There were, according to some, seven and a half million of them ; a man had ten thousand on his right hand and ten thousand on his left. They lived in unclean places, such as tombs and places where there was no cleansing water. They lived in the desert where their howling could be heard—hence the phrase *a howling desert*. They were specially dangerous to the lonely traveller, to the woman in child-birth, to the bride and bridegroom, to children who were out after dark, and to those who voyaged at night. They were specially active in the midday heat and between sunset and sunrise. There was a demon of blindness, and a demon of leprosy and a demon of heart-disease. They could transfer their malign gifts to men. For instance, the evil eye which could turn good fortune into bad and in which all believed was given to a man by the demons. They worked along with certain animals—the serpent,

26

the bull, the donkey and the mosquito. The male demons were known as *shedim*, and the female as *lilin*, after Lilith. The female demons had long hair and were the enemies of children. That is why children had their guardian angels (Matthew 18 : 10).

Now it does not matter whether or not we believe in all this ; whether it is true or not is not the point. The point is that the people in New Testament times did. We still may use the phrase *Poor devil !* That is a relic of the old belief. When a man believed himself to be possessed he was " conscious of himself and also of another being who constrains and controls him from within." That explains why the demon-possessed in Palestine so often cried out when they met Jesus. They knew that Jesus was believed by some at least to be the Messiah ; they knew that the reign of the Messiah was the end of the demons ; and the man who believed himself to be possessed by a demon spoke as a demon when he came into the presence of Jesus. There were many exorcists who claimed to be able to cast out demons. So real was this belief that by A.D. 340 the Christian Church actually possessed an Order of Exorcists. But there was this difference—the ordinary Jewish and pagan exorcist used elaborate incantations, and spells, and magical rites. Jesus with one word of clear, simple, brief authority exorcised the demon from the man. No one had ever seen anything like this before. The power was not in the spell, the formula, the incantation, the elaborate rite ; the power was in Jesus, and men were astonished.

What are we to say to all this ? Paul Tournier in *A Doctor's Casebook* writes, " Doubtless there are many doctors who in their struggle against disease have had, like me, the feeling that they were confronting, not something passive, but a clever and resourceful enemy. Dr. Rendle Short comes tentatively to the conclusion that " the happenings in this world, in fact, and its moral disasters, its wars and wickedness, its physical catastrophes, and its sicknesses, may be part of a great warfare due to the interplay of forces such as we see in the book of Job, the malice of the devil on one hand and the restraints imposed by God on the other.''

This is a subject on which we cannot dogmatize. We may take three different positions. (i) We may relegate the whole matter of demon possession to the sphere of primitive thought. We may say that it was a primitive way of accounting for things in the days before man knew any more about men's bodies and men's minds. (ii) We may accept the fact of demon possession as being true in New Testament times and as being still true to-day. (iii) If we accept the first position we have to explain the attitude and actions of Jesus. Either, He knew no more on this matter than the people of His day, and that is a thing which we can easily accept for Jesus was not a scientist and did not come to teach science. Or, He knew perfectly well that He could never cure the man in trouble unless He assumed the reality of the disease. It was real to the man and had to be treated as real or it could never be cured at all. In the end we come to the conclusion that there are some answers that we do not know.

A PRIVATE MIRACLE

Mark I : 29-31

> And immediately, when they had come out of the Synagogue, they went, along with Peter and John, into the house of Simon and Andrew. Peter's mother-in-law was in bed with an attack of fever. Immediately they spoke to Jesus about her. He went up to her and took her by the hand and raised her up, and the fever left her, and she attended to their needs.

IN the Synagogue Jesus had spoken and had acted in the most amazing way. The Synagogue service ended and Jesus went with His friends to Peter's house. According to Jewish custom the main Sabbath meal came immediately after the Synagogue service, at the sixth hour, that is at

12 o'clock midday. (The Jewish day began at 6 a.m. and the hours are counted from then.) It might well have been that Jesus might have claimed the right to rest after the exciting and exhausting experience that the Synagogue service had brought to Him ; but once again His power was appealed to and once again He had to spend Himself for others. This miracle tells us something about three people.

(i) It tells us something about Jesus. He did not require an audience to exert His power ; He was just as prepared to heal in the little circle of a cottage as in the great crowd of a Synagogue. He was never too tired to help ; the need of others took precedence over His own desire for rest. But above all, we see here, as we saw in the Synagogue, the uniqueness of the methods of Jesus. There were many exorcists in the time of Jesus, but they worked with elaborate incantations, and formulae, and spells, and magical apparatus. In the Synagogue Jesus had spoken one authoritative sentence and the healing was complete. Here we have the same thing again. Peter's mother-in-law was suffering from what the Talmud called " a burning fever." It was, and still is, very prevalent in that particular part of Galilee. The Talmud actually lays down the methods of dealing with it. A knife wholly made of iron was tied by a braid of hair to a thorn bush. On successive days there was repeated, first, Exodus 3 : 2, 3 ; second, Exodus 3 : 4 ; and finally Exodus 3 : 5. Then a certain magical formula was pronounced, and thus the cure was supposed to be achieved. Jesus completely disregarded all the paraphernalia of popular magic, and with a gesture and a word of unique authority and power, He healed the woman. The word that the Greek uses for authority in the previous passage is *exousia* ; and *exousia* was defined as unique knowledge together with unique power ; that is precisely what Jesus possessed, and that is what He was prepared to exercise in a cottage. Paul Tournier, the Christian doctor, writes, " My patients very often say to me, ' I admire the patience with which you listen to everything I tell you.' It is not patience at all, but interest." A miracle to Jesus was not a means of increasing His prestige ; to help was not a laborious and disagreeable duty ; He helped instinctively, because He was supremely interested in all who needed His help.

(ii) It tells us something about *the disciples*. They had not known Jesus long, but even in that short acquaintance-ship they had begun to take all their troubles to Him. Peter's mother-in-law was ill ; the simple home was upset ; and it was for the disciples already the most natural thing in the world to tell Jesus all about it. Paul Tournier tells how one of life's greatest discoveries came to him. He used to visit an old Christian pastor, who never let him go without praying with him. He was struck by the extreme simplicity of the old man's prayers. It seemed just a con-tinuation of an intimate conversation that the old saint was always carrying on with Jesus. Paul Tournier goes on, " When I got back home I talked it over with my wife, and together we asked God to give us also the close fellowship with Jesus the old pastor had. Since then He has been the centre of my devotion and my travelling companion. He takes pleasure in what I do (cp. Eccl. 9 : 7), and concerns Himself with it. He is a friend with whom I can discuss everything that happens in my life. He shares my joy and my pain, my hopes and fears. He is there when a patient speaks to me from his heart, listening to him with me and better than I can. And when the patient is gone I can talk to Him about it." Therein there lies the very essence of the Christian life. As the hymn has it, " Take it to the Lord in prayer." Thus early the disciples had learned that which became the habit of a lifetime—to take all their troubles to Jesus and to ask His help for them.

(iii) It tells us something about *Peter's wife's mother*. No sooner was she healed than she began to attend to their needs. She used her recovered health for renewed service. There is a great Scottish family which has the motto

" Saved to Serve." Jesus helps us that we may help others.

THE BEGINNING OF THE CROWDS

Mark I : 32-34

> When evening had come and when the sun had set, they kept bringing to Him all those who were ill and demon-possessed. The whole city had crowded together to the door ; and He healed many who were ill with various diseases and cast out many demons ; and He forbade the demons to speak because they knew Him.

THE things that Jesus had done in Capernaum could not be concealed. The emergence of so great a new power and authority was not something which could be kept secret. So the evening found Peter's house besieged with crowds seeking Jesus' healing touch. They waited until evening came because the law forbade the carrying of any burden through a town on the Sabbath day (cp. Jeremiah 17 : 24). To have carried such a burden would have been to work and work was forbidden. They had, of course, no clocks or watches in those days ; the Sabbath ran from 6 a.m. to 6 p.m. ; and the law was that the Sabbath was ended and the day had finished when three stars came out in the sky. So the people of Capernaum waited until the sun had set and the stars were out and then they came, carrying their sick, to Jesus ; and He healed them.

Three times we have seen Jesus healing people. First He healed in the Synagogue ; second, He healed in the house of His friends ; and now, third, He healed in the street. Jesus recognized the claim of everyone. It was said of Dr. Johnson that to be in misfortune was to be assured of his friendship and support. Wherever there was trouble Jesus was ready to use His power. He selected neither the place nor the person ; He realized the universal claim of human need.

The people flocked to Jesus because they recognized in

Him a man *who could do things*. There were plenty who could talk and expound and lecture and preach ; but here was one who dealt not in words but in actions. It has been said that " if a man can make a better mousetrap than his neighbours, the public will beat a path to his house even if he lives in the middle of a wood." The person people want is the effective person. Jesus could, and can, pro- duce results.

But there is the beginning of tragedy here. The crowds came, but the crowds came *because they wanted something out of Jesus*. They did not come because they loved Him ; they did not come because they had caught a glimpse of some new vision ; in the last analysis they wanted to use Him. That is what nearly everyone wants to do with God and the Son of God. For one prayer that goes up to God in the days of prosperity ten thousand go up in the time of adversity. Many a man who has never prayed when the sun was shining on life begins to pray when the cold winds come. Someone has said that so many people regard religion as belonging " to the ambulance corps and not to the firing-line of life." Religion to them is a crisis affair. It is only when they have got life into a mess, or when life deals them some knock-out blow that they begin to remember God. It must always remain true that we must all go to Jesus for He alone can give us the things we need for life ; but if that going and these gifts do not produce an answering love and gratitude there is something tragically wrong. God is not someone to be used in the day of misfortune ; He is someone to be loved and remem- bered every day of our lives.

THE QUIET HOUR AND THE CHALLENGE
OF ACTION

Mark I : 35-39

Very early, when it was still night, Jesus rose and went out. He went away to a deserted place and there He was praying. Simon and his friends tracked Him down and said to Him, " They are all searching for you." Jesus said to them, " Let us go somewhere else, to the nearby villages, that I may proclaim the good news there too, for that is why I came forth." So He went to their Synagogues, all over Galilee, proclaiming the good news as He went, and casting out demons.

SIMPLY to read the record of the things that happened at Capernaum is to see that Jesus was left with no time alone at all. Now Jesus knew well that He could not live without God ; that if He was going to be forever giving out, He must be at least sometimes taking in ; that if He was going to spend Himself for others, He must ever and again summon spiritual reinforcements to His aid. That is to say, Jesus knew that He could not live without prayer. In a little book entitled *The Practice of Prayer*, Dr. A. D. Belden has some great definitions of prayer. " Prayer may be defined as the appeal of the soul to God." Not to pray is to be guilty of the incredible folly of ignoring " the possibility of adding God to our resources." " In prayer we give the perfect mind of God an opportunity to feed our mental powers." Jesus knew this ; He knew that if He was to meet men He must first meet God. If prayer was necessary for Jesus, how much more must it be necessary for us ?

But even there they sought Him out. There was no way in which Jesus could shut the door. Once Rose Macaulay, the novelist, said that all she demanded from this life was " a room of her own." That is precisely what Jesus never had. A great doctor has said that the duty of medicine is " sometimes to heal, often to afford relief, and always to bring consolation." That duty was always upon Jesus. It has been said that a doctor's duty is " to help men to live and to die "—and men are always living and dying. It is human nature to try to put up the barriers and to have time and peace to oneself ; that is what Jesus never did. Conscious as He was of His own weariness and exhaustion, He was still more conscious of the insistent cry of human need. So when they came for Him He rose from His knees to meet the challenge of His task. Prayer will never do our work for us ; what it will do is to strengthen us for tasks which must be done.

So Jesus set out on a preaching tour of the Synagogues of Galilee. In Mark this tour is dismissed in one verse, but it must have taken weeks and even months to do it. As He went He *preached* and He *healed*. There were three pairs of things which Jesus never separated. (i) He never separated *words and actions*. He never thought that a work was done when that work was stated ; He never believed that His duty was completed when He had exhorted men to God and to goodness. Always the statement and the exhortation were put into action. Fosdick somewhere tells of a student who bought the best possible books and the best possible equipment, who got a special study chair with a special book-rest to make study easy, and who then sat down in the chair—and went to sleep. The man who deals in words with no actions to follow is very like that.

(ii) He never separated *soul and body*. There have been types of Christianity which spoke as if the body did not matter. But man is *both* soul and body. And the task of Christianity is to redeem the whole man and not just part of him. It is indeed blessedly true that a man may be starving, living in a hovel, in distress and pain and may yet have sweet times with God ; but that is no reason at all for leaving him in such a case. Missions to primitive races do not only take the Bible ; they take education and medicine ; they take the school and the hospital. It is quite wrong to talk about the *social gospel* as if it were an extra, or an addition, or an option, or even a separate part of the Christian message. The Christian message is one message which preaches and works for the good of a man's body and the good of his soul.

(iii) Jesus never separated *earth and heaven*. There are those who are so concerned with heaven that they forget all about earth and so become impractical visionaries and idealists. There are those who are so concerned with earth that they forget about heaven and who limit good to material good. The dream of Jesus was a time when God's will would be done in earth as it is in heaven. (Matthew 6 : 10.) Jesus' dream was a time when earth and heaven would be one.

THE LEPER IS CLEANSED

Mark I : 40-45

A leper came to Him, asking Him to help him and kneeling before Him. " If you are willing to do so," he said, " you are able to cleanse me." Jesus was moved with pity to the depths of His being. He stretched out His hand and touched him. " I am willing," He said, " be cleansed." Immediately the leprosy left him and he was cleansed. Immediately Jesus sent him away with a stern injunction. " See to it," He said to him, " that you tell no man anything about this ; but go and show yourself to the priest, and bring the offering for cleansing which Moses laid down, so that you may prove to them that you really are healed." He went away and began to proclaim the story at length and to spread it all over. The result was that it was not possible for Jesus to come openly into any town, but He had to stay outside in the lonely places ; and they kept coming to Him from all over.

IN the New Testament there is no disease regarded with more terror and pity than the disease of leprosy. When Jesus sent out the Twelve He commanded them, " Heal the sick, cleanse the leper." (Matthew 10 : 8.) The fate of the leper was truly hard. E. W. G. Masterman in his article on leprosy in the *Dictionary of Christ and the Gospels*, from which we have drawn much of the information that follows, says, " No other disease reduces a human being for so many years to so hideous a wreck." Let us look first of all at the facts.

There are three kinds of leprosy. (i) There is *nodular* or *tubercular leprosy*. It begins with an unaccountable lethargy and with unaccountable pains in the joints. Then there appears on the body, especially on the back, symmetrical discoloured patches. On them little nodules form, at first pink, then turning brown. The skin is thickened. The nodules gather specially in the folds of the cheek, the nose, the lips and the forehead. The whole appearance of the face is changed till the man loses his human appearance and looks, as the ancients said, like a lion or a satyr. The nodules grow larger and larger ; they ulcerate and from them there comes a foul discharge. The eye-brows fall out ; the eyes become staring ; the voice becomes hoarse and the breath wheezes because of the ulceration of the vocal chords. The hands and the feet always ulcerate. Slowly the sufferer becomes a mass of ulcerated growths. The average course of the disease is nine years, and it ends in mental decay, coma and ultimately death. The sufferer became utterly repulsive both to himself and to others. (ii) There is *anaesthetic leprosy*. The initial stages are the same ; but in this kind of leprosy the nerve trunks are affected. The infected area loses all sensation. This may happen without the sufferer knowing that it has happened ; and he may not realize that it has happened until he suffers some burning or scalding and finds that there is no pain and no feeling whatsoever where pain ought to be. As the disease develops the injury to the nerves causes discoloured patches and blisters. The muscles waste away ; the tendons contract until the hands become like claws. There is always disfigurement of the finger nails. There ensues chronic ulceration of the feet and of the hands. There comes the progressive loss of fingers and of toes, until in the end a whole hand or a whole foot may drop off. The duration of the disease is anything from twenty to thirty years. It is a kind of terrible and progressive death of the body. (iii) The third kind of leprosy is a type—the commonest of all—where nodular and anaesthetic leprosy are mixed.

That is leprosy proper, and there is no doubt that there

were many lepers like that in Palestine in the time of Jesus. Leprosy is described in Leviticus 13, and from that description it is quite clear that in New Testament times the term *leprosy* was also used to cover other skin diseases. It seems to have been used to include *psoriasis*, a disease which covers the body with white scales, and which would give rise to the phrase " a leper as white as snow." It seems also to have included ring-worm which is still very common in the East. The Hebrew word that is used in Leviticus for leprosy is *tsaraath*. Now Leviticus 13 : 47 speaks of a *tsaraath* of garments, and a *tsaraath* of houses is dealt with in Leviticus 14 : 33. Such a blemish on a garment would be some kind of mould or fungus ; and on a house it would be some kind of dry-rot in the wood or destructive lichen on the stone. The word *tsaraath*, *leprosy* in Jewish thought seems to have covered any kind of creeping skin disease. Very naturally, with medical knowledge in an extremely primitive state, diagnosis did not distinguish between the different kinds of skin disease and included both the deadly and incurable and the non-fatal and comparatively harmless under the one inclusive title.

Any such skin disease rendered the sufferer unclean. He was banished from the fellowship of men ; he must dwell alone outside the camp ; he must go with rent clothes, bared head, a covering upon his upper lip, and as he went he must give warning of his polluted presence with the cry, " Unclean, unclean ! " We may see the same thing in the Middle Ages, which merely applied the Mosaic law. The priest, wearing his stole and carrying a crucifix, led the leper into the church, and read the burial service over him. The leper was a man who was already dead, though still alive. He had to wear a black garment that all might recognize and live in a leper- or lazar-house. He must not come near a church service but might peer through the leper " squint " cut in the walls while the service went on. The leper had not only to bear the physical pain of his disease ; he had to bear the mental anguish and the heart-break of being banished from human society and shunned literally like the plague.

If ever a leper was cured—and real leprosy was incurable, so it is some of the other skin diseases which must be referred to—he had to undergo a complicated ceremony of restoration which is described in Leviticus 14. He was examined by the priest. Two birds were taken and one was killed over running water. In addition there was taken cedar, scarlet and hyssop. These things and the living bird were dipped in the blood of the dead bird and then the live bird was allowed to go free. The man washed himself and his clothes and shaved himself. Seven days then elapsed and he was re-examined. He had then to shave his hair, his head, his eye-brows. Certain sacrifices were made—two male lambs without blemish and one ewe lamb ; three tenth deals of fine flour mingled with oil and one log of oil. The amounts were less for the poor. The restored sufferer was touched on the tip of the right ear, the right thumb and the right great toe with blood and oil. He was finally examined and, if he was clear of the disease, he was allowed to go with a certificate that he was clean.

Here is one of the most revealing pictures of Jesus.

(i) He did not drive away a man who had broken the law. The leper had no right to have spoken to Him at all. Jesus met the desperation of human need with an understanding compassion.

(ii) Jesus stretched out His hand and touched him. Jesus touched the man who was unclean. To Jesus he was not unclean ; he was simply a human soul in desperate need.

(iii) Having cleansed him, Jesus sent him to fulfil the prescribed ritual. Jesus fulfilled the human law and human righteousness. He did not recklessly defy the conventions, but, when need be, submitted to them.

Here we see compassion, power and wisdom all conjoined.

A FAITH THAT WOULD NOT BE DENIED

Mark 2 : 1-6

When, some time afterwards, Jesus had come back to Capernaum, the news went round that He was in a house. Such crowds collected that there was no longer any room left, not even round the door. So He was speaking the word to them. A party arrived bringing to Him a paralysed man carried by four men. When they could not get near Him because of the crowd they unroofed part of the roof of the house in which He was, and when they had dug out part of the roof, they let down the stretcher on which the paralysed man was lying. When Jesus saw their faith, He said to the paralysed man, " Child, your sins are forgiven."

AFTER Jesus had completed His tour of the Synagogues He returned to Capernaum. The news of His coming immediately spread abroad. Life in Palestine was very public. In the morning the door of the house was opened and anyone who wished might come out and in. The door was never shut unless a man deliberately wished for privacy ; an open door meant an open invitation for all to come in. In the humbler houses, such as this must have been, there was no entrance hall ; the door opened direct on to the street. So, in no time, a crowd had filled the house to capacity, and had jammed the pavement round the door ; and they were all eagerly listening to what Jesus had to say. Into this crowd there came four men carrying on a stretcher a friend of theirs who was paralysed. They could not get through the crowd at all, but they were men of resource. The roof of a Palestinian house was flat. It was regularly used as a place of rest and of quiet, and so usually there was an outside stair which ascended to it. The construction of the roof lent itself to what this ingenious four proposed to do. The roof consisted of flat beams laid across from wall to wall, perhaps three feet apart. The space in between the beams was filled with brushwood packed tight with clay. The top was then marled over. Very largely the roof was of earth and often a flourishing crop of grass grew on the roof of a Palestinian house. It was the easiest thing in the world to dig out the filling between two of the beams ; it did not even damage the house very much, and it was easy to repair the breach again. So the four men dug out the filling between two of the beams and let their friend down direct at Jesus feet. When Jesus saw this faith that laughed at barriers He must have smiled an understanding smile. He looked at the man, " Child," He said, " your sins are forgiven."

It may seem an odd way to begin a cure. But in Palestine, in the time of Jesus, it was natural and inevitable. The Jews integrally connected sin and suffering. They argued that if a man was suffering he must have sinned. That is in fact the argument that Job's friends produced. " Who," demanded Eliphaz the Temanite, " ever perished being innocent ? " (Job 4 : 7). The Rabbis had a saying, " There is no sick man healed of his sickness until all his sins have been forgiven him." To this day we get the same idea among primitive peoples. Paul Tournier writes, " Do not missionaries report that disease is a defilement in the eyes of the savage ? Even converts to Christianity do not dare to go to Communion when they are ill, because they consider themselves spurned by God." To the Jews a sick man was a man with whom God was angry. It is still true that a great many illnesses are due to sin ; it is still truer that time and time again they are not due to the sin of the ill man, but to something he has inherited or contracted because of the sin of others. But we do not make that close connection. But the Jews did. Therefore, any Jew would have agreed that forgiveness of sins was a prior condition of cure. But it may well be that there is more than this in this story. The Jews made this connection between illness and sin, and it may well be that, in this case, *the man's conscience agreed*. And it may well be that that consciousness of sin had actually produced the paralysis. The power of mind, especially the sub-conscious mind, over the body is an amazing thing. The psychologists quote a case of a girl who played the piano in a cinema in the days of the silent films. Normally she was quite well, but immediately the lights went out and the cigarette smoke filled the auditorium she began to be paralysed. She fought against it for long, but at last the paralysis became permanent and something had to be done. Examination revealed no physical cause whatever. Under hypnosis it was discovered that when she was very young, only a few weeks old, she had been lying in one of these elaborate old-fashioned cots with an arch of lace over it. Her mother had bent over her smoking a cigarette. The draperies had caught fire. It was immediately extinguished and no hurt was done to her at the time. She did not know that her sub-conscious mind was remembering this terror ; but it was ; and the dark plus the smell of the cigarette smoke in the cinema acted on the unconscious mind and paralysed her body—and she did not know why. Now the man in this story may well have been paralysed because consciously or unconsciously his conscience agreed that he was a sinner, and the thought of being a sinner brought the illness which he believed was the inevitable consequence of sin. The first thing that Jesus said to him was, " Child, God is not angry with you. It's all right." It was like speaking to a frightened child in the dark. The burden of the terror of God and the estrangement from God rolled from his heart, and that very fact made the cure all but complete.

It is a lovely story because the first thing that Jesus does for everyone of us is to say, " Child, God is not angry with you. Come home, and don't be afraid."

THE UNANSWERABLE ARGUMENT

Mark 2 : 7-12

> Some of the experts in the law were sitting there, and they were debating within themselves, " How can this fellow speak like this ? He is insulting God. Who can forgive sins except one person—God ? " Jesus

immediately knew in His spirit that this debate was
going on in their minds, so He said to them, " Why
do you debate thus in your minds ? Which is easier—
to say to the paralysed man, ' Your sins are forgiven,'
or to say, ' Get up, and lift your bed, and walk around '?
Just to let you see that the Son of Man has authority
on earth to forgive sins "—He said to the blind man—
" I say to you, ' Get up ! Lift your bed ! And go
away home ! ' " And he raised himself, and immediately he lifted his bed, and went out in front of them all.
The result was that they were all astonished, and
they kept on praising God. " Never," they kept
repeating, " have we seen anything like this."

JESUS, as we have seen, had already attracted the crowds.
Because of that He had attracted to Himself the notice of
the official leaders of the Jews. The Sanhedrin was the
supreme court of the Jews. One of its great functions was
to be the strict guardian of orthodoxy. For instance, it
was the Sanhedrin's duty to deal with any man who was a
false prophet. It seems that the Sanhedrin had sent out
a kind of scouting party to check up on Jesus ; and they
were there in Capernaum. No doubt they had annexed
an honourable place in the front of the crowd. and they
were sitting there critically watching everything that was
going on. When they heard Jesus say to the man that his
sins were forgiven it came to them as a shattering shock.
It was an essential of the Jewish faith that only God can
forgive sins. For any man to claim to do so was to insult
God ; that was blasphemy and the penalty for blasphemy
was death by stoning (Leviticus 24 : 16). At the moment
they were not ready to launch their attack in public, but
it was not difficult for Jesus to see how their minds were
working. So he determined to fling down a challenge and
to meet them on their own ground. It was their own firm
belief that sin and sickness were indissolubly linked
together. A sick man was a sinning man or a man who
had sinned. So Jesus asked them a question : " Whether
is it easier to say to this man, ' Your sins are forgiven,' or
to say, ' Get up and walk ' ? " Any charlatan could say,

42

" Your sins are forgiven." There was no possibility of ever demonstrating whether his words were effective or not ; such a statement was completely uncheckable. But to say, " Get up and walk " was to say something whose effectiveness would either be proved or disproved there and then. So Jesus said in effect : " You say that I have no right to forgive sins ? You hold as a matter of belief that if this man is ill he is a sinner and he cannot be cured till he is forgiven ? Very well, then, watch this ! " So Jesus spoke the word and the man was cured. The experts in the law were hoist with their own petard. On their own stated beliefs the man could not be cured, unless he was forgiven. He *was* cured, therefore he *was* forgiven. Therefore, Jesus' claim to forgive sin *must* be true. Jesus must have left a completely baffled set of legal experts ; and, worse, He must have left them in a baffled rage. Here was something that must be dealt with ; if this went on all orthodox religion would be shattered and destroyed. In this incident Jesus had signed His own death warrant—and He knew it.

But for all that it is an extremely difficult incident. What does it mean that Jesus can forgive sin ? There are three possible ways of looking at this.

(i) We could take it that what Jesus was doing was that He was *conveying* God's forgiveness to the man. After David had sinned and after Nathan had rebuked him into terror and after David had humbly confessed his sin, Nathan said : " The Lord also hath put away thy sins; thou shalt not die." (2 Samuel 12 : 1-13.) Nathan was not forgiving David's sin, but he was conveying God's forgiveness to David and assuring him of it. So we could say that what Jesus was doing was that He was assuring the man of God's forgiveness, conveying to the man something which God had already given him. That is certainly true, but it does not read as if it was the whole truth.

(ii) We could take it that Jesus was acting as God's representative. John says : " The Father judgeth no man

but hath committed all judgment unto the Son."
(John 5 : 22.) If judgment is committed to Jesus, then
so must forgiveness also be. Let us take a human analogy.
Analogies are always imperfect but we can only think in
human terms. A man may give another man *a power of
attorney* ; that means to say that he has given that man the
absolute disposal of his goods and property. He agrees
that the other man should act for him, and that the other
man's actions should be regarded precisely and exactly as
his own. We could take it that that is what God did with Jesus,
that God entrusted Jesus, delegated to Jesus, His powers
and privileges, and that the word Jesus spoke was none
other than the word of God.

(iii) We can take it in still another way. The whole
essence of Jesus' life is that in Jesus we see clearly displayed the attitude of God to men. Now that attitude was
the very reverse of what men had thought God's attitude
to be. It was not an attitude of stern, severe, austere
justice. It was not an attitude of continual demand. It
was an attitude of perfect love, and of a heart yearning
with love and eager to forgive. Again let us use a human
analogy. Lewis Hind in one of his essays tells us of the
day that he discovered his father. He had always respected
and admired his father ; but he had always been more
than a little afraid of him. He was in church with his
father one Sunday. It was a hot drowsy day. He grew
sleepier and sleepier. He could not keep his eyes open as
the waves of sleep engulfed him. His head nodded. He
saw his father's arm go up ; and he was sure that his
father was going to shake or strike him. And then he
looked up and saw his father smile gently, and the father's
arm went round the boy's shoulder and cuddled the lad
to himself that he might rest the more comfortable and
held him close with the clasp of love. That day Lewis
Hind discovered that his father was not as he had thought
him to be, that his father loved him. That is what Jesus
did for men and for God. Jesus literally brought men God's

forgiveness upon earth. Without Him they would never have even remotely known about it. " I tell you," He said to the man, " and I tell you here and now, upon earth, you are a forgiven man." Jesus showed men perfectly the attitude of God to men. He could say, " I forgive," because in Him God was saying, " I forgive."

THE CALL OF THE MAN WHOM ALL MEN HATED

Mark 2 : 13, 14

> So Jesus went out again to the lakeside, and the whole crowd came to Him, and He went on teaching them. As He walked along, He saw Levi, the son of Alphaeus, sitting in the office where he collected the customs duties. He said to him, " Follow me ! " He rose and followed Him.

STEADILY and inexorably the Synagogue door was shutting on Jesus. Between Him and the guardians of Jewish orthodoxy war had been declared. Now He is teaching, not in the Synagogue, but by the lakeside. The open air is to be His Church, the blue sky His canopy, and a hillside or a fishing boat His pulpit. Here is the beginning of that dreadful situation when the Son of God was banned from the place which was regarded as the House of God.

He was walking by the lakeside and teaching. That was, in fact, one of the commonest ways for a Rabbi to teach. As the Jewish Rabbis walked the roads from one place to another, or as they strolled in the open air, their disciples grouped themselves around them and walked with them and listened as they talked. Jesus was doing what any Rabbi might have done.

Galilee was one of the great road centres of the ancient world. It has been said that, " Judaea is on the way to nowhere ; Galilee is on the way to everywhere." Palestine is the land bridge between Europe and Africa ; all land traffic must go through her. The great road of the Sea led from Damascus, by way of Galilee, through Capernaum, down past Carmel, along the Plain of Sharon, through Gaza and on to Egypt. It is one of the great roads of the world. Another road led from Acre on the coast away across the Jordan out to Arabia and the frontiers of the empire, a road that was trodden by the regiments and the caravans.

Still further—Palestine at this time was partitioned up. Judaea was a Roman province under a Roman procurator ; Galilee was ruled by Herod Antipas, a son of Herod the Great ; to the east the territory which included Gaulonitis, Trachonitis and Batanaea was ruled by Philip, another of Herod's sons. Now on the way from Philip's territory to Herod's domains, Capernaum was the first town to which the traveller came. Capernaum was by its very nature a frontier town ; because of that it was a customs' centre. In those days there were import and export taxes and Capernaum must have been the place where they were collected. That is where Matthew worked. True, he was not, like Zacchaeus, in the service of the Romans ; he must have been working for Herod Antipas ; but a hated tax-collector he was. (The Authorized Version calls the *tax-collectors, publicans ;* that is because the Latin word was *publicanus ;* the translation *publican* is, of course, nowadays quite misleading. The translation actually goes back to Wycliffe.)

This story tells us certain things both about Matthew and about Jesus.

(i) Matthew was a well-hated man. Tax-gatherers can never be a popular section of the community, but in the ancient world they were hated. People never knew just how much they had to pay ; the tax-collectors extracted from them as much as they could possibly get and lined their own pockets with the surplus that remained after the demands of the law had been met. Even a Greek writer like Lucian ranks tax-gatherers with " adulterers, panderers, flatterers and sycophants." Jesus wanted the man no one else wanted. He offered His friendship to the man whom all others would have scorned to call friend.

(ii) Matthew must have been a man at that moment with an ache in his heart. He must have heard about Jesus ; he must have listened on the outskirts of the crowds to His message ; and something must have stirred in his heart, and he must have hated himself and his hated trade. Now Matthew could not possibly have gone to the orthodox good people of his day ; to them he was unclean and they would have refused to have anything to do with him. Hugh Redwood tells of a woman in the dock district in London who came to a women's meeting. She had been living with a Chinese and to him she had a half-caste baby, and she brought the baby with her. She liked the meeting and she came back and back again. Then the vicar came to her. " I must ask you," he said, " not to come to this meeting again." The woman looked her question. " The other women," said the vicar, " say that they will stop coming if you continue to come." She looked at him with a poignant wistfulness. " Sir," she said, " I know I'm a sinner, but isn't there anywhere a sinner can go ? " Fortunately the Salvation Army found that woman and she was reclaimed for Christ. But that is precisely the thing that Matthew was up against until he found the one who came into the world to seek and to save that which was lost.

(iii) But this tells us something about Jesus. It was as He walked along the lakeside that He called Matthew. As a great scholar said, " Even as He was walking along He was looking for opportunities." Jesus was never off duty. If He could find one man for God as He walked He found him. What a harvest we could gather in if we looked for men for Christ as we walked !

(iv) Of all the disciples Matthew gave up most. He, of all of them, literally left all to follow Jesus. Peter and Andrew, James and John could go back to the boats. There were always fish to catch and always the old trade to which to return ; but Matthew burned his boats completely. With one action, in one moment of time, by one swift decision he had put himself out of his job forever, for having left his tax-collector's job, he would never get it back again. It takes a big man to make a big decision, and yet some time in every life there comes the moment to decide. A certain famous man had the habit of going for long country walks on Dartmoor. When he came to a brook that was rather too wide to cross comfortably, the first thing he always did was to throw his coat over to the other side. He made sure first of all that there was to be no turning back. He took the decision to cross and made sure that he was going to stick to it. Matthew was the man who staked everything on Christ ; and Matthew was not wrong.

(v) From his decision Matthew got at least three things. (*a*) *He got clean hands.* From now on he could look the world in the face. He might be very much poorer and life must be very much rougher, and the luxuries and the comforts were gone ; but from now on his hands were clean and, because his hands were clean, his mind was at rest. (*b*) *He lost one job but he got a far bigger one.* It has been said that Matthew left everything but one thing—he did not leave his pen. Scholars do not think that the first gospel, as it stands, is the work of Matthew ; but they do think that it embodies one of the most important documents that was ever written. They believe that it embodies a document which was the first written account of the teaching of Jesus, and that that document was written by Matthew. With his orderly mind, his systematic way of working, his familiarity with the pen, Matthew was the first man to give the world a book on the teaching of Jesus. He lost one job but he got a far bigger one to do. (*c*) The odd thing is that Matthew's reckless decision brought him the one thing he can least have been looking for—*it brought him immortal and world-wide fame.* All men know the name of Matthew as one of the men whose name is for ever connected with the transmission of the story of the life of Jesus. Had Matthew refused the call he would have had a local ill-fame as the follower of a disreputable trade which all men hated ; because he answered the call he gained a world-wide fame as the man who gave to men the record of the words of Jesus. God never goes back on the man who stakes his all on Him.

WHERE THE NEED IS GREATEST

Mark 2 : 15-17

> Jesus was sitting at a meal in Levi's house, and many tax-collectors and sinners were sitting with Jesus and His disciples, for there were many of them, and they sought His company. When the experts in the law, who belonged to the school of the Pharisees, saw that He was eating in the company of sinners and tax-gatherers, they began to say to His disciples, " It is with tax-collectors and sinners that He is eating and drinking." Jesus heard them. " It is not those who are in good health who need a doctor," He said, " but those who are ill. I did not come to bring an invitation to people who think that they have no faults but to those who know that they are sinners."

HERE once again Jesus is flinging down the gauntlet of defiance. When Matthew had yielded himself to Jesus, he invited Him to his house. Very naturally, having discovered Jesus for himself, he wished his friends to share this great new discovery—and his friends were like himself. It could not be any other way. Matthew had chosen a job which cut him off from the society of all respectable and orthodox people, and he had to find his friends among outcasts like himself. Jesus gladly accepted that invitation ; and these outcasts of society sought His company. Nothing could better show the difference between Jesus and the Scribes and Pharisees and orthodox good people of the day. They were not the kind of person whose company a sinner would have sought. The sinner would have been looked at with bleak condemnation, with arrogant superiority. The sinner would have been frozen out of such company even before he had entered it. The orthodox religious people were shocked to the core of their beings. In Palestine a clear distinction was drawn between those who kept the law and the people whom they called *the people of the land*. The people of the land were the common mob who did not observe all the rules and the regulations of conventional Pharisaic piety. By the orthodox it was forbidden to have anything to do with these people at all. The strict law-keeper must have no fellowship with them at all. He must not talk with them nor go on a journey with them ; as far as possible, he must not even do business with them ; to marry a daughter to one of them was as bad as giving her over to a wild beast ; above all, he must not accept hospitality from or give hospitality to such a person. By going to Matthew's house and sitting at his table and companying with his friends Jesus was defying the orthodox conventions of His day.

We need not for a moment suppose that all these people were sinners in the moral sense of the term. The word *sinner (hamartōlos)* had a double significance. It did mean a man who broke the moral law ; but it also meant a man who did not observe the scribal law. The man who committed adultery and the man who ate pork were both sinners ; the man who was guilty of theft and murder and the man who did not wash his hands the required number of times and in the required way before he ate were both sinners. These guests of Matthew no doubt included many who had broken the moral law and played fast and loose with life ; but no doubt they also included many whose only sin was that they did not observe the scribal rules and regulations.

When Jesus was taxed with this shocking conduct His answer was quite simple. " A doctor," he said " goes where he is needed. People in good health do not need him ; sick people do ; I am doing just the same ; I am going to

those who are sick in soul and who need me most."
Verse 17 is a highly concentrated verse. It sounds at first
hearing as if Jesus had no use for good people. But the
point of it is that the one person for whom Jesus can do
nothing is the person who thinks himself so good that he
does not need anything done for him ; and the one person
for whom Jesus can do everything is the person who is a
sinner and a failure and who knows it and who longs in his
heart of hearts for a cure. To have no sense of need is to
have erected a barrier between us and Jesus ; to have a
sense of need is to have the passport to His presence.

The attitude of the orthodox Jews to the sinner was
really compounded of two things.

(i) It was compounded of *contempt*. " The ignorant
man," said the Rabbis, " can never be pious." Heraclitus,
the Greek philosopher, was an arrogant aristocrat. One
called Scythinus undertook to put his discourses into verse
so that ordinary unlettered folk might read and understand
them. The reaction of Heraclitus was put into an epigram.
" Heraclitus am I. Why do ye drag me up and down, ye
illiterate ? It was not for you I toiled, but for such as
understand me. One man in my sight is a match for
thirty thousand, but the countless hosts do not make a
single one." For the mob he had nothing but contempt.
The Scribes and Pharisees despised the common
man ; Jesus loved him. The Scribes and Pharisees stood
on their little eminence of formal piety and looked down
on the sinner ; Jesus came and sat beside him, and by
sitting beside him lifted him up.

(ii) It was compounded of *fear*. The orthodox were
afraid of the contagion of the sinner ; they were afraid
that they might be infected with sin. They were like a
doctor who would refuse to attend a case of infectious
illness lest he himself contracted it. Jesus was the one
who forgot Himself in a great desire to save others. C. T.
Studd, that great missionary of Christ, had four lines of
doggerel that he loved to quote :

> " Some want to live within the sound
>   Of Church or Chapel bell ;
> I want to run a rescue shop
>   Within a yard of hell."

The man with contempt and fear in his heart can never be a fisher of men.

THE JOYOUS COMPANY

Mark 2 : 18-20

> The disciples of John were in the habit of fasting, as were the Pharisees. So they came to Jesus and said, " Why do John's disciples and the disciples of the Pharisees fast, while your disciples do not ? " " Surely," Jesus said to them, " his closest friends cannot fast while the bridegroom is still with them ? So long as they have the bridegroom they do not fast. But the days will come when some day the bridegroom will be taken away from them—and then, in that day, they will fast."

WITH the stricter Jews fasting was a regular practice. In the Jewish religion there was only one day in all the year that was a compulsory fast, and that was the Day of Atonement. The day when the nation confessed and was forgiven its sin was The Fast, *par excellence*. But the stricter Jews fasted on two days every week, on Mondays and Thursdays. It is to be noted that fasting was not as serious as it sounds, for the fast lasted from 6 a.m. to 6 p.m. and after that normal food could be eaten.

It is to be noted that Jesus is not against fasting as such. There are very good reasons why a man might fast. He might deny himself the things he liked for his comfort for the sake of *discipline*, to be certain that he was the master of them and not they of him, to make sure that he never grew to love them so well that he could not give them up. He might deny himself his comforts and his pleasant things that, after self-denial, he might appreciate them all the more. One of the best ways to learn to value our homes is to have to stay away from home for a time ; and one of the best ways to appreciate God's gifts is to do without them for a time. These are good reasons for fasting. The trouble about the Pharisees was that in far too many cases their fasting was for self-display. It was to call the attention of *men* to their own goodness. They actually whitened their faces and went about with dis-shevelled garments on their fast days so that no one could miss the fact that they were fasting and so that everyone would see and admire their devotion. It was to call the attention of *God* to their piety. They felt that this special act of extra piety would bring them to the notice of God. Their fasting was a ritual and a self-displaying ritual at that. To be of any value, fasting must not be the result of a ritual ; it must be the expression of a feeling in the heart. It must not be a mere convention, but a genuine way of expressing a need of the heart.

Jesus uses a vivid picture to tell the Pharisees why His disciples did not fast. After a Jewish wedding the couple did not go away for a honeymoon ; they stayed at home. For a week or so open house was kept and there was con-tinual feasting and rejoicing. In a hard wrought life the wedding week was the happiest week in a man's life. To that week of happiness there were invited the closest friends of the bride and the bridegroom ; and they were called by the name *children of the bridechamber*. Jesus likens his little company to men who were children of the bridechamber, chosen guests at a wedding feast. There was actually a rabbinic ruling which said, " All in atten-dance on the bridegroom are relieved of all religious observances which would lessen their joy." The wedding guests were actually exempt from all fasting.

This incident tells us that the characteristic Christian attitude to life is joy. The discovery of Christ and the company of Christ is the key to happiness. There was a Japanese criminal called Tockichi Ishii. He was utterly and bestially pitiless ; he had brutally and callously murdered men, women and children in his career of crime. He was captured and imprisoned. Two Canadian ladies visited the prison. He could not be induced even to speak ; he only glowered at them with the face of a wild beast. When they left, they left with him a copy of the Bible in the faint hope that he might read it. He read it, and the story of the Crucifixion made him a changed man. " Later when the jailer came to lead the doomed man to the scaffold, he found not the surly, hardened brute he expected, but a smiling, radiant man, for Ishii the murderer had been born again." The mark of his rebirth was a smiling radiance. The life that is lived in Christ cannot be lived other than in joy.

But the story ends with the foreboding cloud across the sky. No doubt when Jesus spoke of the day when the bridegroom would be taken away His friends did not at the moment see the meaning of it. But here, right at the beginning, Jesus saw the Cross ahead. Death did not take Jesus unawares ; even now He had counted the cost and chosen the way. Here is courage ; here is the picture of a man who would not be deflected from the road at whose end there loomed the inevitable Cross.

THE NECESSITY OF STAYING YOUNG IN MIND

Mark 2 : 21, 22

> No one sews a patch of new cloth on to an old garment. If he does the bit that was meant to fill in the hole tears it apart—the new from the old—and the tear is made worse. No one puts new wine into old wine-skins. If he does the wine will burst the wineskins, and the wine will be lost as well as the wineskins. New skins for new wine !

JESUS knew quite well that He was coming with a message which was startlingly new ; and He also knew that His conduct and His way of life was shatteringly different from that of the orthodox rabbinic teacher. He also knew how

difficult it is for the minds of men to accept and to enter-
tain new truth; and here He uses two illustrations to
show how difficult and how necessary it is to have an
adventurous mind.

No one ever had such a gift as Jesus had for the discovery and the use of homely illustrations. Over and over
again He finds in the simple things pathways and pointers
to God. No one was ever such an expert in getting from
" the here and now " to the " there and then." For Jesus
" earth was crammed with heaven." He lived so close to
God that everything spoke to Him of God. Someone tells
how, on Saturday afternoons, he used to go for country
walks with one of the most famous of Scottish preachers.
They used to have long talks together. Telling of it afterwards he said, " Wherever the conversation started, he had
a way of cutting straight across country to God." Where-
ever Jesus' eye lighted it had a way of flashing straight
on to God.

(i) He speaks of the danger of sewing a new patch on an
old garment. The word that is used means that the new
cloth was still undressed ; it had never been shrunk ; so
when the garment got wet in the rain the new patch
shrunk, and being much stronger than the old, it tore the
old apart. There comes a time when the day of patching
is ended. Patching is no more effective and re-creating
must begin. In the time of Luther it was not possible to
patch up the abuses of the Roman Catholic Church ; the
time for patching was done and the time for *reformation*
had come. In the time of John Wesley, for Wesley at least,
the time for patching the Church of England was done.
He did not want to leave it, but in the end he had to, for
only a new fellowship would suffice. It may well be that
there are times when we try to patch and mend and adjust,
when what is wanted is the complete abandonment of the
old and the acceptance of something new altogether.

(ii) In Palestine wine was kept in wineskins. At that

time there was no such thing as a bottle in our sense of the term. When these skins were new they had a certain elasticity ; as they grew old they became hard and unyielding. New wine is still fermenting ; it gives off gases. These gases cause pressure ; and if the skin is new it will yield to the pressure, but if it is old and hard and dry it will explode and wine and skin alike will be lost. Jesus is pleading for a certain elasticity in our minds. It is fatally easy to become set in our way. J. A. Findlay quotes a saying of one of his friends—" When you reach a conclusion you're dead." What he meant was that when our minds become fixed and settled in their ways, when they are quite unable to accept new truth and to contemplate new ways, we may be physically alive but we are mentally dead. As people grow older almost everyone develops a constitutional dislike of that which is new and unfamiliar. We grow very unwilling to make any adjustments in our habits and ways of life. Lesslie Newbigin, who was involved in the discussions about the formation of the United Church of South India, tells how, during these discussions, one of the things that most often held things up was that people would keep asking, " Now, if we do that, just where are we going ? " In the end someone had to say bluntly, " The Christian has no right to ask where he is going." Abraham went out not knowing whither he went. (Hebrews 11 : 8.) There is a great verse in that same chapter of Hebrews : " By faith Jacob, when he was a dying, blessed both the sons of Joseph ; and worshipped, leaning upon the top of his staff." (Hebrews 11 : 21.) With the very breath of death upon him the old traveller still had his pilgrim staff in his hand. To the end of the day, with the evening now upon him, he was still ready for the road. If we are really to rise to the height of the Christian challenge, we must retain the adventurous mind. I received a letter once which ended like this, " Yours aged 83 and still growing "—and indeed, with the inexhaustible riches of Christ still before us, why not ?

PIETY, REAL AND FALSE

Mark 2 : 23-28

> One Sabbath day Jesus was going through the corn
> fields. His disciples began to pluck the ears of corn
> as they made their way along. The Pharisees began
> to say to Him, " Look ! Why are they doing what is
> not allowed on the Sabbath ? " " Have you never
> read," He said, " what David did when he and his
> friends were in need and hungry ? Have you never
> read how he went into the house of God, when
> Abiathar was High Priest, and ate the shewbread—
> which none is allowed to eat except the priests—and
> gave it to his friends as well ? " " The Sabbath,"
> He said to them, "was made for the sake of man and
> not man for the sake of the Sabbath. Therefore the
> Son of Man is lord also of the Sabbath."

ONCE again Jesus cut right across the scribal rules and
regulations. When He and His disciples were going through
the corn fields one Sabbath day, His disciples began to
pluck the ears of corn and to eat them. On any ordinary
day the disciples were doing what was freely permitted
(Exodus 23 : 24). So long as the traveller did not put a
sickle into the field he was free to pluck the corn. But, this
was done on the Sabbath and the Sabbath was hedged
around with literally thousands of petty rules and regulations. All work was forbidden. Work had been classified
under thirty-nine different heads and four of these heads
were, reaping, winnowing, threshing and preparing a meal.
By their action the disciples had technically broken all
these four rules, and they were to be classified as law-
breakers. It seems fantastic to us ; but to the Jewish
rabbis it was a matter of deadly sin and of life and death.

The Pharisees immediately launched their accusation
and pointed out that Jesus' disciples were breaking the law.
They obviously expected Jesus to stop them on the spot.
Jesus answered them in their own language. He cited the
story which is told in I Samuel 21 : 1-6. David was
fleeing for his life ; he came to the tabernacle in Nob ; he

demanded food and there was none except the shewbread. Exodus 25 : 23-30 tells of the shewbread. The shewbread consisted of twelve loaves placed on a golden table three feet long, one and a half feet wide, and one and a half feet high. The table stood in the tabernacle in front of the Holy of Holies and the bread was a kind of offering to God. It was changed once a week ; when it was changed it became the property of the priests and of the priests alone and no one else might eat it (Leviticus 24 : 9). Yet in his time of need David took and ate that bread and thus broke the law. Jesus showed that scripture itself supplies a precedent in which human need took precedence of human and even divine law.

" The Sabbath," He said, " was made for the sake of man and not man for the sake of the Sabbath." That was self-evident. Man was created before ever the elaborate Sabbath law came into existence. Man was not created to be the victim and the slave of Sabbath rules and regulations; the Sabbath rules and regulations were in the beginning created to make life fuller and better for man. Man is not enslaved by the Sabbath ; the Sabbath exists to make his life a better life.

This passage confronts us with certain truly essential truths which we forget at our peril.

(i) Religion does not consist in rules and regulations. To take the matter in question—Sunday Observance is important but there is a great deal more in religion than Sunday Observance. If a man might become a Christian simply by abstaining from work and pleasure on the Sunday, and by attending Church on that day, and saying his prayers and reading his Bible, being a Christian would be a very easy thing. Whenever men forget the love and the forgiveness and the service and the mercy that are at the heart of religion and replace them by the performance of rules and regulations religion is in a decline. Christianity has at all times consisted far more in doing things than in not doing things.

58

(ii) The first claim on any man is the claim of human need. Even the catechisms and the confessions admit that works of necessity and *mercy* are quite legal on the Sabbath. If ever the performance of a man's religion stops him helping someone who is in need, his religion is not religion at all. People matter far more than systems. Persons are far more important than rituals. The best way to worship God is to help men.

(iii) The best way to use sacred things is to use them to help men. That, in fact, is the only way to give them to God. One of the loveliest of all stories is the story of *The Fourth Wise Man*. His name was Artaban. He set out to follow the star and he took with him a sapphire, a ruby and a pearl beyond price as gifts for the King. He was riding hard to meet his three friends, Caspar, Melchior and Balthasar, at the agreed meeting place. The time was short ; they would leave if he was late. Suddenly he saw a dim figure on the ground before him. It was a traveller stricken with fever. If he stayed to help he would be too late. He did stay ; he helped and healed the man. But now he was alone. He needed camels and bearers to help him across the desert because he had missed his friends and their caravan. He had to sell his sapphire to get them because he had helped the man. And he was sad that the King would never have his gem. So he journeyed and in due time he came to Palestine and to Bethlehem, but again he was too late. Joseph and Mary and the baby had gone. Then there came the soldiers to carry out Herod's command that the children should be slain. Artaban was lodging in a house where there was a little child he had come to love. The tramp of the soldiers was at the door ; the weeping of stricken mothers could be heard. Artaban stood in the doorway, tall and dark. He had the ruby in his hand. When the captain came Artaban bribed him with his ruby not to enter. The child was saved ; the mother was overjoyed ; but the ruby was gone ; and Artaban was sad for, as he thought, the King would never have his ruby now. For years he wandered looking for the King. More than thirty years afterwards he came to Jerusalem. There was a crucifixion that day. And when Artaban heard of this Jesus who was being crucified He sounded wondrous like the King. He was going out to Calvary. Maybe his pearl, the loveliest pearl in all the world, could buy the life of the King. Down the street there came a girl fleeing from a band of soldiers. " My father is in debt," she cried, " and they are taking me to sell me as a slave to pay the debt. Save me ! " Artaban hesitated ; then sadly he took out his pearl, gave it to the soldiers, bought the girl's freedom and she was safe. Then on a sudden the skies were dark ; there was an earthquake and a flying tile hit Artaban on the head. He sank half-conscious to the ground. The girl pillowed his head on her lap. Suddenly his lips began to move. " Not so, my Lord. For when saw I Thee anhungered and fed Thee ? Or thirsty, and gave Thee drink ? When saw I Thee a stranger, and took Thee in ? Or naked and clothed Thee ? When saw I Thee sick in prison, and came unto Thee ? Thirty and three years have I looked for Thee ; but I have never seen Thy face, nor ministered to Thee, my King." And then like a whisper from very far away, there came low and sweet a voice. " Verily I say unto you, Inasmuch as thou hast done it unto one of the least of these my brethren, thou hast done it unto me." And Artaban smiled in death because he knew that the King had received his gifts.

The best way to use sacred things is to use them for men. It has been known for children to be barred from a Church because that Church was too ancient and sacred for such as they were. It can be that a Church is more concerned with the elaboration of its services than the help of its simple folk and the relief of its poor. But the sacred things are only truly sacred when they are used for men. The shewbread was never so sacred as when it was used to feed a starving man. The Sabbath was never so sacred as when it was used to help those who needed help. The final arbiter in the use of all things is love and not law.

THE CLASH OF IDEAS

Mark 3 : 1-6

> Jesus went into the Synagogue again ; and there was a man there who had a hand which had withered ; and they were watching Him closely to see if He would heal him on the Sabbath day, so that, if He did, they might be able to formulate a charge against Him. He said to the man who had the withered hand, " Stand up and come out in to the middle of the congregation." He said to them, " Is it lawful to do good on the Sabbath day ? Or to do evil ? To save a life ? Or to kill it ? " But they remained silent. He looked round on them with anger, for He was grieved at the obtuseness of their hearts. He said to the man, " Stretch out your hand ! " He stretched it out ; and his hand was restored. The Pharisees immediately went out and began to concoct a plot with Herod's entourage against Him, with a view to killing Him.

THIS is a crucial incident in the life of Jesus. It was already clear that Jesus and the orthodox leaders of the Jews were quite at variance. For Jesus to go back into the Synagogue at all was a brave thing to do. It was the act of a man who refused to seek safety and who was determined to look a dangerous situation in the face. In the Synagogue there was a deputation from the Sanhedrin. No one could miss them, for, in the Synagogue, the front seats were the seats of honour and they were sitting there. It was the duty of the Sanhedrin to deal with anyone who was likely to mislead the people and seduce them from the right way ; and that is precisely what this deputation conceived of themselves as doing. The last thing they were there to do was to worship and to learn ; they were there to scrutinize Jesus' every action. In the Synagogue there was a man with a paralysed hand. The Greek word means that he had not been born that way but that some illness had taken the strength from him. The gospel according to the Hebrews, a gospel which is lost except for a few fragments, tells us that the man was a stone mason and that he besought Jesus to help him, for his livelihood was in his hands and he was ashamed to beg. If Jesus had been a cautious, prudent person He would have conveniently arranged not to see the man, for He knew that to heal that man was asking for trouble.

It was the Sabbath day ; on the Sabbath day all work was forbidden and to heal was to work. The Jewish law was quite definite and detailed about this. Medical attention could only be given if a life was in danger. To take some examples—a woman in childbirth might be helped on the Sabbath. An affection of the throat might be treated. If a wall fell on anyone, enough might be cleared away to see whether he was dead or alive. If he was alive he might be helped ; if he was dead the body must be left there until the next day. A fracture could not be attended to. Cold water might not be poured on a sprained hand or foot. A cut finger might be bandaged with a plain bandage but not with ointment. That is to say, at the most an injury could be kept from getting worse ; it must not be made better. It is extraordinarily difficult for us to grasp this. The best way in which we can see the strict orthodox view of the Sabbath is to remember that a strict Jew would not even defend his life on the Sabbath. In the wars of the Maccabees, when resistance broke out, some of the Jewish rebels took refuge in some caves. The Syrian soldiers pursued them. Josephus, the Jewish historian, tells us that they gave them the chance to surrender and they would not, so " they fought against them on the Sabbath day, and they burned them as they were in caves, without resistance and without so much as stopping up the entrances of the caves. They refused to defend themselves on that day because they were not willing to break in upon the honour they owed to the Sabbath, even in such distress ; for our law requires that we rest on that day." When

Pompey, the Roman general, was besieging Jerusalem, the defenders took refuge in the Temple precincts. Pompey proceeded to build a mound which would overtop them and from which he might bombard them. He knew the beliefs of the Jews and he built on the Sabbath day, and the Jews lifted not one hand to defend themselves or to hinder the building, although they knew that by their Sabbath inactivity they were signing their own death warrant. The Romans, who had compulsory military service, had in the end to exempt the Jews from army service because no strict Jew would fight on the Sabbath. The orthodox Jewish attitude to the Sabbath was completely rigid and unbending.

Jesus knew that. This man's life was not in the least danger. Physically he would be no worse off if he were left until to-morrow. For Jesus this was a test case, and He met it fairly and squarely. He told the man to rise and to come out of his place and stand where everyone could see him. There were probably two reasons for that. Very likely Jesus wished to make one last effort to waken sympathy for the stricken man by showing everyone his wretchedness. Quite certainly Jesus wished to take the step He was going to take in such a way that no one could possibly fail to see it. He asked the experts in the law two questions. *Is it lawful to do good or to do evil on the Sabbath day?* He put them in a dilemma. They were bound to admit that it was lawful to do good ; and it was a good thing He proposed to do. They were bound to deny that it was lawful to do evil ; and, yet, surely it was an evil thing to leave a man in wretchedness when it was quite possible to help him. Then He asked, *Is it lawful to save a life or to kill it?* Here He was driving the thing home. *He* was taking steps to save this wretched man's life ; *they* were thinking out methods of killing Him. On any reckoning it was surely a better thing to be thinking about helping a man than it was to be thinking of killing a man. No wonder they had nothing to say ! Then Jesus with a word of power

healed the man ; whereat the Pharisees went out and tried
to hatch a plot with the Herodians to kill Him. This shows
the length to which the Pharisees would go. No Pharisee
would have anything to do with a Gentile or a man who
did not keep the law ; such people were unclean. The
Herodians were the court entourage of Herod ; they were
continually coming into contact with Romans and dealing
with them and living with them. For all normal purposes
the Pharisees would have considered them unclean ; but
now they are prepared to enter into, what was for them, an
unholy alliance. In their hearts there was a hate which
would stop at nothing.

Now this passage is fundamental because it shows the
clash of two ideas of religion.

(i) To the Pharisee religion was *ritual* ; it meant obeying
certain rules and laws and regulations. Jesus broke these
regulations and they were genuinely convinced that He
was a bad man. It is like the man who believes that
religion consists in going to Church, reading the Bible,
saying grace at meals, even having family worship, and
carrying out all the external acts which are looked on as
religious, and who yet never put himself out to do anything
for anyone in his life, who has no sense of sympathy, no
desire to sacrifice, who is serene in his rigid orthodoxy, and
deaf to the call of need and blind to the tears of the world.

(ii) To Jesus religion was *service*. It was love of God *and*
love of men. Ritual was irrelevant compared with love
in action.

> " Our Friend, our Brother, and our Lord,
>   What may Thy service be ?
> Nor name, nor form, nor ritual word,
>   But simply following Thee."

To Jesus the most important thing in the world was not
the correct performance of a ritual, but the spontaneous
answer to the cry of human need.

IN THE MIDST OF THE CROWDS

Mark 3 : 7-12

So Jesus withdrew to the lakeside with His disciples, and a great multitude from Galilee followed Him ; and from Judaea and from Jerusalem, and from Idumaea and from the Transjordan country, and from the territory round Tyre and Sidon, there came to Him a great crowd of people, for they were hearing about what great things He was doing. He told His disciples to have a boat ready waiting for Him because of the crowd, so that they would not crush Him ; for He healed many, and the result was that all who were suffering from the scourges of disease rushed upon Him to touch Him. And as often as unclean spirits saw Him, they kept flinging themselves down before Him and shouting, " You are the Son of God." Many times He sternly forbade them to make Him known.

UNLESS Jesus wished to be involved in a head-on collision with the authorities He had to leave the Synagogues. It was not that He withdrew through fear ; it was not the retreat of a man who feared to face the consequences. But His hour was not yet come. There was much that He had still to do and say before the time of final conflict came. So He left the Synagogues and went out to the lakeside and the open sky. Even there the crowds flocked to Him even from far afield. From all over Galilee they came ; many made the hundred-mile journey from Jerusalem in Judaea to see Him and to listen to Him. Idumaea was the ancient realm of Edom, away in the deep south, between the southern borders of Palestine and Arabia. Even from the east side of Jordan they came ; and even from foreign territory, for people came from Phoenicia and from the Phoenician cities of Tyre and Sidon, which lie on the Mediterranean coast, north-west of Galilee. So large were the crowds that it became dangerous and a boat had to be kept ready, just off the shore, in case He might be overwhelmed with the crushing of the mob. His cures brought Him into even greater danger ; for the sick people did not even wait for Him to touch them; they rushed to touch Him.

At this time He was faced with one special problem. There was the problem of those who were possessed by demons. Let us remember that, whatever our belief about demons may be, these people were convinced they were possessed by an alien and an evil power external to themselves. They called Jesus *The Son of God*. What did they mean by that ? They certainly did not use the term in what we might call a philosophical or a theological sense. In the ancient world *Son of God* was by no means an uncommon title. The kings of Egypt were said to be the sons of Ra, their god. From Augustus onwards many of the Roman Emperors were described on inscriptions as sons of God. The Old Testament itself has four ways in which it uses this term. (i) *The angels* are *the sons of God*. The old story in Genesis 6 : 2, says that *the sons of God* saw the daughters of men and were fatally attracted to them. Job I : 6, tells of the day when *the sons of God* came to present themselves before the Lord. It was a regular title for the angels. (ii) *The nation of Israel* is the *son of God*. God called *His son* out of Egypt (Hosea II : I). In Exodus 4 : 22, God says of the nation, " *Israel is my son,* my first-born." (iii) *The king of the nation* is *the son of God*. In 2 Samuel 7 : 14, the promise to the king is, " I will be his father, and he shall be *my son*. (iv) In the later books, which were written between the Testaments, *the good man* is *the son of God*. In Sirach 4 : 10, the promise to the man who is kind to the fatherless is,

" So shalt thou be *a son of the Most High,*
And He shall love thee more than thy mother doth."

In all these cases the term *son* describes someone who is specially near and close to God. We get a parallel to this which shows something of its meaning in the New Testament. Paul calls Timothy *his son* (I Timothy I : 2 ; I : 18). Timothy was no blood relation to Paul at all, but there was no one, as Paul says (Philippians 2 : 19-22), who knew his mind so well. Peter calls Mark *his son* (I Peter 5 : 13), because there was no one who could interpret his mind so well. When we meet this term in the simplicity of the gospel story we are not to think in terms of philosophy or theology or of the doctrine of the Trinity ; we are to think of it as expressing the fact that Jesus' relationship to God was so close that no other word could describe it. Now these demon-possessed men felt that in them there was an independent evil spirit ; they somehow felt that in Jesus here was one near and kin to God ; they felt that in the presence of this nearness to God the demons could not live and therefore they were afraid.

We must ask, " Why did Jesus so sternly bid them to remain silent ? " The reason was very simple and very compelling. Jesus was the Messiah, God's Anointed King ; but His idea of Messiahship was quite different from the popular idea. He saw in Messiahship a way of service, of sacrifice and of love with a cross at the end of it. The popular idea of the Messiah was the idea of a conquering king who, with his mighty armies, would blast the Romans and lead the Jews to world power. Therefore, if a rumour went out that the Messiah had arrived the inevitable consequence would have been rebellions and uprisings and revolts, especially in Galilee where the people were ever ready to follow any nationalist leader. Jesus thought of Messiahship in terms of love ; the people thought of Messiahship in terms of Jewish nationalism. Therefore, before there could be any proclamation of His Messiahship, Jesus had to educate the people into the true idea of what Messiahship means. At this stage nothing but harm and trouble and disaster could come from the proclamation that the Messiah had arrived. Such a proclamation would have issued in nothing but useless war and bloodshed. First of all men had to learn the true conception of what the Messiah was, and a premature announcement such as this could have wrecked Jesus' whole mission.

67

THE CHOSEN COMPANY

Mark 3 : 13-19

> Jesus went up into the mountain and invited to His service the men of His choice ; and He appointed twelve that they might be with Him, and that He might send them out to act as His heralds, and to have power to cast out demons. He chose Simon, and to him He gave the name of Peter ; He chose James, Zebedee's son, and John, James' brother, and to them He gave the name Boanerges, which means Sons of Thunder ; He chose Andrew and Philip and Bartholomew and Matthew and Thomas, and James, Alphaeus' son, and Thaddeus and Simon, the Cananaean, and Judas Iscariot, who also betrayed Him.

JESUS had now come to a very important moment in His life and work. He had emerged with His message ; He had chosen His method ; He had gone throughout Galilee preaching and healing. It is clear that by this time He had made a very considerable impact on the public mind. Now He had to face two very practical problems. First, He had to find some way of making His message permanent if anything happened to Him, and that something would happen He did not doubt. Second, He had to find some way of disseminating His message, and in an age when there was no such thing as a printed book or newspaper, and no way of reaching large numbers of people at the one time, that was no easy task. There was only one way to solve these two problems ; He had to choose certain men on whose hearts and lives He could write His message and who would go out from His presence to carry that message abroad. Here in this passage we see Him doing exactly that.

It is very significant that *Christianity began with a group.* The Christian faith is something which from the beginning had to be discovered and lived out in a fellowship. The whole essence of the way of the Pharisees was that it separated men from their fellow men ; the very name

Pharisee means *the separated one* ; the whole essence of Christianity was that it bound men to their fellow men, and presented them with the task of living with each other and for each other.

Further, Christianity began with a very mixed group. In it the two extremes met. Matthew was a tax-collector and, therefore, an outcast. He was a renegade and a traitor to his fellow countrymen. Simon the Cananaean is correctly called by Luke, Simon the Zealot ; and the Zealots were a band of fiery and violent nationalists who were pledged even to murder and assassination to clear their country of the foreign yoke. The man who was lost to patriotism and the fanatical patriot came together in that group, and no doubt between them there were all kinds of views and backgrounds and opinions. Christianity began by insisting that the most diverse people should live together and by enabling them to do so, because they were all living with Jesus.

Judging them by worldly standards the men Jesus chose had no special qualifications at all. They were not wealthy ; they had no special social position ; they had no special education ; they were not trained theologians ; they were not high-ranking churchmen and ecclesiastics ; they were twelve ordinary men. But they had two special qualifications. First, they had felt the magnetic attraction of Jesus. There was something about Him that made them wish to take Him as their Master. And second, they had the courage to show that they were on His side. Make no mistake, that did require courage. Here was this Jesus calmly crashing through the rules and regulations ; here was this Jesus heading straight for an inevitable collision with the orthodox leaders of His day ; here was this Jesus already branded as a sinner and labelled as a heretic ; and yet they had the courage to attach themselves to Him. No band of men ever staked everything on such a forlorn hope as these Galilaeans, and no band of men ever did it with opener eyes. These twelve had all kinds of faults, but whatever else could be said about them, they loved Jesus and they were not afraid to tell the world that they loved Him—and that is being a Christian.

Jesus called them to Him for two purposes. First, He called them *to be with Him*. He called them to be His steady and consistent companions. Others might come and go ; the crowd might be there one day and away the next ; others might be fluctuating and spasmodic in their attachment to Jesus, but these twelve were to identify their lives with His life ; they were to live with Him all the time. Second, He called them *to send them out*. He wanted them to be His representatives. He wanted them to tell others about Him. They themselves had been won in order to win others.

For their task Jesus equipped them with two things. First, He gave them *a message*. They were to be His heralds. A wise man said that no man has any right to be a teacher unless he has a teaching of his own to offer, or the teaching of another that with all the passion of his heart he wishes to propagate. Men will always listen to the man with a message. Jesus gave these friends of His something to say. Second, He gave them *a power*. They were also to cast out demons. Because they companied with Him something of His power was on their lives.

If we would learn what discipleship is we will do well to think again of these first disciples.

THE VERDICT OF HIS OWN

Mark 3 : 20, 21

Jesus went into a house ; and once again so dense a crowd collected that they could not even eat bread. When His own people heard what was going on, they went out to restrain Him, for they said, " He has taken leave of His senses."

SOMETIMES a man drops a remark which cannot be interpreted otherwise than as the product of bitter experience.

Once when Jesus was enumerating the things which a man might have to face for following Him, He said, "A man's foes shall be they of his own household." (Matthew 10 : 36.) Jesus' own family had come to the conclusion that He had taken leave of His senses, that it was time that He was taken home. Let us see if we can understand what made them feel like that.

(i) Jesus had left home and had left the carpenter's business at Nazareth. No doubt it was a flourishing business from which He could at least have made a living ; and quite suddenly He had flung the whole thing up and had gone out to be a wandering preacher. No sensible man, they must have been thinking, would throw up a business where the money came in every week to become a vagrant who had not any place to lay his head.

(ii) Jesus was obviously on the way to a head-on collision with the orthodox leaders of His day. There are certain people who can do a man a great deal of harm, people on whose right side it is better to keep, people whose opposition can be very dangerous. No sensible man, they must have been thinking, would ever get up against the powers that be, because he would know that in any collision with them he would be bound to come off second best. No one could take on the Scribes and the Pharisees and the orthodox leaders and hope to get away with it.

(iii) Jesus had newly started a little society of His own— and a very queer society it was. There were some fishermen ; there was a reformed tax-collector ; there was a fanatical nationalist. They were not the kind of people whom any ambitious man would particularly want to know. They certainly were not the kind of people who would be any good to a man who was set on a career. No sensible man, they must have been thinking, would pick a crowd of friends like that. They were definitely not the kind of people a prudent man would want to get mixed up with.

By His actions Jesus had made it clear that the three

laws by which men tend to organize their lives meant nothing to Him.

(i) He had thrown away *security*. In point of fact the one thing that most people in this world want more than anything else is security. They want above all things a job and a position which is secure, and where there are as few material and financial risks as possible.

(ii) He had thrown away *safety*. In point of fact most people tend at all times to play safe. They are more concerned with the safety of any course of action than with its moral quality, its rightness or its wrongness. A course of action which involves risk is something from which they instinctively shrink.

(iii) He had shown Himself utterly indifferent to *the verdict of society*. He had shown that He did not much care what men said about Him. In point of fact, as H. G. Wells said, for most people " the voice of their neighbours is louder than the voice of God." " What will people say? " is one of the first questions that most of us are in the habit of asking.

What appalled Jesus' friends was the risks that He was taking, risks which, as they thought, no sensible man would take.

When John Bunyan was in prison he was quite frankly afraid. " My imprisonment," he thought, " might end on the gallows for ought that I could tell." He did not like the thought of being hung. Then there came the day when he was ashamed of being afraid. " Methought I was ashamed to die with a pale face and tottering knees for such a cause as this." So finally he came to a conclusion as he thought of himself climbing up the ladder to the scaffold : " Wherefore, thought I, I am for going on and venturing my eternal state with Christ whether I have comfort here or no ; if God doth not come in, thought I, I will leap off the ladder even blindfold into eternity, sink or swim, come heaven, come hell ; Lord Jesus, if Thou wilt catch me, do : if not, *I will venture for Thy name*." That is precisely what Jesus was willing to do. *I will venture for Thy name.* That was the essence of the life of Jesus, and that—not safety and security—should be the motto of the Christian man and the mainspring of the Christian life.

ALLIANCE OR CONQUEST?

Mark 3 : 22-27

> The experts in the law from Jerusalem came down. They said, " He has Beelzebub on His side." They said, " It is by the ruler of the demons that He casts out the demons." Jesus called them and spoke to them by way of analogy. " How can Satan cast out Satan? If a kingdom is divided against itself, that kingdom cannot stand. And if a house is divided against itself that house will not be able to stand. And if Satan has risen up against himself, and is divided, he cannot stand—he is finished. No one can go into the house of a strong man and plunder his gear unless he first binds the strong man—then he will plunder his house."

THE orthodox officials never questioned Jesus' power to exorcise demons. They did not need to, for exorcism was a common phenomenon then, as it still is now, in the East. What they did say was that Jesus' power over the demons was due to the fact that He was in league with the king of the demons, that, as one commentator puts it, " it was by the great demon He cast out the little demons." People have always believed in " black magic," and that is what they claimed that Jesus was practising. But Jesus had no difficulty in exploding that argument. The essence of exorcism has always been that the exorcist calls in to his aid some stronger power to drive out the weaker demon. So Jesus says : " Just think ! If there is internal dissension in a kingdom, that kingdom cannot last. If there are quarrels in a house, that house will not endure long. If Satan is actually making war with his own demons then he is finished as an effective power, because civil war has begun in the kingdom of Satan." " Put it another way," Jesus said. " Suppose you want to rob a strong man. You have no hope of doing so until you have got the strong man under subjection. Once you have got him tied up you can plunder his goods—but not until then." The defeat of the demons did not show that Jesus was in alliance with Satan ; it showed that Satan's defences had been breached ; a stronger name had arrived ; the conquest of Satan had begun. Two things emerge here.

(i) Jesus accepts the picture of life as a struggle. He sees in life the essential struggle between the power of evil and the power of God. Jesus did not waste His time in speculations about problems to which there is no answer. He did not stop to argue about where evil came from ; but He did deal with it most effectively. One of the odd things is that we spend a good deal of time in discussion groups and the like discussing the origin of evil ; but we spend less time working out practical methods of tackling the problem and dealing with it. Someone put it this way— suppose a man wakes up to find his house on fire, he does not sit down in a chair and embark upon the reading of a treatise entitled " The Origin of Fires in Private Houses." He grabs such defences as he can muster and deals with the fire. Jesus saw the essential struggle between good and evil which is at the heart of life and which is raging in the world ; He did not speculate about it. He dealt with it and gave to others the power to overcome evil and to do the right.

(ii) Jesus regarded the defeat of disease as part of the conquest of Satan. This is an essential part of Jesus' thought. He desired, and He was able, to save men's bodies as well as men's souls. The doctor and the scientist who meet the challenge of disease are sharing in the defeat of Satan as much as the preacher of the word. The doctor and the minister are not doing different work ; they are doing the same work. They are not rivals ; they are allies in God's warfare against the opposing power of evil.

THE SIN FOR WHICH THERE IS NO FORGIVENESS

Mark 3 : 28-30

" This is the truth I tell you—all sins will be forgiven
to the sons of men—I mean all the insulting things
that they say ; but whoever insults the Holy Spirit
will not be forgiven for ever but he has made himself
guilty of the sin that not even eternity can wipe out."
This He said because they were saying, " He has an
unclean spirit."

IF we are to understand what this terrible saying means
we must first understand the circumstances in which it
was said. It was said by Jesus when the Scribes and
Pharisees had declared that the cures He wrought were
wrought not by the power of God, but by the power of the
devil. These men had been able to look at the incarnate
love of God and to think it the incarnate power of Satan.

We must begin by remembering one thing. Jesus could
not have used the phrase the Holy Spirit in the full
Christian sense of the term ; because the Spirit in all His
fulness did not come to men until Jesus had returned to
His glory. It was not until Pentecost that there came to
men the supreme experience of the Holy Spirit. Jesus,
speaking to Jews, must have used the term The Holy
Spirit in the *Jewish* sense of the term. Now in Jewish
thought the Holy Spirit had two great functions. First,
He revealed God's truth to men ; and second, He enabled
men to recognize that truth when they saw it and heard
it. That will give us the key to this passage.

(i) The Holy Spirit enabled men to recognize God's truth
when it entered their lives. But if a man refuses to exercise
any God-given faculty he will in the end lose it. If a man
lived in the dark long enough he would lose the ability
to see. If a man stayed in bed long enough he would lose
the power to walk. If a man refuses to do any serious
study he loses the power to study. And if a man refuses the
guidance of God's Spirit often enough he becomes in the

end incapable of recognizing that truth when he sees it. Evil to him becomes good and good becomes evil. He can look on the goodness of God and call it the evil of Satan.

(ii) Why should such a sin have no forgiveness? H. B. Swete says, " To identify the source of good with the impersonation of evil implies a moral wreck for which the Incarnation itself provides no remedy." A. J. Rawlinson calls it " essential wickedness," as if here we see the quintessence of all evil. Bengel said that all other sins are *human* but this sin is *Satanic*. Why should all this be so? Consider the effect of Jesus on a man. The very first effect of Jesus on any man is to make that man see his own utter unworthiness in comparison with the beauty and the loveliness of the life of Jesus. " Depart from me," said Peter, " for I am a sinful man." (Luke 5 : 8.) When Tokichi Ishii first read the story of the Gospel he said, "I stopped. I was stabbed to the heart as if pierced by a five-inch nail. Shall I call it the love of Christ? Shall I call it His compassion? I do not know what to call it. I only know that I believed and my hardness of heart was changed." The first reaction was that he was stabbed to the heart. Now the result of that sense of unworthiness, and the result of that stabbed heart is a heartfelt penitence, and penitence is the only condition of forgiveness. But, if a man has got himself into such a state, by repeated refusals to listen to the promptings of the Holy Spirit, that he cannot see anything lovely in Jesus at all, then the sight of Jesus will not give him any sense of sin ; because he has no sense of sin he cannot be penitent, and because he is not penitent he cannot be forgiven.

One of the Lucifer legends tells how one day a priest noticed in his congregation a magnificently handsome young man. After the service the young man stayed for confession. He confessed so many and such terrible sins that the priest's hair stood on end. " You must have lived long to have done all that," the priest said. " My name is

Lucifer and I fell from heaven at the beginning of time,"
said the young man. "Even so," said the priest, "say
that you are sorry, say that you repent and even you can
be forgiven." The young man looked at the priest for a
moment and then turned and strode away. He would not
and could not say it ; and therefore he had to go on still
desolate and still damned.

There is only one condition of forgiveness and that is
penitence. But if a man, by repeated refusals of God's
guidance, has lost the ability to recognize goodness when
he sees it, if he has got his moral values inverted until evil
to him is good and good to him is evil, then, even when he
is confronted by Jesus, he is conscious of no sin ; he cannot
repent and therefore he can never be forgiven. That is the
sin against the Holy Spirit. So long as a man sees loveliness
in Christ, so long as he hates his sin even if he cannot
leave it, even if he is in the mud and the mire, he can still
be forgiven. It is only when he has made himself such
that the sight of Christ is nothing to him that he has shut
himself out forever from the love of God, for then, even the
Incarnation itself, has been unable to move his heart.

THE CONDITIONS OF KINSHIP

Mark 3 : 31-35

His mother and His brothers came. They stood outside and sent someone in with a message to Him. The
crowd were sitting round Him. "Look !" they said,
your mother and your brothers are outside inquiring
for you." "Who," He answered, "is my mother and
my brothers?" He looked round those who were
sitting in a circle round about Him. "Look !" He
said, "my mother and my brothers ! Whoever does
God's will, he is my brother, my sister and my mother."

HERE Jesus lays down the conditions of true kinship.
Kinship is not solely a matter of flesh and blood. It can

happen that a man is really nearer to someone who is not blood relation to him at all than he is to those who are bound to him by the closest ties of kin and blood. Wherein then lies this true kinship?

(i) True kinship lies in *a common experience*, especially when it is an experience where two people have really come through things together. It has been said that two people really become friends when they are able to say to each other, " Do you remember? " and then to go on and talk about the things they have come through together. Someone once met an old negro woman. An acquaintance of hers had died. " You will be sorry," he said, " that Mrs. So-and-so is dead." " Yes," she said but without showing any great grief. " I saw you just last week," he said, " laughing and talking with each other. You must have been great friends." " Yes," she said, " I was friendly with her. I used to laugh with her ; but to be real friends folk have got to weep together." That is profoundly true. The basis of true kinship lies in a common experience, and Christians have the common experience of being forgiven sinners.

(ii) True kinship lies in *a common interest*. A. M. Chirgwin tells us a very interesting thing in *The Bible in World Evangelism*. One of the greatest difficulties that colporteurs and distributors of the Scriptures have is not so much to sell their books as to keep people reading them. He goes on, "A colporteur in pre-Communist China had for years been in the habit of going from shop to shop and house to house. But he was often disappointed because many of his new Bible readers lost their zeal, until he hit upon the plan of putting them in touch with one another and forming them into a worshipping group which in time became a duly organized Church." Only when these isolated units became part of a group which was bound together by a common interest did real fellowship and real kinship come into being. The common interest bound them into kinship. The Christian has that common interest because all Christians are people who desire to know more about Jesus Christ.

(iii) True kinship lies in *a common obedience*. The disciples were a very mixed group. All kinds of beliefs and opinions were mixed up among them. A tax-collector like Matthew and a fanatical nationalist like Simon the Zealot ought to have hated each other like poison, and no doubt at one time did. But they were bound together because they both had accepted Jesus Christ as Master and Lord. Any platoon of soldiers will be made up of men from different backgrounds aud from different walks of life and holding very different opinions; yet, if they are long enough together, they will be welded into a band of comrades because of the common obedience to the army which they all share. Men can become friends of each other when they share a common master. Men can only love each other when they all love Jesus Christ.

(iv) True kinship lies in *a common goal*. There is nothing for binding men together like a common aim. Here there is a great lesson for the Church. A. M. Chirgwin, talking of the renewed interest in the Bible, asks, does this " point to the possibility of a new approach to the ecumenical problem based on biblical rather than on ecclesiastical considerations? " The Churches will never draw together so long as they argue about the ordination of their ministers, the form of Church government, the administration of the sacraments and all the rest of it. The one thing on which they can all come together is the fact that all of them are seeking to win men for Jesus Christ. If kinship comes from a common goal then Christians above all men possess its secret, for all of us are seeking to know Christ better and to bring others within His Kingdom. On whatever else we differ on that we can agree.

TEACHING IN PARABLES

Mark 4 : 1, 2

> Jesus began again to teach by the lakeside. A very great crowd collected to hear Him, so great that He had to go on board a boat and sit in it on the lake. The whole crowd was on the land facing the lake. He began to teach them many things in parables, and, in His teaching, He began to say to them, " Listen ! Look ! The sower went out to sow."

IN this section we see Jesus making a new departure. He was no longer teaching in the Synagogue ; He was teaching by the lakeside. He had made the orthodox approach to the people ; now He had to take unusual methods. We do well to note that Jesus was prepared to use new methods. He was ready and willing to take religious preaching and teaching out of its conventional setting in the Synagogue into the open air and among the crowds of ordinary men and women. John Wesley was for many years a faithful and orthodox servant of the Church of England. Down in Bristol his friend George Whitefield was preaching to the miners, to as many as twenty thousand of them at a time, in the open air ; and his hearers were being converted by the hundred. He sent for John Wesley. Wesley himself said, " I love a commodious room, a soft cushion, a handsome pulpit." This whole business of open air preaching rather offended him. He said himself, " I could scarcely reconcile myself at first to this strange way—having been all my life (till very lately) so tenacious of every point relating to decency and order, that I should have thought the saving of souls almost a sin if it had not been done in a Church." But Wesley saw that field preaching won souls and, as he said, " I cannot argue against a matter of fact." There must have been many amongst the orthodox Jews who regarded this new departure of Jesus as stunting and sensationalism ; but Jesus was wise enough to know when new methods were necessary and adventurous enough to use them. It would be well if His Church was equally wise and equally adventurous.

Now this new departure needed a new method ; and the new method Jesus chose was to speak to the people *in parables*. A *parable* is literally *something thrown beside something else* ; that is to say, a parable is basically *a comparison*. A parable is an *earthly story with a heavenly meaning*. Something on earth is compared with something in heaven, that the heavenly truth may be better grasped and understood in light of the earthly illustration. Why did Jesus choose this method? And why did He use it so much that it became so characteristic of Him that He is known forever as the master of the parable?

(i) First and foremost, Jesus chose the parabolic method simply to make people listen. He was not now dealing with an assembly of people who were in a Synagogue and who were more or less bound to remain there until the end of the service. He was dealing with a crowd in the open air who were quite free to walk away at any time. Therefore, the first essential was *to interest the crowd*. Unless their interest was aroused they would simply drift away. Sir Philip Sidney speaks of the poet's secret : " With a tale forsooth he cometh unto you, with a tale that holdeth children from play and old men from the chimney-corner." The surest way to awaken men's interest is to tell them stories and Jesus knew that.

(ii) Further, when Jesus used the parabolic method He was using something with which Jewish teachers and audiences were entirely familiar. There are parables in the Old Testament of which the most famous is the story of the one ewe lamb that Nathan told to David when he had treacherously eliminated Uriah and taken possession of Bathsheba (2 Samuel 12 : 1-7). The Rabbis habitually used parables in their teaching. It was said of Rabbi Meir that he spoke one-third in legal decisions ; one-third in exposition ; and one-third in parables. Here are two examples of Rabbinic parables. The first is the work of

Rabbi Judah the Prince (c. A.D. 190). Antoninus, the Roman Emperor, asked him how there could be punishment in the world beyond, for, since body and soul after their separation could not have committed sin they could blame each other for the sins committed upon earth. The Rabbi answered in a parable :

> A certain king had a beautiful garden in which was excellent fruit ; and over it he appointed two watchmen, one blind and one lame. The lame man said to the blind man, " I see exquisite fruit in the garden. Carry me thither that I may get it and we will eat it together." The blind man consented and both ate of the fruit. After some days the Lord of the garden came and asked the watchmen concerning the fruit. Then the lame man said, "As I have no legs I could not go to it, so it is not my fault." And the blind man said, " I could not even see it so it is not my fault." What did the Lord of the garden do? He made the blind man carry the lame and thus passed judgment on them both. So God will replace the souls in their bodies and will punish both together for their sins.

When Rabbi Chiyya's son Abin died at the early age of twenty-eight, Rabbi Zera delivered the funeral oration, which he put in the form of a parable :

> A king had a vineyard for which he engaged many labourers, one of whom was specially apt and skilful. What did the king do? He took this labourer from his work, and walked through the garden conversing with him. When the labourers came for their hire in the evening the skilful labourer appeared among them and received a full day's wages from the king. The other labourers were very angry at this, and said, " We have toiled the whole day, while this man has worked but two hours. Why does the king give him the full hire even as unto us? " The king said to them, " Why are you angry? Through his skill he has done more in the two hours than you have done all day." So it is with Rabbi Abin ben Chiyya. In the twenty-eight years of his life he has learned more than others learn in a hundred years. Hence he has fulfilled his life work, and is entitled to be called to Paradise earlier than others from his work on earth ; nor will he miss aught of his reward.

When Jesus used the parabolic method of teaching, He was using a method with which the Jews were familiar and which they could understand.

(iii) Still further when Jesus used the parabolic method of teaching He was making the abstract idea concrete. There are very few people who can grasp abstract ideas. Most people think in pictures. We could talk about *beauty* for long enough and no one would be any the wiser ; but, if we can point at a person and say, " That is a beautiful person," then beauty becomes clear. We could talk about goodness for long enough and fail to arrive at a definition of it ; but every one recognizes a good deed when he sees one. There is a sense in which *every* word must become flesh ; every idea must be actualized in a person. When the New Testament talks about faith it takes the example of Abraham so that the idea of faith becomes flesh in the person of Abraham. Jesus was a wise teacher. He knew that it was useless to expect simple minds to cope with abstract ideas ; and so He put the abstract ideas into concrete stories ; He showed them in action ; He made them into persons, so that men might grasp and understand them.

(iv) Lastly, the great virtue of the parable is that it compels a man to think for himself. It does not do his thinking for him. It compels him to make his own deduction and to discover the truth for himself. The very worst way to help a child is to do his work for him. It does not help him at all to do his sums, write his essay, work out his problems compose his Latin prose for him. It does help very greatly to give him the necessary help to do it *for himself.* That is what Jesus was aiming at. Truth has always a double impact when it is a personal discovery. Jesus did not wish to save men the mental sweat of thinking ; He wished to make them think. He did not wish to make their minds lazy ; He wished to make them active. He did not wish to take the responsibility from them ; He wished to lay the responsibility on them. So He used the parabolic method, not to do men's thinking for them, but to encourage them to do their own thinking. He presented them with truth which, if they would make the right effort in the right frame of mind, they could discover for themselves, and therefore possess it in a way that made it really and truly theirs.

FROM EARTH TO HEAVEN

Mark 4 : 3-9

" Listen ! Look ! The sower went out to sow. As he was sowing, some seed fell along the roadside ; and the birds came and devoured it. Some fell upon rocky ground where it did not have much earth ; and it sprang up immediately, because it had no depth of earth, but, when the sun rose, it was scorched, and it was withered away, because it had no root. Some fell among thorns ; and the thorns crowded in on it until they choked the life out of it, and it did not yield any fruit. And some fell on good ground ; and, as it grew up and grew greater, it yielded fruit and bore as much as thirtyfold and sixtyfold and a hundred-fold." And He said, " Who has ears to hear, let him hear."

WE shall leave the interpretation of this parable until we come to the interpretation which Mark gives to us, and for the moment we shall only consider it as a specimen of Jesus' parabolic teaching in action. The scene is the lake-side ; Jesus is sitting in the boat just off the shore. The shore shelves gently down to the water's edge, and makes a natural amphitheatre for the crowd to stand on, Even as He talks Jesus sees a sower busy sowing seed in the fields within sight of the lake. " Look ! " He said, " The sower went out to sow." Herein is the whole essence of the parabolic method.

(i) Jesus started from the *here and now* to get to *the there and then*. He started from a thing that was happening at that moment on earth in order to lead men's thoughts to heaven ; He started from something which all men could see to get to the things that are invisible ; He started from something which all men knew to get to something which they had never as yet realized. That was the very essence of Jesus' teaching. He did not bewilder men by starting with things which were strange and abstruse and involved ; He started with the simplest things that even a child could understand.

(ii) By so doing Jesus showed that He believed that there was a real kinship between earth and heaven. Jesus would not have agreed that " earth was a desert drear." He believed that in the ordinary, common, everyday things of life men could see God. As William Temple put it : " Jesus taught men to see the operation of God in the regular and the normal—in the rising of the sun and the falling of the rain and the growth of the plant." Long ago Paul had the same idea when he said that the visible world is designed to make known the invisible things of God (Romans I : 20). For Jesus this world was not a lost and evil place ; it was the garment of the living God. Sir Christopher Wren lies buried in St. Paul's Cathedral, the great Church that his own genius planned and built. On his tombstone there is a simple Latin inscription which means, " If you wish to see his monument, look around you." Jesus would have said, " If you wish to see God, look around you." Jesus finds in the common things of life a countless source of signs which lead men to God if they will only read them aright.

(iii) The very essence of the parables is that they were spontaneous, extempore and unrehearsed. They were spoken on the spur of the moment. Jesus looks round, seeking a point of contact with the crowd. He sees the sower and on the spur of the moment that sower becomes His text. The parables are not stories which were wrought out in the quiet of a study ; they were not carefully thought out and polished and rehearsed. The supreme greatness of them is that Jesus thought of and composed these immortal short stories on the spur of the moment. They were produced by the demand of the moment and in the cut and thrust of debate. C. J. Cadoux said of the parables : "A parable is art harnessed for service and conflict. . . . Here we find the reason why the parable is so rare. It requires a considerable degree of art, but art exercised under hard conditions. In the three typical parables of the Bible the speaker takes his life in his hands. Jotham (Judges 9 : 8-15) spoke his parable of the trees to the men of Shechem and then fled for his life. Nathan (2 Samuel 12 : 1-7), with the parable of the ewe-lamb, told an oriental despot of his sin. Jesus in the Parable of the Wicked Husbandmen used His own death sentence as a weapon for His cause. . . . In its most characteristic use the parable is a weapon of controversy, not shaped like a sonnet in undisturbed concentration but improvised in conflict to meet the unpremeditated situation. In its highest use it shows the sensitiveness of the poet, the penetration, rapidity and resourcefulness of the protagonist, and the courage that allows such a mind to work unimpeded by the turmoil and danger of mortal conflict." We have always admired these parables of Jesus, but when we remember that they were flashed out extempore, unprepared, on the spur of the moment their wonder is increased a hundredfold.

(iv) That brings us to a point that we must always remember in our attempts to interpret the parables. The parables were, in the first instance, not meant to be read but to be *heard*. That is to say, in the first instance, no one could possibly sit down and investigate and study them phrase by phrase and word by word. They were spoken not to be studied at length and at leisure, but to produce an immediate impression and reaction. That is to say, *the parables must never be treated as allegories*. In an allegory every part and action and detail of the story have an inner meaning and significance. *The Pilgrim's Progress* and the *Faerie Queene* are allegories ; in them every event

86

and person and detail has a symbolic meaning ; but, if that be so, clearly an allegory is something to be read and studied and examined and investigated ; but a parable is something which was heard once and once only. Therefore what we must look for in a parable is not a situation in which every detail stands for something ; we must look for a situation in which one great idea leaps out and shines like a flash of lightning. It is always wrong to attempt to make every detail of a parable mean something. It is always right to say : " What one idea would flash into a man's mind when he heard this story for the first time? "

THE MYSTERY OF THE KINGDOM

Mark 4 : 10-12

When He was alone, His own circle of people, together with The Twelve, asked Him about the parables. He said to them, " To you there is given the knowledge of the Kingdom of God which only the initiated can know. To those who are outside, everything is expounded by means of parables, so that they may indeed see and yet not perceive the meaning of things, and may indeed hear and not understand, lest at any time they should turn and be forgiven."

THIS has always been one of the most difficult passages to understand in all the gospels. The Authorised Version speaks of the *mystery* of the Kingdom of God. Now this word *mystery* has in Greek a technical meaning ; it does not mean something which is complicated and mysterious in our sense of the term. It means something which is quite unintelligible to the person who has not been initiated into its meaning, but which is perfectly clear and plain to the person who has been so initiated. In New Testament times, in the pagan world one of the great features of popular religion was what were called the *Mystery Religions*. These religions promised communion and union with and even identity with some god, whereby all the fears and the terrors of life and of death would be taken away. Now nearly all these Mystery Religions were based on the story of some god who had suffered and died and risen again ; they were nearly all in the nature of passion plays. One of the most famous of them was called the Mystery of Isis. Osiris was a wise and good king. Seth, his wicked brother, hated him and along with seventy-two conspirators persuaded him to come to a banquet. There he persuaded him to enter into a cunningly made coffin which exactly fitted him. When he was inside it the lid was snapped down and the coffin was cast into the Nile. Isis, his faithful wife, after a long and weary search, found the coffin and brought it home in mourning. When she was absent the wicked Seth came again, stole away the body, cut it into fourteen pieces and scattered them throughout all Egypt. Once again Isis set out on her sad and weary search. In the end she discovered all the pieces and by her magical powers put them together and restored Osiris to life again ; and from that time he became the immortal king of the living and the dead. Now what happened was this. The candidate underwent a long preparation of purification and of fasting and of asceticism and of instruction as to the inner meaning of the story. Then the dramatic story with its grief and its sorrow and its resurrection and its triumphal ending was played out as a passion play. Music and incense and lighting and a splendid liturgy were all used to enhance the emotional atmosphere. As the play was played out the worshipper felt himself one with the god both in his sufferings and in his triumph. He passed through death to immortality by union with the god. Now the point is that to an uninitiated person the whole thing would have been meaningless ; but to the initiated the thing was full of meaning which he had been taught to see. That is the technical meaning of this Greek word *musterion*. When the New Testament talks of the *mystery* of the Kingdom, it does not mean that the Kingdom is remote and abstruse and recondite and hard to understand ; but it does mean that it is quite unintelligible to the man who has not given his heart to Jesus, and that only the man who has taken Jesus as Master and Lord can understand what the Kingdom of God means.

But the real difficulty of the passage lies in the section that follows. If we take it at its face value it sounds as if Jesus taught in parables deliberately to cloak His meaning, purposely to hide it from all ordinary men and women. Whatever else the passage originally meant it cannot mean that ; and whatever else Jesus said He did not say that ; for, if one thing is crystal clear, it is that Jesus used parables not to cloak His meaning and to hide His truth but to compel men to recognize the truth and to enable them to see it.

How then did this passage come to be in the form in which it is? It is a quotation from Isaiah 6 : 9, 10. From the beginning it worried people. It was worrying people more than two hundred years before Jesus made use of it. The Hebrew of it literally runs (the following two trans lations are by W. O. E. Oesterley) :

> And He said, Go, and say to this people, " Go on hearkening, but understand not ; go on looking, but perceive not." Make fat the heart of this people, and its ears make heavy, and its eyes besmear ; lest it see with its eyes, and with its ears hear, and its heart understand, so that it should be healed again.

That seems on the face of it that God is telling Isaiah that he is to pursue a course deliberately designed to make the people fail to understand. In the third century B.C. the Hebrew scriptures were translated into Greek, and the Greek version, the Septuagint, as it is called, became one of the most influential books in the world, for it carried the Old Testament everywhere Greek was spoken. The Septuagint translators were worried at this strange passage and they translated it differently :

And He said, Go and say to this people, " Ye shall hear indeed, but ye shall not understand ; and seeing, ye shall see, and not perceive." For the heart of this people has become gross, and with their ears they hear heavily, and their eyes they have closed ; lest at any time they should see with their eyes and hear with their ears, and understand with their heart, and should be converted, and I should heal them.

The Greek version does not say that God intended that the people should be so dull that they would not understand ; it says that they had made themselves so dull that they could not understand—which is a very different thing. The explanation is that no man can translate or set down in print a tone of voice. When Isaiah spoke he spoke half in irony and half in despair and altogether in love. He was thinking, " God sent me to bring His truth to this people ; and for all the good I am doing I might as well have been sent to shut their minds to it. I might as well be speaking to a brick wall. You would think that God had shut their minds to it." So Jesus spoke His parables ; He meant them to flash into men's minds and to illuminate the truth of God. But in so many eyes He saw a dull incomprehension. He saw so many people blinded by prejudice, deafened by wishful thinking, too lazy to think. He turned to His disciples and He said to them : " Do you remember what Isaiah once said? He said that when he came with God's message to God's people Israel in his day they were so dully un-understanding that you would have thought that God had shut instead of opening their minds ; I feel like that to-day." When Jesus said this, He did not say it in anger, or irritation, or bitterness, or exasperation. He said it with the wistful longing of frustrated love, the poignant sorrow of a man who had a tremendous gift to give which people were to blind to take. If we read this, not hearing a tone of bitter exasperation, but a tone of regretful love, it will sound quite different. It will tell us not of a God who deliberately blinded men and hid His truth, but of men who were so dully uncomprehending that it seemed no use even for God to try to penetrate the iron curtain of their lazy incomprehension. God save us from hearing God's truth like that !

THE HARVEST IS SURE

Mark 4 : 13-20

" Don't you understand this parable? " He said to them. " How then will you understand all the parables? What the sower is sowing is the word. The kind of people represented by the case in which the seed fell by the side of the road, are those in whose case the word is sown, and whenever they hear it, immediately Satan comes, and snatches away the word that was sown into them. Just so, the kind of people represented by the case in which the seed was sown on the rocky ground, are those, who, whenever they hear the word, immediately gladly welcome it. They have no root in themselves, but they are quite impermanent ; and then, when trouble or persecution happens because of the word, they immediately stumble and collapse. Then there are the others who are represented by the case in which the seed was sown among thorns. These are the people who hear the word, but the anxieties of this world and the deceptive attraction of wealth and the desires for other things enter into them and choke the life out of the word, and it never gets a chance to bear fruit. The kind of people who are represented by the case in which the seed fell on good ground are such as hear the word and receive it and bring forth fruit, thirty and sixty and a hundredfold."

EVERY detail of this parable would be real to the hearers of Jesus, because every detail of it came from everyday life. In it four kinds of ground are mentioned. (i) There is the hard ground at the side of the road. The seed might fall on this kind of ground in two ways. The fields in Palestine were in the form of long, narrow strips ; these strips were divided by little grass paths ; these paths were rights of way ; the result was that they became beaten as hard as the pavement by the feet of those who used them. As the sower scattered his seed some might well fall there ; and there it had not a chance to grow. But in Palestine there was another way of sowing. Sometimes a sack of seed was put on the back of an ass ; a hole was cut in the corner of the sack ; and then the beast was led up and down as the seed flowed out. Inevitably as the ass was brought along the road to the field some of the seed fell on the road ; and just as inevitably the birds swooped on it and gobbled it up. There are some people into whose hearts Christian truth can find no entry. Its failure to find an entry is due to the hearer's lack of interest ; and that lack of interest comes from a failure to realize how important the Christian decision is. Christianity fails to make an impact on so many people, not because they are hostile to it, but because they are indifferent to it. They think that it is irrelevant to life and that they can get on well enough without it. That might be true if life was always an easy way where there were neither tensions nor tears ; but in point of fact there comes to every man in life a time when he needs a power not his own. It is the tragedy of life that so many people discover that too late.

(ii) There was the rocky ground. This was not ground full of stones ; it was a narrow skin of earth over a shelf of limestone rock. Much of Galilee was like that. In many fields the outcrop of the rock through the shallow soil could be seen. Seed which fell there germinated all right ; but because the soil was so shallow and held so little nourishment and moisture, the heat of the sun soon withered the sprouting seed so that it died. It is always easier to begin a thing than it is to finish it. A certain famous evangelist is quoted as saying : " We have learned that it takes about five per cent. effort to win a man to Christ, and ninety-five per cent. to keep him in Christ and growing into maturity in the Church." Many a man begins the Christian way ; and of that many, many fall out by the wayside. There are two troubles which cause this collapse. The one is the failure to think the thing out and to think it through, the failure to realize what it means and what it costs before we start. The other is the fact that there are thousands of people who are attracted by Christianity but who never let it get beyond the surface and the circumference of their lives. The fact is that with Christianity it is a case of all or nothing. A man is only safe when he has given himself in total yieldedness to Christ :

> " Is there a thing beneath the sun,
> That strives with Thee my heart to share?
> Ah ! tear it thence, and reign alone,
> The Lord of every motion there."

(iii) The third kind of ground was the ground that was full of thorns. The Palestinian farmer was lazy. He cut off the top of the fibrous rooted weeds ; he even burned off the top ; and the field might look clean ; but in below the surface the roots were still there ; and in due time the weeds revived in all their strength. The weeds grew with such rapidity and such virulence that they choked the life out of the seed. It is easy to pack life with such a multiplicity of interests that there is no time left for Christ. As the poet said, the cares of life can be like the clogging dust until " we forget because we must and not because we will." The more complicated life becomes, the more necessity there is to see that our priorities are right, for there are so many things which seek to shoulder Christ from out the topmost niche.

(iv) Finally there was the good, clean, deep soil in which the seed might flourish. If we are really to benefit by the Christian message the parable tells us that we must do three things. (a) We must *hear* it. We cannot hear unless we listen. It is characteristic of the life of so many of us that we are so busy talking that we have no time to hear, so engaged in arguing that we have no time to listen, so occupied in advancing our own opinions and our own views that we have no time to listen to the views of Christ, so much on the move that we have no time for the essential stillness. (b) We must *receive* it. When we hear the Christian message we must really take it into our minds. The human mind is an odd and a dangerous machine. We are so constructed, in the wise providence of creation, that, whenever a foreign body threatens to enter the eye, the eye automatically closes. That is an instinctive, reflex action. Whenever the mind hears something that it does not want to hear it automatically closes its door and forgets. There are times when truth can hurt ; but sometimes a distasteful drug or an unpleasant treatment must be accepted if health is to be preserved. To shut the mind to truth we do not want to hear is the straight road to disaster and to tragedy. (c) We must *put it into action*. The yield in the parable was thirty, sixty and a hundredfold. That is a large yield but the volcanic soil of Galilee was famous for its crops. Christian truth must always emerge in action. In the last analysis the Christian is challenged, not to speculate, but to act.

Now all that is the meaning of this parable *when we sit down and study it at leisure.* But we are reading it with time to think. It is quite impossible that all that would flash upon men's minds as they heard it for the first time and, we must remember, as we have already seen, that originally the parable was spoken to a crowd. What would be the one thing which flashed out on a crowd who heard it for the first time? Surely this—that, *although part of the seed never grew, the fact remained that at the end of the day there was a splendid harvest.* This is the parable to end despair. It may seem that much of our effort achieves no result ; it may seem that much of our labour is wasted. That is what the disciples were feeling, when they saw Jesus banished from the Synagogue and regarded with suspicion. In many places His message seemed to have failed, and they were discouraged and down-hearted. But this parable said to them, and says to us, " Patience ! Do your work. Sow the seed. Leave the rest to God. The harvest is sure."

THE LIGHT WHICH MUST BE SEEN

Mark 4 : 21

> This was one of Jesus' sayings : " Surely a lamp is not brought in to be put under a peck measure or under the bed? Is it not brought in to be set upon a lamp stand? "

VERSES 21-25 are interesting because they show the problems that confronted the writers of the gospels. These verses give us four different sayings of Jesus. In verse 21 there is the saying about the lamp. In verse 22 there is the saying about the revealing of secret things. In verse 24 there is the saying which lays it down that we shall receive back with the same measure as we have given. In verse 25 there is the saying that says that to him who has still more will be given. Now in Mark these verses come one after another in immediate succession. But verse 21 is repeated in Matthew 5 : 15 ; verse 22 is repeated in Matthew 10 : 26 ; verse 24 is repeated in Matthew 7 : 2 ; and verse 25 is repeated in Matthew 13 : 12 and also in Matthew 25 : 29. That is to say that four consecutive verses in Mark's gospel are scattered all over Matthew's gospel. One practical thing emerges for our study of them. We must not try to find any connection between them, for clearly there is none. They are quite disconnected and we must take them one by one.

How did this happen? How did it come about that these sayings of Jesus are given by Mark one after another and scattered by Matthew all over his gospel? The reason is just this. Jesus had a unique command of language. He could say the most vivid and pithy things. He could say things that stuck in the memory and refused to be forgotten. Further, He must have said many of these things far more than once. He was moving from place to place and from audience to audience ; and He must have repeated much of His teaching wherever He went. The consequence was that men remembered the things that Jesus said—they were said with such vividness that they could not be forgotten—but they forgot the occasion on which they were said. The result was that there are a great many of what one might call " orphan " sayings of Jesus. The saying itself is embedded in men's minds and remembered for ever, but the context of it, the occasion of it is forgotten. So then we have to take these vivid sayings by themselves individually and examine them.

One of Jesus' memorable sayings was that men do not light a lamp and put it under a peck measure, which would be like putting a bowl on the top of it, nor do they put it under a bed. A lamp is meant to be seen and to make men able to see ; and it is put in a place where all men can see it. From this saying we may learn two things.

(i) *Truth is meant to be seen.* The truth is not meant to be concealed ; it is meant to be displayed. There may be times when it is dangerous to tell the truth ; there may be times when to tell the truth is the quickest way to persecution and to trouble. But the true man and the true Christian stands by the truth in face of all men. When Luther decided to take up his stand against the Roman Catholic Church he decided first of all to attack *indulgences.* *Indulgences* were to all intents and purposes remissions of sins which a man could buy from a priest at a price. He drew up ninety-five theses against these indulgences. And what did he do with his ninety-five theses? There was a church in Wittenberg called the Church of All Saints. It was closely connected with the University ; on its door University notices were posted, and the subject of academic debates displayed. There was no more public notice-board in the town. To that door Luther affixed his theses. When did he do it? The day when the largest congregation came to the church and the town was All Saints' Day, the first of November. It happened to be the anniversary of the founding of that church and many services were held and crowds came. It was on All Saints' Day that Luther nailed his ninety-five theses to the church door. If Luther had been a prudent and a cautious man he would not have drawn up his ninety-five theses at all. If he had been a man with an eye on safety he would never have nailed them to the church door. And, if he must nail them to the door, if he had had any thought of personal safety he would never have chosen All Saints' Day to make his declaration. But Luther felt that he had discovered the truth ; and his one thought was to display the truth and to align his life with it. In every walk of life there are times when we know quite well what the truth demands, what the right thing to do is, what a Christian man ought to do. In every walk of life there are times when we fail to do it, because to do it would be to court unpopularity and perhaps worse. We ought to remember that the lamp of truth is something to be held aloft and not concealed in the interests of a cowardly safety.

(ii) *Our Christianity is meant to be seen.* In the early Church sometimes to show one's Christianity meant death. The Roman Empire was as vast as the world. In order to get some sort of binding unity into that vast empire Emperor worship was started. The Emperor was the embodiment and the impersonation of the state and he was worshipped as a god. On certain stated days it was demanded that everyone should come and sacrifice to the godhead of the Emperor. It was really a test of political loyalty. After a man had done so he got a certificate to say he had done so ; and, having got that certificate, he could go away and worship any god he liked. We still have many of these certificates. They run like this :

> To those who have been put in charge of the sacrifices from Inareus Akeus from the village of Theoxenis, together with his children Aias and Hera, who stay in the village of Theadelpheia. We sacrifice regularly to the gods and now in your presence, as the regulations demand, we have sacrificed and poured our libation and have tasted the offerings, and we ask you to give us the required certificate. May you fare well.

Then there follows the attestation.

> We, Serenas and Hermas, have witnessed your sacrificing.

All a Christian had to do was to go through that formal act, receive that certificate, and he was safe. And the fact of history is that thousands of Christians died rather than do so. They could have concealed the fact that they were Christians with the greatest of ease ; they could have gone on being Christians, as it were, privately, with no trouble at all. But to them their Christianity was something which had to be attested and witnessed to in presence of all men. They were proud that all should know where they stood. To such we owe our Christian faith to-day. It is often easier to keep quiet the fact that we belong to Christ and His Church ; but our Christianity must always be like the lamp that can be seen of all men.

THE TRUTH THAT CANNOT BE SUPPRESSED

Mark 4 : 22, 23

> For there is nothing secret that will not be brought into the open ; nothing is done that it should be hidden away, but that it should lie open for all to see. If a man has ears to hear let him hear.

IT was Jesus' certain conviction that the truth cannot ultimately be hidden. This saying applies in two directions.

(i) *It applies to truth itself.* There is something about the truth which is indestructible. Men may refuse to face the truth ; they may try to suppress the truth ; they may even try to obliterate the truth ; they may refuse to accept the truth, but " great is the truth and in the end it will prevail." In the early sixteenth century there was an astronomer called Copernicus who made the discovery that the earth is not the centre of the universe, that in fact the earth goes round the sun and not the sun round the earth. He was a cautious man and for thirty years he kept this discovery to himself. Then in 1543, when death's breath was on him, he persuaded a terrified printer to print his great work, *Revolutions of Heavenly Bodies*. Soon Copernicus died but others inherited the storm. In the early seventeenth century Galileo accepted the theory of Copernicus and stated publicly his belief in it. In 1616 he was summoned to the inquisition in Rome and his beliefs were condemned. Judgment was passed. " The first proposition that the sun is the centre and does not revolve about the earth, is foolish, absurd, false in theology, and heretical because contrary to Holy Scripture. . . . The second proposition, that the earth is not the centre, but revolves about the sun, is absurd, false in philosophy, and from a theological point of view at least, opposed to the true faith." Galileo gave in. It was easier to conform than to die ; and for years he remained silent. A new pope came to the papal throne and Galileo thought that Urban the Eighth was a man of wider sympathy and greater culture than his predecessor, so once again he came out into the open with his theory. He was mistaken in his hopes. This time he had to sign a recantation or undergo torture. He signed. " I, Galileo, being in my seventieth year, being a prisoner and on my knees, and before your Eminences, having before my eyes the Holy Gospel, which I touch with my hands, abjure, curse and detest the error and the heresy of the movement of the earth." His recantation saved him from death but not from prison. And in the end he was even denied burial in the family tomb. It was not only the Roman Catholic Church which tried to avoid the truth. Luther wrote : " People gave ear to an upstart astrologer (he meant Copernicus) who strove to show that the earth revolves, not the heavens or the firmament, the sun and the moon. . . . This fool wishes to reverse the entire science of astronomy ; but sacred Scripture tells us that Joshua commanded the sun to stand still, and not the earth." But time goes on

You can threaten to torture a man for discovering the truth ; you can call him a fool and try to laugh him out of court ; but that does not alter the truth. " It lies not in your power," said Andrew Melville, " to hang or exile the truth." Truth may be attacked, delayed, suppressed, mocked at ; but time brings in its revenges and in the end truth prevails. A man must have a care that he is not fighting against the truth.

(ii) *It applies to ourselves and to our own life and to our own life and conduct.* When a man does a wrong thing his first instinct is to hide. That is what Adam and Eve did when they broke the commandment of God (Genesis 3 : 8). But truth has a way of emerging. In the last analysis no man can hide the truth from himself, and the man with a secret is never a happy man. The web of deception is never a permanent concealment. And, when it comes to ultimate things, no man can have any secrets from God. In the end it is literally true that there is nothing secret which will not be revealed in the presence of God. When we remember that we are bound to be filled with the desire to make life such that all men may look on it and God survey it, without shame to ourselves.

THE BALANCE OF LIFE

Mark 4 : 24

> This was another of Jesus' sayings : " Pay attention to what you hear ! What you get depends on what you give. What you give you will get back, only more so."

In life there is always a balance. A man's getting will in every case be determined by his giving.

(i) This is true of *study.* The more study a man is prepared to give to any subject, the more he will get from it. It is told that the ancient nation of the Parthians would never give their young men a meal until they had broken sweat. They had to work before they ate. All subjects of study are like that. They give pleasure and satisfaction in proportion to the effort that we are prepared to spend upon them. It is specially so in regard to the study of the Bible. We sometimes feel that there are certain parts of the Bible with which we are out of sympathy ; if we study these parts they are often the very parts which end by giving us the richest harvest. A superficial study of any subject will often leave us quite uninterested ; a really intensive study of any subject will leave us thrilled and fascinated.

(ii) It is true of *worship*. The more we bring to the worship of God's house the more we will get from it. When we come to worship in the house of God, there are three wrong ways in which we may come. (*a*) We may come entirely to get. If we come in such a way the likelihood is that we will criticize the organist and the choir and find fault with the minister's preaching. We will regard the whole service as a performance laid on for our special entertainment. We must come prepared to give ; we must remember that worship is a corporate act, and that each of us can contribute something to it. If we ask, not, " What can I get out of this service? " but, " What can I contribute to this service? " we will in the end get far more out of it than if we simply came to take. (*b*) We may come without expectation. Our coming may be the result of habit and routine. Our coming may be simply part of the time-table into which we have divided the week. But, after all, we come to meet God, and when we meet God anything may happen. (*c*) We may come without preparation. It is so easy to leave for the worship of God's house with no preparation of mind or heart at all. It is easy to do that for often it is a rush to get there at all. But it would make all the difference in the world, if, before we came, we were for a moment or two still and silent and quiet, and, if, before we came, we companied for a moment or two with God in prayer. As the Jewish Rabbis told their disciples : " They pray best together who first pray alone."

(iii) It is true of *personal relationships*. One of the great facts of life is that we see our own reflection in other people. If we are cross and irritable and bad-tempered, we will find other people equally unpleasant. If we are critical and fault-finding, the chances are that we will find other people the same. If we are suspicious and distrustful, the likelihood is that others will be so to us. If we wish others to love us, we must first love them. The man who would have friends must show himself friendly. It was because Jesus believed in men that men believed in Him.

THE LAW OF INCREASE

Mark 4 : 25

To him who already has still more will be given : and from him who has not, even what he has will be taken away.

THIS may seem at first sight a hard saying ; but the whole lesson of life is that it is inevitably and profoundly true.

(i) It is true of *knowledge*. The more a man knows the more he is capable of knowing. A man cannot enter into the riches of Greek literature before he has ploughed his way through Greek grammar. When he has the basic grammar still more will be given to him. A man cannot really get the best out of music until he learns something of the structure of a symphony. But when he possesses that knowledge still more and more loveliness will be given to him. It is equally true that unless a man is consistently bent on the task of increasing his knowledge such knowledge as he has will in the end be taken away from him. Many a man in his youth had a working knowledge of French at school and has now forgotten even the little that he knew because he made no attempt to develop it. In knowledge the more knowledge a man has the more he can acquire. When he has it, more will be given to him. And, if he is not always out to increase that knowledge, such knowledge as he has will soon slip from his grasp. The Jewish teachers had an oddly expressive saying. They said that the scholar should be treated like a young heifer—because every day a little heavier burden should be laid upon him. In knowledge we cannot stand still ; we are gaining or losing it all the time.

(ii) It is true of *effort*. The more physical strength a man has, the more, within the limits of his bodily frame, he can acquire. The more he trains his body, the more his body will be able to do. On the other hand, if he allows his physical frame to grow slack and flabby and soft he will end by losing even the fitness that he had. We would sometimes do well to remember that our bodies belong to God as much as our souls. Many a man has been hindered from doing the work he might do because he has made himself physically unfit to do it.

(iii) It is so with *any skill or craft*. The more a man develops the skill of his hand, or eye, or mind, the more he is able to develop it. If he is content to drift along, never trying anything new, never adopting any new technique, he remains stuck in the one job with no progress. If he neglects his particular skill he will find in the end that he has lost it altogether.

(iv) It is so with *the ability to bear responsibility*. The more responsibility a man shoulders the more he can shoulder ; the more decisions he compels himself to take the better he is able to take them. But if a man shirks his responsibilities, if he evades his decisions and vacillates all the time, in the end he will become a flabby, spineless creature totally unfitted for responsibility and totally unable to come to any decision at all. Again and again in his parables Jesus goes on the assumption that the reward of good work is still more work to do. It is one of the essential laws of life, a law which a man forgets at his peril, that the more he has won the more he can win, and that, if he will not make the effort, he will lose even that which once he had won.

THE UNSEEN GROWTH AND THE CERTAIN END

Mark 4 : 26-29

> He said to them : " This is what the Kingdom of God is like. It is like what happens when a man casts seed upon the earth. He sleeps and he wakes night and day, and the seed sprouts and grows—and he does not know how it does it. The earth produces fruit with help from no one, first the shoot, then the ear, then the full corn in the ear. When the time allows it, immediately he despatches the sickle, for the time to harvest has come."

THIS is the only parable which is peculiar to Mark. He alone relates it to us. The Kingdom of God really means *the reign of God* ; it means the day when all the world will accept the will of God, and when God's will will be done as perfectly in earth as it is in heaven. That is the aim and the goal of God for the whole universe. This parable is short but it is filled with unmistakable truths.

(i) It tells us of *the helplessness of man.* The farmer does not make the seed grow. In the last analysis he does not even understand how it grows. It has the secret of life and of growth within itself. No man has ever possessed the secret of life ; no man has ever created anything in the full and literal sense of the term. Man can discover things ; he can rearrange them ; he can develop them ; but create them he cannot. We do not create the Kingdom of God ; the Kingdom is God's. It is true that we can frustrate it and hinder it. We can make a situation in the world where it is given the opportunity to come more fully and more speedily. But behind all things is God and the power and will of God.

(ii) It tells us something about *the Kingdom.* It is a notable fact that Jesus so often uses illustrations from the growth of nature to describe the coming of the Kingdom of God. (a) Nature's growth is often *imperceptible.* We do not see a plant growing. If we see it every day we cannot see the growth taking place. It is only when we see it, and then go away, and then come back after an interval of time that we see the difference. It is so with the Kingdom. There is not the slightest doubt that the Kingdom is on the way if we compare, not to-day with yesterday, but this century with the century which went before. When Elizabeth Fry went to Newgate Prison in 1817 she found in the women's quarters three hundred women and numberless children crammed into two small wards. They lived and cooked and ate and slept on the floor. The only attendants were one old man and his son. They crowded, half naked, almost like beasts, begging for money which they spent on drink at a bar in the prison itself. She found there a boy of nine who was waiting to be hung for poking a stick through a window and stealing paints valued at twopence. In 1853 the weavers of Bolton were striking for a pay of 7½d. a day ; and the miners of Stafford were striking for a pay of 2s. 6d. a week. Nowadays things like that are unthinkable. Why? Because the Kingdom is on the way. The growth of the Kingdom may, like the growth of the plant, be imperceptible from day to day ; but over the years that growth is plain. (b) Nature's growth is *constant*. Night and day, while man sleeps, growth goes on. There is nothing spasmodic about God. The great trouble about human effort and human goodness is in fact that they are spasmodic. One day we take one step forward ; the next day we take two steps back. But the work of God goes on quietly; unceasingly God unfolds His plan.

> " God is working His purpose out, as year succeeds
>   to year :
> God is working His purpose out, and the time is
>   drawing near—
> Nearer and nearer draws the time—the time tha
>   shall surely be,
> When the earth shall be filled with the glory of God
>   as the waters cover the sea."

(c) Nature's growth is *inevitable*. There is nothing so powerful as growth. A tree can split a concrete pavement with the power of its growth. A weed can push its green head through an asphalt path. Nothing can stop growth. It is so with the Kingdom. In spite of man's rebellion and disobedience, God's work goes on ; and nothing in the end can stop the purposes of God.

(iii) It tells us that there is *a consummation.* There is a day when the harvest comes. Now inevitably when the harvest comes two things happen—things which are opposite sides of the same thing. The good fruit is gathered in, and the weeds and the tares are destroyed. Harvest and judgment go hand in hand. When we think of this coming day three things are laid upon us. (*a*) It is a summons to *patience.* We are creatures of the moment and inevitably we think in terms of the moment. God has all eternity in which to work. "A thousand years in Thy sight are but as yesterday when it is past, and as a watch in the night." (Psalm 90 : 4.) Instead of our petulant, fretful, irritable human hastiness we should cultivate in our souls the patience which learned to wait on God. (*b*) It is a summons to *hope.* We are living to-day in an atmosphere of despair. People despair of the Church ; they despair of the world ; they look with shuddering dread on the future. " Man," said H. G. Wells, " who began in a cave behind a windbreak will end in the disease-soaked ruins of a slum." Between the wars Sir Philip Gibbs wrote a book in which he looked forward. He was thinking of the possibility of a war of poison gas. He said something like this. " If I smell poison gas in High Street, Kensington, I am not going to put on a gas-mask. I am going to go out and breathe deeply of it, because I will know that *the game is up.*" So many people feel that for humanity the game is up. Now no man can think like that *and* believe in God. If God is the God we believe Him to be there is no room for pessimism in life. There may be remorse, regret ; there may be penitence, contrition ; there may be heart-searching, the realization of failure and of sin ; but there can never be despair.

" Workman of God ! O lose not heart,
    But learn what God is like,
And, in the darkest battle-field,
    Thou shalt know where to strike.

" For right is right, since God is God,
    And right the day must win :
To doubt would be disloyalty,
    To falter would be sin."

(c) It is a summons to *preparedness*. If there comes the consummation we must be ready for it. It is too late to prepare for it when it is upon us. We have literally to prepare to meet our God. But if we live in patience which cannot be defeated, in hope which cannot despair, and in preparation which ever sees life in the light of eternity, we shall, by the grace of God, be ready for God's consummation when it comes.

FROM SMALL TO GREAT

Mark 4 : 30-32

He said : " How shall we find something with which to compare the Kingdom of God, or what picture will we use to represent it? It is like a grain of mustard seed, which, when it is sown upon the ground, is the least of all the seeds upon the earth. But, when it is sown, it springs up and it becomes greater than all the herbs ; and it sends out great branches so that the birds of the heaven can find a lodging under its shade."

THERE are in this parable two pictures which every Jew would readily recognize. First, in Palestine a grain of mustard seed stood proverbially for the smallest possible thing. For instance, " faith as a grain of mustard seed," means " the smallest conceivable amount of faith." In Palestine this mustard seed did grow into something very like a tree. A traveller in Palestine speaks of seeing a mustard plant which, in its height, overtopped a horse and its rider. The birds were in fact very fond of the little black seeds of the tree, and a cloud of birds over a mustard plant was a common sight. Second, in the Old Testament one of the commonest ways to describe a great empire was to describe it as a tree, and the tributary nations who are within it are said to be like birds finding shelter within the shadow of its branches (Ezekiel 17 : 22ff ; 31 : 1ff ; Daniel 4 : 10, 21). The figure of a tree with birds in the branches therefore stands for a great empire and the nations who form part of it.

(i) This parable says to us, *Never be daunted by small beginnings*. It may seem that at the moment we can pro- duce only a very small effect ; but if that small effect is repeated and repeated the small effect will become very great. There is a scientific experiment to show the effect of dyes. A large vessel of clear water is taken and a little phial of dye. Drop by drop the dye is dropped into the clear water. At first it seems to have no effect at all and the water does not seem to be coloured in the least. Then quite suddenly the water begins to tinge with the colour ; bit by bit the colour deepens, until the whole vessel of water is coloured by the colour of the dye. It was the repeated drops that produced the effect. We often feel that for all that we can do it is hardly worth while starting a thing at all. But we must remember this—*somebody* must start everything ; *everything* must have a beginning. Nothing emerges full-grown. It is our duty to do what we can ; and the cumulative effect of all the small efforts can in the end produce an amazing result.

(ii) This parable speaks to us of *the empire of the Church*. The tree and the birds, we have seen, stand for the great empire and for all the nations who find shelter within it. The Church began with an individual and it is meant to end with the world. There are two directions in which this is true. (*a*) The Church is an Empire in which all kinds of opinions and all kinds of theologies can find a place. We have a tendency to brand as a heretic anyone who does not think as we do. John Wesley was the greatest example of tolerance in the world. " We think," he said,

" and we let think." " I have no more right," he said,
" to object to a man for holding a different opinion from
mine than I have to differ with a man because he wears
a wig and I wear my own hair." Wesley had one greeting,
" Is thy heart as my heart? Then give me thy hand ! "
It is good for a man to have the assurance that he is right,
but that is no reason why he should have the conviction
that everyone else is wrong. (*b*) The Church is an Empire
in which all nations meet. Once a new church was being
built. One of the great features of it was to be a stained
glass window. The committee in charge searched for a
subject for the window and finally decided to take as its
subject the lines of the hymn,

> " Around the throne of God in heaven
> Thousands of children stand."

They employed a great artist to paint the picture from
which the window would be made. The artist began the
work and fell in love with the task. Finally he finished the
picture. He went to bed and fell asleep but in the night he
seemed to hear a noise in his studio ; it seemed to him
that he went into the studio to investigate ; and there he
seemed to see a stranger with a brush and a palette in his
hands working at his picture. " Stop ! " he cried. " You'll
ruin my picture." " I think," said the stranger, " that you
have ruined it already." " How that? " said the artist.
" Well," said the stranger, " you have many colours on
your palette but you have used only one for the faces of
the children. Who told you that in heaven there were
only children whose faces were white? " " No one," said
the artist. " I just thought of it that way." " Look ! "
said the stranger. " I will make some of their faces yellow,
and some brown, and some black, and some red, for they
are all there for they have all answered my call." " Your
call? " said the artist. " Who are you? " The stranger
smiled. " Once, long ago," He said, " I said, ' Let the
children come to me and don't stop them, for of such is the
Kingdom of Heaven '— and I'm still saying it." And then

the artist knew that it was the Master Himself, and as he knew it, He vanished from his sight. The picture looked so much more wonderful now with the little black negroes, the little yellow, slant-eyed Chinese, and with the red for the Red Indians and the Arabs burnt with the sun and the sand, and with the little white children too. In the morning the artist awoke and rushed through to his studio. His picture was just the same as he had left it ; and he knew that it had all been a vision and a dream. Although that very day the committee was coming to examine the picture he seized his brushes and his paints, and began to paint the children of every colour and of every race throughout all the world. And when the committee arrived they thought the picture very beautiful and one whispered gently, " Why ! It's God's family at home." The Church is the family of God ; and that Church which began in Palestine, small as the mustard seed, has room in it for every nation in the world. There are no barriers in the Church of God. Man made the barriers and God in Christ tore them down.

THE WISE TEACHER AND THE WISE SCHOLAR

Mark 4 : 33, 34

> It was with many such parables that He kept speaking the word to them, suiting His instruction to their ability to hear it. It was His custom not to speak to them without a parable ; and when they were by themselves, He unfolded the meaning of everything to His own disciples.

IN this passage we have a short but perfect definition of both the wise teacher and the wise learner. Jesus suited His instruction to the ability of those who were listening to Him. That is the first essential in wise teaching.

There are two dangers that the wise teacher must at all

costs avoid. (*a*) He must avoid all *self-display*. A teacher's duty is not to draw attention to himself but to draw attention to his subject. A love of self-display can make a man attempt to scintillate at the expense of truth. It can make him think more of clever ways of saying a thing than of the thing itself. Or, it can make him so desirous of displaying his own erudition that he becomes so obscure and elaborate and involved that the ordinary man cannot understand him at all. There is no virtue in talking over the head of an audience. As someone said, " The fact that a man shoots above the target only proves that he is a bad shot." A good teacher must be in love with his subject and not in love with himself. (*b*) He must avoid *a sense of superiority*. True teaching does not consist in telling people things. It consists in learning things together. It was Plato's idea that teaching simply meant extracting from people's minds and memories what they already knew. The teacher who stands on a pedestal and talks down will never be successful. True teaching consists in sharing and discovering truth together. It is a joint exploration of the countries of the mind.

There are certain qualities which he who would teach must ever seek to acquire and to possess. (*a*) The teacher must possess *understanding*. One of the great difficulties of the expert is to understand why the non-expert finds a thing so difficult to understand or to do. It is necessary for the teacher to think with the learner's mind and to see with the learner's eyes, before he can really explain and impart any kind of knowledge. (*b*) The teacher must possess *patience*. The Jewish Rabbi Hillel laid it down, " An irritable man cannot teach," and insisted that the first essential of a teacher is that he must be even-tempered. The Jews laid it down that if a teacher found that his scholars did not understand a thing he must begin again without rancour and without irritation and explain it all over again. That is precisely what Jesus did all His life. (*c*) The teacher must possess *kindness*. Jewish teaching regulations forbade all excessive punishment. Especially they forbade all punishment which would humiliate the scholar. The teacher's duty was always to encourage, and never to discourage. Anna Buchan tells how her old grandmother had a favourite phrase, " Never daunton youth." It is easy for the teacher to use the lash of his tongue on the pupil with the limping mind ; it is often a temptation to score a cheap triumph by making such a pupil the target of such sarcasms and witticisms as will make him a laughing-stock. The teacher who is kind will never do that.

But this passage also shows us the wise learner. It gives us a picture of an inner circle to whom Jesus could really and fully explain things. (a) The wise learner *does not go away to forget*. He goes away to think over what he has heard. He ought to chew it over until he has finally digested it. Epictetus, the wise Stoic teacher, used to be grieved by some of his pupils. He used to say that men ought to use the philosophy they learned, not to talk about, but to live by. In a crude metaphor, he said that sheep do not vomit up the grass that they have eaten to show the shepherd how much they have eaten ; they digest it and use it to produce wool and milk. The wise scholar goes away, not to forget what he has learned, and not to display what he has learned, but quietly to think over it until he has discovered what it means for life and for living for him. (b) Above all, the wise learner *seeks the master's company*. After Jesus had spoken the crowds dispersed ; but there was a little company who lingered with Him and who did not want to leave Him. It was to them that He unfolded the meaning of everything. In the last analysis, if a man is a really great teacher, it is not so much the man's teaching that we wish to know, but the man himself. His message will always lie not so much in what he says as in what he is. The man who wishes to learn from Christ must company with Christ. If he does that he will win, not only learning, but even life itself.

THE PEACE OF THE PRESENCE

Mark 4 : 35-41

> When on that day evening had come, He said to them,
> " Let us cross over to the other side." So they left
> the crowds and took Him, just as He was, in their
> boat. And there were other boats with Him. A great
> storm of wind got up and the waves dashed upon the
> boat, so that the boat was on the point of being
> swamped. And He was in the stern sleeping upon a
> pillow. They woke Him. " Teacher," they said,
> " don't you care that we are perishing? " So, when
> He had been wakened, He spoke sternly to the wind
> and said to the sea, " Be silent ! Be muzzled ! "
> and the wind sank to rest and there was a great calm.
> He said to them, " Why are you afraid? Have you
> still no faith? " And they were stricken with a great
> awe, and kept saying to each other, " Who then can
> this be, because the wind and the sea obey Him? "

THE Lake of Galilee was notorious for its storms. They
were storms which came literally out of the blue with
shattering and terrifying suddenness. A writer describes
them like this : " It is not unusual to see terrible squalls
hurl themselves, even when the sky is perfectly clear, upon
these waters which are ordinarily so calm. The numerous
ravines which to the north-east and east debouch upon the
upper part of the lake operate as so many dangerous defiles
in which the winds from the heights of Hauran, the
plateaux of Trachonitis, and the summit of Mount Hermon
are caught and compressed in such a way that, rushing
with tremendous force through a narrow space and then
being suddenly released, they agitate the little Lake of
Gennesaret in the most frightful fashion." The voyager
across the lake was always liable to encounter just such
sudden storms as this.

Jesus was in the boat in the position in which any distinguished guest would be conveyed. We are told that,
" In these boats ... the place for any distinguished stranger
is on the little seat placed at the stern, where a carpet and
cushion are arranged. The helmsman stands a little farther

forward on the deck, though near the stern, in order to have a better look-out ahead."

It is interesting to note that the words that Jesus addressed to the wind and the waves are exactly the same words as he addressed to the demon-possessed man in Mark 1 : 15. Just as an evil demon possessed that man, so the destructive power of the storm was, as people in Palestine believed in those days, the evil power of the demons at work in the realm of nature.

We do this story far less than justice if we merely take it in a literalistic sense. If this describes simply a physical miracle in which an actual storm was stilled, it is a very wonderful story, and it is something about which we read and at which we marvel, but nonetheless it is something which happened once and which cannot happen again. In that case it is quite external to us. But if we read it in a symbolic sense it is far more valuable. When the disciples realized the presence of Jesus with them the storm became a calm. Once they knew He was there there was a calm, fearless peace in their hearts no matter what any storm was like. To voyage with Jesus was to voyage in peace even in a storm. Now that is universally true. That is not something which happened once ; it is something which still happens and which can happen for us. In the presence of Jesus we can have peace in even the wildest storms of life.

(i) He gives us peace in the storm of *sorrow*. When sorrow comes to us, as come it must, He tells us of the glory of the life to come. He changes the darkness of death into glory of the thought of life eternal. He tells us of the love of God. There is an old story of a gardener who in his garden had a favourite flower which he loved much. One day he came to the garden to find that flower gone. He was vexed and angry and full of complaints. In the midst of his resentment he met the master of the garden and hurled his complaints at him. " Hush ! " said the master, " I plucked it for myself." In the storm of sorrow Jesus tells us that those we love have gone to be with God, and gives us the certainty that we shall meet again those whom we have loved and lost awhile.

(ii) He gives us peace when life's *problems* involve us in a tempest of doubt and tension and uncertainty. There come times when we do not know what to do ; when we stand at some cross-roads in life and do not know which way to take. If then we turn to Jesus and say to Him, " Lord, what wilt Thou have me to do? " the way will be clear and plain. The real tragedy is not that we do not know what to do ; it is that so often we do not humbly submit to His guidance. To ask His will and to submit to it is the way to peace at such a time.

(iii) He gives us peace in the storms of *anxiety* which can attack this life. The enemy of peace is worry, worry for ourselves, worry about the unknown future, worry about those we love. But Jesus speaks to us of a Father whose hand will never cause His child a needless tear and of a love beyond which neither we nor those we love can ever drift. In the storm of anxiety He brings us the peace of the love of God.

THE BANISHING OF THE DEMONS

Mark 5 : 1-13

> They came to the other side of the lake, to the territory of the Gerasenes. Immediately Jesus had disembarked from the boat, there met him from the tombs a man in the grip of an unclean spirit. This man lived amongst the tombs. No one had ever been able to bind him with a chain, because he had often been bound with fetters and chains, and the chains had been wrenched apart by him and the fetters shattered ; and no one was strong enough to tame him. Continually, night and day, in the tombs and in the hills, he kept shrieking and gashing himself with stones. He saw Jesus when He was still a long way away, and he ran and knelt before Him. " What," he said, " have you and I to do with each other, Jesus, you son of the most high God? In God's name, I

adjure you, do not torture me ! " For Jesus had been
saying to him, " Unclean spirit, come out of the man ! "
" What is your name? " He asked him. " Legion is
my name," he said, " for we are many." And he
kept begging Him with many an entreaty not to send
them out of the country. Now a great herd of swine
was feeding on the mountain-side. " Send us into the
swine," they urged Him, " that we may go into them."
And Jesus permitted them to go into them. And the
unclean spirits came out and entered into the swine
and the herd—there were about two thousand of
them—rushed down the precipice into the lake, and
were drowned in the lake.

HERE is a vivid and rather eerie story. It is the kind of
story in which we have to do our best to try to read between
the lines, because it is thinking and speaking in terms
which were quite familiar to people in Palestine in the
days of Jesus, but quite alien to us.

If this is to be taken in close connection with what
goes before—and that is Mark's intention—it must have
happened late in the evening or even when the night had
begun, in the dusk or in the dark. The story becomes all
the more weird and frightening when it is seen as
happening in the shadows of the night. Verse 35 tells us
that it was late in the evening when Jesus and His friends
had set sail. The Lake of Galilee is 13 miles long at its
longest, and 8 miles wide at its widest. At this particular
part it was about 5 miles across. They had made the
journey and, on the way, they had encountered the storm,
and now they had reached land. It was a part of the lakeside where there were many caves in the limestone rock,
and many of these caves were used as tombs in which
bodies were laid. At the best of times it was an eerie place ;
as night fell it must have been grim indeed. Out of the
tombs there came a demon-possessed man. It was a
fitting place for him to be, for demons, so they believed in
those days, dwelt in woods and gardens and vineyards and
dirty places, in lonely and desolate spots and among the
tombs. The demon-possessed man dwelt in the haunt of

demons. It was in the night-time and before cock-crow
that the demons were specially active. To sleep alone in
an empty house at night was dangerous ; to greet any
person in the dark was perilous, for the person might be a
demon. To go out at night without a lantern or a torch
was to court trouble. It was a perilous place and a
perilous hour, and the man was a dangerous man.

How completely this man felt himself to be possessed is
seen in his way of speaking. Sometimes he uses the
singular, as if he himself was speaking ; sometimes he uses
the plural, as if all the demons in him were speaking. He
was so convinced that the demons were in him, that he
felt that they were speaking through him. When asked
his name he said his name was Legion. There were probably
two reasons for that. A legion was a Roman regiment of
6,000 troops. Very likely the man had seen one of these
Roman regiments clanking along the road, and he felt that
there was a whole solid battalion of demons inside him.
In any event the Jews believed that no man would survive
if he realised the number of demons with which he was
surrounded. They were " like the earth that is thrown up
around a bed that is sown." There were a thousand at a
man's right hand and ten thousand at his left. The queen
of the female spirits had no fewer than 180,000 followers.
There was a Jewish saying, " A legion of hurtful spirits is
on the watch for men, saying, ' When shall he fall into the
hands of one of these things and be taken?' " No doubt
this wretched man knew all about this, and his poor,
wandering mind was certain that a mass of those demons
had taken up their residence in him. But further, Palestine
was an occupied country. The legions, at their wildest and
most irresponsible, could sometimes be guilty of atrocities
that would make the blood run cold. It may well be that
this man had seen, had suffered from, or had seen his loved
ones suffer from, the murder and the rapine that could
sometimes follow the legions. It may well be that it was

some such terrible experience which had driven him insane. The word *Legion* conjured up for him a vision of terror and death and destruction. He was convinced that demons like that were inside him.

We shall not even begin to understand this story unless we see clearly how serious a case of demon possession this man was. It is clear that Jesus made more than one attempt to heal this man. Verse 8 tells us that Jesus had begun by using his usual method—an authoritative order to the demon to come out. On this occasion that was not successful. Next, Jesus demanded what the demon's name was. It was always supposed in those days that, if a demon's name could be discovered, it gave a certain power over the demon. An ancient magical formula says, " I adjure thee, every demonic spirit, Say whatsoever Thou art." The belief was that if the name was known the demon's power was broken. In this case even that did not prove enough.

Jesus saw that there was only one thing that could cure this man—and that was something which would be to the man an unanswerable demonstration that the demons had gone out of him, at least, unanswerable as far as his own mind was concerned. It does not matter whether we believe in demon-possession or not ; this man did believe in it. Even if it all lay in his disordered mind, the demons were terribly real to him. Dr. Rendle Short, speaking about the supposed evil influence of the moon (Psalm 121: 6) which emerges in the words *lunatic* and *moonstruck*, says, " Modern science does not recognize any particular harm as coming from the moon. Yet it is a very widespread belief that the moon does affect people mentally. . . . It is good to know that the Lord can deliver us from imaginary dangers as well as from real ones. Often the imaginary are harder to face." This man needed deliverance ; whether that deliverance was from literal demon-possession, or

from an all-powerful delusion does not matter. This is
where the herd of swine comes in. They were grazing on
the hillside. The man felt that the demons were asking,
not to be totally destroyed, but to be sent into the swine.
All the time he was uttering these shrieks and going through
these paroxysms which were the sign of his malady.
Suddenly, as his yells reached a new pitch of intensity, the
whole herd took flight and plunged down a steep slope
into the sea. *There* was the very proof that the man
needed. This was almost the only possible thing on earth
that could have convinced him that he was cured. Jesus,
like a wise healer, like one who understood, so kindly and
sympathetically the psychology of a mind diseased, used
the event to help the man in his climb back to sanity, and
his disordered mind was restored to peace.

There are ultra-fastidious people who will blame Jesus
because the healing of the man involved the death of the
pigs. They complain about the cruelty to these animals
involved in this miracle. Surely it is a singularly blind way
in which to look at things. How could the fate of the pigs
possibly be compared with the fate of a man's immortal
soul? We do not, presumably, have any objections to
eating meat for our dinner, nor will we refuse pork because
it involved the killing of some pig. Surely if we kill
animals to avoid going hungry, we can raise no objection if
the saving of a man's mind and soul involved the death
of a herd of these same animals. There is a cheap senti-
mentalism which will languish in grief over the pain of an
animal and will never turn a hair at the wretched state of
millions of God's men and women. This is not to say that
we need not care what happens to God's animal creation,
for God loves every creature whom His hands have made,
but it is to say that we must preserve a sense of proportion ; and in God's scale of proportions, there is
nothing so important as a human soul.

BIDDING CHRIST BE GONE

Mark 5 : 14-17

> The men who were feeding the pigs fled, and brought news of what had happened to the town and to the farms. They came to see what it was that had happened. They came to Jesus, and they saw the demon-possessed man—the man who had had the legion of demons—sitting fully clothed and in his senses, and they were afraid ; and those who had seen what had taken place told them what had happened to the demon-possessed man, and told them about the pigs ; and they began to urge Him to get out of their territory.

VERY naturally the men who had been in charge of the pigs went to the town and to the farms with news of this astounding happening. When the curious people arrived on the spot they found the man who had once been so mad sitting fully clothed and in full possession of his faculties. The wild and naked madman had become a sane and sensible citizen. And then there comes the surprise, the paradox, the thing that no one would really expect. One would have thought that they would have regarded the whole matter with joy ; but they regarded it with terror. And one would have thought that they would have besought Jesus to stay with them and to exercise still further His amazing power ; but they besought Him to get out of their district as quickly as possible. Why? A man had been healed but their pigs had been destroyed, and therefore they wanted no more of this. The routine of life had been unsettled and disturbed, and they wanted the disturbing element removed as quickly as possible.

The one battle-cry of the human mind is, " Please don't disturb me." On the whole, the one thing that people want is to be let alone.

(i) Instinctively people say, " *Don't disturb my comfort.*" If someone came to us who are reasonably comfortably off and said, " I can give you a world that will be a better world for the mass of people in general, but it will mean that your comfort will, at least for a time, be disturbed and upset, and you will have to do with less for the sake of others," most people would say, " I would much rather that you would leave things as they are." In point of fact that is almost precisely the situation through which we are living in the present social revolution. We are living through a time of redistribution ; we are living through a time when life is a great deal better than ever it was for a great many people. But it has meant that life is not so comfortable as it was for quite a number of people ; and for that very reason there is a resentment abroad because some of the comforts of life have gone. There is a great deal of talk about what life *owes* us. Life owes us precisely nothing ; the debt is all the other way round. It is we who owe life all that we have to give. We are followers of one who gave up the glory of heaven for the narrowness of earth, who gave up the joy of God for the pain of the Cross. It is human not to want to have our comfort disturbed ; it is divine to be willing to be disturbed that others may have more.

(ii) Instinctively people say, " *Don't disturb my possessions.*" Here is another aspect of the same thing. No man really willingly gives up anything he may possess. The older we get the more we want to clutch it to us. Borrow, who knew the gipsies, tells us that it is the fortune-telling gipsy's policy to promise to the young various pleasures, and to foretell to the old riches, and only riches " for they have sufficient knowledge of the human heart to be aware that avarice is the last passion that becomes extinct within." We can soon see whether a man really accepts his faith and whether he really believes in his principles, by seeing if he is willing to become poorer for them.

(iii) Instinctively people say, " *Don't disturb my religion.*" (*a*) People say, " Don't let unpleasant subjects disturb the pleasant decorum of my religion." Edmund Gosse points out a curious omission in the sermons of the famous divine, Jeremy Taylor. " These sermons are amongst the most able and profound in the English language, but they hardly ever mention the poor, hardly ever refer to their sorrows, and show practically no interest in their state. The sermons were preached in South Wales where poverty abounded. The cry of the poor and the hungry, the ill-clothed and the needy ceaselessly ascended up to heaven, and called out for pity and redress, but this eloquent divine never seemed to hear it, he lived and wrote and preached surrounded by the suffering and the needy, and yet remained scarcely conscious of their existence." It is much less disturbing to preach about the niceties of theological beliefs and doctrines than it is to preach about the needs of men and the abuses of life. We have actually known of congregations who informed ministers that it was a condition of their call that they would not preach on certain subjects. It was a notable thing that it was not what Jesus said about God, that got Him into trouble ; it was what He said about *man* and about the needs of man that disturbed the orthodox of His day. (*b*) People have been known to say, " Don't let personal relationships disturb my religion." James Burns quotes an amazing thing in this connection from the life of Angela di Foligras, the famous Italian mystic. She had the gift of completely withdrawing herself from this world, and from returning from her trances with tales of ineffably sweet communion with God. It was she herself who said : " In that time, and by God's will, there died my mother, who was a great hindrance unto me in following the way of God ; my husband died likewise, and in a short time there died all my children. And because I had commenced to follow the aforesaid way, and had prayed God that He would rid me of them, I had great consolation of their deaths, albeit I did also feel some grief." Her family was a trouble to her religion. There is a type of religion which is fonder of committees than it is of housework, which is more set on quiet times than it is on human service. It prides itself on serving the Church and spending itself in devotion—but nonetheless in God's eyes it has got things the wrong way round. (c) People say, " Don't disturb my beliefs." There is a type of religion which says, " What is good enough for my fathers is good enough for me." There are people who do not want to know anything new, for they know that if they did they might have to go through the mental sweat of rethinking things and coming to new conclusions. There is a cowardice of thought and a lethargy of mind and a sleep of the soul which are terrible things.

The Gerasenes banished the disturbing Christ—and still men seek to do the same.

A WITNESS FOR CHRIST

Mark 5 : 18-20

> As Jesus was getting into the boat, the man who had been demon-possessed kept begging Him that he might be allowed to stay with Him. He did not allow him, but said to him, " Go back to your home and your own people, and tell them all that the Lord has done for you." And he went away and began to proclaim the story throughout the Decapolis of all that Jesus had done for him.

THE interesting thing about this passage is that it tells us where this whole incident happened. It happened in the Decapolis. Decapolis literally means The Ten Cities. Near to the Jordan, and especially on the East side of the Jordan, there were ten cities which were of rather a special character. They were essentially Greek. Their names were Scythopolis, which was the only one on the west side of the Jordan, Pella, Dion, Gerasa, Philadelphia, Gadara, Raphana, Kanatha, Hippos and Damascus. With the conquests of Alexander the Great there had been a Greek penetration into Palestine and Syria. These Greek cities which had been then founded were in rather a curious position. They were within Syria ; but they were very largely independent. They had their own councils and their own coinage ; they had the right of local administration, not only of themselves but of an area around them ; they had the right of association for mutual defence and for commercial purposes. They remained in a kind of semi-independence down until the time of the Maccabees, about the middle of the second century B.C. The Maccabees were the Jewish conquerors, and they subjected most of these cities to Jewish rule. They were liberated from Jewish rule by the Roman Emperor Pompey about 63 B.C. They were still in a curious position. They were to some extent independent, but they were liable to Roman taxation and Roman military service. They were not garrisoned, but frequently they were the headquarters of Roman legions in the eastern campaigns. Now Rome governed most of this part of the world by a system of tributary kings. The result was that Rome could give these cities very little actual protection ; and so they banded themselves together into a kind of corporation to defend themselves against Jewish and Arab encroachment. They were stubbornly Greek. They were beautiful cities ; they had their Greek gods and their Greek temples and their Greek amphitheatres ; they were devoted to the Greek way of life. Here, then, is a most interesting thing. If Jesus was in the Decapolis this is one of the first hints of things to come. There would be Jews there, but it was fundamentally a Greek area. Here is a foretaste of a world for Christ. Here is the first sign of Christianity bursting the bonds of Judaism and going out to all the world. Just how Greek these cities were, and just how important they were, can be seen from the fact that from Gadara alone there came Philodemus, the great Epicuraean philosopher, who was a contemporary of Cicero, Meleager, the master of the Greek epigram, Menippus, the famous satirist, and Theodorus, the rhetorician, who was no less a person than the tutor of Tiberius, the reigning Roman Emperor. Something happened on that day that Jesus set foot in the Decapolis.

There is now good reason to see why Jesus sent the man back.

(i) He was to be a witness for Christianity. He was to be a living, walking, vivid, unanswerable demonstration of what Christ can do for a man. Our glory must always be not in what we can do for Christ but in what Christ can do for us. The unanswerable proof of Christianity is a re-created man.

(ii) He was to be the first seed which in time was to become a mighty harvest. The first contact with Greek civilization was made in the Decapolis. Everything must start somewhere ; and the glory of all the Christianity which one day flowered in the Greek mind and genius began with a man who had been possessed by demons and whom Christ healed. Christ must always begin with someone. In our own circle and society why should He not begin with us?

IN THE HOUR OF NEED

Mark 5 : 21-24

> When Jesus had crossed over in the boat back again to the other side, a great crowd gathered together to Him ; and He was by the lakeside. One of the rulers of the Synagogue, Jairus by name, came to Him ; and, when he saw Him, he threw himself at His feet. He pled with Him, " My little daughter is lying at death's door. Come and lay your hands on her, that she may be cured and live." Jesus went away with him ; and the crowd were following Him, and crushing in upon Him on all sides.

THERE are all the elements of tragedy here. It is always tragic when a child is ill. The story tells us that the Ruler's daughter was twelve years of age. According to the Jewish custom a girl became a woman at twelve years and one day. This girl was just on the threshold of womanhood, and when death comes at such a time it is doubly tragic.

The story tells us something about this man who was the Ruler of the Synagogue. He must have been a person of some considerable importance. The Ruler of the Synagogue was the administrative head of the Synagogue. He was the president of the board of elders who were responsible for the good management of the Synagogue. He was responsible for the conduct of the services. He did not usually take part in them himself, but he was responsible for the allocation of duties, and for seeing that they were carried out with all seemliness and good order. The Ruler of the Synagogue was one of the most important and the most respected men in the community. But something had happened to him when his daughter fell ill and when he thought of Jesus.

(i) His *prejudices* were forgotten. There can be no doubt that he must have regarded Jesus as an outsider, as a dangerous heretic, as one to whom the Synagogue doors were closed, and one whom anyone who valued his orthodoxy would do well to avoid. But he was a big enough man to abandon his prejudices in his hour of need. Prejudice really means *a judging beforehand*. It is a judging before a man has examined the evidence, or a verdict given because of refusal to examine the evidence. Few things have done more to hold things up than prejudice. Nearly every forward step has had to fight against the initial prejudice against it. When Sir James Simpson discovered the use of chloroform as an anaesthetic, especially in the case of childbirth, chloroform was held to be, " a decoy of Satan, apparently opening itself to bless women, but in the end hardening them, and robbing God of the deep, earnest cries, that should arise to Him in time of trouble." A prejudiced mind shuts out a man from many a blessing.

(ii) His *dignity* was forgotten. He, the Ruler of the Synagogue, came and threw himself at the feet of Jesus, the wandering teacher. Not a few times a man has had to forget his dignity to save his life and to save his soul.

In the old story that is precisely what Naaman had to do
(2 Kings 5). He had come to Elisha to be cured of his
leprosy. Elisha's prescription was that he should go and
wash in the Jordan seven times. That was no way to treat
the Syrian Prime Minister ! Elisha had not even delivered
the message personally ; he had sent it by a messenger !
And, had they not far better rivers in Syria than the
muddy little Jordan? These were Naaman's first thoughts ;
but he swallowed his pride and lost his leprosy. There is a
famous story of Diogenes, the Cynic philosopher. He was
captured by pirates and he was being sold as a slave. As
he gazed at the bystanders who were bidding for him, he
looked at a man. " Sell me to that man," he said. " He
needs a master." The man bought him ; handed over the
management of his household and the education of his
children to him. " It was a good day for me," he used to
say, " when Diogenes entered my household." True, but
that required an abrogating of dignity. It frequently
happens that a man stands on his dignity and falls from
grace.

(iii) His *pride* was forgotten. It must have taken a conscious effort of humiliation for this Ruler of the Synagogue
to come and ask for help from Jesus of Nazareth. It is true
to say that no one wishes to be indebted to anyone else.
We would like to run life on our own. The very first step
of the Christian life is to realize that we cannot be anything
other than indebted to God.

(iv) Here we enter the realm of speculation, but it seems
to me that we can say of this man that his *friends* were
forgotten. It may well be that, to the end, they objected
to him calling in this Jesus. It is rather strange that he
came himself and did not send a messenger. It seems
unlikely that he would consent to leave his daughter when
she was on the point of death. Maybe he came because no
one else would go. His household were suspiciously quick
to tell him not to trouble Jesus any more. It sounds almost
as if they were glad not to call upon His help. It may well

be that this ruler defied public opinion and home advice in order to call in Jesus. Many a man is wisest when his worldly wise friends think that he is acting like a fool.

Here was a man who forgot everything except that he wanted the help of Jesus ; and, just because he forgot, he would remember for ever after that Jesus is a Saviour.

A SUFFERER'S LAST HOPE

Mark 5 : 25-29

> Now there was a woman who was suffering from a hemorrhage which had lasted for twelve years. She had gone through many things at the hands of many doctors ; she had spent everything she had ; and it had not helped her at all. Indeed she rather got worse and worse. When she heard the stories about Jesus, she came up behind Him in the crowd, and she touched His robe, for she said, " If I touch even His clothes I will be cured." And immediately the fountain of her blood was staunched, and she knew in her body that she was healed from her scourge.

THE woman in this story suffered from a trouble which was very common and very hard to deal with. The Talmud itself gives no fewer than eleven cures for such a trouble. Some of them are tonics and astringents ; but some of them were sheer superstitions like carrying the ashes of an ostrich-egg in a linen rag in summer and a cotton rag in winter ; or carrying a barley corn which had been found in the dung of a white she-ass. No doubt this poor woman had tried even these desperate remedies. The trouble was that not only did this affect a woman's health, but it also rendered her continuously unclean, and shut her off from the worship of God and the fellowship of her friends (Leviticus 15 : 25-27).

Mark here has a gentle jibe at the doctors. She had tried them all and had suffered much and had spent everything she had, and the result was that she was worse instead of better. Jewish literature is interesting on the subject of doctors. " I used to go to the physicians," says one person, " to be healed, and the more they anointed me with their medicaments, the more my eyes were blinded by the films, until they were totally blinded." (Tobit 2 : 10.) There is a passage in the *Mishnah*, which is the written summary of the traditional law, which is talking about the trades that a man may teach his son. " Rabbi Judah says : 'Ass-drivers are most of them wicked, camel-drivers are most of them proper folk, sailors are most of them saintly, the best among physicians is destined for Gehenna, and the most seemly among butchers is a partner of Amalek '." But, fortunately and justly, there are voices on the other side. One of the greatest of all tributes to doctors is in *The Book of Sirach* (one of the apocryphal books written in the time between the Old and the New Testaments) in chapter 38 : 1-15.

" Cultivate the physician in accordance with the need
        of him,
    For him also hath God ordained.
It is from God that the physician getteth wisdom,
    And from the king he receiveth gifts.

" The skill of the physician lifteth up his head,
    And he may stand before nobles.
God hath created medicines out of the earth,
    And let not a discerning man reject them.

" By means of them the physician assuageth pain,
    And likewise the apothecary prepareth an oint-
        ment :
That His work may not cease,
    Nor health from the face of the earth.

" And to the physician also give a place ;
    Nor should he be far away for of him there is need.
For there is a time when successful help is in his
        power ;
    For he also maketh supplication to God,
To make his diagnosis successful,
    And the treatment that it may promote recovery."

The physicians had had no success with the treat-ment of this woman's case, and she had heard of

Jesus. But she had this problem—her trouble was an embarrassing thing ; to go in the crowd and to state it openly was something that she could not face ; and so she decided to try to touch Jesus in secret. In the time of Jesus every devout Jew wore an outer robe with four tassels on it, one at each corner. These tassels were worn in obedience to the command in Numbers 15 : 38-40, and they were to signify to others, and to remind a man himself, that a man was a member of the chosen people of God. They were the badge of a devout Jew. It was one of these tassels that the woman slipped through the crowd and touched ; and, having touched it, she was thrilled to find herself cured.

Here was a woman who came to Jesus as a last resort ; having tried every other cure that the world had to offer she finally tried Jesus. Many and many a man has come to seek the help of Jesus Christ when he himself was at his wits' end. He may have battled with temptation until he could fight no longer and until he stretched out a hand, crying, " Lord, save me ! I perish ! " He may have struggled on with some exhausting task until he has reached the breaking-point and cried out for a strength which is not his strength. He may have laboured to attain the goodness which haunts him, only to see it recede ever farther away, until he is utterly frustrated. No man should need to be driven to Christ by the force of circumstances, and yet many come that way ; and, even if it is thus we come, He will never send us empty away.

> " When other helpers fail and comforts flee,
>   Help of the helpless, O abide with me."

THE COST OF HEALING
Mark 5 : 30-34.

Jesus was well aware in Himself that the power which issued from Him had gone out of Him ; and immediately, in the middle of the crowd, He turned and said :

" Who touched my clothes? " The disciples said to Him : " Look at the crowd that are crushing you on every side—what's the point of saying, ' Who touched me? ' " He kept looking all round to see who had done this. The woman was terrified and trembling. She knew well what had happened to her. She came and threw herself down before Him, and told Him the whole truth. " Daughter ! " He said to her, " Your faith has cured you ! Go, and be in good health, free from the trouble that was your scourge."

THIS passage tells us something about three people.

(i) It tells us something about Jesus. It tells us *the cost of healing.* Every time Jesus healed anyone it took something out of Him. Here is a universal rule of life. We will never produce anything great unless we are prepared to put something of ourselves, of our very life, of our very soul into it. No pianist will ever give a really great performance if he glides through a piece of music with faultless and effortless technique and nothing more. The performance will not be great unless at the end of it there is the exhaustion which comes of the outpouring of self. No actor will ever give a great performance who repeats his words with every inflection right and every gesture correct, like a perfectly designed automaton. His tears must be real tears ; his feelings must be real feelings ; something of himself must go into the acting. No preacher who ever preached a real sermon descended from his pulpit without a feeling of being drained of something. If we are ever to help men, we must be ready to spend ourselves. It all comes from our attitude to men. Once Matthew Arnold, the great literary critic, said of the middle classes : " Look at these people ; the clothes they wear ; the books they read ; the texture of mind that composes their thoughts ; would any amount of money compensate for being like one of these? " Now the *sense* of that saying may or may not be true ; but the point is that it was *contempt* that gave it birth. He looked on men with a kind of shuddering loathing ; and no one who looks on men like that can ever help them. Think on the other hand of Moses, after the people had made the golden calf when he was on the mountain top. Remember how he besought God to blot him out of the book of remembrance if only the people might be forgiven. (Exodus 32 : 30-32.) Think of how Myers makes Paul speak when he looks upon the lost and pagan world :

" Then, with a thrill, the intolerable craving,
　　Shivers throughout me like a trumpet call—
　O to save these, to perish for their saving—
　　Die for their life, be offered for them all."

The greatness of Jesus was that He was prepared to pay the price of helping others, and that price was the outgoing of His very life. We only follow in His steps when we are prepared to spend, not our substance, but our souls and strength for others.

(ii) It tells us something about the disciples. It shows us very vividly the limitations of what is called common sense. The disciples took the common sense point of view. How could Jesus avoid being touched and jostled in a crowd like that? That was the sensible way to look at things. There emerges the strange and poignant fact that they had never recognized or realized that it cost Jesus anything at all to heal others. One of the tragedies of life is the strange insensitiveness of the human mind. We so often utterly fail to realize what others are going through. Because we may have no experience of something, we never think what that something is costing someone else. Because something may be quite easy for us we never realize what a costly effort it is for someone else. That is why we so often hurt worst of all those we love. A man may pray for common sense, but sometimes he would do well to pray for that sensitive, imaginative insight which can see into the hearts of others.

(iii) It tells us something about the woman. It tells us of the relief of confession. It was all so difficult ; it was all so humiliating. But once she had told the whole truth

to Jesus, the terror and the trembling were gone and a
wave of relief flooded her heart. And when she had made
her pitiful confession she found Him very kind.

> " Let not conscience make you linger,
>   Nor of fitness fondly dream ;
> All the fitness He requireth
>   Is to feel your need of Him."

It is never hard to confess to one who understands like
Jesus.

DESPAIR AND HOPE

Mark 5 : 35-39

> While He was still speaking, messages came from the
> household of the Ruler of the Synagogue. " Your
> daughter," they said, " has died. Why trouble the
> teacher any more? " Jesus overheard this message
> being given. He said to the Ruler of the Synagogue,
> " Don't be afraid ! Only keep on believing ! " He
> allowed no one to accompany Him except Peter and
> James and John, James' brother. They came to the
> house of the Ruler of the Synagogue. He saw the
> uproar. He saw the people weeping and wailing. He
> came in. " Why," He said to them, " are you so
> distressed? And what are you weeping for? The
> little girl has not died—she is sleeping." They
> laughed Him to scorn.

JEWISH mourning customs were very vivid and very
detailed, and practically all of them were designed to
stress the desolation and the final separation of death.
The triumphant victorious hope of the Christian faith was
totally absent from them.

Immediately death had taken place a loud wailing was
set up so that all might know that death had struck. The
wailing was repeated at the grave side. The mourners
hung over the dead body, begging for a response from the
silent lips. They beat their breasts ; they tore their hair ;
and they rent their garments. The rending of garments

was done according to certain rules and regulations. It was done just before the body was finally hid from sight. Garments were to be rent to the heart, that is, until the skin was exposed, but were not to be rent beyond the navel. For fathers and mothers the rent was on the left side, over the heart ; for others it was on the right side. A woman was to rend her garments in private ; she was then to reverse the inner garment, so that it was worn back to front ; she then rent her outer garment, so that her body was not exposed. The rent garment was worn for thirty days. After seven days the rent might be roughly sewn up, in such a way that it was still clearly visible. After the thirty days the garment was properly repaired. Flute-players were essential. Throughout most of the ancient world, in Rome, in Greece, in Phoenicia, in Assyria and in Palestine, the wailing of the flute was inseparably connected with death and tragedy. It was laid down that, however poor a man was, he must have at least two flute-players at his wife's funeral. W. Taylor Smith in Hastings' *Dictionary of Christ and the Gospels* quotes two interesting instances of the use of flute-players, which show how widespread the custom was. There were flute-players at the funeral of Claudius, the Roman Emperor. When in A.D. 67 news reached Jerusalem of the fall of Jotapata to the Roman armies, Josephus tells us that " most people engaged flute-players to lead their lamentations." The wail of the flutes, the screams of the mourners, the passionate appeals to the dead, the rent garments, the torn hair, must have made a Jewish house a poignant and pathetic place on the day of mourning.

When death came a mourner was forbidden to work, to anoint himself or to wear shoes. Even the poorest man must cease from work for three days. He must not travel with goods ; and the prohibition of work extended even to his servants. He must sit with head bound up. He must not shave, or " do anything for his comfort." He must not read the Law or the Prophets, for to read these books is joy. He was allowed to read Job, Jeremiah and Lamentations. He must eat only in his own house, and he must abstain altogether from flesh and wine. He must not leave the town or village for thirty days. It was the custom not to eat at a table, but to eat, sitting on the floor, using a chair as a table. It was the custom, which still survives, to eat eggs dipped in ashes and salt. There was one curious custom. All water from the house, and from the three houses on each side, was emptied out, because it was said that the Angel of Death procured death with a sword which was dipped in water taken from close at hand. There was one peculiarly pathetic custom. In the case of a young life cut off too soon, if the young person had never been married, a form of marriage service was part of the burial rites. For the time of mourning the mourner was exempt from the keeping of the law, because he was supposed to be beside himself, mad with grief.

The mourner must go to the Synagogue ; and when he entered the people faced him and said, " Blessed is He that comforteth the mourner." The Jewish prayer book has a special prayer to be used before meat in the house of the mourner.

" Blessed art Thou, O God, our Lord, King of the Universe, God of our fathers, our Creator, our Redeemer, our Sanctifier, the Holy One of Jacob, the King of Life, who art good and doest good ; the God of truth, the righteous Judge who judgest in righteousness, who takest the soul in judgment, and rulest alone in the universe, who doest in it according to His will and all His ways are in Judgment, and we are His people, and His servants, and in everything we are bound to praise Him and to bless Him, who shields all the calamities of Israel, and will shield us in this calamity, and from this mourning will bring us to life and peace. Comfort, O God, our Lord, all the mourners of Jerusalem that mourn in our sorrow. Comfort them in their mourning, and make them rejoice in their agony as a man is comforted by his mother. Blessed art Thou, O God, the Comforter of Zion, Thou that buildest again Jerusalem."

That prayer is later than New Testament times, but it is against the background of the earlier, unrestrained expressions of grief that we must read this story of the girl who had died.

THE DIFFERENCE FAITH MAKES

Mark 5 : 40-43

> But He put them all out, and He took with Him the father of the little girl, and the mother and His own friends, and went into the room where the little girl was. He took the little girl by the hand, and He said to to her, " Maid ! I say to you, Arise ! " Immediately the maid arose and walked around, for she was about twelve years of age. And immediately they were amazed with a great astonishment. He gave them strong injunctions that no one should know about this. And He ordered that something to eat should be given to her.

THERE is one very lovely thing here. " Talitha cumi " is Aramaic for " Maid ! Arise ! " How did this little bit of Aramaic get itself embedded in the Greek of the gospels? There can only be one reason. Mark got his information from Peter. For the most part, outside of Palestine at least, Peter, too, would have to speak in Greek. But Peter had been there ; he was one of the chosen three, the inner circle, who had seen this happen. And he could never forget Jesus' voice. In his mind and memory he could hear that " Talitha cumi " all his life. The love, the gentleness, the caress of it lingered with him forever, so much so that he was unable to think of it in Greek at all, because he could only hear it in memory in the voice of Jesus, in the very words that Jesus spoke.

The great characteristic of this passage is that it is a story of contrasts.

(i) There is the contrast between *the despair* of the mourners and *the hope* of Jesus. " Don't bother the Teacher," they said. " There's nothing anyone can do now." " Don't be afraid," said Jesus, " only believe."

In the one place it is the voice of despair that speaks ; in the other the voice of hope.

(ii) There is the contrast between *the unrestrained distress* of the mourners and *the calm serenity* of Jesus. They were wailing and weeping and tearing their hair and rending their garments in a paroxysm of distress ; He was calm and quiet and serene and in control.

Why should this difference be? The difference came because of Jesus' perfect confidence and trust in God. The worst human disaster can be met with courage and gallantry when we meet it with God. They laughed Him to scorn because they thought that His hope was groundless and His calm mistaken. But the great fact of the Christian life is that that which looks completely impossible with men is possible with God. That which on merely human grounds is far too good to be true, becomes blessedly true when God is there. They laughed Him to scorn, but that laughter must have turned to amazed wonder, when they realized what God can do. There is nothing beyond facing, and there is nothing beyond conquest—not even death— when it is faced and conquered in the love of God which is in Christ Jesus our Lord.

WITHOUT HONOUR IN HIS OWN COUNTRY

Mark 6 : 1-6

Jesus left there and came into His own native place, and His disciples went with Him. When the Sabbath came He began to teach in the Synagogue. Many, as they listened, were amazed. " Where," they said, " did this man get this knowledge? What wisdom is this that has been given to Him? And how can such wonderful things keep happening through His hands? Is not this the carpenter, Mary's son, the brother of James and Joses and Judah and Simon? Are His sisters not here with us?" And they took offence at Him. So Jesus said to them, "A prophet is not without honour except in his own native place, and amongst his own kinsmen and in his own family." And He was not able to do any wonderful deeds there, except that He laid His hands on a few sick people and healed them. And He was amazed by their unwillingness to believe. He made a tour of the villages teaching.

WHEN Jesus came to Nazareth He put Himself to a very severe test. He was coming to His home town ; and there are no severer critics of any man than those who have known him since his boyhood. It was never meant to be a private visit simply to see His old home and His own people. He came attended by His disciples. That is to say He came as a Rabbi. The Rabbis moved about the country accompanied by their little circle of disciples, and it was as a teacher, with his disciples, that Jesus came.

He went into the Synagogue and He taught. His teaching was greeted not with wonder but with a kind of contempt. " They took offence at Him." They were scandalised that a man who came from a background like Jesus should say and do things like that. Familiarity had bred a mistaken contempt.

They refused to listen to what He had to say for two reasons.

(i) They said, " Is not this the carpenter? " The word used for *carpenter* is *tektōn*. Now *tektōn* does mean a worker in wood, but it means more than merely a joiner. It means a *craftsman*. In Homer the *tektōn* is said to build ships and houses and temples. In the old days, and still to-day in many places, there could be found in little towns and villages a craftsman who would build you anything from a chicken-coop to a house ; the kind of man who could build a wall, mend a roof, repair a gate ; the craftsman, the handy-man, who with few or no instruments and with the simplest tools could turn his hand to any job. That is what Jesus was like. But the point is that the people of Nazareth despised Jesus *because He was a working-man*. He was a man of the people, a layman, a simple man— and therefore they despised him. One of the great leaders of the Labour movement was that great soul Will Crooks.

He was born into a home where one of his earliest recollections was seeing his mother crying because she had no idea where the next meal was to come from. He started work in a blacksmith's shop at five shillings a week. He became a fine craftsman and one of the bravest and straightest men who ever lived. He entered municipal politics and became the first Labour Mayor of any London borough. There were people who were offended when Will Crooks became Mayor of Poplar. In a crowd one day a lady said with great disgust, " They've made that common fellow, Crooks, Mayor, and he's no better than a working man." A man in the crowd—Will Crooks himself— turned round and raised his hat. " Quite right, madam," he said. " I am not better than a working man." The people of Nazareth despised Jesus because He was a working man. To us that is His glory, because it means that God, when He came to earth, claimed no exemptions. He took upon Himself this common life with all its common tasks. The accidents of birth and fortune and pedigree have nothing to do with manhood. As Pope had it,

> " Worth makes the man, and want of it the fellow ;
> The rest is all but leather or prunello."

As Burns had it,

> " A prince can mak' a belted knight,
> A marquis, duke, an' a' that !
> But an honest man's aboon his might—
> Guid faith, he mauna fa' that !
> For a' that, an' a' that,
> Their dignities an' a' that,
> The pith o' sense an' pride o' worth
> Are higher rank than a' that."

We must ever beware of the temptation to evaluate men by externals and incidentals, and not by native worth.

(ii) They said, " Is not this Mary's son? Do we not know His brothers and His sisters? " The fact that they called Jesus *Mary's son* tells us that Joseph must have been dead. Therein we have the key to one of the enigmas of Jesus' life. Jesus was only thirty-three when He died ; and yet

He did not leave Nazareth until He was thirty. (Luke 3:23.) Why this long delay? Why this lingering in Nazareth while a world waited to be saved? The reason was that Joseph died young and Jesus took upon Himself the support of His mother and of His brothers and sisters ; and only when they were old enough to fend for themselves did He go forth. He was faithful in little, and therefore in the end God gave Him much to do. But the people of Nazareth despised Him because they knew His family. Thomas Campbell was a very considerable poet. His father had no sense of poetry at all. When Thomas's first book emerged with Thomas's name on it, he sent a copy to his father. The old man took it up and looked at it. It was really the binding and not the contents at all that he was looking at. " Who would have thought," he said in wonder, " that our Tom could have made a book like that?" Sometimes when familiarity should breed a growing respect it breeds an increasing and easy-going familiarity. Sometimes we are too near people to see their greatness.

The result of all this was that Jesus could do no mighty works in Nazareth. The atmosphere was wrong. There are some things that cannot be done if the atmosphere is wrong.

(i) It is still true that no man can be healed if he refuses to be healed. Margot Asquith tells of the death of Neville Chamberlain. Everyone knows how Neville Chamberlain's policy turned out in such a way that it broke his heart. Margot Asquith met his doctor, Lord Horder. " You can't be much of a doctor," she said, " as Neville Chamberlain was only a few years older than Winston Churchill, and I should have said he was a strong man. Were you fond of him? " Lord Horder replied, " I was very fond of him. I like all unlovable men. I have seen too many of the other kind. Chamberlain suffered from shyness. He did not want to live ; and when a man says that, *no doctor can save him*." We may call it faith ; we may call it the will to live ; but without it no man can live.

(ii) There can be no preaching in the wrong atmosphere. Our Churches would be different places if congregations would only remember that they preach far more than half the sermon. In an atmosphere of expectancy the poorest effort can catch fire. In an atmosphere of critical coldness or bland indifference, the most Spirit-packed utterance can fall lifeless to the earth.

(iii) There can be no peace-making in the wrong atmosphere. If men have come together to hate, they will hate. If men have come together to refuse to understand, they will misunderstand. If men have come together to see no other point of view but their own, they will see no other. But if men have come together, loving Christ and seeking to love each other, even those who are most widely separated can come together in Christ.

There is laid on us the tremendous responsibility that we can either help or hinder the work of Jesus Christ. We can open the door wide to Him—or we can slam it in His face.

HERALDS OF THE KING

Mark **6 :** **7-11**

Jesus called The Twelve to Him and He began to send them out in twos. He gave them power over unclean spirits. He ordered them to take nothing for the road except a staff. He ordered them not to take bread, or a wallet, or a copper coin in their belts. He ordered them to wear sandals and, He said, "You must not put on two tunics." He said to them, "Wherever you enter into a house, stay there, until you leave that place; and, if any place refuses to give you hospitality, and, if in any place they will not listen to you, when you leave there, shake off the dust from the soles of your feet, to bear witness to the fact that they were guilty of such conduct."

WE will understand all the references in this passage better if we have in our minds a picture of what the Jew in Palestine in the time of Jesus ordinarily wore. He had five articles of dress.

(i) The innermost garment was the *chitōn,* or *sindōn,* or *tunic.* It was very simple. It was simply a long piece of cloth folded over and sewn down one side. It was long enough to reach almost to the feet. Holes were cut in the top corners for the arms. Such garments were commonly sold without any hole for the head to go through. That was to prove that the garment was in fact new, and it was to allow the buyer to arrange the neck-line as he or she wished. For instance, the neckline was different for men and women. It had to be lower in the case of women so that a mother could suckle her baby. At its simplest, then the inner garment was little more than a sack with holes cut in the corners. In a more developed form it had long close-fitting sleeves ; and sometimes it was opened up so that it was made to button down the front like a cassock.

(ii) The outer garment was called the *himation.* It was used as a cloak by day and as a blanket by night. It was composed of a piece of cloth seven feet from left to right and four and a half feet from top to bottom. One and a half feet at each side was folded in and in the top corner of the folded in part holes were cut for the arms to go through. It was therefore almost square. Usually it was made of two strips of cloth, each seven feet by a little more than two feet, sewn together. The seam came down the back. But a specially carefully made *himation* might be woven of one piece, as Jesus' robe was (John 19 : 23). This was the main article of dress.

(iii) There was the *girdle.* It was worn over the two garments we have already described. The skirts of the tunic could be hitched up under the girdle for work or for running. Sometimes the tunic was hitched above the girdle, and in the hollow place so made above the girdle a parcel or a package could be carried. The girdle was often double for the eighteen inches from each end. The double part formed a pocket like a money-belt, and in that pocket money was carried.

(iv) There was the *head-dress*. The head-dress was a piece of cotton or linen about a yard square. It could be white, or blue, or black. Sometimes it was made of coloured silk. It was folded diagonally and then placed on the head so that it protected the back of the neck, the cheek-bones, and the eyes from the heat and glare of the sun. It was held in place by a circlet of easily stretched, semi-elastic wool, which was worn round the head.

(v) There were the *sandals*. The sandals were merely flat soles of leather, wood or matted grass. The soles had thongs at the edges through which a strap passed, and so held the sandal on to the foot.

The wallet may be one of two things. (*a*) It may be the ordinary travellers' bag. This bag was made of a kid's skin. Often the animal was skinned whole and the skin retained the original shape of the animal, legs, and tail, and head and all ! It had a strap at each side and was slung over the shoulder. In it the shepherd, or pilgrim, or traveller carried bread and raisins, and olives, and cheese enough to last him for a day or two. (*b*) There is a very interesting suggestion. The Greek word is *pēra* ; and it can mean a *collecting-bag*. Very often the priests and devotees went out with these collecting bags to collect contributions for their temple and their god. They have been described as " pious robbers with their booty growing from village to village." There is an inscription in which a man who calls himself a slave of the Syrian goddess says that he brought in seventy bags full each journey for his lady. If the first meaning is taken, Jesus meant that His disciples must take no supplies for the road, but must trust God for everything. If the second meaning is taken, it means that they must not be like the rapacious priests. They must go about giving and not getting.

There are two other interesting things here.

(i) It was the Rabbinic law that when a man entered the

Temple courts he must put off his staff and shoes and money girdle. All ordinary things were to be set aside on entering the sacred place. It may well be that Jesus was thinking of this, and that He meant His men to see that the humble homes they were to enter were every bit as sacred as the Temple courts.

(ii) Hospitality was a sacred duty in the East. When a stranger entered a village, it was not his duty to search for hospitality ; it was the duty of the village to offer it. Jesus told His disciples that if hospitality was refused, and if doors and ears were shut, they must shake off the dust of that place from their feet when they left. The Rabbinic law said that the dust of a Gentile and a heathen country was defiled, and that when a man entered Palestine from another country he must shake off every particle of dust of the unclean land. It was a pictorial formal denial that a Jew could have any fellowship even with the dust of a heathen land. It is as if Jesus said, " If they refuse to listen to you, the only thing you can do is to treat them as a rigid Jew would treat a Gentile house. There can be no fellowship between them and you."

So we can see that the mark of the Christian disciple was to be utter simplicity, complete trust, and the generosity which is out always to give and never to demand.

THE MESSAGE AND THE MERCY OF THE KING

Mark 6 : 12, 13

> So they went out and heralded forth the summons to repentance ; and they cast out many demons, and anointed many sick people with oil and healed them.

HERE in brief summary is an account of the work that The Twelve did when Jesus sent them out.

(i) They heralded forth the message of Jesus. The word

that is used is literally the word that is used for *a herald's proclamation*. When the apostles went out to preach to men, they did not *create* a message ; they *brought* a message. They did not tell people what they believed and what they considered probable ; they told people what God had told them. It was not their opinions that they brought to men ; it was God's truth. The message of the prophets always began, " Thus saith the Lord." The man who would bring an effective message to others must first receive it from God.

(ii) To the people they brought *the King's Message* ; and the King's message was, " Repent ! " Now, clearly, that was a disturbing message. To repent means to change one's mind, and then to fit one's actions to this change of mind. Repentance means a change of heart and a change of action. Repentance is bound to *hurt*, for it involves the bitter realization that the way we were following is wrong. Repentance is bound to *disturb*, because it means a complete and total reversal of life. That is precisely why so few people do repent—for the last thing that most people desire is to be disturbed. Lady Asquith, in a vivid phrase, speaks of people who " dawdle towards death." So many people do that. They resent all strenuous activity. Life for them is " a land where it is always afternoon." In some ways the positive, vivid, swashbuckling sinner who is crashing his way to some self-chosen goal is a more attractive person than the negative, nebulous, loiterer who drifts spinelessly and without direction through life. There is a passage in the novel *Quo Vadis?* Vinicius, the young Roman, has fallen in love with a girl who is a Christian. Because he is not a Christian she will have nothing to do with him. He follows her to the secret night gathering of the little group of Christians, and there, unknown to anyone, he listens to the service. He hears Peter preach, and, as he listens, something happens to him. " He felt that if he wished to follow that teaching, he would have to place on a burning pile all his thoughts, habits and character, his whole nature up to that moment, burn them into ashes and then fill himself with a life altogether different, and an entirely new soul." That *is* repentance. But what if a man has no other desire than to be left alone? The change is not necessarily from robbery, theft, murder, adultery, the glaring sins. The change may be from a life that is completely selfish, instinctively demanding, totally inconsiderate, the change from a self-centred to a God-centred life—and a change like that hurts. W. M. Macgregor quotes a saying of the Bishop in *Les Misérables*. " I always bothered some of them ; for through me the outside air came at them ; my presence in their company made them feel as if a door had been left open and they were in a draught." Repentance is no sentimental feeling sorry ; repentance is a revolutionary thing—that is why so few repent.

(iii) To the people they brought *the King's mercy*. Not only did they bring this shattering demand upon men. They brought also help and healing. They brought liberation to poor, demon-possessed men and women. From the beginning Christianity has aimed to bring health to body and to soul ; it has always aimed not only at soul salvation, but at whole salvation. It brought not only a hand to lift from moral wreckage, but a hand to lift from physical pain and suffering. It is a most suggestive thing that they anointed with oil. In the ancient world oil was regarded as a panacea. Galen, the great Greek doctor, said, " Oil is the best of all instruments for healing diseased bodies." In the hands of the servants of Christ the old cures acquired a new virtue. The strange thing is that they used the things which men's limited knowledge knew at that time ; but the spirit of Christ gave the healer a new power and the old cure a new virtue. The power of God became available in common things to the faith of men.

So The Twelve brought to men the message and the mercy of the King, and that remains the Church's task to-day and every day.

THREE VERDICTS ON JESUS

Mark 6 : 14, 15

> King Herod heard about Jesus, for His name was known everywhere. He said, " John the Baptizer has risen from the dead. That is why these wonderful powers work through him." Others said, " It is Elijah." Others said, " He is a prophet, like one of the famous prophets."

By this time news of Jesus had penetrated all over the country. The tale of Jesus had reached the ears of Herod. The reason why Herod had not up to this time heard of Jesus may well be due to the fact that Herod's official residence in Galilee was in Tiberias. Tiberias was largely a Gentile city, and, as far as we know, Jesus never set foot in it. But the mission of The Twelve had taken Jesus' name and fame all over Galilee, so that His name was upon every lip. Here in this passage we have three verdicts upon Jesus.

(i) There is the verdict of a guilty conscience. As we shall see Herod had been guilty of allowing the execution of John the Baptizer, and now he was haunted by what he had done. Whenever a man does an evil thing, the whole world becomes his enemy. Inwardly, he cannot command his thoughts ; and, whenever he allows himself to think, his thoughts return to the wicked thing that he has done. No man can avoid living with himself ; and when his inward self is an accusing self life becomes intolerable. Outwardly, he lives in the fear that he will be found out, that some day the consequences of his evil deed will catch up on him, in the uncertainty as to who knows what he has done. Some time ago a convict escaped from a Glasgow prison. After forty-eight hours of liberty he was recaptured, cold and hungry and exhausted. He, himself, said that it was not worth it. " I didn't have a minute," he said. " Hunted, hunted all the time. You don't have a chance. You can't stop to eat. You can't stop to sleep." *Hunted*—that is the word which so well describes the life of the man who has done some evil thing, When Herod heard of Jesus, the first thing that flashed into his mind was that this was John the Baptizer, whom he had killed, come back to reckon with him. Because the sinning life is the haunted life, sin is never worth the cost.

(ii) There is the verdict of the nationalist. Some thought that this Jesus was Elijah come again. The Jews waited for the Messiah. There were many ideas about the Messiah, but the commonest of all was that the Messiah would be a conquering king who would first give the Jews back their liberty and their freedom, and who would then lead them on a triumphant campaign of victory throughout the world. Now it was an essential part of that belief that, before the coming of the Messiah, Elijah, the greatest of the prophets, would come again to be his herald, and his forerunner. Even to this day, when the Jews celebrate the Passover Feast, they leave at the table an empty chair called Elijah's chair. They place that empty chair there with a glass of wine before it, and at one part of their service they go to the door and fling it wide open that Elijah may come in and bring at last the long-awaited news that the Messiah has come. This is the verdict of the man who desires to find in Jesus the realizations of *his own ambitions*. He thinks of Jesus, not as someone to whom he must submit, and someone whom he must obey ; he thinks of Jesus as someone whom he can use. Such a man thinks more of his own ambitions than of the will of God.

(iii) There is the verdict of the man who is waiting for the voice of God. There were those who saw in Jesus a prophet. In those days the Jews were pathetically conscious that for three hundred years the voice of prophecy had been silent. Men had listened to the arguments and the legal disputations of the Rabbis ; men had listened to the moral lectures of the Synagogue ; but it was three long centuries since men had listened to a voice which pro-

claimed, " Thus saith the Lord." Men in those days were
listening for the authentic voice of God—and in Jesus they
heard it. It is true that Jesus was more than a prophet.
He did not bring only the voice of God. He brought to
men the very power, and the very life, and the very being
of God. But those who saw in Jesus a prophet were at
least more right than the conscience-stricken Herod and
the expectant nationalists. If they had got that length in
their thoughts of Jesus, it was not impossible that they
might take the further step and see in Him the Son
of God.

AN EVIL WOMAN'S REVENGE

Mark 6 : 16-29

But when Herod heard about it, he said, " This is
John, whom I beheaded, risen from the dead." For
Herod had sent and seized John and had bound him
in prison because of the affair of Herodias, his brother
Philip's wife—because he had married her. For John
had said to Herod, " It is not right for you to have
your brother's wife." Herodias set herself against him,
and wished to kill him, and she could not succeed in
doing so, for Herod was afraid of John, because he
well knew that he was a just and holy man, and he
kept him safe. When Herod listened to John he did
not know what to do, and yet he found a certain
pleasure in listening to him. But a day of opportunity
came, when, on his birthday, Herod was giving a
banquet to his courtiers and to his captains and to the
leading men of Galilee. Herodias' daughter herself
came in and danced before them, and she pleased
Herod and those who were reclining at table with him.
The king said to the maiden, " Ask me for anything
you like and I will give it to you." He swore to her,
" Whatever you ask me for, I will give you, even up
to half of my kingdom." She went out and said to her
mother, " What am I to ask for myself? " She said,
" John the Baptizer's head." At once she hurried into

THE GOSPEL OF MARK

the king and made her request. " I wish," she said,
" that here and now you will give me the head of John
the Baptizer on a plate." The king was grief-stricken,
but, because of the oath he had taken, and because he
had taken it in front of his guests, he did not wish to
break his word to her. So immediately the king
despatched an executioner with orders to bring his
head. The executioner went away and beheaded him
in prison, and brought his head on a plate, and gave
it to the maiden, and the maiden gave it to her
mother. When his disciples heard about it, they came
and took away his body and laid it in a tomb.

THERE is in this story all the simplicity of tremendous
drama.

First, let us look at *the scene*. The scene was the Castle
of Machaerus. Machaerus stood on a lonely ridge,
surrounded by terrible ravines, overlooking the east side
of the Dead Sea. It was one of the loneliest and grimmest
and most unassailable fortresses in the world. To this day
the dungeons are there, and the traveller can still see the
staples and the iron hooks in the wall to which John must
have been bound. It was in that bleak and desolate fortress
that the last act of John's life was played out.

Second, let us look at *the characters*. The marriage
tangles of the Herod family are quite incredible, and their
inter-relations are so complicated that they become almost
impossible to work out. When Jesus was born Herod the
Great was king. He was the king who was responsible for
the massacre of the children in Bethlehem when Jesus was
born. (Matthew 2 : 16-18.) Herod the Great was married
many times. Towards the end of his life he became almost
insanely suspicious, and murdered member after member
of his own family, until it became a Jewish saying, " It is
safer to be Herod's pig than Herod's son." First, he
married Doris, by whom he had a son, Antipater, whom he
murdered. Then he married Mariamne, the Hasmonean,
by whom he had two sons, Alexander and Aristobulus,

whom he also murdered. Herodias, the villainess of the present passage, was the daughter of this Aristobulus. Herod the Great then married another Mariamne, called the Boethusian. By her he had a son called Herod Philip. This Herod Philip married Herodias, who was the daughter of his half-brother, Aristobulus, and who was therefore his own niece. By Herodias, this Herod Philip had a daughter called Salome, who is the girl who danced before Herod the ruler of Galilee in our passage. Herod the Great then married Malthake, by whom he had two sons—Archelaus and Herod Antipas who is the Herod of our passage and who was the ruler of Galilee. The Herod Philip who married Herodias originally, and who was the father of Salome, inherited none of Herod the Great's dominions. He lived as a wealthy private citizen in Rome. Herod Antipas—the Herod of this passage—visited him in Rome. There he seduced his wife Herodias and persuaded her to leave her husband and marry him. Now note who Herodias was : (a) she was the daughter of his half-brother, Aristobulus, and therefore his niece ; and (b) she was the wife of his half-brother Herod Philip, and therefore his sister-in-law. Previously this Herod Antipas had been married to a daughter of the king of the Nabataeans, an Arabian country. She escaped to her father who invaded Herod's territory to avenge his daughter's honour and heavily defeated Herod. To complete this astounding picture— Herod the Great finally married Cleopatra of Jerusalem, by whom he had a son called Philip the Tetrarch. This Philip married Salome who was at one and the same time (a) the daughter of Herod Philip, his half brother, and (b) the daughter of Herodias, who herself was the daughter of Aristobulus, another of his half brothers. Salome was therefore at one and the same time his niece and his grand-niece. If we put this in the form of a table it will be easier to follow.

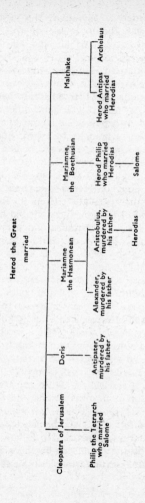

Seldom in history can there have been such a series of matrimonial entanglements as existed in the Herod family. By marrying Herodias, his brother's wife, Herod had broken the Jewish law (Leviticus 18 : 16 ; 20, 21) and had outraged the laws of decency and of morality.

Because of this adulterous marriage, and because of Herod's deliberate seduction of his brother's wife, John had publicly rebuked him. It took courage to rebuke in public an oriental despot who had the power of life and death, and this courage of John in rebuking evil wherever he saw it is commemorated in the Prayer-book collect for St. John the Baptist's Day.

> " Almighty God, by whose providence thy servant, John the Baptist, was wonderfully born, and sent to prepare the way of Thy Son our Saviour, by preaching of repentance ; Make us so to follow his doctrine and holy life, that we may truly repent according to his preaching ; and after his example constantly speak the truth, boldly rebuke vice, and patiently suffer for the truth's sake."

In spite of John's rebuke Herod still feared and respected him, for John was so obviously a man of sincerity and of goodness ; but with Herodias it was different. She was implacably hostile to John and determined to eliminate him. She got her chance at Herod's birthday feast which he was celebrating with his courtiers and his captains. Into that feast Salome, the daughter of Herodias, came to dance. The fact that she did so at all is an incredible thing. Solo dances in those days in such society were disgusting and licentious pantomimes. That a princess of the royal blood should so expose and demean herself is beyond belief because those dances were the art of professional prostitutes. The very fact that she did so dance is a grim commentary on the character of Salome, and of the mother who allowed and encouraged her to do so. But Herod was pleased ; and Herod offered her any reward ; and thus Herodias got the chance she had plotted for so long ; and John, to gratify her spleen, was executed.

There is something to learn from every character in this story.

(i) Herod stands revealed before us. (*a*) He was an odd mixture. At one and the same time he feared John and respected him. At one and the same time he dreaded John's tongue and yet found pleasure in listening to him. There is nothing in this world so queer a mixture as a human being. The characteristic fact about man is that he is a mixture. Boswell, in his *London Diary*, tells us how he sat in Church enjoying the worship of God, and yet at the same time he was planning how to pick up a prostitute in the streets of London that same night. The strange fact about man is that he is haunted both by sin and by goodness. Robert Louis Stevenson speaks about people " clutching the remnants of virtue in the brothel or on the scaffold." Sir Norman Birkett the great Q.C. and judge speaks of the criminals he has defended and tried. " They may seek to escape but they cannot ; they are condemned to some nobility ; all their lives long the desire for good is at their heels, the implacable hunter." Herod could sin, could fear John and love him, could hate his message and yet not be able to free himself from its insistent fascination. Herod was simply a human being. Are we so very different? (*b*) Herod was a man who acted on impulse. He made his reckless promise to Salome without thinking. It may well be that he made it when he was more than a little drunk and flown with wine. Let a man have a care. Let a man think before he speaks. Let him never by self-indulgence get into a state when he loses his powers of judgment, and is liable to do things for which afterwards he will be very sorry. (*c*) Herod feared what men might say. He kept his promise to Salome because he had made it in front of his cronies and he could not break it. He feared their jeers, their laughter ; he feared that they would think him weak. Many a man has done things he afterwards bitterly regretted because he had not the moral courage to do the right thing. Many a man has made himself far worse than he is because he feared the laughter of his so-called friends.

(ii) Salome and Herodias stand revealed before us. There is a certain greatness about Herodias. Years after this her Herod sought the title of King. He went to Rome to plead for it ; instead of giving him the title the Emperor banished him to Gaul for having the insolence and the insubordination to ask for such a title. Herodias was told that she need not share this exile, that she might go free, and she proudly answered that where her husband went she went too. Herodias shows us what an embittered woman can do. There is nothing in this world as good as a good woman, and nothing as bad as a bad woman. The Jewish Rabbis had a quaint saying. They said that a *good woman* might marry a *bad man,* for by so doing she would end by making him as good as herself. But they said that *a good man* might never marry *a bad woman,* for she would inevitably drag him down to her own level. The trouble with Herodias was that she wished to eliminate the one man who had the courage to confront her with her sin. She wished to do as she liked with no one to remind her of the moral law. She murdered John that she might sin in peace. She forgot that she need no longer meet John, but that she still had to meet God.

(iii) John the Baptizer stands revealed before us. He stands as the man of courage. He was a child of the desert and of the wide open spaces, and to imprison him in the dark dungeons of Machaerus must have been for him the last refinement of torture. But John was the man who preferred death to falsehood. He lived for the truth and he died for the truth. The man who brings to men the voice of God acts on men as a conscience. Many a man would silence his conscience if he could, and therefore the man who speaks for God must always take his life and his fortune in his hands.

THE PATHOS OF THE CROWD

Mark 6 : 30-34

The apostles came together again to Jesus, and they told Him all that they had done and taught. He said to them, " Come you by yourselves into a lonely place, and rest for a while." For there were many coming and going and they could not find time even to eat. So they went away in the boat to a lonely place all by themselves. Now many saw them going away and recognized them ; and they ran together there on foot from all the towns and went on ahead of them. When Jesus disembarked He saw a great crowd, and He was moved to the depths of His being with pity for them, because they were like sheep who had no shepherd ; and He began to teach them many things.

WHEN the disciples came back from their mission they reported to Jesus all that they had done. The demanding crowds were so insistent that they had no time even to eat ; so Jesus told them to come with Him to a lonely place on the other side of the lake that they might have peace and rest for a little time.

Here we see what might be called *the rhythm of the Christian life*. For the Christian life is a continuous going into the presence of God from the presence of men, and coming out into the presence of men from the presence of God. It is like the rhythm of sleep and work. We cannot work unless we have our time of rest ; and sleep will not come unless we have worked until we are tired. There are two dangers in life. First, there is the danger of a too constant activity. No man can work without rest ; and no man can live the Christian life unless he gives himself times with God. It may well be that the whole trouble in our lives is that we give God no opportunity to speak to us, because we do not know how to be still and to listen ; we give God no time to recharge us with spiritual energy and strength, because there is no time when we wait upon Him. How can we shoulder life's burdens if we have no contact with Him who is the Lord of all good life? How can we do God's work unless in God's strength? And how can we receive that strength unless we seek in quietness and in loneliness the presence of God? Second, there is the danger of too much withdrawal. Devotion that does not issue in action is not real devotion. Prayer that does not issue in work is not real prayer. We must never seek the fellowship of God to avoid the fellowship of men but to fit ourselves better for it. The rhythm of the Christian life is the alternate meeting with God in the secret place and serving men in the market place.

But the rest which Jesus sought for Himself and for His disciples was not to be. The crowds saw Jesus and His men going away. At this particular place it was four miles across the lake by boat and ten miles round the top of the lake on foot. On a windless day, or with a contrary wind, a boat might take some time to make the passage, and an energetic person could walk round the top of the lake and be there before the boat arrived. That is exactly what happened ; and when Jesus and His men stepped out of the boat the very crowd from which they had sought some little peace was there waiting for them.

Any ordinary man would have been intensely annoyed. The rest Jesus so much desired and which He had so well earned was denied to Him. His privacy was invaded. Any ordinary man would have resented it all, but Jesus was moved with pity at the pathos of the crowd. He looked at them ; they were so desperately in earnest ; they wanted so much what He alone could give them ; to Him they were like sheep who had no shepherd. What did He mean?

(i) A sheep without the shepherd cannot find the way. Left to ourselves we get lost in life. Principal Cairns spoke of people who feel like " lost children out in the rain." Dante has a line where he says, " I woke up in the middle of the wood, and it was dark, and there was no clear way before me." Life can be so bewildering. We can stand at some cross-roads of life and not know what way to take.

It is only when Jesus leads that we can find the way by following Him.

(ii) A sheep without the shepherd cannot find its pasture and its food. In this life we are bound to seek for sustenance for life. We need the strength which can keep us going ; we need the inspiration which can lift us out of ourselves and above ourselves. When we seek it elsewhere our minds are still unsatisfied, our hearts are still restless, our souls are still unfed. We can only gain strength for life from Him who is the living bread.

(iii) A sheep without the shepherd has no defence against the dangers which threaten it. It can defend itself neither from the robbers or the wild beasts. If life has taught us one thing it must be that we cannot live it alone. No man can defend himself from the temptations which assail him and from the evil of the world which attacks him. Only in the company of Jesus can we walk in the world and keep our garments unspotted from the world. Without Him we are defenceless ; with Him we are safe.

LITTLE IS MUCH IN THE HANDS OF JESUS

Mark 6 : 35-44

When it was now late the disciples came to Jesus. " The place," they said, " is lonely, and it is now late. Send them away that they may go into the surrounding countryside and villages and buy themselves something to eat." He answered, " You give them something to eat." " Are we," they said to Him, " to go away and buy ten pounds worth of loaves and so give them something to eat ? " " How many loaves have you ? " He said to them. " Go and see ! " When they had found out, they said, " Five and two fishes." He ordered them to make them all sit down in groups on the green grass. So they sat down in sections of hundreds and of fifties. He took the five loaves and the two fishes, and He looked up into the heaven and blessed them and broke the loaves. He gave them to the disciples to serve the people with them. And He divided up the two fishes among them all. And they all ate until they were completely satisfied ; and they gathered up the broken pieces of bread and what was left of the fishes—twelve baskets-ful. And those who ate the loaves amounted to five thousand men.

It is a notable fact that no miracle seems to have made such an impression on the disciples as this, because this is the only miracle of Jesus which is related in all the four gospels. We have already seen how Mark's gospel really embodies the preaching material of Peter. To read this story, so simply and yet so dramatically told, is to read something that reads exactly like an eye-witness account. Let us note some of the vivid and realistic details.

They sat down on *the green grass*. It is as if Peter was seeing the whole thing in his mind's eye again. It so happens that this little descriptive phrase provides us with quite a lot of information. The only time when the grass would be green would be in the late spring time, in mid-April. So it is then that this miracle must have taken place. At that time the sun set at 6 p.m., so this must have happened some time in the late afternoon. Mark tells us that they sat down in *sections* of a hundred and of fifty. The word used for *sections* (*prasiai*) is a very pictorial word. It is the normal Greek word for the rows of vegetables in a vegetable garden. When you looked at the little groups, as they sat there in their orderly rows, they looked for all the world like the rows of vegetables in a series of garden plots. At the end they took up *twelve basketsful* of fragments. No orthodox Jew travelled without his basket (*kophinos*). The Romans made a jest of the Jew and his basket. There were two reasons for the basket. It was a wicker-work basket shaped like a narrow-necked pitcher, broadening out as it went down. First, the very orthodox Jew carried his own food supplies in his basket, so that he would be certain of eating food that was ceremonially clean and pure. Second, many a Jew was an accomplished beggar, and into his basket went the proceeds of his begging. The reason that there were *twelve* baskets is simply that there were *twelve* disciples. It was into their own baskets that they frugally gathered up the fragments so that nothing would be lost.

The wonderful thing about this story is that, all through it, there runs an implicit contrast between the attitude of Jesus and the attitude of the disciples.

(i) It shows us *two reactions to human need*. When the disciples saw how late it was, and how tired and hungry the crowd were, they said, " Send them away so that they can find something to eat." In effect they said, " These people are tired and hungry. Get rid of them and let some-one else worry about them." Jesus said, " *You* give them something to eat." In effect Jesus said, " These people are tired and hungry. We must do something about it." There are always the people who are quite aware that others are in difficulty and trouble, but who wish to push off the responsibility for doing something about it on to someone else ; and there are always the people who when they see someone up against it feel compelled to do some-thing about it themselves. There are those who say, " Let others worry." And there are those who say, " I must worry about my brother's need."

(ii) It shows us *two reactions to human resources*. When the disciples were asked to give the people something to eat, they insisted that two hundred " pence " was not enough to buy bread for them. The word the Authorised Version translates *penny* is the word *denarius*. The *denarius* was a Roman silver coin worth about 9d. Further, it was the standard day's wage of a working man. In effect the disciples are saying, " We could not earn enough in more than six months' work to give this crowd a meal." They are saying, "Anything we have got is no use at all." Jesus said, " What have you got? " They had five loaves. These loaves were nothing like the size of an English loaf : they were more like rolls. John (6 : 9) tells us that they were barley loaves ; and barley loaves were the food of the poorest of the poor. Barley bread was the cheapest and the coarsest of all bread. They had two fishes. They would be about the size of sardines. Tarichaea —which means The Salt-fish Town—was a well known place on the lake from which salt-fish went out to all over the world. The little salt-fishes were eaten as relish with the dry rolls. It did not seem much. But Jesus took it and worked wonders with it. In the hands of Jesus, little is always much. We may think that we have little of talent or ability or substance to give to Jesus. That is no reason for a hopeless pessimism such as the disciples had. The one fatal thing to say is, " For all I could do, it is not worth my while trying to do anything." If we put ourselves into the hands of Jesus Christ, there is no telling what He can do with us and through us.

THE CONQUEST OF THE STORM

Mark 6 : 45-52

Immediately He made the disciples embark on the boat and go across ahead to Bethsaida while He sent the crowd away. When He had taken leave of them, He went away into a mountain to pray. When it was late the boat was half way across the lake and He was alone upon the land. He saw that they were sore beset as they rowed, for the wind was against them. About the fourth watch of the night He came to them walking on the sea, and it looked as if He meant to pass them by. When they saw Him walking on the sea they thought it was a ghost, and they cried out in terror, for they all saw Him and they were distracted with fear. At once He spoke with them. Courage ! " He said. " It is I. Don't be afraid." And He came into the boat with them, and the wind sank to rest. And they were exceedingly astonished within themselves, because they did not understand about the loaves because their minds were obtuse.

AFTER the hunger of the crowd had been satisfied Jesus immediately sent His disciples away before He dismissed the crowd. Why should He do that? Mark does not tell us, but most probably we have the explanation in John's account of this incident. John tells us that after the crowd had been fed there was a move to take Jesus, and, even against His will, to make Him king. That was the last thing Jesus desired. It was that very way of power that once, finally and for all, He had rejected at the time of His temptations. He could see it coming. He did not want His disciples to be infected and caught up in this nationalistic outburst. Galilee was the hotbed of revolution. If this movement was not checked there might well emerge amongst the excitable people a rebellion which would wreck everything, and which could only lead to disaster for all concerned. So Jesus sent away His disciples lest they too should become inflamed by this movement, and then He calmed the crowd and bade them farewell.

When He was alone He went up into a mountain to pray Thick and fast the problems were descending upon Him. There was the hostility of the orthodox people ; there was the frightened suspicion of Herod Antipas, the ruler of Galilee ; there were the political hotheads who would make Him a nationalistic Messiah against His will. At this particular time there was many a problem on Jesus' mind and many a burden on His heart.

So for some hours He was alone amidst the hills with God. As we have seen this must have happened about mid-April, and mid-April was the Passover time. Now the Passover time was deliberately fixed for the full moon, as Easter time still is. The Jewish night ran from 6 p.m. to 6 a.m. and it was divided into four watches—6 p.m. to 9 p.m., 9 p.m. to 12 midnight, 12 midnight to 3 a.m., and 3 a.m. to 6 a.m. About three o'clock in the morning Jesus looked from the mountainside out across the lake. The lake was only four miles across, and in the light of the moon it lay stretched out before Him. The wind was up, and there He saw the boat, with His men in it, having a hard struggle to reach the other side. See what happened. Immediately Jesus saw His friends in trouble His own problems were set aside ; the moment for prayer was past : the time for action had come ; He forgot Himself and went to the help of His friends. That is of the very essence of Jesus. The cry of human need to Him surpassed all other claims. His friends needed Him ; He must go.

What happened we do not know, and will never know. The story is cloaked in mystery which defies explanation. What we do know is that He came to them and their storm became a calm. With Him beside them nothing mattered any more.

When Augustine was writing about this incident He said, " He came treading the waves ; and so He puts all the swelling tumults of life under His feet. Christians— why afraid? " It is the simple fact of life, a fact which has been proved by countless thousands of men and women in every generation, that when Christ is there the storm becomes a calm, the tumult becomes a peace, the undoable becomes doable, the unbearable becomes bearable, and men pass the breaking point and do not break. To walk with Christ is for us also the conquest of the storm.

THE DEMANDING CROWDS

Mark 6 : 53-56

When they had crossed over and reached land they came to Gennesareth, and moored the boat there. When they had disembarked from the boat the people immediately recognized Him ; and they ran all over that countryside, and, wherever they knew He was, they began to carry to Him on pallets those who were ill. And whenever He came into villages or towns or country places, they laid the sick in the open spaces, and they kept begging Him to be allowed to touch even the tassel of His robe ; and all who touched it were restored to health.

No sooner had Jesus landed on the other side of the lake than once again He was surrounded by crowds. Just sometimes Jesus must have looked on the crowds with a certain wistfulness, because there was hardly a person in them who had not come to get something out of Him. They came to get. They came with their insistent demands. They came—to put it bluntly—to use Him. What a difference it would have made if, among these crowds, there had been some few who came to give and not to get. In a way it is natural that we should come to Jesus to get things from Him, for there are so many things that He alone can give ; but it is always a shameful thing to take everything and to give nothing, and yet it is very characteristic of human nature.

(i) There are those who simply make use of their *homes*. It is specially so with young people. They regard their homes as being there to cater for their comfort and their convenience. It is there they eat and sleep and get things done for them ; but surely a home is a place to which we ought to contribute, and from which we ought not to be taking all the time.

(ii) There are those who simply make use of their *friends*. There are some people from whom we never receive a letter unless they want something from us. There are those who regard other people as existing to help them when they need their help, and to be forgotten when they cannot be made of use.

(iii) There are those who simply make use of the *Church*. They desire the Church to baptize their children, to marry their young people and bury their dead. They are seldom to be seen there unless they wish some service from the Church. It is their unconscious attitude that the Church exists to serve them, but that they have no duty whatever towards the Church.

(iv) There are those who seek simply to make use of *God*. They never remember God unless they need Him. Their only prayers are requests and even demands made of God. Someone has put it this way. In American hotels there is a boy called the "bell-hop." The hotel guest rings the bell and the bell-hops appears. He will fetch anything the guest wishes on demand. There are some people who regard God as a kind of universal bell-hop, only to be summoned when something is needed.

If we examine ourselves we are all, to some extent, guilty of these things. It would rejoice the heart of Jesus if more often we came to Him to offer our love, our service, our devotion, and less often to demand from Him the help we need.

CLEAN AND UNCLEAN

Mark 7 : 1-4

There gathered together to Jesus the Pharisees, and some of the experts in the law who had come down from Jerusalem. They saw that some of His disciples ate their bread with hands which were ceremonially unclean, that is to say hands which had not undergone the prescribed washings ; for the Pharisees, and all the Jews, who hold to the traditions of the elders, do not eat unless they wash their hands, using the fist as the law prescribes ; and when they come in from the market-place they do not eat unless they immerse their whole bodies ; and there are many other traditions which they observe which relate to the prescribed washings of cup and pitchers and vessels of bronze.

THE difference and the argument between Jesus and the Pharisees and the experts in the law, which this chapter relates, are of tremendous importance, for they show us the very essence and core of the divergence between Jesus and the orthodox Jew of His time.

The question asked is, Why do Jesus and His disciples not observe the tradition of the elders? What was this tradition, and what was its moving spirit? Originally, for the Jew, the Law meant two things ; it meant, first and foremost, the Ten Commandments, and, second, the first five books of the Old Testament, or, as they are called, the Pentateuch. Now it is true that the Pentateuch contains a certain number of detailed regulations and instructions ; but, in the matter of moral questions, what is laid down is a series of great moral principles which a man must interpret and apply for himself. For long the Jews were content with that. But in the fourth and fifth centuries before Christ there came into being a class of legal experts, whom we know as the *Scribes*. They were not content with great moral principles ; they had, what can only be called, a passion for definition. They wanted these great principles amplified, expanded, broken down until they issued in thousands and thousands of little rules and regulations governing every possible action and every possible situation in life. Life was no longer to be governed by principles, but by rules and regulations. These rules and regulations were never written down until long after the time of Jesus. They are what is called the *Oral Law* ; it is they which are *the tradition of the elders*. The word *elders* does not mean, in this phrase, the officials of the Synagogue ; rather it means *the ancients*, the great legal experts of the old days, like Hillel and Shammai. Much later, in the third century after Christ, a summary of all these rules and regulations was made and written down, and that summary is known a the *Mishnah*. There are two aspects of these scribal rules and regulations which emerge in the argument in this passage. One is about *the washing of hands*. The Scribes and Pharisees accused the disciples of Jesus of eating with unclean hands. The Greek word is *koinos*. Ordinarily, *koinos* means common ; then it comes to describe something which is ordinary in the sense that it is not sacred, something that is *profane* as opposed to sacred things ; and finally it describes something, as it does here, which is ceremonially unclean and unfit for the service and worship of God. There were definite and rigid rules for the washing of hands. Now, note, that this hand-washing was *not* in the interests of hygienic purity ; it was *ceremonial cleanness* which was at stake. Before every meal, and between each of the courses, the hands had to be washed, and they had to be washed in a certain way. The hands, to begin with, had to be free of any coating of sand or mortar, or gravel or any such substance. The water for washing had to be kept in special large stone jars, so that it itself was clean in the ceremonial sense, and so that it might be certain that it had been used for no other purpose, and that nothing had fallen into it or had been mixed with it. First, the hands were held with the finger tips *pointing upwards* ; the water was poured over them and must run at least down to the wrist ; the minimum amount of water was one quarter of a log, which is equal to one and a half egg-shells full of water. While the hands were still wet each hand had to be cleansed with the fist of the other. That is what the phrase about using the fist means ; the fist of one hand was rubbed into the palm and against the surface of the other. This meant that at this stage the hands were wet with water ; but that water was now itself unclean because it touched unclean hands. So, second, the hands had to be held with finger tips pointing downwards and the water had to be poured over them in such a way that it began at the wrists and ran off at the finger tips. After all that had been done the hands were clean.

Now, note, that to fail to do this was in Jewish eyes, not to be guilty of bad manners, not to be dirty in the health sense, but to be unclean in the sight of God. The man who ate with unclean hands was subject to the attacks of a demon called Shibta. To omit so to wash the hands was to become liable to poverty and destruction. Bread eaten with unclean hands was no better than excrement. A Rabbi who once omitted the ceremony was buried in excommunication. Another Rabbi, imprisoned by the Romans, used the water given to him for this handwashing rather than for drinking and in the end nearly perished of thirst, because he was determined to observe the rules of handwashing rather than satisfy his thirst.

That to the Pharisaic and Scribal Jew was religion. It was ritual, ceremonial, rules and regulations like that which they considered to be the essence of the service of God. Ethical religion was buried under a mass of tabus and rules and regulations.

The last verses of the passage deal further with this conception of uncleanness. A thing might in the ordinary sense be completely clean and yet in the legal sense be unclean. There is something about this conception of uncleanness in Leviticus chapters 11 to 15, and in Numbers 19. Nowadays we would talk rather of things being *tabu* than of being *unclean*. Certain animals were unclean (Leviticus 11). A woman after child-birth was unclean ; a leper was unclean ; anyone who touched a dead body was unclean. And anyone who had so become unclean made unclean anything he in turn touched. A Gentile was unclean ; food touched by a Gentile was unclean ; any vessel touched by a Gentile was unclean. So, then, when a strict Jew returned from the market place he immersed his whole body in clean water to take away the taint he might have acquired.

Obviously vessels could easily become unclean ; they might be touched by an unclean person or by unclean food. This is what our passage means by the washings of cups and pitchers and vessels of bronze. In the *Mishnah* there are no fewer than twelve treatises on this kind of uncleanness. If we take some actual examples we will see how far this went. A *hollow* vessel made of pottery could contract uncleanness *inside* but not outside ; that is to say, it did not matter who or what touched it outside, but it did matter what touched it inside. If it became unclean it must be broken ; and no unbroken piece must remain which was big enough to hold enough oil to anoint the little toe. A flat plate without a rim cannot become unclean at all ; but a plate with a rim can. If vessels made with leather, bone or glass are *flat* they cannot contract uncleanness at all ; if they are *hollow* they can become unclean *outside and inside*. If they are unclean they must be broken ; and the break must be a hole at least big enough for a medium-sized pomegranate to pass through. To cure uncleanness earthen vessels must be broken ; other vessels must be immersed, boiled, purged with fire—in the case of metal vessels—and polished. A three-legged table can contract uncleanness ; if it loses one or two legs it cannot ; if it loses three legs it can, for then it can be used as *a board* and a board can become unclean. Things made of metal can become unclean, except a door, a bolt, a lock, a hinge, a knocker and a gutter. Wood used in metal utensils can become unclean ; but metal used in wood utensils cannot. Thus a wooden key with metal teeth can become unclean ; but a metal key with wooden teeth cannot.

We have taken some time over these scribal laws, this tradition of the elders, because *that is what Jesus was up against*. To the scribes and Pharisees these rules and regulations were the essence of religion. To observe them was to please God ; to break them was to sin. This was their idea of goodness and of the service of God. In the religious sense Jesus and these people spoke different languages. It was precisely because He had no use for all these regulations that they considered Him a bad man. There is a fundamental cleavage here—the cleavage between the man who sees religion as ritual, ceremonial, rules and regulations, and the man who sees in religion loving God and loving his fellow-men.

The next passage will develop this ; but it is clear that Jesus' idea of religion and the idea of religion of the Scribes and Pharisees had nothing in common at all.

GOD'S LAWS AND MEN'S RULES

Mark 7 : 5-8

So the Pharisees and the experts in the law asked Him, " Why do your disciples not conduct themselves as the tradition of the elders prescribes, but eat bread with hands that are unclean?" He said to them, "Isaiah did well when he prophesied about you hypocrites, as it stands written, 'This people honour me with their lips, but their heart is far away from me. This so-called reverence of men is an empty thing, for they teach as doctrine human rules and regulations.' While you hold fast the tradition of men you abandon the command of God."

THE Scribes and Pharisees saw that the disciples of Jesus did not observe the niceties of the tradition and the code of the oral law in regard to the washing of hands before and during meals, and they demanded why. Jesus began by quoting to them a passage from Isaiah 29 : 13. There Isaiah accused the people of his day of honouring God with their lips while their hearts were really far away. In principle, Jesus accused the Scribes and Pharisees of two things.

(i) He accused them of *hypocrisy*. The word *hupokrites* has an interesting and revealing history. It begins by meaning simply *one who answers* ; it goes on to mean one who answers in a set dialogue or a set conversation, that is to say *an actor* ; and finally it means, not simply an actor on the stage, but *one whose whole life is a piece of acting without any sincerity behind it at all.* Anyone to whom religion is a legal thing, anyone to whom religion means carrying out certain external rules and regulations, anyone to whom religion is entirely connected with the observation of a certain ritual and the keeping of a certain number of tabus is in the end bound to be, in this sense, a hypocrite. The reason for that is this—he believes that he is a good man, if he carries out the correct external acts and practices, *no matter what his heart and his thoughts are like.* To take the case of the legalistic Jew in the time of Jesus, he might in his heart of hearts hate his fellow man with all his heart, he might be full of envy and jealousy and concealed bitterness, and pride ; that did not matter so long as he carried out the correct handwashings, and observed the correct laws about cleanness and uncleanness. Legalism takes account of a man's outward actions ; but it takes no account at all of his inward feelings. He may well be meticulously serving God in outward things, and bluntly disobeying God in inward things—and that is hypocrisy. The Mohammedan must pray to God a certain number of times each day. To do so he carries his prayer mat ; wherever he is he will unroll the prayer mat, fall upon his knees, say his prayers and then go on. There is a story of a Mohammedan who was pursuing a man with upraised knife to murder him. Just then the call to prayer rang out. Immediately he stopped, spread out his prayer mat, knelt, said his prayer as fast as he could ; and then rose and continued his murderous pursuit. The prayer was simply a form and a ritual, and an outward observance, merely the correct interlude in the career of murder. There is no greater religious peril than the peril of identifying religion with outward observance. There is no commoner religious mistake than in identifying goodness with certain so-called religious acts. Church-going, bible-reading, careful financial giving, even time-tabled prayer do not make a man a good man. The fundamental question is, how is a man's heart towards God and towards his fellow-men? And if in his heart there are enmity, bitterness, grudges, pride, not all the outward religious observances in the world will make him anything other than a hypocrite.

(ii) The second accusation that Jesus implicitly levelled against these legalists was that *they substituted the efforts of human ingenuity for the laws of the voice of God.* For their guidance for life they did not depend on listening to God ; they depended on listening to the clever arguments and debates, the fine-spun niceties, the ingenious interpretations of the legal experts. Cleverness never can be the basis of true religion. True religion can never be the product of man's mind. True religion must always come, not from a man's ingenious discoveries, but from the simple listening to and accepting of the voice of God.

AN INIQUITOUS REGULATION

Mark 7 : 9-13

> He said to them, " You make an excellent job of completely nullifying the command of God in order to observe your own tradition. For Moses said, ' Honour your father and your mother.' And, ' He who speaks evil of his father or mother shall certainly die.' But you say, that, if a man says to his father or mother, ' That by which you might have been helped by me is *Korban*,'—that is to say, *God-dedicated*—you no longer allow him to do anything for his father and mother, and you thereby render invalid the word of God by your tradition which you hand on. You do many things like that."

THE exact meaning of this passage is very difficult to discover. It hinges on the word *Korban*. It would seem that this word *Korban* really underwent two stages of meaning in Jewish usage.

(i) The word means a *gift*. It was used to describe something which was specially given and dedicated to God. A thing which was *Korban* was as if it had already been laid upon the altar. That is to say, it was completely set apart from all ordinary purposes and usages and became the property of God. If a man wished to dedicate some of his money or his property to God, he declared it *Korban*, and thereafter it might never again be used for any ordinary or any secular purpose. It does seem that, even at this stage, the word was capable of very shrewd usage. For instance, a creditor might have a debtor who refused or was unwilling to pay. The creditor might then say, " The debt you owe me is *Korban*," that is to say, " The debt you owe me is dedicated to God." From then on the debtor ceased to be in debt to a fellow-man and began to be in debt to God, which was far more serious. It may well be that the creditor could discharge his part of the matter by making a quite small symbolic payment to the Temple, and then keeping the rest for himself. In any event, to introduce the idea of *Korban* into this kind of debt was a kind of religious blackmail, which transformed a debt owed to man into a debt owed to God. It does seem that the idea of *Korban* was already capable of misuse. If that be the idea that is behind this, the passage means that a man has declared his property *Korban*, sacred to and dedicated to God, as if laid upon the altar, and then when his father or mother is in dire need and comes to him for help, he says, " I am sorry that I cannot give you any help because nothing that I have is available for you because it is dedicated to God." The vow was made an excuse or a reason to avoid helping a parent in need. The vow which the scribal legalist insisted upon was a vow which involved breaking one of the Ten Commandments which are the very law of God.

(ii) It seems that there came a time when the word *Korban* became a much more generalized oath. When a person declared anything *Korban* he entirely alienated it, and separated it from the person to whom he was talking. A man might say, " *Korban* that by which I might be profited by you," and, in so doing, he bound himself never to touch, taste, have or handle anything possessed by the person so addressed. Or, he might say, " *Korban* that by which you might be profited by me," and, in so saying, he bound himself never to help or to benefit the person so addressed by him by anything that belonged to himself. If that be the use which is meant here, the passage means that, at some time, perhaps in a fit of anger or rebellion, a man had said to his parents, " *Korban* anything by which you may ever be helped by me," and that afterwards, even if he repented from his rash vow, the scribal legalists declared that it was unbreakable and that he might never again render his parents any assistance. Whichever be the case—and it is not possible to be certain—this much is certain, that there were cases in which the strict performance of the scribal law made it impossible for a man to carry out the law of the Ten Commandments.

Jesus was attacking a system which put rules and regulations before the claim of human need. The commandment of God was that the claim of human love and human ties should come first ; the commandment of the scribes was that the claim of legal rules and regulations should come first. Jesus was quite sure that any rule and regulation which prevented a man from giving help where help was needed was nothing less than a contradiction of the law of God. We must have a care that we never allow rules and regulations to paralyse the claims of charity and love. Nothing that prevents us helping a fellow-man can ever be a rule approved by God.

THE REAL DEFILEMENT

Mark 7 : 14-23

> He called the crowd to Him again and said, " Listen to me, all of you and understand. There is nothing which goes into a man from outside which can render him unclean ; but it is the things which come out of a man which render the man unclean." When He came into the house, away from the crowd, His disciples asked Him about this hard saying. He said to them, " So, then, are you too unable to grasp things? Do you not understand that everything that goes into a man from outside cannot render him unclean, because it does not go into his heart, but into his stomach, and it is then evacuated from him by natural bodily processes? " (The effect of this saying is to render all foods clean.) But He went on to say, " What comes out of a man, *that* is what renders the man unclean. It is from within, from the heart, that there come evil designs, fornications, thefts, murders, adulteries, covetous deeds, evil deeds, guile, wanton wickedness, envy, slander, pride, folly. All these evil things come from within, and they render a man unclean."

ALTHOUGH it may not seem to be so now, this passage when it was first spoken, is well-nigh the most revolutionary passage in the New Testament. Jesus has been arguing with the legal experts about different aspects of the traditional law. He has shown the irrelevance of the elaborate handwashings. He has shown how rigid adherence to the traditional law can actually mean disobedience of the law of God. But here He says something more startling yet. He declares that nothing that goes into a man can possibly defile that man, for it is received only into his body and his body rids itself of it in the normal, physical way. Now, no Jew ever believed that, and no orthodox Jew believes it yet. Leviticus 11 has a long list of animals that are unclean and may not be used for food. How very seriously this was taken can be seen from many an incident in the Maccabean times. At that time the Syrian king, Antiochus Epiphanes, was determined to root out the Jewish faith. One of the things he demanded was that the Jews should eat pork, swine's flesh. The Jews died in their hundreds rather than do so. " Howbeit many in Israel were fully resolved and confirmed in themselves not to eat any unclean thing. Wherefore they chose rather to die, that they might not be defiled with meats, and that they might not profane the holy covenant ; so then they died." (I Maccabees I : 62, 63.) Fourth Maccabees (chapter 7) tells the story of a widow and her seven sons. It was demanded that they should eat swine's flesh. They refused. The first had his tongue cut out, the ends of his limbs cut off ; and he was then roasted alive in a pan ; the second had his hair and the skin of his skull torn off ; one by one they were tortured to death while their aged mother looked on and cheered them on ; they died rather than eat meat which to them was unclean. It is in face of that that Jesus made this revolutionary statement that nothing that goes into a man can make him unclean. He was wiping out at one gesture the laws for which Jews had suffered and died. No wonder the disciples were amazed.

In effect Jesus was saying that *things* cannot be either unclean or clean in any real religious sense of the term. Only *persons* can be really defiled ; and what defiles a person is his own actions, which are the product of his own heart. This was new doctrine and shatteringly new doctrine. The Jew had, and still has, a whole system of *things* which are clean and unclean. With one sweeping pronouncement Jesus declared the whole thing irrelevant, and declared that uncleanness has nothing to do with what a man takes into his body, and everything to do with what comes out of his heart.

Let us see the things that Jesus lists as coming from the heart and making a man unclean.

He begins with *evil designs* (*dialogismoi*). Every outward act of sin is preceded by an inward act of choice ; therefore Jesus begins with the evil thought from which the evil action comes. Next there come *fornications* (*porneiai*) ; later He is to list *acts of adultery* (*moicheiai*) ; but this first word is a wide word—it means every kind of traffic in sexual vice. There follow *thefts* (*klopai*). In Greek there are two words for a robber—*kleptēs* and *lēstēs*. *Lēstēs* is a *brigand* ; Barabbas was a *lēstēs* (John 18 : 40) and a brigand may be a very brave man although an outlaw. *Kleptēs* is a thief ; Judas was a *kleptēs* when he pilfered from the bag (John 12 : 6). A *kleptēs* is a mean, deceitful, dishonourable pilferer, without even the redeeming quality of a certain audacious gallantry that a brigand must have. *Murders* and *adulteries* come next in the list and their meaning is clear. Next there comes *covetous deeds* (*pleonexiai*). *Pleonexia* comes from two Greek words meaning *to have more*. It has been defined as *the accursed love of having*. It has been defined as " the spirit which snatches at that which it is not right to take," " the baneful appetite for that which belongs to others." It is the spirit which snatches at things, not to hoard them like a miser, but to spend them in lust and luxury. Cowley defined it as, " Rapacious appetite for gain, not for its own sake, but for the pleasure of refunding it immediately through all the channels of pride and luxury." It is not

the desire for money and things ; it includes the desire
for power, the insatiable lust of the flesh. Plato said,
" The desire of man is like a sieve or pierced vessel which
he ever tries to, and can never fill." *Pleonexia* is that lust
for having which is in the heart of the man who sees
happiness in things instead of in God. There follows *evil
deeds*. In Greek there are two words for evil—*kakos*, which
describes a thing which in itself is an evil thing, and
poneros, which describes a person or a thing which is
actively evil. It is *poneriai* which is the word that is used
here. The man who is *poneros* is the man in whose heart
there is the desire to harm. He is, as Bengel said, " trained
in every crime and completely equipped to inflict evil on
any man." Jeremy Taylor defined this *poneria* as " aptness
to do shrewd turns, to delight in mischiefs and tragedies ;
loving to trouble our neighbour, and to do him ill offices ;
crossness, perverseness and peevishness of action in our
intercourse." *Poneria* not only corrupts the man who has
it ; it corrupts others too. *Poneros*—The Evil One—is the
title of Satan. The worst of men, the man who is doing
Satan's work, is the man who, being bad himself, makes
others as bad as himself. There follows *dolos* ; it is translated *guile*. It comes from a word which means *bait* ; it
means trickery and deceit. It is used for instance of a
mousetrap. When the Greeks were besieging Troy and
could not gain an entry they sent to the Trojans the
present of a great wooden horse, as if it was a token of
good will. The Trojans opened their gates and took it in.
But the horse was filled with Greeks who in the night broke
out and dealt death and devastation to Troy. That exactly
is *dolos*. *Dolos* is crafty, cunning, deceitful, clever
treachery. Next on the list comes *wanton wickedness*
(*aselgeia*). The Greeks defined *aselgeia* as " a disposition
of soul that resents all discipline," as " a spirit that
acknowledges no restraints, dares whatsoever its caprice
and wanton insolence may suggest." The great characteristic of the man who is guilty of *aselgeia* is that he is lost

to decency and to shame. The evil man may hide his sin, and will always try to hide it, but the man who has *aselgeia* sins without a qualm and never hesitates to shock his fellowmen. Jezebel was the classic instance of *aselgeia* when she built a heathen shrine in Jerusalem the Holy City. *Envy* is literally *the evil eye*, the eye that looks on the success amd happiness of another in such a way that it would cast an evil spell upon it if it could. Next there comes *slander*. The word is *blasphēmia*. When this word is used of words against man, it means *slander* ; when it is used of words against God, it means *blasphemy*. It means insulting man or God. There follows *pride* (*huperēphania*). The Greek word literally means " showing oneself above." It describes the attitude of the man " who has a certain contempt for everyone except himself." The interesting thing about this word, as the Greeks used it, is that it describes an attitude that may never become *public*. It may be that in his heart of hearts a man is always secretly comparing himself with others. He might even ape humility and yet in his heart be proud. Sometimes, of course, the pride is evident. The Greeks had a legend of this pride. They said that the Giants, the sons of Tartarus and Gē, in their pride, sought to storm heaven and were cast down by Hercules. That is *huperēphania*. It is setting oneself up against God ; it is " invading God's prerogatives." That is why it has been called " the peak of all the vices," and that is why " God resists the proud." (James 4 : 6.) Lastly, there comes *folly* (*aphrosunē*). This does not mean the foolishness that is due to weakness of intellect and lack of brains ; it means moral folly. It describes, not the man who is a brainless fool, but the man who, as we say, is playing the fool.

It is a truly terrible list which Jesus cites of the things that come from the human heart. When we go into it and examine it a shudder surely passes over us. Nonetheless it is a summons, not to a fastidious shrinking from such things, but to an honest self-examination of our own hearts.

THE FORECAST OF A WORLD FOR CHRIST

Mark 7 : 24-30

> He left there and went away into the regions of Tyre
> and Sidon. He went into a house and He did not wish
> anyone to know about it, but He could not be there
> without people knowing about it. When a woman
> whose daughter had an unclean spirit heard about Him,
> she immediately came and threw herself at His feet.
> The woman was a Greek, a Syrophoenician by birth.
> She asked Him to cast the demon out of her daughter.
> He said to her, " First of all you must let the children
> eat their fill ; it is not right to take the bread that
> belongs to the children and to throw it to the dogs."
> " True, sir," she answered, " but even the dogs below
> the table eat some of the bits of bread that the children
> throw away." He said to her, " Because of this word,
> go your way ! The demon has come out of your
> daughter ! " She went away and found the child
> thrown upon her bed and the demon gone.

WHEN this incident is seen against its background and in
its implications it becomes one of the most moving and
extraordinary incidents in the life of Jesus.

First, let us look at the geography of the incident. Tyre
and Sidon were cities of Phoenicia, and Phoenicia was a
part of Syria. Phoenicia stretched north from Carmel,
right along the coastal plain. It was Phoenicia which came
between Galilee and the sea coast. Phoenicia indeed, as
Josephus puts it, " encompassed Galilee." Tyre lay 40
miles north-west of Capernaum. Its name means *The Rock*.
It was so called because off the shore there lay two great
rocks joined by a three-thousand-feet-long ridge. This
formed a natural breakwater and Tyre was one of the
great natural harbours of the world from the earliest times.
Not only did the rocks form a breakwater, but they also
formed a defence, and Tyre was not only a famous harbour ;
she was also a famous fortress. It was from Tyre and
Sidon that there came the first sailors who steered by the
stars. Until men learned to find their way by the stars,
ships had to hug the coast and to lay up by night : but the

Phoenician sailors had circumnavigated the Mediterranean and had found their way through the Pillars of Hercules until they came to Britain and the tin mines of Cornwall. It may well be that in their adventuring they had even circumnavigated Africa. Sidon was 26 miles north-east of Tyre, and 60 miles north of Capernaum. Like Tyre it had a natural breakwater, and its origin as a harbour and a city was so ancient that no man knew who had founded it. Although the Phoenician cities were part of Syria, they were all independent, and they were all rivals. They had their own kings, their own gods and their own coinage. Within a radius of 15 or 20 miles they were supreme. Outwardly they looked to the sea ; and inland they looked to Damascus ; and the ships of the sea and the caravans of many lands flowed into them. In the end Sidon lost her trade to Tyre and lost her greatness and sunk into a demoralised degeneracy. But the name of the Phoenician sailors will always be famous as the men who first found their way by following the stars.

(i) So, then, the first tremendous thing which meets us here is that *Jesus is in Gentile territory.* Is it any accident that this incident comes here? The previous incident shows Jesus wiping out the distinction between clean and unclean foods. Can it be that here, in symbol, we have Jesus wiping out the difference between clean and unclean people? Just as the Jew would never soil his lips with forbidden foods, so he would never soil his life by contact with the unclean Gentile. It may well be that here Jesus is saying by implication that the Gentiles are not unclean but that they, too, have their place within the Kingdom. Jesus must have come north to this region for temporary escape. In his own country He was under attack from every side. Long ago the Scribes and Pharisees had branded Him as a sinner because He broke through their rules and regulations. Herod had regarded Him as a menace. The people of Nazareth had treated Him with scandalized dislike. The hour would come when He would face His

enemies with blazing defiance, but that hour had not yet
come. Before it came, He would seek the peace and quiet
of seclusion, and in that withdrawal from the enmity of the
Jews the foundation of the Kingdom of the Gentiles was
laid. It is the forecast of the whole history of Christianity.
The rejection of the Jews had become the opportunity of
the Gentiles.

(ii) But there is more to it than that. Ideally these
Phoenician cities were part of the realm of Israel. When,
under Joshua, the land was being partitioned out the tribe
of Asher was allocated the land even unto great Zidon . . .
and to the strong city Tyre (Joshua 19 : 28, 29). They had
never been able to subdue their territory, and they had
never entered into it. Again is it not symbolic? Where
the might of arms was helpless, the conquering love of
Jesus Christ was victorious. The earthly Israel had failed
to gather in the people of Phoenicia ; now the true Israel
had come upon them. It was not a strange land into which
Jesus came ; it was a land which long ago God had given
Him for His own. He was not so much coming amongst
strangers as He was entering into His inheritance.

(iii) The story itself must be read with insight. The
woman came asking Jesus' help for her daughter. Jesus'
answer was that it is not right to take the children's bread
and give it to dogs. At first it is an almost shocking saying.
The dog was not the well-loved guardian that it is to-day.
More commonly the dog was a symbol of dishonour. To
the Greek, the word *dog* meant a shameless and audacious
woman ; it was used exactly with the connotation that
we use the word *bitch* to-day. To the Jew it was equally a
term of contempt. " Give not that which is holy unto
dogs." (Matthew 7 : 6 ; cp. Philippians 3 : 2 ;
Revelation 22 : 15). The word dog was in fact sometimes
a Jewish term of contempt for the Gentiles. Rabbi Joshua
ben Levi had a parable. He saw the blessings of God
which the Gentiles enjoy ; he asked, " If the Gentiles
without the law enjoy blessings like that, how many more

blessings will Israel, the people of God, enjoy?" "It is like a king who made a feast and brought in the guests and placed them at the door of his palace. They saw the dogs come out, with pheasants, and heads of fatted birds, and calves in their mouths. Then the guests began to say, 'If it be thus with the dogs, how much more luxurious will the meal itself be.' And the nations of the world are compared to dogs, as it is said (Isaiah 56 : 11), 'Yea, the dogs are greedy '." No matter how you look at it, the term *dog* is an insult. How, then, are we to explain Jesus' use of it here? (*a*) He did not use the usual word ; He used a diminutive word which described, not the wild dogs of the streets, but the little pet lap-dogs of the house. In Greek diminutives are characteristically affectionate. Jesus took the sting out of the word. (*b*) Without a doubt His tone of voice makes all the difference. The same word can be a deadly insult and an affectionate address, according to the tone of voice. We can call a man " an old rascal " in a voice of contempt or a voice of affection. Jesus' tone took all the poison out of the word. (*c*) In any event Jesus did *not* shut the door. *First*, He said, the children must be fed ; but only first ; there is meat left for the household pets. True, Israel had the *first* offer of the gospel, but only the first ; there were others still to come. Now the woman was a Greek, and the Greeks had a gift of repartee ; and she saw at once that Jesus was speaking with a smile. She knew that the door was swinging on its hinges. In those days people did not have either knives or forks or table-napkins. They ate with their hands ; they wiped the soiled hands on chunks of bread and then flung the bread away and the house-dogs ate it. So the woman said, " I know the children are fed first, but can't I even get the scraps the children throw away?" And Jesus loved her. Here was a sunny faith that would not take no for an answer, here was a woman with the tragedy of an ill daughter at home, and there was still light enough in her heart to answer with a smile. Her faith was tested and her faith was real, and her prayer was answered. Symbolically she stands for the Gentile world which so eagerly seized on the bread of heaven which the Jews had rejected and thrown away.

DOING ALL THINGS WELL

Mark 7 : 31-37

> He went away again from the regions of Tyre and came through Sidon to the Sea of Galilee, through the regions of the Decapolis. They brought to Him a man who was deaf and who had an impediment in his speech, and they asked Him to lay His hands on him. He took him aside from the crowd all by himself. He thrust His fingers into his ears, and spat, and touched his tongue. Then He looked up into heaven, and sighed, and said to him, " Ephphatha ! " which means, " Be opened ! " And his ears were opened, and the bond which held his tongue was loosed, and he spoke correctly. He enjoined them to tell no one ; but the more He enjoined them the more exceedingly they proclaimed the story of what He had done. They were all amazed beyond measure. " He has done all things well," they said. And He made the deaf to hear and the dumb to speak.

THIS story begins by describing what is on the face of it an amazing journey. Jesus was going from Tyre to the territory around the Sea of Galilee. That is to say, He was going from Tyre, in the north, to Galilee in the south ; and, according to this story, He started by going to Sidon. That is to say, He started going due south by going due north ! As one scholar has put it, it would be like going from London to Cornwall *via* Manchester; or it would be like going from Glasgow to Edinburgh *via* Perth. Because of that difficulty some people have thought that the text is wrong, and that Sidon should not enter into it at all. But almost certainly the text is correct as it stands. Another great scholar thinks that this journey took no less than eight months, and that, indeed, is far more likely. It may well be that this long journey is the peace before the storm; it is the long communion with the disciples before the final storm breaks. In the very next chapter Peter makes the great discovery that Jesus is the Christ (Mark 8: 27-29), and it may well be that it was in this long, lonely time together that that impression became a certainty in Peter's heart. Jesus needed this long time with His men before the storm and tension of the approaching end.

When Jesus did arrive back in the regions of Galilee, He came into the district of the Decapolis, and there they brought to Him a man who was deaf and who had an impediment in his speech. As Tyndale vividly translates it the man was " deffe and stambed in his speech." No doubt the two things went together ; it was the man's inability to hear which made his speech so imperfect. There is no miracle which so beautifully shows Jesus' way of treating people.

(i) Jesus took the man aside from the crowd, all by himself. Here is the most tender considerateness. Deaf folk are always a little embarrassed. In some ways it is more embarrassing to be deaf than it is to be blind. A deaf person knows he cannot hear ; and when someone in a crowd shouts at him and tries to make him hear, in his excitement, he becomes all the more helpless. Jesus shows the most tender consideration for the feelings of a man for whom life was very difficult.

(ii) Throughout the whole miracle Jesus acted what He was going to do in dumb-show. He put His hands in the man's ears. In those days people believed that spittle had a curative quality. Suetonius, the Roman historian, tells of an incident in the life of Vespasian, the Roman Emperor. " It fortuned that a certain mean commoner stark-blind, another likewise with a feeble and lame leg, came together unto him as he sat upon his tribunal, craving that help and remedy for their infirmities which had been shown unto them by Serapis in their dreams ; that he should restore the one to his sight, if he did but spit into his eyes, and strengthen the other's leg, if he vouchsafed only to touch it with his heel. Now when as he could hardly believe that the thing any way would find success and speed accordingly, and therefore durst not so much as put it to the venture, at the last, through the persuasion of his friends, openly before the assembly he assayed both means, neither missed he of the effect." (Suetonius, Life of Vespasian 7. Holland's translation.) Jesus then looked up to heaven to show that it was from God that help was to come. Then He spoke the word and the man was healed. The whole story shows us most vividly that Jesus did not consider the man merely *a case* ; He considered him as *an individual*. The man had a special need and a special problem, and with the most tender considerateness Jesus dealt with him in a way that spared his feelings, and in a way that he could understand.

When it was done the people declared that He had done all things well. That is none other than the verdict of God upon His own creation in the very beginning (Genesis 1: 31). When Jesus came, bringing healing to men's bodies and salvation to their souls, He had begun the work of creation all over again. In the beginning everything had been good ; man's sin had spoiled it all ; and now Jesus was bringing back the beauty of God to the world which man's sin had rendered ugly.

COMPASSION AND CHALLENGE

Mark 8 : 1-10

> In those days, when there was again a great crowd, and when they had nothing to eat, Jesus called His disciples to Him and said, " My heart is moved with pity for the crowd, because they have stayed with me now for three days, and they have nothing to eat. If I send them away to their homes still fasting, they will faint on the road ; and some of them have come from a long distance." His disciples answered Him, " Where could anyone get bread to satisfy them in a

desert place like this? " He asked them, " How many loaves have you? " They said, " Seven." He ordered the crowd to sit down on the ground. He took the seven loaves and gave thanks for them and broke them, and gave them to His disciples to set before the people. So they set them before the crowd, and they had a few small fishes. So He blessed them and told them to set them before them too. So they ate until they were completely satisfied. They gathered up what remained over of the broken pieces—seven baskets. There were about four thousand people there. So He sent them away, and immediately He embarked on the boat with His disciples and came to the district of Dalmanutha.

THERE are two things closely intertwined in this incident.

(i) There is the compassion of Jesus. Over and over again we see Jesus moved with compassion for men. The most amazing thing about Jesus is His sheer considerateness. Now considerateness is a virtue which never forgets the details of life. Jesus looked at the crowd ; they had been with Him for three days ; and then He remembered that they had a long walk home. It might have been thought that He whose task it was to bring the splendour and the majesty of the truth and love of God to men would have had a mind above thinking of what was going to happen to His congregation on their walk home. But Jesus was not like that. Confront Jesus with a lost soul or a tired body and His first instinct was to help. It is all too true that the first instinct of too many people is *not* to help. I met a man once at a conference and was discussing with him the dangers of a certain stretch of road on the way to the town where we were. " Yes," he said. " It's a right bad bit of road. I saw a crash on it as I drove here to-day." " Did you stop and help? " I asked. " Not me," he said, " I wasn't going to be held up by getting mixed up in a thing like that." It is human to want to avoid the trouble of giving help ; it is divine to be moved with such a compassion and a pity that we are compelled to help.

(ii) There is the challenge of Jesus. When Jesus had

pity on the crowd, and when He wished to give them
something to eat, the disciples immediately pointed out
the practical difficulty that they were in a desert place,
and that there was nowhere within miles where any food
could be got. At once Jesus flashed the question back at
them, " What have *you* got wherewith you may help? "
The compassion has become a challenge. In effect Jesus
was saying, " Don't try to push the responsibility for
helping on to someone else. Don't say that you would
help if you had only something to give. Don't say that in
these circumstances to help is impossible. Take what you
have got and give it and see what happens." One of the
most joyous of all Jewish feasts is the Feast of Purim. It
falls on the 14th March, and commemorates the deliverance
of which the Book of Esther tells. Above all it is a time
of giving gifts ; and one of its regulations is that, no
matter how poor a man is, he must seek out someone
poorer than himself and give him a gift. Jesus has no time
for the spirit which waits until all the circumstances are
perfect before it thinks of helping. Jesus says, " If you see
someone in trouble, help him with what you have got.
You never know what you may do."

There are two interesting things in the background of
this story.

The first is this. This incident happened on the far side
of the Sea of Galilee in the district called the Decapolis.
Why did this tremendous 4,000 crowd assemble? There is
no doubt that the healing of the deaf man with the impediment in his speech would help to arouse interest and to
collect the crowd. But one commentator has made a most
interesting suggestion. In Mark 5 : 1-20, we have already
read how Jesus cured the Gerasene demoniac. That
incident also happened in the Decapolis. At the moment
the result of that incident was that they besought Jesus
to go away. But we remember that the cured demoniac
had wished to follow Jesus, and that Jesus had sent him
back to his own people to tell them what great things the

Lord had done for him. Is it just possible that part of this great crowd was due to the missionary activity of the healed demoniac? Have we got here a glimpse of what the witness of one man can do for Christ? Were there people in the crowd that day who came to Christ and found their souls because of the story that a man had told about what Christ had done for his soul? John Bunyan tells how he owed his conversion to the fact that he heard three or four old women talking, as they sat in the sun, " about a new birth, the work of God in their hearts." They were talking of what God had done for them. It may well be that there were many that day in that crowd in Decapolis who were there because they had heard a man telling of what Jesus Christ had done for him.

The second thing at the back of this story is this. It is an odd thing that the word for *basket* is different in this story from the word which is used in the similar story in Mark 6. In Mark 6 : 44, the word for basket is *kophinos*, which describes the basket in which the Jew carried about his food, a basket shaped narrow at the top and wider at the foot, and rather like a water pot in shape. The word used here is *sphuris*, which describes a basket like a hamper, a *frail*, is the technical term ; it was in that kind of basket that Paul was let down over the wall of Damascus (Acts 9 : 25) ; and it describes the basket which the Gentiles used. As we have already said this incident happened in the Decapolis, which was on the far side of the lake and which had a large Gentile population. Is it possible that we are to see in the feeding of the multitude, in Mark 6, the coming of the bread of God to the Jews, and in this incident, the coming of the bread of God to the Gentiles? When we put these two stories together, is there somewhere at the back of them the suggestion and the forecast and the symbol that Jesus came to satisfy the hunger of Jew and Gentile alike, that in Him, in truth, there was the God who opens His hand and who satisfies the desire of every living thing?

THE BLINDNESS WHICH DESIRES A SIGN

Mark 8 : 11-13

> The Pharisees came out and began to ask Him
> questions. They were looking for a sign from heaven,
> and they were trying to test Him. He sighed in His
> spirit and said to them, " Why does this generation
> look for a sign? This is the truth I tell you—no sign
> will be given to this generation." He sent them away
> and He again embarked on the boat, and went away to
> the other side.

THE whole tendency of the age in which Jesus lived was to
look for God in the abnormal. It was believed that when
the Messiah came the most startling and shattering things
would happen. Before we reach the end of this chapter
we shall examine more closely, and in detail, the kind of
signs which were expected. We may note just now that
when false Messiahs arose, as they frequently did, they
lured the people to follow them by promising them astonishing signs. They would promise, for instance, to cleave
the waters of the Jordan in two and to leave a pathway
through it, or they would promise, with a word, to make
the city walls fall down. It was a sign like that that the
Pharisees were demanding. They wished to see some
shattering event blazing across the horizon, defying the
laws of nature and astonishing men. Now to Jesus such
a demand was not due to the desire to see the hand of God ;
it was due to the fact that they were blind to the hand of
God. To Jesus the whole world was full of signs of God.
The corn in the field, the leaven in the loaf, the scarlet
anemones on the hillside all spoke to Him of God. He
did not think that God had to break in, in some staggering
way, from outside the world ; He knew that God was
already in the world for anyone who had eyes to see. The
sign of the truly religious man is not that he comes to
Church to find God but that he finds God everywhere, not
that he makes a great deal of sacred places, but that he
sanctifies common places. That is what the poets knew

and felt, and that is why they were poets. Elizabeth
Barret Browning wrote :

> " Earth's crammed with heaven,
> And every common bush afire with God ;
> But only he who sees, takes off his shoes,
> The rest sit round it and pluck blackberries."

Thomas Edward Brown wrote :

> " A garden is a lovesome thing God wot !
>   Rose plot,
>   Fringed pool,
>   Fern'd grot—
>   The veriest school
>   Of peace ; and yet the fool
> Contends that God is not—
> Not God ! In gardens ! when the eve is cool?
>   Nay, but I have a sign ;
>   'Tis very sure God walks in mine."

And still another poet wrote :

> " One asked a sign from God ; and day by day
>   The sun arose in pearl ; in scarlet set ;
> Each night the stars appeared in bright array ;
>   Each morn the thirsty grass with dew was wet ;
> The corn failed not its harvest, nor the vine—
>   And yet he saw no sign ! "

For him who has eyes to see and a heart to understand the
daily miracle of night and day, and the daily splendour of
all common things is sign enough from God.

THE FAILURE TO LEARN FROM EXPERIENCE

Mark 8 : 14-21

They had forgotten to bring loaves, and they had only
one loaf with them in the boat. Jesus enjoined them,
" Look to it ! Beware of the evil influence of the
Pharisees and of the evil influence of Herod ! " They
kept discussing the situation among themselves, and
saying, " We have no loaves." Jesus knew what they
were saying. " Why," He said, " do you keep talking
about the fact that you have no loaves? Do you not
yet see and understand? Is your mind completely

obtuse? Do you not see although you have eyes? Do you not hear although you have ears? Do you not remember? When I broke the five loaves and gave them to the five thousand how many basketsful of broken pieces did you take up? " " Twelve," they said to Him. " When I broke the seven loaves among the four thousand how many basketsful of broken pieces did you take up? " " Seven," they said to Him. So He said to them, " Do you still not understand? "

THIS passage sheds a very vivid light on the minds of the disciples. They were crossing over to the other side of the Sea of Galilee, and they had forgotten to bring bread with them. We will best get the meaning of this passage if we connect it closely with what goes before. Jesus was thinking of the demand of Pharisees for a sign, and He was also thinking of Herod's terrified reaction to Himself. " Beware," He said, to translate it literally, " of the leaven of the Pharisees and the leaven of Herod." To the Jew leaven was the symbol of evil. Leaven was a piece of dough which had been kept over from a previous baking. In the keeping it fermented, and that fermented dough was leaven. To the Jew fermentation was identified with putrefaction, and therefore leaven stood for evil. Sometimes the Jew used the word leaven much as we would use the term *original sin*, or the natural evil of human nature. Rabbi Alexander said, " It is revealed before Thee that our will is to do Thy will. And what hinders? The leaven that is in the dough and slavery to the kingdoms of the world. May it be Thy will to deliver us from their hand." It was, so to speak, the taint of human nature, original sin, the corrupting leaven which kept man from doing the will of God. So when Jesus said this, He was saying, " Be on your guard against the evil influence of the Pharisees and of Herod. Don't you go the same way that the Pharisees and Herod have already gone."

What is the point? What possible connection is there between the Pharisees and Herod? The Pharisees had just asked for a sign. For a Jew—we shall see this more fully shortly—nothing was easier than to think of the Messiah in terms of wonders and conquests and miraculous happenings, and nationalistic triumphs and political supremacy. Herod had tried to build up happiness through the gaining of power and wealth and influence and prestige. In one sense, for both the Pharisees and Herod, the Kingdom of God was an earthly Kingdom ; it was based on earthly power and greatness, and on the victories that force could win. It is as if Jesus by this detached hint was already preparing the disciples for something that was very soon to come. It was as if He was saying, " Maybe soon it will dawn on you that I am God's Annointed One, the Messiah. When that thought does come don't think in terms of earthly power and glory as the Pharisees and Herod do." Of the true meaning at the moment He said nothing. That grim revelation was still to come.

In point of fact this hint of Jesus passed clean over the disciples' heads. They could think of nothing but the fact that they had forgotten to bring loaves, and that, unless something happened, they would go hungry. Jesus saw their preoccupation with bread. It may well be that He asked His questions, not with anger, but with a smile, like one who tries to lead a slow child to see a self-evident truth. He reminded them that twice He had satisfied the hunger of huge crowds with food enough and to spare. It is as if He said, " Why all the worry? Don't you remember what happened before? Hasn't experience taught you that you don't need to worry about things like that if you are with me? "

The odd fact is that we only learn half the lessons of experience. Too often experience fills us with pessimism, teaches us what we cannot do, teaches us to view life with a kind of resigned hopelessness. But there are other experiences. Sorrow came—and we came through it still erect. Temptation came—and somehow we did not fall. Illness took us—and somehow we recovered. A problem seemed insoluble—and somehow it was solved. We were at our wits' end—and somehow we went on. We reached the breaking point—and somehow we did not break. We, too, are blind. If we would only read the lessons of experience aright, it would teach us not the pessimism of the things that cannot be, but the hope which stands amazed that God has brought us thus far in safety and in certainty, that the lesson of the past is that God can bring us through anything that may happen.

A BLIND MAN LEARNS TO SEE

Mark 8 : 22-26

> They came to Bethsaida ; and they brought a blind man to Him and asked Him to touch him. He took the blind man's hand and took him outside the village. He spat into his eyes and laid His hands on him, and asked him, " Do you see anything? " He looked up and said, " I see men, but I see them walking looking like trees." Again He laid His hands on his eyes. He gazed intently, and his sight was restored and he saw everything clearly. He sent him away to his home. " Do not," he said, " even enter into the village."

BLINDNESS was, and still is, one of the great curses of the East. It was caused partly by ophthalmia and partly by the pitiless glare of the sun. It was greatly aggravated by the fact that people knew nothing of hygiene and of cleanliness. It was common to see a person with matter-encrusted eyes on which the flies persistently settled. Very naturally this carried the infection far and wide, and blindness was a scourge of Palestine.

Only Mark tells us this story, and yet there are certain extremely interesting things in it.

(i) Here again we see the unique considerateness of Jesus. Jesus took the blind man out of the crowd and out of the village that He might be alone with Him. Why? Think of it. This man was blind and apparently had been born blind. If he had been suddenly given back his sight amidst a crowd, there would have flashed upon his newly-seeing eyes the sight of hundreds of people and things, and dazzling colours, so that he would have been completely bewildered. Jesus knew it would be far better if he could be taken to a place where the thrill of seeing would break less suddenly upon him. Every great doctor and every great teacher has one outstanding characteristic and ability. The great doctor is able to enter into the very mind and heart of his patient ; he understands his fears and his hopes ; he literally sympathises—suffers—with him. The great teacher enters into the very mind of his scholar. He sees his problems, his difficulties, his stumbling-blocks. That is why Jesus was so supremely great. He could enter into the mind and heart of the people whom He sought to help. He had the gift of considerateness, because He could think with their thoughts and feel with their feelings. God grant to us this Christlike gift.

(ii) Jesus used methods that the man could understand. The ancient world had a curious belief in the healing power of spittle. The belief is not so strange when we remember that it is a first instinct to put a cut or burned finger into our mouths to ease the pain. Of course the blind man knew of this, and Jesus used a method of curing him which he could understand. Jesus was wise. He did not begin with words and methods which were far above the heads of simple folk. He spoke to them and acted on them in a way that simple minds could grasp and understand. There have been times when unintelligibility has been accounted a virtue and a sign of greatness. Jesus had the still greater greatness—the greatness which a simple mind could grasp.

(iii) In one thing this miracle is unique—it is the only miracle which can be said to have happened gradually. Usually Jesus' miracles happened suddenly and completely. In this miracle the blind man's sight came back in stages. There is symbolic truth here. No man sees all God's truth all at once. One of the dangers of a certain type of evangelism is that it encourages the idea that when a man has taken his decision for Christ he is a full-grown Christian. One of the dangers of Church membership is that it can be presented in such a way as to imply that when a person becomes a pledged member of the Church he has come to the end of the road. So far from that being the case the decision and the pledge of membership are the beginning of the road. They are the discovery of the riches of Christ which are inexhaustible, and if a man lived a hundred, or a thousand, or a million years, he would still have to go on growing in grace, and learning more and more about the infinite wonder and beauty of Jesus Christ. F. W. H. Myers, in his poem *Saint Paul*, makes Paul say :

> " Let no man think that sudden in a minute
>   All is accomplished and the work is done—
> Though with thine earliest dawn thou shouldst
>   begin it
>   Scarce were it ended in thy setting sun."

It is gloriously true that sudden conversion is a gracious possibility, but it is equally true that every day a man should be re-converted. With all God's grace and glory before him he can go on learning for a life time and still need eternity to know as he is known.

THE GREAT DISCOVERY

Mark 8 : 27-30

Jesus and His disciples went away to the villages of Caesarea Philippi. On the road He asked His disciples a question. " Who," He said to them, " do men say that I am? " They said to Him, " Some say, John the Baptizer ; others say, Elijah ; others, one of the prophets." He asked them, " You—who do you say that I am? " Peter answered Him, " You are God's Anointed One." And He insisted that they should tell no man about Him.

CAESAREA PHILIPPI was outside Galilee altogether. It was not in the territory of Herod, but in the territory of Philip.

It was a town with an amazing history. In the oldest days it was called *Balinas*, for it had once been a great centre of the worship of Baal. To this day it is called *Banias*, which is a form of *Panias*. It had been called *Panias* because up on the hillside there was a cavern which was said to have been the birthplace of the Greek God, Pan, who was the god of nature. Again, from a cave in the hillside there gushed forth a stream, and that stream was held to be the source of the River Jordan. Still farther up on the hillside there rose a gleaming temple of white marble which Philip had built to the godhead of Caesar, the Roman Emperor, the ruler of the world, who was regarded as a God. It is an amazing thing that it was here of all places that Peter saw in a homeless Galilaean carpenter the Son of God. The ancient religion of Palestine was in the air, and the memories of Baal clustered around. The gods of classical Greece brooded over the place, and no doubt men heard the pipes of Pan and caught a glimpse of the woodland nymphs. The Jordan would bring back to memory episode after episode in the history of Israel and the conquest of the land. And, clear in the eastern sun, there gleamed and glinted the marble of the holy place which reminded all men that Caesar was a god. There, of all places, as it were, against the background of all religions and all history, Peter discovered that a wandering teacher from Nazareth, who was heading for a cross, was the Son of God. There is hardly anything in all the gospel story which shows the sheer force of the personality of Jesus as does this incident.

This incident comes in the very middle of Mark's gospel sand it does so designedly, for it comes at the peak momen of the gospel. In one way at least this moment was the crisis of Jesus' life. Whatever His disciples might be thinking, He knew for certain that ahead there lay an inescapable cross. Things could not go on much longer. The opposition was gathering itself to strike. Now the problem and the question confronting Jesus was this— had He had any effect at all? Had he achieved anything?

Or, to put it in another way, had anyone discovered who He really was? If he had lived and taught and moved amongst men, and if no one had glimpsed God in Him then all His work had gone for nothing. There was only one way He could leave a message with men, and that was to write it on the heart of some man. So, in this moment, Jesus put all things to the test. He asked His disciples what men were saying about Him, and He heard from them the popular rumours and reports. Then there came a breathless silence and He put the question which meant so much, " Who do *you* say that I am? " And suddenly Peter realized what he had always known deep down in his heart. This was the Messiah, the Christ, the Anointed One, the Son of God. And in that answer Jesus knew that He had not failed.

But now we come to a question which has been half-put and half-answered more than once before, but which now has to be answered in detail or the whole gospel story is not fully intelligible. No sooner had Peter made this discovery than Jesus told him that at this stage he must tell no man of it. Why? Because, first and foremost, Jesus had to teach Peter and the others what Messiahship really meant. Now, to understand the task that Jesus had in hand, and to understand the real meaning of this necessity, we have to enquire at some length what the Messianic ideas of the time of Jesus really were.

THE JEWISH IDEAS OF THE MESSIAH

Throughout all their existence the Jews never forgot that they were in a very special sense God's chosen people. Because of that, they very naturally looked to a very special place in the world. In the early days they looked forward to achieving that position by what we might call natural means. They always regarded the greatest days in their history as the days of David ; and they dreamed of a day when there would arise another king of David's line, a king who would make them great in righteousness and in power. (Isaiah 9 : 7 ; 11 : 1 ; Jeremiah 22 : 4 ; 23 : 5 ; 30 : 9.) But as time went on it came to be pitilessly clear that this dreamed of greatness would never be achieved by natural means. The ten tribes were carried off to Assyria and lost forever. The Babylonians conquered and blasted Jerusalem and carried the Jews away captive. Then came the Persians as their masters ; then came the Greeks ; then came the Romans. So far from knowing anything like dominion, for centuries the Jews never even knew what it was to be completely free and independent. So another line of thought grew up. It is true that the idea of a great king of David's line never entirely vanished and was always intertwined in some way with their thought ; but more and more they began to dream of a day when God would intervene in history and achieve by supernatural means that which natural means could never achieve. They looked for divine power to do what human power was helpless to do. In between the Testaments there were written a whole flood of books which were dreams and forecasts of this new age and this intervention of God. As a class they are called by the name *Apocalypses*. The word literally means *unveilings*. These books were meant to be unveilings of the future. It is to them that we must turn to find out what the Jews believed in the time of Jesus about the Messiah, and the work of the Messiah, and the new age. It is against their dreams and visions and hopes that we must set the dream of Jesus.

In these books certain basic ideas occur. We follow here the classification of these ideas that Schürer, who wrote the great book *The History of the Jewish People in the Time of Christ*, gives.

(i) Before the Messiah came there would be a time of terrible tribulation. There would be a Messianic travail. It would be the birth-pangs of a new age. Every conceivable terror would burst upon the world ; every

standard of honour and decency would be torn down ; the
world would become a physical and moral chaos.

> " And honour shall be turned into shame,
> And strength humiliated into contempt,
> And probity destroyed,
> And beauty shall become ugliness . . .
> And envy shall rise in those who had not thought
>   aught of themselves,
> And passion shall seize him that is peaceful,
> And many shall be stirred up in anger to injure many,
> And they shall rouse up armies in order to shed blood,
> And in the end they shall perish together with them."
>
> (2 Baruch 27.)

There would be, " quakings of places, tumult of peoples,
schemings of nations, confusion of leaders, disquietude
of princes." (4 Ezra 9 : 3.)

> " From heaven shall fall fieryswords down to the
> earth. Lights shall come, bright and great, flashing
> into the midst of men ; and earth, the universal
> mother, shall shake in these days at the hand of the
> Eternal. And the fishes of the sea and the beasts of
> the earth and the countless tribes of flying things and
> all the souls of men and every sea shall shudder at the
> presence of the Eternal and there shall be panic. And
> the towering mountain peaks and the hills of the
> giants he shall rend, and the murky abyss shall be
> visible to all. And the high ravines in the lofty
> mountains shall be full of dead bodies and rocks shall
> flow with blood and each torrent shall flood the
> plain. . . . And God shall judge all with war and
> sword, and there shall be brimstone from heaven, yea
> stones and rain and hail incessant and grievous. And
> death shall be upon the four-footed beasts. . . . Yea
> the land itself shall drink of the blood of the perishing
> and beasts shall eat their fill of flesh." (The Sibylline
> Oracles 3 : 363 ff.)

The Mishnah enumerates as signs that the coming of the
Messiah is near,

> " That arrogance increases, ambition shoots up,
> that the vine yields fruit yet wine is dear. The govern-
> ment turns to heresy. There is no instruction. The
> synagogue is devoted to lewdness. Galilee is

destroyed, Gablan laid waste. The inhabitants of a district go from city to city without finding compassion. The wisdom of the learned is hated, the godly despised, truth is absent. Boys insult old men, old men stand in the presence of children. The son depreciates the father, the daughter rebels against the mother, the daughter-in-law against the mother-in-law. A man's enemies are his house-fellows."

The time which preceded the coming of the Messiah was to be a time when the world was torn in pieces and every bond relaxed. The physical and the moral order would collapse.

(ii) Into this chaos there would come Elijah as the forerunner and herald of the Messiah. He was to heal the breaches and bring order into the chaos to prepare the way for the Messiah to come. In particular he was to mend disputes. In fact the Jewish oral law laid it down that money and property the ownership of which was disputed, or anything found whose owner was unknown, must wait " till Elijah comes." When Elijah came the Messiah would not be far behind.

(iii) Then there would enter the Messiah. The word *Messiah* and the word *Christ* mean the same thing. *Messiah* is the Hebrew and *Christ* is the Greek for *The Anointed One*. A king was made king by anointing and the Messiah was God's Anointed King. It is important to remember that *Christ* is not a *name* ; it is a *title*. Sometimes the Messiah was thought of as a king of David's line, but more often he was thought of as a great, divine, super-human figure, crashing into history to remake the world and in the end to vindicate God's people.

(iv) The nations would ally themselves and gather themselves together against the champion of God.

" The kings of the nations shall throw themselves against this land bringing retribution on themselves. They shall seek to ravage the shrine of the mighty God and of the noblest men whensoever they come to the land. In a ring round the city the accursed kings shall place each one his throne with his infidel people by him. And then with a mighty voice God shall speak unto all the undisciplined, empty-minded people and judgment shall come upon them from the mighty God, and all shall perish at the hand of the Eternal." (Sibylline Oracles 3 : 363-372.)

" It shall be that when all the nations hear his (The Messiah's) voice, every man shall leave his own land and the warfare they have one against the other, and an innumerable multitude shall be gathered together desiring to fight against him." (4 Ezra 13 : 33-35.)

(v) The result would be the total destruction of these hostile powers. Philo said that the Messiah would "take the field and make war and destroy great and populous nations."

" He shall reprove them for their ungodliness,
  Rebuke them for their unrighteousness,
  Reproach them to their faces with their treacheries—
  And when he has rebuked them he shall destroy
      them." (4 Ezra 12 : 32, 33.)

" And it shall come to pass in those days that none
      shall be saved,
  Either by gold or by silver,
  And none shall be able to escape.
  And there shall be no iron for war,
  Nor shall one clothe oneself with a breastplate.
  Bronze shall be of no service,
  And tin shall not be esteemed,
  And lead shall not be desired.
  And all things shall be destroyed from the surface
      of the earth." (Enoch 52 : 7-9.)

The Messiah will be the most destructive conqueror in history, smashing his enemies into utter extinction.

(vi) There would follow the renovation of Jerusalem. Sometimes this was thought of as the purification of the existing city. More often it was thought of as the coming down of the new Jerusalem from heaven. The old house was to be folded up and carried away, and, in the new one, " All the pillars were new and the ornaments larger than those of the first." (Enoch 90 : 28, 29.)

(vii) The Jews who were dispersed all over the world would be gathered into the city of the new Jerusalem. To this day the Jewish daily prayer includes the petition, " Lift up a banner to gather our dispersed and assemble us from the four ends of the earth." The eleventh of the Psalms of Solomon has a noble picture of that return.

> " Blow ye in Zion on the trumpet to summon the saints,
>> Cause ye to be heard in Jerusalem the voice of him that bringeth good tidings ;
>> For God hath had pity on Israel in visiting them.
> Stand on the height, O Jerusalem, and behold thy children,
>> From the East and the West, gathered together by the Lord ;
> From the North they come in the gladness of their God,
>> From the isles afar off God hath gathered them.
> High mountains hath he abased into a plain for them ;
>> The hills fled at their entrance.
> The woods gave them shelter as they passed by ;
>> Every sweet-smelling tree God caused to spring up for them,
>> That Israel might pass by in the visitation of the glory of their God.
> Put on, O Jerusalem, thy glorious garments ;
>> Make ready thy holy robe ;
>> For God hath spoken good for Israel forever and ever,
> Let the Lord do what he hath spoken concerning Israel and Jerusalem ;
>> Let the Lord raise up Israel by His glorious name.
> The mercy of the Lord be upon Israel forever and ever."

It can easily be seen how Jewish this new world is to be. The nationalistic element is dominant all the time.

(viii) Palestine will be the centre of the world and all the world will be subject to it. All the nations would be subdued. Sometimes it was thought of as a peaceful subjugation.

> " And all the isles and the cities shall say, How doth
> the Eternal love those men ! For all things work in
> sympathy with them and help them. . . . Come let us
> all fall upon the earth and supplicate the eternal King,
> the mighty, everlasting God. Let us make procession
> to His Temple, for He is the sole Potentate."
> (Sibylline Oracles 3 : 690 ff.)

More often the fate of the Gentiles is utter destruction at
which Israel will exult and rejoice.

> " And He will appear to punish the Gentiles,
> And He will destroy all their idols.
> Then, thou, O Israel, shalt be happy.
> And thou shalt mount upon the necks and the wings
>   of the eagle
>   (i.e., Rome, the eagle is to be destroyed)
> And they shall be ended and God will exalt thee.
>
> .   .   .   .
>
> " And thou shalt look from on high
> And see thine enemies in Gehenna,
> And thou shalt recognize them and rejoice."

> (Assumption of Moses 10 : 8-10.)

It is a grim picture. Israel will rejoice to see her enemies
broken and in hell. Even the dead Israelites are to be
raised up to share in the new world.

(ix) Finally, there will come the new age of peace and
goodness which will last forever.

These are the Messianic ideas which were in the minds
of men when Jesus came. They were violent, nationalistic,
destructive, vengeful. True, they ended in the perfect reign of
God, but they came to it through a bath of blood and a career
of conquest. Think of Jesus set against a background like
that. No wonder He had to re-educate His disciples in the
meaning of Messiahship ; and no wonder they crucified
Him in the end as a heretic. There is no room for a cross
and there is little room for suffering love in a picture like
that.

THE TEMPTER SPEAKS IN THE VOICE
OF A FRIEND

Mark 8 : 31-33

> He began to teach them that it was necessary that the
> Son of Man should suffer many things, and should be
> rejected by the elders and chief priests and scribes, and
> be killed and rise again after three days. He kept
> telling them this plainly. And Peter caught Him and
> began to rebuke Him. He turned round ; He looked
> at His disciples ; and He rebuked Peter. " Get
> behind me, Satan," He said. " These are not God's
> thoughts but men's."

IT is against the background of what we have just seen of
the common conception of the Messiah that we must read
this. When Jesus connected Messiahship with suffering
and death, He was making what were to the disciples
statements which were both incredible and incompre-
hensible. All their lives they had thought of the Messiah
in terms of irresistible conquest, and they were now being
presented with an idea which staggered them. That is
why Peter so violently protested. To him the whole thing
was impossible.

Why did Jesus so sternly rebuke Peter? Because Peter
was putting into words the very temptations which were
assailing Jesus at that moment. Jesus did not want to die.
He knew that He had powers which He could use for
conquest. At this moment He was refighting the battle of
temptations in the wilderness. This was the devil tempting
Him again to fall down and worship him, to take his way
instead of God's way.

It is a strange thing, and sometimes a terrible thing,
that the tempter speaks to us in the voice of a well-meaning
friend. We may have decided on a course which is the
right course but which will inevitably bring trouble, loss,
unpopularity, sacrifice. And at that moment some well-
meaning friend may come and try, with the best intentions

in the world, to stop us. I knew a man who decided to take a course which would almost inevitably land him in trouble. A friend came to him and tried to dissuade him. " Remember," said the friend, " that you have a wife and a family. You can't do this." It is quite possible for some-one to love us so much that he or she wants us to avoid trouble and to play safe.

In *Gareth and Lynette* Tennyson tells the story of the youngest son of Lot and Bellicent. He has seen the vision and he wishes to become one of Arthur's knights. Bellicent, his mother, does not wish to let him go.

" Hast thou no pity on my loneliness? " she asks. His father, Lot, is old and " lies like a log and all but smouldered out." Both his brothers are already at Arthur's court. " Stay, my best son," she says, " ye are yet more boy than man." If he stays she will arrange the hunt to keep him happy in the chase and find some princess to be his bride. The boy had had the vision, and, one by one the mother, who loves him dearly, produces reasons, excellent reasons, why he should stay at home. It is someone who loves him who is speaking with the tempter's voice all unaware that she is doing it. But Gareth answers,

> " O Mother,
> How can ye keep me tethered to you—Shame.
> Man am I grown and man's work must I do.
> Follow the deer? follow the Christ, the King,
> Live pure, speak true, right wrong, follow the King—
> Else, wherefore born? "

So Gareth went when the vision called.

The tempter can make no more terrible attack than when he attacks in the voice of those who love us, and who think they seek only our good. That is what happened to Jesus that day ; that is why He answered so sternly. Not even the pleading voice of love must silence for us the imperious voice of God.

THE WAY OF THE DISCIPLE

Mark 8 : 34, 35

> He called the crowd to Him, together with His disciples, and said to them, " If anyone wishes to come after me, let him deny himself, and let him take up his cross, and let him follow me."

WHEN we come to this part of Mark's gospel we are so near the heart and centre of the Christian faith that we must take it almost sentence by sentence. If each day a man could go out with only one of these sentences locked in his heart and dominating his life, it would be far more than enough to be going on with.

Two things stand out here even at first sight.

(i) There is the almost startling honesty of Jesus. No one could ever say that he followed Jesus under false pretences. Jesus never tried to bribe men by the offer of an easy way. He did not offer men peace ; He offered them glory. To tell a man that he must be ready to take up a cross was to tell him that he must be ready to be regarded as a criminal and to die. The honesty of the great leaders has always been one of their great characteristics. In the days of the Second World War, when Sir Winston Churchill took over the leadership of the country, all that he offered men was " blood, sweat and tears." After the siege of Rome in 1849, Garibaldi, the great Italian patriot, made the famous proclamation : " Soldiers, all our efforts against superior forces have been unavailing. I have nothing to offer you but hunger and thirst, hardship and death ; but I call on all who love their country to join with me." Jesus never sought to lure men to Him by the offer of an easy way ; He sought to challenge them, to waken the sleeping chivalry in their souls, by the offer of a way than which none could be higher and harder. He came not to make life easy, but to make men great.

(ii) There is the fact that Jesus never called upon men to do or face anything which He was not prepared to do

206

and face Himself. That indeed is the characteristic of the
leader whom men will follow. When Alexander the Great
set out in pursuit of Darius, he made one of the wonder
marches of history. In eleven days he marched his men
thirty-three hundred furlongs. His men were very nearly
giving up, mainly because of thirst, for there was no water.
Plutarch relates the story. " While they were in this distress, it happened that some Macedonians who had fetched
water in skins upon their mules from a river they had
found out came about noon to the place where Alexander
was, and seeing him almost choked with thirst, presently
filled an helmet and offered it to him. He asked them to
whom they were carrying the water ; they told him to
their children, adding, that if his life were but saved, it
was no matter for them, they should be well enough able to
repair that loss, though they all perished. Then he took
the helmet into his hands, and looking round about, when
he saw all those who were near him stretching their heads
out and looking earnestly after the drink, he returned it
again with thanks without tasting a drop of it. ' For,' he
said, ' if I alone should drink, the rest would be out of
heart.' The soldiers no sooner took notice of his temperance
and magnanimity upon this occasion, but they, one and all,
cried out to him to lead them forward boldly, and began
whipping on their horses. For while they had such a king
they said they defied both weariness and thirst, and looked
upon themselves to be little less than immortal." It was
easy to follow a leader who never demanded from his men
what he would not endure himself. There was a famous
Roman general, Quintus Fabius Cunctator. He was discussing with his staff how to take a difficult position.
Someone suggested a certain course of action to capture it.
" It will only cost the lives of a few men," this counsellor
said. Fabius looked at him. " Are you," he said,
" willing to be one of the few ? " Jesus was not the kind
of leader who sat remote and played with the lives of men
like expendable pawns. What He demanded that they

should face, He, too, was ready to face. Jesus had a right
to call on us to take up a cross, for He, Himself, first bore
one.

(iii) Jesus said of the man who would be His disciple,
" Let him deny himself." We will understand the meaning
of this demand best if we take it very simply and very
literally. " Let him say no to himself." If a man will
follow Jesus Christ he must ever say no to himself and yes
to Christ. He must say no to his own natural love of ease
and comfort. He must say no to every course of action
which is based on self-seeking and self-will. He must say
no to the instincts and the desires which prompt him to
touch and taste and handle the forbidden things. He must
unhesitatingly say yes to the voice and the command of
Jesus Christ. He must be able to say with Paul that it is
no longer he who lives but Christ who lives in him. He
lives no longer to follow his own will, but to follow the will
of Christ, and, in that service, he finds his perfect freedom.

FINDING LIFE BY LOSING LIFE

Mark 8 : 36

> Whoever seeks to save his life shall lose it ; and who-
> ever loses his life for my sake and for the sake of the
> gospel shall save it.

THERE are certain things which are lost by being kept and
saved by being used. Any talent that a man possesses is
like that. If he uses it, it will develop into something
still greater. If he refuses to use it he will in the end lose
it. Supremely so, life is like that.

History is full of examples of men, who by throwing
away their lives, gained life eternal. Somewhere, late in
the fourth century, there was in the East a monk called
Telemachus. He had determined to leave the world and
to live all alone in prayer and meditation and fasting, and

so to save his soul. So in his lonely life he sought nothing but contact with God. But somehow he felt that there was something wrong. One day he rose from his knees and it suddenly dawned upon him that this life that he was living was based, not on a self-less, but on a selfish love of God. It came to him that if he was to serve God he must serve men, that the desert was no place for a Christian to live, that the cities were full of men and women ; that the cities were full of sin and therefore full of need. So he determined to bid farewell to the desert and to set out to the greatest city in the world, the city of Rome, which was at the other side of the world. He begged his way across lands and seas to Rome. By this time Rome was officially Christian. He arrived at a time when Stilicho, the Roman general, had gained a mighty victory over the Goths. To Stilicho there was granted a Roman triumph. There was this difference from the old days—now it was to the Christian Churches the crowds poured and not to the heathen temples. There were the processions and the celebrations and Stilicho rode in triumph through the streets, with the young Emperor Honorius by his side. But one thing had lingered on into Christian Rome. There was still the arena ; there were still the gladiatorial games. Nowadays Christians were no longer thrown to the lions ; but still those captured in war had to fight and to kill each other to make a Roman holiday for the populace. Still men roared with the blood lust as the gladiators fought. Telemachus found his way to the arena. There were eighty-thousand people there. The chariot races were ending ; and there was a tenseness in the crowd as the gladiators prepared to fight. Into the arena they came with their greeting. " Hail, Caesar ! We who are about to die salute you ! " The fight was on and Telemachus was appalled. Men for whom Christ had died were killing each other to amuse an allegedly Christian populace. He leapt the barrier. He was in between the gladiators, and, for a moment they stopped. " Let the games go on," roared the crowd. They pushed the old man aside ; he was still in his hermit's robes. Again he came between them. The crowd began to hurl stones at him ; they urged the gladiators to kill him and get him out of the way. The commander of the games gave an order ; a gladiator's sword rose, and flashed and stabbed ; and Telemachus lay dead. And suddenly the crowd were silent. They were suddenly shocked that a holy man should have been killed in such a way. Quite suddenly there was a mass realization of what this killing really was. The games ended abruptly that day—and they never began again. Telemachus, by dying, had ended them. As Gibbon said of him, " His death was more useful to mankind than his life." By losing his life he had done more than ever he could have done if he had husbanded it out in lonely devotion in the desert.

God gave us life to spend and not to keep. If we live carefully, husbanding life, always thinking first of our own profit, ease, comfort, security, if our sole aim is to make life as long and as trouble-free as possible, if we will make no effort except for ourselves, we are losing life all the time. But if we spend life for others, if we forget health and time and wealth and comfort in our desire to do something for Jesus and for the men for whom Jesus died, we are winning life all the time. What would have happened to the world if doctors and scientists and inventors had not been prepared to risk experiments often on their own bodies? What would have happened to life if everyone had wished for nothing but to remain comfortably at home, and there had been so such person as an explorer or a pioneer? What would happen if every mother refused to take the risk of bearing a child? What would happen if all men spent all they had upon themselves? The very essence of life is in risking life and spending life, not in saving it and hoarding it. True, it is the way of weariness, of exhaustion, of giving to the uttermost—but it is better any day to burn out than to rust out, for that is the way to happiness and the way to God.

THE SUPREME VALUE IN LIFE

Mark 8 : 37

> What profit is it for a man to gain the whole world and
> to forfeit his life? For what is a man to give in exchange
> for his life?

IT is quite possible for a man in one sense to make a huge
success of life and in another sense to be living a life that is
not worth living. The real question of this saying of Jesus
is, " Where do you put your values in life? " It is possible
for a man to put his values on the wrong things and to discover it too late.

(i) A man may sacrifice honour for profit. He may
desire material things and not be over-particular how he
gets them. The world is full of temptations towards
profitable dishonesty. George Macdonald tells in one of
his books about a draper who always used his thumb to
make the measure just a little short. " He took from his
soul," he said, " and put it in his siller-bag." The real
question, the question which sooner or later will have to
be answered is, " How does life's balance sheet look in the
sight of God? " After all, God is the auditor whom, in the
end, all men must face.

(ii) A man may sacrifice principle for popularity. It
may happen that the easy-going, agreeable, pliable man
will save himself a lot of trouble. It may happen that the
man inflexibly devoted to principle will find himself dis-
liked. Shakespeare paints the picture of Wolsey, the great
Cardinal, who served Henry the Eighth with all the
ingenuity and wit he possessed.

> " Had I but serv'd my God with half the zeal
> I serv'd my king, he would not in mine age
> Have left me naked to mine enemies."

The real question, the question that every man in the end
will have to face, is not, " What did men think of this? "
but, " What does God think of it? " It is not the verdict
of public opinion, but the verdict of God that settles
destiny.

(iii) A man may sacrifice the lasting things for the cheap things. It is always easier to have a cheap success. An author may sacrifice that which would be really great for the cheap success of a moment. A musician may produce cheap, ephemeral trifles when he might be producing something that was real and lasting. A man may choose a job which will bring him more money and more comfort, and turn his back on a job where he could render more service to his fellow-men. A man may spend his life in little things and let the big things go. A woman may prefer a life of pleasure and of so-called freedom to the service of her home and the upbringing of a family. But life has a way of revealing the true values and condemning the false as the years pass on. A cheap thing never lasts.

(iv) We may sum it all up by saying—a man may sacrifice eternity for the moment. We would be saved from all kinds of mistakes if we always looked at things in the light of eternity. There is many a thing pleasant for the moment but ruinous in the long run. The test of eternity, the test of seeking to see the thing as God sees it, is the realest test of all.

The man who sees things as God sees them will never spend his life on the things that lose his soul.

WHEN THE KING COMES INTO HIS OWN

Mark 8 : 38 ; 9 : 1

"Whoever is ashamed of me and of my words in this adulterous and sinful generation, of him also shall the Son of Man be ashamed when He comes in the glory of His Father with the holy angels." And He used to say to them, " This is the truth I tell you—there are some of those who are standing here who will not taste of death until they shall see the Kingdom of God coming with power."

ONE thing leaps out from this passage to meet us—the confidence of Jesus. He has just been speaking of His death ; He has no doubt that the Cross stands out ahead of Him ; but nonetheless He is absolutely sure that in the end there will be triumph. The first part of this passage states a very natural and simple truth. When the King comes into His Kingdom He will be loyal to those who have been loyal to Him. No man can expect to dodge all the trouble of some great undertaking and then to reap all the benefit of it. No man can expect to refuse service in some campaign and then to share in the decorations when the campaign is brought to a successful conclusion. Jesus is saying, " In a difficult and a hostile world Christianity is up against it in these days. If a man is ashamed under such conditions to show that he is a Christian, if he is afraid to show what side he is on, he cannot expect to gain a place of honour when the Kingdom comes."

The last part of this passage has caused many people much serious thought. Jesus says that many who are standing there will not die until they see the Kingdom coming with power. What worries some people is that they take this as a reference to the Second Coming ; and if it is such a reference, then Jesus was mistaken, because He did not return in power and glory in the lifetime of those who were there. But this is not a reference to the Second Coming at all. Consider the situation in which Jesus was speaking. At the moment He had only once been outside of Palestine, and on that occasion he was just over the border in Tyre and Sidon. Only a very few men in a very small country had ever heard of Him. Palestine was only about 120 miles from north to south and about 40 miles from east to west ; her total population was 4,000,000 or thereby. To speak in terms of world conquest when He had never been outside the smallest country of all was a strange thing. To make matters worse, even in that small country, He had so provoked the enmity of the orthodox leaders, and of those in whose hands lay power, that it was quite certain that He could hope for nothing other than death as a heretic and an outlaw. In face of a situation like that there must have been many who felt despairingly that

Christianity had no possible future, that in a short time now it would be wiped out completely and eliminated from the world. And, humanly speaking, these pessimists were right. And now consider what did happen. Scarcely more than 30 years later, Christianity had swept through Asia Minor. Antioch had become a great Christian Church. It had penetrated to Egypt. The Christians were strong in Alexandria. It had crossed the sea and had come to Rome and swept through Greece. Christianity had spread like an unstoppable tide throughout the world. It was literally and astonishingly true that in the life time of many there, against all expectations, Christianity had come with power. So far from being mistaken Jesus was absolutely right.

The amazing thing about Jesus is that He never knew despair. In face of the dullness of the minds of men, in face of the opposition, in face of crucifixion and of death, He never doubted his final triumph because He never doubted God. He was always certain that what is impossible with man is completely possible with God.

THE GLORY OF THE MOUNTAIN TOP

Mark 9 : 2-8

> Six days after Jesus took Peter and James and John along with Him and brought them up into a high mountain, all by themselves, alone. And He was transfigured in their presence. His clothes became radiant, exceedingly white, such that no fuller on earth could have made them so white. And Elijah and Moses appeared to them, and they were talking with Jesus. Peter said to Jesus, " Teacher, it is good for us to be here. So let us make three booths, one for you, and one for Moses and one for Elijah." He said this because he did not know what he was saying, for they were awe-struck. And there came a cloud overshadowing them. And there came a voice from the cloud, " This is my beloved Son. Hear Him ! " And immediately, when they had looked round, they saw no one any more except Jesus alone with them.

HERE we are face to face with an incident in the life of Jesus that is cloaked in mystery. We can only try to understand what happened. Mark says that this happened six days after the incidents near Caesarea Philippi. Luke says that it happened eight days afterwards. There is no discrepancy here. They both mean what we would express by saying, "About a week afterwards." Both the Eastern and the Western Church hold their remembrance of the Transfiguration on 6th August. It does not matter whether or not that is the actual date, but it is a time which we would do well to seek to remember. Tradition says that the Transfiguration took place on the top of Mount Tabor. The Eastern Church actually calls the Festival of the Transfiguration the *Taborion*. It may be that the choice of Mount Tabor is based on the mention of Mount Tabor in Psalm 89 : 12, but it is an unfortunate choice. Tabor is in the *south* of Galilee, and Caesarea Philippi is away to the north. Tabor is no more than 1,000 feet high, and, in the time of Jesus, there was a fortress on the top. It is much more likely that this happened amidst the eternal snows of Mount Hermon which is 9,200 feet high, which is much nearer Caesarea Philippi and where the solitude would be much more complete.

What happened we cannot tell. We can only bow in reverence as we try to understand. Mark tells us that the garments of Jesus became radiant. The word he uses (*stilbein*) is the word which is used for the glistening gleam of burnished brass or gold, or of polished steel, or of the golden glare of the sunlight. When the incident came to an end a cloud overshadowed them. In Jewish thought the presence of God is regularly connected with the cloud. It was in the cloud that Moses met God. It was in the cloud that God came to Tabernacle. It was the cloud which filled the Temple when it was dedicated after Solomon had built it. And it was the dream of the Jew's that when the Messiah came the cloud of God's presence would return to the Temple. (Exodus 16 : 10, 19 : 9,

33 : 9, I Kings 8 : 10, 2 Maccabees 2 : 8). The descent
of the cloud is a way of saying that the Messiah had come,
and any Jew would understand it like that.

The Transfiguration has a double significance.

(i) It did something very precious for Jesus. Jesus
had to take His own decisions. He had taken the decision
to go to Jerusalem and that decision was the decision
to face and to accept the Cross. Obviously He had to be
absolutely sure that was right before He could go on. On
the mountain top He received a double approval of His
decision and His choice. (a) Moses and Elijah met with
Him. Now Moses was the *supreme law-giver* of the nation
of Israel. To him the nation owed the laws which were
the laws of God. Elijah was *the first and the greatest of the
prophets*. Always men looked back to him as the prophet
who brought to men the very voice of God. When these
two great figures met with Jesus it meant that the greatest
of the law-givers and the greatest of the prophets said to
Jesus, " Go on! " It meant that they saw in Jesus the
consummation of all that they had dreamed of in the past.
It meant that they saw in Him all that history had longed
for and hoped for and looked forward to. It is as if at
that moment Jesus was assured that He was on the right
way because all history had been leading up to the Cross.
(b) God spoke with Jesus. As always, Jesus did not consult
His own wishes. He went to God and said, " What wilt
Thou have me to do? " He put all His plans and intentions
before God. And God said to Him, " You are acting as my
own beloved Son should act and must act. Go on! " On
the Mountain of the Transfiguration Jesus was assured
that He had not chosen the wrong way. He saw, not
only the inevitability, but the essential rightness of the
Cross.

(ii) It did something very precious for the disciples.
(a) They had been shattered by Jesus' statement that
He was going to Jerusalem to die. That seemed to them
the complete negation and denial of all that they under-

stood of the Messiah. They were still bewildered and puzzled and uncomprehending. Things were happening which not only baffled their minds but which were also breaking their hearts. What they saw on the Mountain of the Transfiguration would give them something to hold on to, even when they could not understand. Cross or no Cross, they had heard God's voice acknowledge this Jesus as His Son. (b) It made them in a special sense witnesses of the glory of Christ. A witness has been defined as a man who first *sees* and then *shows*. This time on the Mount had shown them the glory of Christ, and now, not at the moment, but when the time came, they had the story of this glory to hide in their hearts and to tell to men.

THE FATE OF THE FORERUNNER

Mark 9 : 9-13

> As they were coming down from the mountain, Jesus enjoined them that they must not relate to anyone what they had seen, except when the Son of Man should have risen from the dead. They clung to this word, asking among themselves, what this phrase about rising from the dead could mean. They asked Jesus, " Do the experts in the Law not say that Elijah must come first? " " It is true," He said to them, " that Elijah comes first and sets all things in order. And yet how does it stand written about the Son of Man that He must suffer many things and be treated with contempt? But, I say to you, Elijah, too, *has* come, and they treated him as they wished, even as it stands written about him."

VERY naturally the three disciples were thinking hard as they came down the mountain-side.

First, Jesus began with an injunction. They must tell no one of what they had seen. Jesus knew quite well that their minds were still haunted by the conception of a Messiah of might and power. If they were to tell of what had happened on the mountain top, of how the glory of God had appeared, of how Moses and Elijah had appeared how that could be made to chime in with the popular expectations! How it could be made to seem a prelude to the burst of God's avenging power on the nations of the world! The disciples still had to learn what Messiahship meant. There was only one thing that could teach them what it meant—the Cross and the Resurrection to follow. When the Cross had taught them what Messiahship meant, and when the Resurrection had convinced them that Jesus was the Messiah, *then,* and then only, they might tell of the glory of the mountain top for then, and then only, would they see it as it ought to be seen—as the prelude, not to the unleashing of God's force, but to the crucifying of God's love.

Still their minds worked on. They could not understand what Jesus' words about resurrection meant. Their whole attitude shows that in fact they never understood them. Their whole outlook when the Cross came was the outlook of men to whom the end had come. We must not blame the disciples. It was simply that they had been so schooled in a completely different idea of Messiahship that they literally could not take in what Jesus had said.

Then they asked something that was puzzling them. The Jew believed that before the Messiah came Elijah would come to be His herald and forerunner. (Malachi 3 : 5, 6). They had a rabbinic tradition that Elijah would come three days before the Messiah. On the first day he would stand on the mountains of Israel, lamenting the desolation of the land. And then in a voice that would be heard from one end of the world to the other, he would cry, " *Peace* cometh to the world. *Peace* cometh to the world." On the second day he would cry, " *Good* cometh to the world. *Good* cometh to the world." And on the third day he would cry " *Jeshuah* (*salvation*) cometh to the world. *Jeshuah* cometh to the world." He would restore all things. He would mend the family breaches of the grim last days. He would settle all doubtful points of ritual and ceremonial. He would cleanse the nation of Israel by bringing back those wrongfully excluded and driving out those wrongfully included. Elijah had an amazing place in the thought of Israel. He was conceived of as being continuously active in heaven and on earth in their interest, and being the herald of the final consummation. Inevitably the disciples were wondering " If Jesus is the Messiah what has happened to Elijah?" Jesus' answer was in terms that any Jew would understand. " Elijah," He said, " has come and men treated him as they willed. They took him and they arbitrarily applied their will to him and forgot God's will." Jesus was referring to the imprisonment and the death of John the Baptist at the hands of Herod. And then, by implication, He drove them back to that thought that they would not face and that He was determined that they must face. By implication He demanded, " If they have done that to the forerunner, what will they do to the Messiah?" Jesus was overturning all the preconceived notions and ideas of His disciples. They looked for the emergence of Elijah, the coming of the Messiah, the irruption of God into time and the shattering victory of heaven, which they identified with the triumph of Israel. He was trying to compel them to see that in fact the herald had been cruelly killed and the Messiah must end on a Cross. They still did not understand, and their failure to understand was due to the cause which always makes men fail to understand—they clung to their way and refused to see God's way. They wished things as they desired them and not as God had ordered them. The error of men's thoughts had blinded them to the revelation of God's truth.

COMING DOWN FROM THE MOUNT

Mark 9 : 14-18

When they came to the disciples, they saw a great crowd gathered around them, and the experts in the law engaged in discussion with them. And as soon as they saw Him the whole crowd were amazed and ran to Him and greeted Him. He asked them, " What are you discussing among yourselves? " And one of the crowd answered Him, " Teacher, I brought my son to you because he has a spirit which makes him dumb. And whenever the spirit seizes him, it convulses him, and he foams at the mouth and grinds his teeth, and he is wasting away. And I asked your disciples to cast it out and they could not."

THIS is the very kind of thing that Peter had wanted to avoid. On the mountain top, in the presence of the glory, Peter had said, " This is a good place for us to be." Then he had wanted to build three booths for Jesus and Moses and Elijah, and to stay there. Life was so much better, so much nearer God there on the mountain top. Why ever come down again? But it is of the very essence of life that we must come down from the mountain top. It has been said that in religion there must be *solitude*, but there must not be *solitariness*. The solitude is necessary, for a man must keep his contact with God, but if a man, in his search for the essential solitude, shuts himself off from his fellow-men, if he shuts his ears to the appeal of men for help, if he shuts his heart to the cry of the tears of things, then that is not religion. The solitude is not meant to make us solitary. It is meant to make us better able to meet and cope with the demands of everyday life.

Jesus came down to a very delicate situation. A father had brought his boy to the disciples, and the boy was an epileptic. All the symptoms are there. The disciples had been quite unable to deal with this case, and that had given the scribes, the experts in the law, their chance. The helplessness of the disciples was a first-rate opportunity to belittle not only them but their Master. That is what made the situation so delicate, and that is what makes every human situation so delicate for the Christian. His conduct, his words, his behaviour, his ability or inability to cope with the demands of life, are used as a yard-stick, not only to judge him, but to judge Jesus Christ.

A. Victor Murray, in his book on *Christian Education*, writes, " There are those into whose eyes comes a far-away look when they talk about the Church. It is a super-natural society, the body of Christ, His spotless bride, the custodian of the oracles of God, the blessed company of the redeemed, and a few more romantic titles, none of which seem to tally with what the outsider can see for himself in ' St. Agatha's Parish Church,' or ' High Street Methodists.' " It does not matter how high-sounding a man's professions may be, it is by his actions that people judge him, and, in judging him, judge his Master. In this particular situation the scribes found what was to them a heaven-sent opportunity to belittle not the disciples but Jesus Himself.

And then Jesus arrived. When the people saw Him they were astonished. We are not for one moment to think that the radiance of the Transfiguration still lingered on Him. That would have been to undo His own instructions that it be kept as yet a secret. The crowd had thought Him away up in the lonely slopes of Hermon. They had been so engrossed in their argument that they had not seen Him come, and now, just when the moment was most opportune, here He was in the midst of them. It was at His sudden, unexpected arrival, just at the right moment, that they were surprised.

Here we learn two things about Jesus.

(i) He was ready to face the Cross, and He was ready to face the common problem just as either came. It is characteristic of human nature that we can face the great crisis-moments of life with honour and dignity, but we allow the routine demands of everyday to irritate and distract and annoy us. We can face the shattering blows of life with a certain heroism, but we allow the petty pinpricks to upset and distress us. Many a man can face a great disaster or a great loss with a calm serenity and yet loses his temper if a meal be badly cooked or a train be late. It was the amazing thing about Jesus that He could serenely face the Cross, and at the same time just as calmly deal with the day to day emergencies of life. The reason was that He did not keep God for the crisis as so many of us do. He walked the daily paths of life with God.

(ii) He had come into the world to save the world, and yet He could give Himself in His entirety to the helping of one single person. It is much easier to preach the gospel of love for mankind than it is to love single, individual, not very lovable sinners. It is easy to be filled with a sentimental affection for the human race, and just as easy to find it too much bother to go out of our way to help an individual member of the human race. Jesus had the gift, which is the gift of a regal nature, of giving Himself entirely to every person with whom He happened to be.

THE CRY OF FAITH

Mark 9 : 19-24

"O faithless generation!" Jesus answered. "How long am I to be with you? How long am I to bear you? Bring him to me!" They brought him to Him. When he saw Him, immediately the spirit sent him into a convulsion, and he fell upon the ground, and rolled about, foaming at the mouth. Jesus asked his father, "How long is it since this happened to him?" He said, "He has been like this since he was a child. Often it throws him into the fire and into waters for it is out to destroy him. But, if you can, let your heart be moved with pity, and help us." Jesus said to him, "You say, 'If you can.' All things are possible to him who believes." Immediately the father of the boy cried out, "I *do* believe. Help my unbelief."

THIS passage begins with a cry wrung from the heart of Jesus. He had been on the mountain top, and He had faced the tremendous task that lay ahead of Him. He had decided to stake His life on the redemption of the world.

And now He had come back down from the mountain top to find His nearest followers, His own chosen men beaten and baffled and helpless and ineffective. The thing, for the moment, must have daunted even Jesus. He must have had a sudden realization of what anyone else would have called the hopelessness of His task. He must at that moment have almost despaired of the attempt to change human nature and to make men of the world into men of God. How did He meet that moment of despair? " Bring the boy to me," He said. When we cannot deal with the ultimate situation, then the thing to do is to deal with the situation which at the moment confronts us. It was as if Jesus said, " I do not know how I am ever to change these disciples of mine, but I *can* at this moment help this boy. Let me get on with the present task, and not despair of the future." Again and again that is the way to avoid despair. If we sit and think about the state of the world, we may well despair. Then let us get to action and do what we can about our small corner of the world. We may sometimes despair of the Church. Then let us get to action in our own part of the Church. Jesus did not sit appalled and paralysed at the slowness of men's minds. He dealt with the immediate situation. As Kingsley had it,

> " Do the work that's nearest,
> Though it's dull at whiles,
> Helping when you meet them
> Lame dogs over stiles."

The surest way to avoid pessimism and despair is to take what immediate action we can take—and there is always something to be done.

To the father of the boy Jesus stated the conditions of a miracle. " To him that believeth," said Jesus, " all things are possible." It was as if Jesus said, " The cure of your boy depends, not on me, but on you." This is not a specially theological truth. It is a universal truth. To approach anything in the spirit of hopelessness is to make it hopeless. To approach anything in the spirit of faith is to make it a possibility. Cavour once said that what a statesman needed above all was " a sense of the possible." Most of us are cursed with a sense of the impossible, and that is precisely why miracles do not happen.

The whole attitude of the father of the boy is most illuminating. Originally he had come seeking for Jesus Himself. Since Jesus was on the mountain top he had had to deal with the disciples. His experience of the disciples was discouraging. His faith was badly shaken, so badly shaken that when he came to Jesus all he could say was, " Help me, *if you can*." And then, face to face with Jesus, suddenly his faith blazed up again. " I believe," he cried. " If there is still some discouragement in me, still some doubts, take them away and fill me with an unquestioning faith." It sometimes happens that people get less than they hoped for from some Church or from some servant of the Church. They come to some Church, or they come to some man, who, they think, is a man of God and they find themselves disappointed. When that happens such people must press beyond the Church to the Master of the Church, beyond the servant of Christ to Christ Himself. The Church may at times disappoint us, and God's servants on earth may at times disappoint us. But when we battle our way face to face with Jesus Christ He never disappoints us.

THE CAUSE OF FAILURE

Mark 9 : 25-29

When Jesus saw that the crowd was running together, He rebuked the unclean spirit. " Spirit of dumbness and deafness," He said, " I order you, come out of him, and don't go into him again." When it had cried and violently convulsed him it came out, and he became like a dead man, so that many said, " He is dead." But Jesus took him by the hand, and raised him up, and he stood up. When He had gone into the house, and when they were by themselves, His disciples asked Him, " Why were we not able to cast it out? " " This kind," He said to them, " cannot come out except by prayer."

JESUS must have taken the father and the son aside. But the crowd, hearing the cries of both father and son, had come running up, and then Jesus acted. There was one last struggle, a struggle to complete exhaustion, and the boy was cured.

When they were by themselves the disciples asked the cause of their failure. They were no doubt remembering that Jesus had sent them out that they might preach and heal and cast out devils. (Mark 3 : 14, 15). Why, then, had they this time so signally failed? Jesus answered quite simply that this kind of cure demanded prayer.

In effect He said to them, " You don't live close enough to God." They had been equipped with power, but it needed prayer to keep and to maintain that power.

There is a deep lesson for us here. God may have given us some gift, but unless we maintain close contact with him that gift may wither and die. That is true of any gift. God may give a man great natural gifts as a preacher, but unless a man maintains his contact with God, he may in the end become only a man of words and not a man of power. God may give a person a gift of music or of song, but unless that person maintains contact with God, he or she may become a mere professional, who uses the gift only for gain, which is a dreary thing. That is not to say a person should not use a gift for gain. A man has a right to capitalize any talent. But it does mean that, even when he is so using it, he should be joying in it because he is using it for God. It is told of Jenny Lind, the famous Swedish soprano, that before every performance, she would stand alone in her dressing-room and pray, " God, help me to sing true to-night."

Unless we maintain this contact with God we lose two things however great our gift may be.

(i) We lose *vitality*. We lose that living power, that something plus which makes for greatness. The thing becomes a performance, instead of an offering to God. What should be a breathing, vital, living body becomes a beautiful corpse.

(ii) We lose *humility*. What should be used for the glory of God we begin to use for the glory of ourselves, and the virtue goes out of it. What should have been used to set God before men is used to set ourselves before men, and the breath of loveliness is gone.

Here is a warning thought. The disciples had been equipped with power direct from Jesus Himself, but they had not nurtured power with prayer, and power had vanished. Whatever gifts God has given us, we lose them when we use them for ourselves. We keep them when we enrich them by continual contact with the God who gave them.

FACING THE END

Mark 9 : 30, 31

> When they left there, they made their way through Galilee, and Jesus did not wish anyone to know where He was, for He kept teaching the disciples and saying to them, " The Son of Man is being delivered into the hands of men, and they will kill Him, and, when He has been killed, after three days He will rise again." But they did not understand what He said, and they were afraid to ask Him what it meant.

THIS passage marks a mile-stone. Jesus had now left the north country where He was safe, and He was taking the first step towards Jerusalem and to the Cross which awaited Him there. For once He did not want the crowds around Him. Jesus knew one thing quite clearly, that, unless He could write His message on the hearts of His chosen men, He had failed. Any teacher can leave behind him a series of propositions, but Jesus knew that that was not enough. He had to leave behind Him a band of persons on whom these propositions were written. He had to make sure, before He left this world in the body, that there were some who understood, however dimly, what He had come to say. This time the tragedy of His warning is even more poignant. If we compare this passage with the previous passage in which He foretold His death (Mark 8 : 31), we see that one phrase is added, " The Son of Man is being delivered into the hands of men." There was a traitor in the little band, and Jesus knew it. He could see the way in which the mind of Judas was working. Maybe He could see it better than Judas could himself. And when Jesus said, " The Son of Man is being delivered into the hands of men," He was not only announcing a fact and giving a warning, He was also making a last appeal to the man in whose heart there was forming the purpose of betrayal.

Even yet the disciples did not understand. The thing that they did not understand was the bit about rising again. By this time they were aware of the atmosphere of tragedy, but to the end of the day they never grasped the certainty of the Resurrection. That was a wonder that was too great for them, a wonder that they only grasped when it became an accomplished fact.

When they did not understand they were afraid to ask any further questions. They were like men who knew so much that they were afraid to know any more. A man might receive a verdict from a doctor. He might think that the general purport of the verdict was bad, but he might not understand all the details, and he might be afraid to ask any questions, for the simple reason that he was afraid to know any more. The disciples were like that.

Sometimes we are amazed that the disciples did not grasp that which was so plainly spoken. The human mind has an amazing faculty for rejecting that which it does not wish to see. Are we so very different? Over and over again we have heard the Christian message. We know the glory of accepting it, and we know the tragedy of rejecting it, but there are many of us just as far off as ever we were from giving it our full allegiance and moulding our lives to fit it. Men still accept the parts of the Christian message which they like and which suit them, and refuse to understand the rest.

THE TRUE AMBITION

Mark 9 : 32-35

> So they came to Capernaum. When Jesus was in the house He asked them, " What were you arguing about on the road? " They remained silent, for on the road they had been arguing with each other who was to be greatest. So Jesus sat down, and called The Twelve, and said to them, " If anyone wishes to be first, he must be the last of all, and the servant of all."

NOTHING so well shows how far the disciples were from realizing the real meaning of Jesus' Messiahship than this incident. Repeatedly He had told them of what awaited Him in Jerusalem, and yet, it is clear, they were still thinking of Jesus' Kingdom in terms of an earthly kingdom, and of themselves as His chief ministers of state. There is something heart-breaking in the thought of Jesus going towards a Cross and His disciples arguing about who would be greatest. And yet in their heart of hearts they knew they were wrong. When He asked them what they had been arguing about they had nothing to say. It was the silence of shame. They had nothing to say for themselves. They had no defence. It is strange how a thing takes its proper place and acquires its true character when it is set in the eyes of Jesus. So long as they had thought that Jesus was not listening and that Jesus had not seen, the argument about who should be greatest seemed fair enough, but when that argument had to be stated in the presence of Jesus it was seen in all its unworthiness. If we took everything and set it in the sight of Jesus it would make all the difference in the world to life. If of everything we did, we asked, " Could I go on doing this if Jesus was watching me? " ; if of everything we said, we asked, " Could I go on talking like this if Jesus was listening to me? " there would be many things which we would be saved from doing and saying. And the fact of Christian belief is that there is no " if " about it. All deeds are done, all words are spoken in His presence. God keep us from the words and deeds which we would be ashamed that He should hear and see.

Jesus dealt with this very seriously. It says that He sat down and called The Twelve to Him. When a Rabbi was really teaching as a Rabbi, when he was teaching as a master teaches his scholars and disciples, when he was really making a pronouncement, he sat to teach. Jesus deliberately took up the position of a Rabbi teaching his pupils before He spoke. And then He told them that if they sought for greatness in His Kingdom they must find that greatness, not by being first but by being last, not by being masters, but by being servants of all. It was not that Jesus abolished ambition. Rather He recreated and sublimated ambition. For the ambition to rule He substituted the ambition to serve. For the ambition to have things done for us He substituted the ambition to do things for others.

So far from being an impossibly idealistic view this is a view of the soundest common-sense. The really great men, the men who are remembered as having made a real contribution to life, are the men who said to themselves, not, " How can I use the state and society to further my own prestige and my own personal ambitions? " but, " How can I use my own personal gifts and talents to serve the state? " Mr. Baldwin, as he then was, paid a noble tribute to Lord Curzon when he died. In it he said, " I want, before I sit down, to say one or two things that no one but I can say. A Prime Minister sees human nature bared to the bone, and it was my chance to see him twice when he suffered great disappointment—the time when

I was preferred to him as Prime Minister, and the time when I had to tell him that he could render greater service to the country as chairman of the Committee of Imperial Defence than in the Foreign Office. Each of these occasions was a profound and bitter disappointment to him, but never for one moment did he show by word, look, or innuendo, or by any reference to the subject afterwards, that he was dissatisfied. He bore no grudge, and he pursued no other course than the one I expected of him, of doing his duty where it was decided he could best render service." Here was a man whose greatness lay, not in the fact that he reached the highest offices of state, but in the fact that he was ready to serve his country anywhere.

True selflessness is rare, and when it is found it is remembered. The Greeks had a story of a Spartan called Paedaretos. Three hundred men were to be chosen to govern Sparta and Paedaretos was a candidate. When the list of the successful was announced his name was not on it. " I am sorry," said one of his friends, " that you were not elected. The people ought to have known what a wise officer of state you would have made." " I am glad," said Paedaretos, " that in Sparta there are three hundred men better than I am." Here was a man who became a legend because he was prepared to give to others the first place and to bear no ill will.

Every economic problem would be solved if men lived for what they could do for others and not for what they could get for themselves. Every political problem would be solved if the ambition of men was only to serve the state and not to enhance their own prestige. The divisions and disputes which tear the Church asunder would for the most part never occur if the only desire of the Church and its office-bearers was to serve the Church, and not to care in what position so long as the service was given. When Jesus spoke of the supreme greatness and value of the man whose ambition was to be a servant He laid down one of the greatest practical truths in the world.

HELPING THE HELPLESS IS HELPING CHRIST

Mark 9 : 36, 37

> Jesus took a little child and set him in the midst of them. And He took him up in the crook of His arm and said to them, " Whoever receives one little child like this in my name receives me, and whoever receives me, receives not me, but Him who sent me."

LET us remember that Jesus is here still dealing with the worthy and the unworthy ambition.

Jesus took a child and set him in the midst. Now a child has no influence at all. A child cannot advance a man's career nor enhance a man's prestige. A child cannot give us things. It is the other way round. A child needs things. A child must have things done for him. So Jesus says, " If a man welcomes the poor, ordinary people, the people who have no influence and no wealth and no power, the people who need things done for them, he is welcoming me. More than that, he is welcoming God." The child is typical of the person who needs things, and it is the society of the person who needs things that we must seek.

There is a warning here. It is easy to cultivate the friendship of the person who can do things for us, and whose influence can be useful to us. And it is equally easy to avoid the society of the person who inconveniently needs our help. It is easy to curry favour with the influential and the great, and to neglect the simple, humble, ordinary folk. It is easy at some function to seek the society and the notice of some distinguished person, and to avoid the poor relation. In effect Jesus here says that we ought to seek out not those who can do things for us, but those for whom we can do things, for by so doing we are seeking the society of Himself. This is another way of saying, " Inasmuch as ye have done it unto one of the least of these my brethren ye have done it unto me."

A LESSON IN TOLERANCE

Mark 9 : 38-40

> John said to Jesus, " Teacher, we saw a man casting
> out demons by the use of your name, and we tried
> to stop him because he is not one of our company."
> " Don't stop him," said Jesus. " There is no one who
> can do a work of power in the strength of my name
> and lightly speak evil of me. He who is not against
> us is for us."

As we have seen over and over again, in the time of Jesus
everyone believed in demons. Everyone believed that
both mental and physical illness was caused by the malign
influence of these evil spirits. Now there was one very
common way to exorcise these demons. If one could get
to know the name of a still more powerful spirit, and then
command the evil demon in that name to come out of a
person the demon was supposed to be powerless to resist.
The demon could not stand against the might of the more
powerful name. This is the kind of picture we have here.
John had seen a man using the all-powerful name of Jesus
to defeat the demons and he had tried to stop him, because
he was not one of the intimate band of the disciples. But
Jesus declared that no man could do a mighty work in
His name and be altogether His enemy. And then Jesus
laid down the great principle that " he who is not against
us is for us."

Here then is a lesson in tolerance, and it is a lesson that
nearly everyone needs to learn.

(i) Every man has a right to his own thoughts. Every
man has a right to think things out and to think them
through until he comes to his own conclusions and his
own beliefs. And that is a right that we should respect.
We are always very apt to condemn what we do not understand. William Penn once said, " Neither despise nor
oppose what thou dost not understand." Kingsley Williams
in his new translation of the New Testament, *The New
Testament in Plain English,* translates a phrase in Jude 10

like this—"Those who speak abusively of everything they do not understand." And that is a very common malady among Christians. There are two things which we must remember. (a) There is far more than one way to God. "God," as Tennyson has it, "fulfils Himself in many ways." Cervantes once said, "Many are the roads by which God carries His own to heaven." After all the world is round, and two people can get to precisely the same destination by starting out in precisely opposite directions. In the Roman Empire there was in the centre of the forum at Rome the golden milestone. Throughout all the provinces the mileages were marked to that famous milestone. It was true that, "All roads lead to Rome." And it is also true that all roads, if we pursue them long enough and far enough, lead to God. It is a fearful thing for any man or any church to think that he or it has a monopoly of salvation. (b) It is necessary always to remember that truth is always bigger than any man's grasp of it. No man can possibly grasp all truth. The basis of tolerance is not a lazy acceptance of anything. It is not the feeling that there cannot be assurance anywhere. The basis of tolerance is simply the realization of the magnitude of the orb of truth. John Morley wrote, "Toleration means reverence for all the possibilities of truth, it means acknowledgment that she dwells in divers mansions, and wears vesture of many colours, and speaks in strange tongues. It means frank respect for freedom of indwelling conscience against mechanic forms, official conventions, social force. It means the charity that is greater than faith or hope." Intolerance is a sign both of arrogance and ignorance, for it is a sign that a man believes that there is no truth beyond the truth that he sees.

(ii) Not only must we concede to every man the right to do his own thinking, but we must also concede the right to a man to do his own speaking. Of all democratic rights the dearest is that of liberty of speech. There are of course limits. If a man is inculcating doctrines which are calculated

233

to destroy morality, and to remove the foundations from all civilized and Christian society, he must be combatted. But the way to combat him is certainly not to eliminate him by force, but to prove him wrong. Once Voltaire laid down the conception of freedom of speech in a vivid sentence. " I hate what you say," he said, " but I would die for your right to say it."

(iii) We must in the end remember that any doctrine and any belief must finally be judged by the kind of people it produces. Dr. Chalmers once put the matter in a nut-shell. " Who cares," he demanded, " about any Church but as an instrument of Christian good? " The question must always ultimately be, not, " How is a Church governed? " but, " What kind of people does a Church produce? " There is an old eastern fable. There was a man who possessed a ring set with a wonderful opal. Whoever wore the ring became so sweet and true in character that all men loved him. The ring was a charm. Always this ring was passed down from father to son, and always it did its work. But, as time went on, it came to a father who had three sons whom he loved with an equal love. What was he to do when the time came to pass on the ring, when he knew that he was to die? The father got other two rings made, precisely the same so that none could tell the difference. On his death-bed he called each of his sons in and spoke some words of love to them and to each of them, without telling the others, gave a ring. Soon the three sons discovered that each had had a ring, and a great dispute arose as to which was the true ring, which could do so much for its owner. The case was taken to a wise judge. The judge examined the rings and was silent, and then he spoke. " I cannot tell which is the magic ring," he said, " but you yourselves can prove it." " We? " asked the sons in astonishment. " Yes," said the judge, " for if it is true that the true ring gives sweetness to the character of the man who wears it, then I and all the other people in the city will know the man who possesses the true ring by the goodness of his life. So, go your ways, and be kind, be truthful, be brave, be just in your dealings, and he who does these things will be the owner of the true ring." The matter was to be proved by life. No man can entirely condemn beliefs which make a man a good man. If we remember that we will be less intolerant than heretofore.

(iv) And, lastly, there is one thing always to remember—we may hate a man's beliefs, but we must never hate the man. We may wish to eliminate what he teaches, but we must never wish to eliminate him.

> " He drew a circle that shut me out—
> Rebel, heretic, thing to flout.
> But love and I had the wit to win—
> We drew a circle that took him in."

REWARDS AND PUNISHMENTS

Mark 9 : 41, 42

> Whoever gives you a cup of water to drink on the ground that you belong to Christ, I tell you truly he will not lose his reward. And whoever puts a stumbling-block in the path of one of these little ones who believe in me, it is better for him that a great millstone hangs about his neck and he was cast into the sea.

THE teaching of this passage is simple, unmistakable, direct and salutary.

(i) It declares that any kindness shown, any help given to the people of Christ will not lose its reward. The reason for helping is that the person in need belongs to Jesus Christ. It is therein that others have a claim upon us. Every man in need has a claim upon us because every man is dear to Christ. Had Jesus still been here in the flesh He would have helped that man in the most practical way, and the duty of help has devolved on us. It is to be noted how simple the help and the gift is. The gift is a cup of cold water. We are not asked to do great things for others, things beyond our power. We are asked to give the simple things that any man can give.

A missionary tells a lovely story. She had been telling a class of the African primary children about giving a cup of cold water in the name of Jesus. She was sitting on the verandah of her house. Into the village square there came a company of native bearers. They had heavy packs. They were tired and thirsty, and they sat down to rest. Now they were men of another tribe, and had they asked the ordinary non-Christian native for water they would have been told to go and find it for themselves, because of the barrier between the tribes. But as the men sat wearily there, and as the missionary watched, from the school there emerged a little line of tiny African girls. On their heads they had pitchers of water. Shyly and fearfully they approached the tired bearers, knelt and offered their pitchers of water. In surprise the bearers took them and drank and handed them back, and then suddenly the little African girls took to their heels and ran to the missionary. " We have given a thirsty man a drink," they said, " in the name of Jesus." The little children took the story and the duty literally. Would that more would do so! It is the simple kindnesses that are needed. As Mahomet said long ago, " Putting a lost man on the right road, giving a thirsty man a drink of water, smiling in your brother's face—that too is charity."

(ii) But the converse is also true. To help is to win the eternal reward. To cause a weaker brother to stumble is to win the eternal punishment. The passage is deliberately stern. The mill-stone that is mentioned is a great mill-stone. There were two kinds of mills in Palestine. There was the hand-mill that the women used in the house. And there was the mill whose stone was so great that it took an ass to turn it. This mill-stone is literally an ass's mill-stone. To be cast into the sea with that attached was very certainly to have no hope of return. This was in fact a punishment and a means of execution both in Rome and in Palestine. Josephus tells us that when certain Galilaeans had made a successful revolt " they took those of Herod's party and drowned them in the lake." Suetonius, the Roman historian, tells us of Augustus that, " Because the tutor and attendants of his son Gaius took advantage of their master's illness to commit acts of arrogance and greed to his province, he had them thrown into a river with heavy weights about their necks."

To sin oneself is a terrible thing, but to teach another to sin is infinitely worse. O. Henry, the American master of the short story, has a story in which he tells of a little girl whose mother was dead. Her father used to come home from work and sit down and take off his jacket and open his paper and light his pipe and put his feet on the mantelpiece. The little girl would come in and would ask him to play with her for a little for she was lonely. He told her he was tired, to let him be at peace. He told her to go out to the street and play. She played on the streets. The inevitable happened—she took to the streets. The years passed on and she died. Then O. Henry's vision extended to heaven. The girl's soul arrived in heaven. Peter saw her and said to Jesus, " Master, here's a girl who was a bad lot. I suppose we send her straight to hell? " " No," said Jesus gently, " let her in. Let her in." And then His eyes grew stern, " But look for a man who refused to play with his little girl and who sent her out to the streets *and send him to Hell*." God is not hard on the sinner, but God will be stern to the person who makes it easier for another to sin, and whose conduct, either thoughtless or deliberate, puts a stumbling-block in the path of the weaker brother.

THE GOAL WHICH IS WORTH ANY SACRIFICE
Mark 9 : 43-48

If your hand proves a stumbling-block to you, cut it off. It is better for you to enter life maimed than

to go away to Gehenna with two hands, to the fire
that can never be quenched. And if your foot is a
stumbling-block to you, cut it off. For it is better
for you to enter into life lame than to be cast into
Gehenna with two feet. And if your eye proves a
stumbling-block to you, cast it away. For it is better
for you to enter into the Kingdom of God with one
eye than to be cast into Gehenna with two eyes, where
their worm does not die and the fire is never quenched.

THIS passage lays down in vivid eastern language the
basic and fundamental truth that there is one goal in
life which is worth any sacrifice. In physical matters it
may be that a man may have to consent to part with a
limb or with some part of the body to preserve the life
of the whole body. There can come a situation in which
the amputation of some limb or the excision of some part
of the body by surgical means is the only way to preserve
the life of the whole body. In the spiritual life the same
kind of thing can happen.

The Jewish Rabbis themselves had sayings based on
the way in which some parts of the body can lend themselves
to sin. " The eye and the heart are the two brokers of
sin." " The eye and the heart are the two handmaids of
sin." " Passions lodge only in him who sees." " Woe to
him who goes after his eyes for the eyes are adulterous."
There are certain instincts in man, and certain parts of
man's physical constitution, which minister to sin. This
saying of Jesus is not to be taken literally, but it is a vivid
eastern pictoral way of saying that there is a goal in life
which is worth any sacrifice which must be made to attain it.

There are in this passage repeated references to *Gehenna*.
Gehenna is spoken of in the New Testament in Matthew
5 : 22, 29, 30 ; 10 : 28 ; 18 : 9 ; 23 : 15, 33 ; Luke
12 : 5 ; James 3 : 6. The word is regularly translated
Hell. It is a word with a history. It is a form of the word
Hinnom. The valley of Hinnom was a ravine outside
Jerusalem. It had an evil history. It was the valley in
which Ahaz, in the old days, had instituted fire worship

and the sacrifice of little children in the fire. " He burnt incense in the valley of the son of Hinnom, and burnt his children in the fire." (2 Chronicles 28 : 3). That terrible heathen worship was also followed by Manasseh (2 Chronicles 33 : 6). The valley of Hinnom, Gehenna, therefore, was the scene of one of Israel's most terrible lapses into heathen customs. In his reformations Josiah declared the valley of Hinnom an unclean place. " He defiled Topheth, which is in the valley of Hinnom, that no man might make his son or his daughter pass through the fire to Molech." (2 Kings 23 : 10). When the valley had been so declared unclean and had been so desecrated it was set apart as the place where the refuse of Jerusalem was thrown to be burned. The consequence was that it was a foul, unclean place, where loathsome worms bred on the refuse, and where it smoked and smouldered at all times like some vast incinerator. The actual phrase about the worm which does not die, and the fire which is not quenched, comes from a description of the fate of Israel's evil enemies in Isaiah 66 : 24. Because of all this the valley of Hinnom, Gehenna, had become a kind of type or symbol of Hell, of the place where the souls of the wicked will be tortured and destroyed. It is so used in the Talmud. " The sinner who desists from the words of the Law will in the end inherit Gehenna." So then Gehenna stands of the place of punishment, and the word roused in the mind as every Israelite the grimmest and most terrible pictures.

But what was the goal for which everything must be sacrificed? It is described in two ways. Twice it is called *life*, and once it is called *The Kingdom of God*. How may we define *The Kingdom of God*? We may take our definition of it from the Lord's Prayer. In that prayer two petitions are set beside each other. " Thy Kingdom come. Thy will be done in earth as it is in heaven." There is no literary device so characteristic of Jewish style as *parallelism*. In parallelism two phrases are set side by side, the one of which either restates the other, or amplifies, explains and develops it. Any verse of the Psalms will show this device in action. So, then, we may take it that in the Lord's Prayer the one petition is an explanation and amplification of the other. When we set the two together we get the definition that, " The Kingdom of Heaven is a society upon earth in which God's will is as perfectly done in earth as it is in heaven." We may then go on to say quite simply that perfectly to do God's will is to be a citizen of the Kingdom of Heaven. And if we take that and apply it to the passage that we are now studying it will mean that *it is worth any sacrifice and any discipline and any self-denial to do the will of God*, that only in doing the will of God is there real life and ultimate and completely satisfying peace.

Origen takes this symbolically. He says that it may be necessary to excise some heretic, some evil person from the fellowship of the Church in order to keep the body of the Church pure. But this saying is meant to be taken very personally. It means that it may be necessary to excise some habit, to abandon some pleasure, to give up some friendship, to cut out some thing which has become very dear to us, which has become a part of our very lives, in order to be fully obedient to the will of God. This is not a matter with which anyone can deal for anyone else. It is solely a matter of a man's individual conscience, and it means that, if there is anything in our lives which is coming between us and a perfect obedience to the will of God, however dear that thing or person is to us, however much habit and custom may have made it part of our lives, it must be rooted out. The rooting out may be as painful as a surgical operation, it may seem like cutting out part of our own body, but if we are to know real *life*, real happiness and real peace it must go. This may sound bleak and stern, but in reality it is only a facing of the facts of life.

THE GOSPEL OF MARK

THE SALT OF THE CHRISTIAN LIFE

Mark 9 : 49, 50

> Everyone must be salted with fire.
> Salt is good, but, if the salt has become saltless, with what will you season it?
> Have salt in yourselves, and so live at peace with each other.

THESE three verses are amongst the most difficult in the New Testament to interpret. The commentarors produce literally scores of different interpretations. The interpretation will become easier if we remember one thing, which we have already had cause to note. Often Jesus dropped pithy sayings which stuck in men's minds because they could not possibly forget them. But often, although men remembered the saying, they did not remember the context and the occasion on which it was said. The result is that we often get a series of quite disconnected sayings of Jesus set together because they stuck in the writer's mind in that order. It was in that order that He had taught Himself to remember them. Here is an instance of this. We will not make sense of these two verses at all unless we recognize that here we have *three quite separate sayings of Jesus* which have nothing to do with each other. They came together in the compiler's mind and stuck there together in this order because they all contain the word *salt.* They are a little collection of the sayings of Jesus in which He used *salt* in its various uses as a metaphor or illustration. All this is to say that we must not try to find some remote connection between these sayings. We must take them individually, one by one, and interpret each one as it comes.

(i) Everyone must be salted by fire. According to the Jewish Law every sacrifice must be salted with salt before it was offered to God on the altar (Leviticus 2 : 13). That sacrificial salt was called *the salt of the covenant* (Numbers 18 : 9 ; 2 Chronicles 13 : 5). It was the addition of that salt which made the sacrifice acceptable to God, and which

His covenant law laid down as necessary. This saying of Jesus will then mean, " Before a Christian life becomes acceptable to God it must be treated with fire just as every sacrifice is treated with salt." The fire is the salt which makes the life acceptable to God. What then does that mean? In ordinary New Testament language, fire has two connections. (*a*) Fire is connected with *purification*. It is the fire which purifies the base metal, by which the alloy is separated, and the metal left pure. Fire then will mean everything which purifies life, the discipline by which a man conquers his sin, the experiences of life which purify and strengthen the sinews of the soul. In that case this will mean, " The life which is acceptable to God is the life which has been cleansed and purified by the discipline of Christian obedience and Christian acceptance of the guiding hand of God." (*b*) Fire is connected with *destruction*. In that case this saying will have to do with *persecution*. It will mean that the life which has undergone the trials and destructions and hardships and perils of persecution is the life which is acceptable to God. The man who has voluntarily faced the danger of the destruction of his goods, and the destruction of his own life, because of his loyalty to Jesus Christ, is the man who is dear to God. So, then, we may take this first saying of Jesus to mean that the life which is purified by discipline, and the life which has faced the danger of persecution because of its loyalty is the sacrifice which is precious to God.

(ii) Salt is good, but if the salt has become saltless, with what will you season it? This is an even harder saying to interpret. We would not say that there are no other possible interpretations, but we would suggest that it may be understood on the following lines. Salt has two characteristic virtues. First, it lends *flavour* to things. An egg without salt is an insipid thing. Anyone knows how unpleasant many a dish is when the salt which should have been included is accidentally omitted in the preparation of it. Second, salt was the earliest of all *preservatives*. To keep a thing from going rotten and bad salt was used. The Greeks used to say that salt acted like a soul in a dead body. Dead meat left to itself goes bad, but, pickled in salt, it retains its freshness. The salt seemed to put a kind of life into it. Salt, then, defended against rottenness and corruption. Now the Christian was sent into a heathen society to live there and to do something for that society. Heathen society had two characteristics. First, it was bored and world-weary. The very luxuries and excesses of that ancient world were a proof that in its bored weariness it was looking for some thrill in a life from which all thrill had gone. As Matthew Arnold wrote,

> " On that hard pagan world, disgust
>   And secret loathing fell ;
> Deep weariness and sated lust
>   Made human life a hell.
> In his cool hall, with haggard eyes,
>   The Roman noble lay ;
> He drove abroad in furious guise
>   Along the Appian Way ;
> He made a feast, drank fierce and fast,
>   And crowned his hair with flowers—
> No easier nor no quicker passed
>   The impracticable hours."

Now into that bored and weary world Christianity came, and it was the task of the Christian to impart to society a new flavour and a new thrill as salt does to the dish with which it is used. Second, that ancient world was a corrupt world. No one knew that better than the ancients themselves. Juvenal likened Rome to a filthy sewer. Purity was gone and chastity was unknown. Now into that corrupt and rotten world Christianity came, and it was the task of the Christian to bring an antiseptic to the poison of life, to bring a cleansing, purifying influence into that corruption. Just as salt defeated the corruption which inevitably attacked dead meat, so Christianity was to attack the corruption of the world. So then in this saying Jesus was challenging the Christian. " The world," He said, " needs the flavour and the purity that only the Christian can bring into it. And if the Christian himself has lost the thrill and the purity of the Christian life, where will the world ever get these things?" Jesus is pointing out that unless the Christian brings the Christian zest and the Christian cleanness to life there is nowhere else where the world can find these things. Unless the Christian, in the power of Christ, defeats world-weariness and world corruption, these things must flourish unchecked.

(iii) Have salt in yourselves and live at peace with each other. Here we must take salt in the sense of *purity*. The ancients declared that there was nothing in the world purer than salt because it came from the two purest things, the sun and the sea. The very glistening whiteness of salt was a picture of purity. So this will mean, " Have within yourselves the purifying influence of the Spirit of Christ. Be purified from selfishness and self-seeking, from bitterness and anger and grudge-bearing. Be cleansed from irritation and moodiness and self-centredness, and then, and then only, you will be able to live in peace with your fellow men." In other words, Jesus is saying that it is only the life that is cleansed of self and filled with Christ which can live in real fellowship with men.

FOR BETTER OR FOR WORSE

Mark 10 : 1-12

Leaving there, Jesus came into the hill-country of Judaea and to the district across the Jordan, and once again crowds came together to Him. As His custom was, He again continued to teach them. Some Pharisees came to Him and asked Him if it was lawful for a man to put away his wife. They asked this question to test Him. He asked them, " What commandment did Moses lay down for you?" They answered, " Moses allowed a man to write a bill of divorcement and then to put her away." Jesus said

to them, " It was to meet the hardness of your heart
that he wrote this commandment for you. From the
beginning of creation male and female He created
them. For this cause a man will leave his father and
his mother and will cleave to his wife. And the two
will become one flesh, so that they are no longer two
but one flesh. So then what God has joined together
let not man separate." In the house His disciples
again asked Him about this. He said to them,
" Whoever puts away his wife and marries another
woman commits adultery against her. And if a woman
divorces her husband and marries another man, she
commits adultery."

JESUS was pursuing His way south. Now He had left
Galilee and He had come into Judaea. He had not yet
entered Jerusalem, but step by step and stage by stage
He was approaching the final scene. Certain Pharisees
came to Him with a question about divorce, by which
they hoped to test Him. There may have been more than
one motive behind the question of these Pharisees. The
question of divorce was a burning question, a crux of
rabbinic discussion, and it may quite well be that they
honestly wished for Jesus' opinion and verdict on it. They
may have wished to test His orthodoxy. It may well be
that Jesus had already had something to say on this matter.
Matthew 5 : 31, 32, shows us Jesus speaking about
marriage and re-marriage, and it may be that these
Pharisees had the hope that He might contradict Himself
and entangle Himself in His own words. It may be that
they knew what He would answer, and they wished to
involve Him in enmity with Herod who had in fact
divorced his wife and married another. It may well be
that they wished to hear Jesus contradict the law of
Moses, as indeed He did, and thereby to formulate a charge
of heresy against Him. One thing is certain—the question
they asked Jesus was no academic question of interest only
to the rabbinic schools. It was a question which dealt with
something which was one of the acutest issues of the time
in which Jesus lived.

In theory nothing could be higher than the Jewish ideal of marriage. Chastity was held to be the greatest of all the virtues. "We find that God is long-suffering to every sin except the sin of unchastity." "Unchastity causes the glory of God to depart." "Every Jew must surrender his life rather than commit idolatry, murder or adultery." "The very altar sheds tears when a man divorces the wife of his youth." The ideal was there but practice fell very far short of it.

The basic fact that vitiated the whole situation was that in Jewish law a woman was regarded as a thing. She had no legal rights whatever. She was at the complete disposal of the male head of the family. The result was that a man could divorce his wife on almost any grounds, while there were very few grounds on which a woman could seek divorce. At best she could only ask her husband to divorce her. "A woman may be divorced with or without her will, but a man only with his will." The only grounds on which a woman could claim a divorce were if her husband became a leper, if he engaged in a disgusting trade such as that of a tanner, if he ravished a virgin, or if he falsely accused her of pre-nuptial sin.

The law of Jewish divorce goes back to Deuteronomy 24 : 1. That passage was the foundation and the crux of the whole matter. It runs thus : "When a man hath taken a wife, and married her, and it come to pass that she find no favour in his eyes, because he hath found some uncleanness in her, then let him write her a bill of divorcement, and give it in her hand, and send her out of his house."

At first the bill of divorcement was very simple. It read like this : "Let this be from me thy writ of divorce and letter of dismissal and deed of liberation, that thou mayest marry whatsoever man thou wilt." In later days the bill became more elaborate : "On the........day, of the ....week, of the........month, year........of the world, according to the calculation in use in the town of ...., situated by the river........, I, A.B., son of

C.D., and by whatsoever name I am called here, present this day........, native of the town of........, acting of my free-will, and without any coercion, do repudiate, send back, and put away thee E.F., daughter of G.H., and by whatsoever name thou art called, and until this present time my wife. I send thee away now E.F., daughter of G.H., so that thou art free and thou canst at thy pleasure marry whom thou wilt and no one will hinder thee. This is thy letter of divorce, act of repudiation, certificate of separation, according to the law of Moses and of Israel."

In New Testament times this document took a skilled Rabbi to draw it up. It was afterwards proved by a court of three rabbis, and then lodged with the Sanhedrin. But the process of divorce remained on the whole exceedingly easy, and at the entire discretion of the man.

But the real crux of the problem was the interpretation of the law as it is in Deuteronomy 24 : 1. There it is laid down that a man can divorce his wife if he finds in her *a matter of uncleanness*. How was that phrase to be interpreted? There were in this matter two schools of thought. There was the school of Shammai. They interpreted the matter with utter strictness. A matter of uncleanness was adultery and adultery alone. Let a woman be as bad as Jezebel, the wife of Ahab, unless she was guilty of adultery there could be no divorce. The other school was the school of Hillel. They interpreted that crucial phrase as widely as possible. They said that it could mean if the wife spoiled a dish of food, if she spun in the streets, if she talked to a strange man, if she spoke disrespectfully of her husband's relations in his hearing, if she was a brawling woman, which was defined as a woman whose voice could be heard in the next house. Rabbi Akiba even went the length of saying that it meant if a man found a woman who was fairer in his eyes than his wife was. Human nature being as it is, it was the laxer view which prevailed. The result was that divorce for the most trivial reasons, or for no reason at all, was tragically common. To such a pass had things come that, in the time of Jesus, women hesitated to marry at all because marriage was so insecure. When Jesus spoke as He did He was speaking on a subject which was a burning issue, and He was striking a blow for women by seeking to restore marriage to the position it ought to have.

Certain things are to be noted. Jesus quoted the Mosaic regulation, and then He said that Moses only laid that down " to meet the hardness of your hearts." That may mean one of two things. It may mean that Moses laid it down because it was the best that could be expected from people such as those for whom he was legislating. Or, it may mean that Moses laid it down in order to try to control a situation which even then was degenerating, that in fact it was not so much a permission to divorce as it was in the beginning an attempt to control divorce, to reduce it to some kind of law, and to make it more difficult. In any event Jesus made it quite clear that He regarded Deuteronomy 24 : 1, as being laid down for a definite situation and being in no sense permanently binding. The authorities which He quoted went much further back. For His authorities He went right back to the Creation story and quoted Genesis 1 : 27 and 2 : 24. It was His view that in the very nature of things marriage was a permanency which indissolubly united two people into one, in such a way that the bond could never be broken by any human laws and regulations. It was His belief that in the very constitution of the universe marriage is meant to be an absolute permanency and unity, and no Mosaic regulation dealing with a temporary situation could alter it.

The difficulty is that in the parallel account in Matthew there is a difference. In Mark, Jesus' prohibition of divorce and of remarriage is absolute. In Matthew 19 : 3-9, He is shown as still absolutely forbidding remarriage, but as permitting divorce on one ground—the ground of adultery. Almost certainly the Matthew version is correct, and is indeed implied in the Mark version. It was Jewish law that adultery did in fact compulsorily dissolve any marriage. And the truth is that adultery, and infidelity does in fact dissolve the bond and unity of marriage. Once the sin of adultery has been committed the unity is in any case destroyed and divorce merely attests the fact.

But the real essence of the passage is that Jesus insisted that the loose sexual morality of His day must be mended. Those who sought marriage only for pleasure must be reminded that marriage is also for responsibility. Those who regarded marriage simply as a means of gratifying their physical passions must be reminded that it was also a spiritual unity. Jesus was building a rampart round the home.

OF SUCH IS THE KINGDOM OF HEAVEN

Mark 10 : 13-16

> They brought little children to Jesus that He might touch them. But the disciples rebuked them. When Jesus saw what they were doing He was vexed and said to them, " Let the little children come to me, and don't try to stop them for of such is the Kingdom of God. This is the truth I tell you, whoever does not receive the Kingdom of God as a little child will not enter into it." And He took them up in the crook of His arm and blessed them and laid His hands upon them."

It was the very natural thing that Jewish mothers should wish their children to be blessed by a great and distinguished Rabbi. Especially they brought their children to such a person on the child's first birthday. It was in that way that they brought the children to Jesus on this day.

We will only fully understand the almost poignant beauty of this passage if we remember when it happened. We must remember that Jesus was on the way to the Cross—and He knew it. That cruel shadow can never have been far from His mind. It was at such a time as that that He had time for the children. Even with such a tension in

249

His mind as that He had time to take them in His arms and He had the heart to smile into their faces and maybe to play with them awhile. That is precisely why the disciples sought to keep the children away. It was not that they were boorish and ungracious men. It was that they wanted to protect Jesus. They did not know what was going on, but they knew quite clearly that tragedy lay ahead, and they could see the tension under which Jesus laboured. They did not want Him to be bothered. They could not conceive that He could want the children about Him at such a time as that. But even then Jesus said, " Let the children come to me."

Quite incidentally, as it were in the passing, this tells us a great deal about Jesus. It tells us that He was the kind of person who cared for children and for whom children cared. He could not have been a stern and gloomy and joyless person. There must have been a kindly sunshine on Him. He must have smiled easily and laughed joyously. Somewhere George Macdonald says that he does not believe in a man's Christianity if the children are never to be found playing around his door. This little, precious incident throws a flood of light on the human kind of person that Jesus was.

" Of such," said Jesus, " is the Kingdom of God." What was it about the child that Jesus liked and valued so much?

(i) There is the child's *humility*. There is the child who is an exhibitionist, but such a child is rare and is almost always the product of misguided adult treatment. Ordinarily the child is embarrassed by prominence and publicity. He has not yet learned to think in terms of place and pride and prestige. He has not yet learned to discover the importance of himself.

(ii) There is the child's *obedience*. True, a child is often disobedient, but, paradox though it may seem, a child's natural instinct is to obey. The child has not yet learned the pride and the false independence which separates a man from his fellow men and from God.

(iii) There is the child's *trust*. That is seen in two things. (*a*) It is seen in the child's acceptance of authority. There is a time when the child thinks his father knows everything, and that his father is always right. To our shame, he soon grows out of that. But instinctively the child realizes his own ignorance and his own helplessness and trusts the one who, as he thinks, knows. (*b*) It is seen in the child's confidence in other people. It is the unique fact about a child that he does not expect any person to be a bad person. The child will make friends with a perfect stranger. A very great man once said that the greatest compliment that was ever paid to him was when a very little boy came up to him, a complete stranger, and asked him to tie his shoe lace. The child has not yet learned to suspect the world. He still believes the best about others. Sometimes that very trust leads him into danger for there are those who are totally unworthy of it and who abuse it, but that trust is a very lovely thing.

(iv) The child has *a short memory*. He has not yet learned to bear grudges and nourish bitterness. Even when he is unjustly treated—and who among us is not sometimes unjust to our children?—he forgets, and he forgets so completely that he does not even need to forgive.

Indeed, of such is the Kingdom of God.

HOW MUCH DO YOU WANT GOODNESS?

Mark 10 : 17-22

As Jesus was going along the road, a man came running to Him and threw himself at His feet and asked Him, " Good teacher, what am I to do to inherit eternal life? " Jesus said to him, " Why do you call me good? There is no one who is good, except one—God. You know the commandments. You must not kill, you must not commit adultery, you must not steal, you must not bear false witness, you must not defraud anyone, you must honour your father and mother." He said to Him, " Teacher, I have kept all these from my youth." When Jesus looked at him He loved him, and He said to him, " You still lack one thing. Go, sell all that you have, and give it to the poor and you will have treasure in heaven. And come ! Follow me ! " But he was grieved at this saying, and he went away in sadness, for he had many possessions.

HERE is one of the most vivid stories in the gospels.

(i) We must note how the man came and how Jesus met him. He came running. He flung himself at Jesus' feet. There is something amazing in the sight of this rich, young aristocrat falling at the feet of the penniless prophet from Nazareth, who was on the way to being an outlaw. " Good teacher ! " he began. And straight away Jesus answered back, " No flattery ! Don't call me good ! Keep that word for God ! " It looks almost as if Jesus was trying to freeze him and to pour cold water on that young enthusiasm. There is a lesson here. It is clear that this man came to Jesus, swept to Him in a moment of overflowing emotion. It is also clear that Jesus exercised a personal fascination over him. Jesus did two things that every evangelist and every preacher and every teacher ought to remember and to copy. First, Jesus said in effect, " Stop and think ! You are all wrought up and palpitating with emotion ! I don't want you swept to me by a moment of emotion. Think calmly what you are doing." Jesus was not freezing the man. He was telling him even at the very outset to count the cost. Second, Jesus said in effect, " You cannot become a Christian by a sentimental passion for me. *You must look at God.*" Preaching and teaching always mean the conveying of truth through personality, and thereby lies the greatest danger of the greatest teachers. The danger is that the pupil, the scholar, the young person can form a personal attachment to the teacher or the preacher and think that it is an attachment to God. The teacher and preacher must never point to himself. He must always point to God. There is in all true teaching a certain self-obliteration. True, we cannot keep personality and warm personal loyalty out of it altogether, and we would not if we could. But the matter must not stop there. The teacher and the preacher are in the last analysis only finger-posts to God.

(ii) Never did any story so lay down the essential Christian truth that *respectability is not enough*. Jesus quoted the commandments which were the basis of the decent, respectable life. Without hesitation the man said he had kept them all. Now note one thing—with one exception they were all negative commandments, and that one exception was one which operated only in the family circle. In effect the man was saying, " I never in my life did anyone any harm." That was perfectly true. But the real question is, " What good have you done people? " And the question to this man was even more pointed for it was, " With all your possessions, with your wealth, with all that you could give away, what positive good have you done to others? How much have you gone out of your way to help and comfort and strengthen others as you might have done? " Respectability, on the whole, consists in *not doing things*. Christianity consists in *doing things*. That was precisely where this man—and so many of us—fall down.

(iii) So Jesus confronted this man with a challenge. In effect He said, " Get out of this moral respectability. Stop looking at goodness as consisting in not doing things. Take yourself, take all that you have, and spend yourself and your possessions on others. Then you will find true happiness in time and in eternity." And the man could not do it. He had great possessions, and it had never entered his head to give them away and when it was suggested to him he could not. True, he had never stolen, and he had never defrauded anyone—but neither had he ever been, nor could he compel himself to be, positively and sacrificially generous. It may be respectable never to take anything from anyone. It is Christian to give everything to someone. In reality Jesus was confronting this man with a basic and essential question—" How much do you want real Christianity? Do you want it enough to give your possessions away?" And the man had to answer in effect, "I want it—but I don't want it as much as all that." Robert Louis Stevenson in *The Master of Ballantrae* draws a picture of the master leaving the ancestral home of Durrisdeer for the last time. Even he is sad. He is talking to the faithful family steward. "Ah! M'Kellar," he said, "Do you think I have never a regret." "I do not think," said M'Kellar, "that you could be so bad a man unless you had all the machinery for being a good one." "Not all," said the master, "not all. It is there you are in error. *The malady of not wanting.*" It was the malady of not wanting enough which meant tragedy for the man who came running to Jesus. It is the malady from which most of us suffer. We all want goodness, but so few of us want it enough to pay the price.

Jesus looking at him loved him. There were many things in that look of Jesus. (*a*) There was the appeal of love. Jesus was not angry with him. He loved him too much for that. It was not the look of anger but the appeal of love. (*b*) There was the challenge to chivalry. It was a look which sought to pull the man out of his comfortable, respectable, settled life into the adventure of being a real Christian. (*c*) It was the look of grief. And that grief was the grief that is the sorest grief of all—the grief of seeing a man deliberately choose to fail to be what he might have been and had it in him to be. Jesus looks at us with the appeal of love, with the challenge to the knightliness of the Christian way. God grant that He may never have to look at us with the sorrow of one who looks at a loved one who refuses to be what he might have been and could have been.

THE PERIL OF RICHES

Mark 10 : 23-27

Jesus looked round and said to His disciples, "With what difficulty will those who have money enter into

254

the Kingdom of God !" His disciples were amazed at His words. Jesus repeated, "Children, how difficult it is for those who trust in money to enter into the Kingdom of God ! It is easier for a camel to go through the eye of a needle than for a rich man to enter the Kingdom of God." They were exceedingly astonished. "Who then," they said to Him, "can be saved?" Jesus looked at them and said, "With man it is impossible, but not with God. All things are possible with God."

THE ruler who had refused the challenge of Jesus had walked sorrowfully away, and, no doubt, as he went, the eyes of Jesus and the company of the apostles followed him until his figure receded into the distance. Then Jesus turned and looked round His own men. " How very difficult it is," He said, "for a man who has money to enter into the Kingdom of God." The word that is used for money is *chremata*, which is defined by Aristotle as, "All those things of which the value is measured by coinage." We may perhaps wonder why this saying so astonished the disciples. Twice their amazement is stressed. The reason for their amazement was that when Jesus said this He was turning accepted Jewish popular standards completely upside down. Popular Jewish morality was simple. It believed quite simply that prosperity was a sign of God's favour, and that therefore prosperity was the sign of a good man. If a man was rich and prosperous, they believed that God must have honoured and blessed him. Wealth was the proof of excellence of character and of favour with God. The Psalmist sums it up, " I have been young and now am old, yet I have not seen the righteous forsaken, nor his seed begging bread." (Psalm 37 : 25.) That is not a point of view which appeals to us at all. But it must be remembered that that was the Jewish point of view. No wonder the disciples were surprised ! They would have argued that the more prosperous a man was the more certain he was of entry into the Kingdom. So Jesus repeated His saying in a slightly different way to

255

make it clearer what He meant. "How difficult it is," He said, "for those who have put their trust in riches, for those who rely on riches to enter the Kingdom."

No one ever saw the danger of prosperity and of material things more clearly than Jesus did. What are these dangers?

(i) Material possessions tend to fix a man's heart to this world. He has so large a stake in this world, he has so great an interest in this world, that it is difficult for him to think beyond it, and it is specially difficult for him to contemplate leaving it. It is told that Dr. Johnson was once shown round a famous castle and its lovely grounds. After he had seen it all, he turned to his friends and said, "These are the things that make it difficult to die." The danger of possessions is that they fix a man's thoughts and interests to this world.

(ii) If a man's main interest is in material possessions it tends to make him think of everything in terms of price. A hill shepherd's wife wrote a most interesting letter to a newspaper some time ago. Her children had been brought up in the loneliness of the hills. They were simple and unsophisticated. Then her husband got a position in a town and the children who had been brought up in the hills were introduced to the town. They changed and they changed very considerably—and they changed for the worse. The last paragraph of her letter reads like this— "Which is preferable for a child's upbringing—a lack of worldliness, but with better manners and sincere and simple thoughts, or worldliness and its present-day habit of knowing the price of everything and the true value of nothing?" If a man's main interest is in material things, he will think in terms of price and not in terms of value. He will think in terms of what money can get and money can buy. And he may well forget that there are values in this world far beyond money, that there are things which have no price, and that there are precious things that money cannot buy. It is fatal when a man begins to think that everything worth having has a money price.

(iii) Jesus would have said that the possession of material things is two things. (*a*) It is an acid test of a man. For a hundred men who can stand adversity only one can stand prosperity. Prosperity can so very easily make a man arrogant, proud, self-satisfied, worldly. It takes a really big and good man to be worthy of prosperity. (*b*) It is a responsibility. A man will always be judged by two standards—how he got his possessions and how he uses his possessions. The more he has the greater the responsibility that rests upon him. Will he use what he has selfishly or generously? Will he use it as if he had undisputed possession of it, or will he use it, remembering that he holds it in stewardship from God?

The reaction of the disciples was that, if what Jesus was saying was true, to be saved at all was well-nigh impossible. Then Jesus stated the whole doctrine of salvation in a nutshell. " If," He said, " salvation depended on a man's own efforts it would be impossible for anyone. But salvation is the gift of God, for all things are possible to God." The man who trusts in himself and in his possessions can never be saved. The man who trusts in the saving power and the redeeming love of God can enter freely into salvation. This is the thought that Jesus stated. This is the thought that Paul wrote letter after letter to prove. And this is the thought which is still for us also the very basis and foundation of the Christian faith.

CHRIST IS NO MAN'S DEBTOR.

Mark 10 : 28-31

Peter began to say to Him, " Look now ! We have left everything and have become your followers." Jesus said, " This is the truth I tell you—there is no one who has left house or brothers or sisters or mother or father or children or lands for my sake and for the sake of the good news who will not get it back a hundred times over in this present time—homes and brothers and sisters and mothers and children and lands—with persecutions, and in the world to come eternal life. But many who are first will be last, and the last first.

PETER'S mind had been working, and, characteristically, Peter's tongue could not stay still. He had just seen a man deliberately refuse Jesus' "Follow me!" and turn his back on that invitation. He had just heard Jesus say in effect that that man by his action had shut himself out from the Kingdom of God. Peter could not help drawing the contrast between that man and himself and his friends. Just as the man had refused Jesus' "Follow me!" he and his friends had accepted it, and Peter with that almost crude honesty of his wanted to know what he and his friends were to get out of it. Jesus' answer falls into three sections.

(i) Jesus said that no man ever gave up anything for the sake of Himself and of His good news without getting it back a hundredfold. It so happened that in the early Church that was literally true. A man's Christianity might involve the loss of home and friends and loved ones and dear ones, but his entry into the Christian Church brought him into a far greater and wider family than ever he had left, a family who were all spiritually kin to him. We can see the thing actually happening in the life of Paul. No doubt when Paul became a Christian, the door of his home slammed in his face and his family disowned him. But equally without doubt there was city upon city, town upon town, village upon village in Europe and in Asia Minor where Paul could find a home waiting for him and a family in Christ to welcome him. It is strange how he uses the very family terms. In Romans 16 : 13, he tells how the mother of Rufus was as good as a mother to him. In Philemon 10, he speaks of Onesimus as the son whom he had begotten in his bonds. It would be so of every Christian in the early days. When his own family rejected him he entered into the wider family of Christ.

When Egerton Young first preached the gospel to the Red Indians in Saskatchewan the idea of the fatherhood of God fascinated men who had hitherto seen God only in the thunder and the lightning and the storm blast. An old chief said to Egerton Young, " Did I hear you say to God ' Our Father ' ? " " I did," said Egerton Young. " God is your Father? " asked the chief. " Yes," said Egerton Young. " And," went on the chief, " He is also my Father? " " He certainly is," said Egerton Young. Suddenly the chief's face lit up with a new radiance. His hand went out. " Then," he said like a man making a dazzling discovery, " you and I are brothers." It may be that a man may have to sacrifice ties that are very dear in order to become a Christian, but when he does so he becomes a member of a family and a brotherhood as wide as earth and heaven.

(ii) Jesus added two things to this. First, He added the simple words *and persecutions*. Straightaway these words remove the whole matter from the world of *quid pro quo*. They take away the idea of a material reward for a material sacrifice. They tell us of two things. They speak of the utter honesty of Jesus. He never offered an easy way. He told men straightly that to be a Christian is a costly thing. Second, they tell us that Jesus never used a *bribe* to make men follow Him. He used a *challenge*. It is as if He said, " Certainly you will get your reward, but you will have to show yourself a big enough man and a gallant enough adventurer to get it." The second thing that Jesus added was the idea of the world to come. He never promised that within this world of space and time there would be a kind of squaring up of the balance sheet and settlement of accounts. He did not call men to win the rewards of time. He called men to earn the blessings of eternity. God had not only this world in which to repay.

(iii) Then Jesus added one warning epigram—" Many

who are first shall be last, and the last first." This was in reality a warning to Peter. It may well be that by this time Peter was assessing his own worth and his own reward and assessing them high. What Jesus was saying was, " The final standard of judgment is with God. Many a man may stand well in the judgment of the world, but the judgment of God may well upset the world's judgment. Still more—many a man may stand well in his own judgment, and find that God's evaluation of him is very different." It is a warning against all pride. It is a warning that the ultimate judgments belong to God who alone knows the motives of men's hearts. It is a warning that the judgments of heaven may well upset the reputations of earth.

THE APPROACHING END

Mark 10 : 32-34

They were on the road, on their way up to Jerusalem, and Jesus was walking ahead of them. They were in a state of astonished bewilderment, and, as they followed Him, they were afraid. Once again He took The Twelve to Him, and began to tell them what was going to happen to Him. " Look you ! " He said, " We are going up to Jerusalem, and the Son of Man will be handed over to the chief priests and experts in the law, and they will condemn Him to death, and they will hand Him over to the Gentiles, and they will make a jest of Him, and they will spit on Him, and they will scourge Him and they will kill Him. And after three days He will rise again."

HERE is a vivid picture, all the more vivid because of the stark economy of words with which it is told. Now Jesus and His men were entering upon the last scene. Jesus had set His course definitely and irrevocably to Jerusalem and to the Cross. Mark marks the stages very definitely. There had been the withdrawal to the north, to the territory round Caesarea Philippi. There had been the journey south, and the brief halt in Galilee. There had been the way to Judaea and the time in the hill-country and beyond Jordan. And now there is the final stage, the road to Jerusalem.

This picture tells us something about Jesus.

(i) It tells us of the loneliness of Jesus. They were going along the road, and He was out ahead of them—alone. And they were so amazed and bewildered, so conscious of the sense of impending tragedy, that they were afraid to go up to Him. There are certain decisions which a man must take alone. Had Jesus tried to share this decision with The Twelve their only contribution would have been to try to stop Him. There are certain things which a man must face alone. Matthew Arnold, in his poem *Isolation*, speaks of,

> " This truth—to prove and make thine own :
> ' Thou hast been, shalt be, art alone '."

There are certain decisions which must be taken, and certain roads that must be walked in the awful loneliness of a man's own soul. And yet, in the deepest sense of all, even in these times a man is not alone, for never is God nearer to Him. Whittier writes of such a time,

> " Nothing before, nothing behind.
>   The steps of faith
> Fall on the seeming void, and find
>   The rock beneath."

Here we see the essential loneliness of Jesus, a loneliness that was comforted by God.

(ii) It tells us of the courage of Jesus. Three times Jesus foretold the things that were to happen to Him in Jerusalem, and it is to be noted that, as Mark tells us of these warnings and forecasts, each time they grow grimmer, and each time some further detail of horror is included. At first (Mark 8 : 31) it is the bare announcement. At the second time the hint of betrayal is there (Mark 9 : 31). And now at the third time the jesting, the mocking and the scourging appear. It would seem as if Mark meant us to see that the picture became ever clearer in the mind of Jesus as He became more and more aware of the cost of redemption. There are two kinds of courage. There is the courage which is a kind of instinctive reaction, the courage which is almost a reflex action, the courage of the man confronted out of the blue with a crisis and emergency, to which he instinctively reacts with courage and gallantry, about which he has not even time to think. Many a man has become a hero in the heat of the moment. But there is also the courage of the man who sees the grim thing approaching far ahead, of the man who has plenty time to turn back, of the man who could, if he chose to do so, evade the issue, and who yet inflexibly goes on. There is no doubt which is the higher courage. This cold, deliberate facing of the future which is known is a far higher thing. That is what Jesus did. If no higher verdict was possible, it would still be true to say of Jesus that He ranks with the heroes of the world.

(iii) It tells us of the personal magnetism of Jesus. It is quite clear that by this time the disciples did not know what was going on. They were sure that Jesus was the Messiah. They were equally sure that He was going to die. To them these two facts did not make sense when put together. They were completely bewildered, *and yet they followed*. To them everything was dark but one thing—they loved this Jesus, and, however much they wished to, they could not leave Him. They had learned something which is of the very essence of life and faith—they loved so much that they were compelled to accept what they could not understand.

THE REQUEST OF AMBITION

Mark 10 : 35-40

James and John, the sons of Zebedee, came to Jesus. " Teacher," they said, " We want you to do for us whatever we ask you." " What do you want me to do for you? " He said to them. They said to Him,

" Grant to us that, in your glory, we may sit one on
your right hand and one on your left." " You do not
know what you ask," Jesus said to them. " Can you
drink the cup which I am drinking? Or, can you go
through the experience through which I am going? "
" We can," they said to Him. Jesus said to them,
" You will drink the cup which I am drinking. You
will go through the experience through which I am
going. But to sit on my right hand and on my left
is not mine to give you. That place belongs to those
for whom it has been prepared."

THIS is a very revealing story.

(i) It tells us something about Mark. Matthew retells
this story (Matthew 20 : 20-23), but in Matthew the
request for the first places is not made by James and
John, but by their mother Salome. Matthew must have
felt that such a request was unworthy of an apostle, and,
to save the reputation of James and John, he attributed
the request to the natural ambition of their mother. This
is a story which shows us the honesty of Mark. It is told
that a court painter painted the portrait of Oliver Cromwell.
Cromwell was afflicted with warts on the face. Thinking
to please him, the court painter omitted the warts in the
painting. When Cromwell saw it, he said, " Take it away !
and paint me warts and all ! " It is Mark's aim to show us
the disciples' warts and all. And Mark was right, because
The Twelve were not a company of saints. They were very
ordinary men. It was with people like ourselves that
Jesus set out to change the world—and did it.

(ii) It tells us something about James and John. (a) It
tells us that they were ambitious. When, as they thought,
the victory was won and the triumph was complete, they
aimed at being Jesus' chief ministers of state. Maybe
their ambition was kindled because more than once Jesus
had made them part of His inner circle, the chosen three.
Maybe they were a little better off than the others.
Their father was well enough off to employ hired servants
(Mark I : 20), and it may be that they rather snobbishly
thought that their social superiority entitled them to the

first place. In any event they show themselves as men in whose hearts there was ambition for the first place in an earthly kingdom. (*b*) It tells us that they had completely failed to understand Jesus. The amazing thing is not the fact that this incident happened, but *the time* at which it happened. It is the juxtaposition of Jesus' most definite and detailed forecast of His death and this request that is staggering. It shows, as nothing else could, how little they understood what Jesus was saying to them. Words were powerless to rid them of the idea of a Messiah of earthly power and glory. Only the Cross could do that. (*c*) But when you have said all that is to be said against James and John, this story tells us one shining thing about them— bewildered they might be, *they still believed in Jesus*. It is an amazing thing that these two could still connect glory at all with a Galilaean carpenter who had incurred the enmity and the bitter opposition of the orthodox religious leaders of His day, and who was apparently heading inevitably for a cross. There is an amazing confidence and an amazing loyalty there. Misguided James and John might be, the fact remains their hearts were in the right place. They never doubted Jesus' ultimate triumph.

(iii) It tells us something of Jesus' standard of greatness, In the Authorised Version Jesus says to them—and the translation is literally accurate—" Can ye drink of the cup that I drink of? And be baptized with the baptism that I am baptized with?" Jesus uses two Jewish metaphors there. It was the custom at a royal banquet for the king to hand the cup to his guests. *The cup* therefore became a metaphor for the life and experience that God handed out to men. "My cup runneth over," said the Psalmist (Psalm 23 : 5), when he spoke of a life and experience of happiness given to him by God. "In the hand of the Lord there is a cup," said the Psalmist (Psalm 75 : 8), when he was thinking of the fate in store for the wicked and the disobedient. Isaiah, thinking of the disasters which had come upon the people of Israel, describes them as having

drunk " at the hand of the Lord the cup of His fury."
(Isaiah 51 : 17.) *The cup* then speaks of the experience
allotted to men by God. The other phrase which Jesus
uses is actually misleading in the literal English version.
He speaks of the baptism with which He was baptized.
The Greek verb *baptizein* means *to dip*. Its past participle
(*bebaptismenos*) means *submerged*, and it is regularly used
of being *submerged in any experience*. For instance, a spend-
thrift is said to be *submerged* in debt. A drunk man is said
to be *submerged* in drink. A grief-stricken person is said to
be *submerged* in sorrow. A lad before a cross-examining
teacher is said to be *submerged* in questions. The word is
regularly used for a ship that has been wrecked and *submerged* beneath the waves. The metaphor is very closely
related to a metaphor which the Psalmist often uses.
In Psalm 42 : 7 we read, "All Thy waves and Thy billows
are gone over me." In Psalm 124 : 4 we read, " Then the
waters had overwhelmed us, the stream had gone over our
soul." The expression, as Jesus used it here, had nothing
to do with technical baptism. What He is saying is, " Can
you bear to go through the terrible experience which I
have to go through? Can you face being submerged in
hatred and pain and death, as I have to be?" Jesus was
telling these two disciples that without a cross there can
never be a crown. The standard of greatness in the
Kingdom is the standard of the Cross. It was true that in
the days to come these two did go through the experience
of their Master, for James was beheaded by Herod Agrippa
(Acts 22 : 2), and, though John was not likely martyred,
he suffered much for Christ. They accepted the challenge
of their Master—even if they did so blindly.

(iv) Jesus told them that the ultimate issue of things
belonged to God. The final assignment of destiny is the
prerogative of God. Jesus never usurped the place of God.
His own whole life was one long act of submission to the
will of God, and He knew that in the end the will of God
was supreme.

THE PRICE OF MAN'S SALVATION

Mark 10 : 41-45

> When the ten heard about this, they began to be vexed about the action of James and John. Jesus called them to Him. " You are well aware," He said, " that those who are esteemed good enough to rule over the Gentiles lord it over them, and their great ones exercise authority over them. It is not so amongst you, but, amongst you, whoever wishes to be great will be your servant, and amongst you, whoever wishes to be first will be the slave of all. For the Son of Man did not come to be served but to serve, and to give His life a ransom for many."

INEVITABLY the action of James and John aroused deep resentment amongst the other ten. It seemed to them that James and John had tried to steal a march upon them, and to take an unfair advantage. Immediately the old controversy about who was to be greatest began to rage again. This was a serious situation. It could well have been that the fellowship of the apostolic band might have been wrecked, had Jesus not taken immediate action. He called them to Him, and He made quite clear the different standards of greatness in His Kingdom and in the kingdoms of the world. In the kingdoms of the world the standard of greatness was power. The test was : How many people does a man control? How great an army of servants has he at his beck and call? On how many people can he impose his will? How many people can he compel to be obedient to his word of command and to do things for him? Not very much later than this, Galba was to sum up the heathen idea of kingship and greatness when he said that now he was Emperor he could do what he liked and do it to anyone. In the Kingdom of Jesus the standard was that of service. Greatness consisted, not in reducing other men to one's service, but in reducing oneself to their service. The test was not, What service can I extract?, but, What service can I give?

We tend to think of this as an ideal state of affairs, but, in point of fact, it is the soundest common sense. It is in fact the first principle of ordinary everyday business life. Bruce Barton points out that the basis on which a motor company will claim the patronage of prospective customers is the claim that they will crawl under your car oftener and get themselves dirtier than any of their competitors. They are in other words prepared to give more service. He points out that when the ordinary clerk goes home at 5.30 p.m. the light will be seen to be burning in the office of the chief executive long into the night. It is his willingness to give the extra service that made him the head of the firm. The basic trouble in the human situation is that men wish to do as little as possible and to get as much as possible. It is only when men are filled with the desire to put into life more than they take out, that is, to serve others, that life for themselves and for others can be happy and prosperous. Kipling has a poem called *Mary's Son* which is advice on the spirit in which a man must work :

> " If you stop to find out what your wages will be
> And how they will clothe and feed you,
> Willie, my son, don't you go to the Sea,
> For the Sea will never need you.

> " If you ask for the reason of every command,
> And argue with people about you,
> Willie, my son, don't you go on the Land,
> For the Land will do better without you.

> " If you stop to consider the work that you've done
> And to boast what your labour is worth, dear,
> Angels may come for you, Willie, my son,
> But you'll never be wanted on earth dear ! "

The world needs people whose ideal is service—that is to say the world needs people who have realized what sound sense Jesus spoke.

To clinch His words Jesus pointed to His own example. With such powers as He had He could have arranged and dictated life entirely to suit Himself, but He had spent Himself and given all His powers to the service of others.

He had come, He said, *to give His life a ransom for many.*
This is one of the great phrases of the gospel, and yet it is a
phrase which has been sadly mishandled and maltreated.
People have tried to erect a theory of the atonement on
what is a saying of love. It was not long until people were
asking to whom this ransom of the life of Christ had been
paid? Origen asked the question. " To whom did He give
His life a ransom for many? It was not to God. Was it
not then to The Evil One? For the devil was holding us
fast until the ransom should be given to him, even the life
of Jesus, for he was deceived with the idea that he could
have dominion over it and did not see that he could not
bear the torture involved in retaining it." It is an odd
conception—that the life of Jesus was paid as a ransom
to the devil, in order to pay him to release men from the
bondage in which he held them, but that the devil found
that in demanding and accepting that ransom, he had, so
to speak, bitten off more than he could chew. Gregory of
Nyssa saw the flaw in that theory. The flaw is that it
really puts the devil on an equality with God. It allows
the devil to make a bargain with God on equal terms. So
Gregory of Nyssa conceived of the extraordinary idea of
a trick played on the devil by God. The devil was tricked
by the seeming helplessness and weakness of the incarnation.
He mistook Jesus for a mere man. He tried to exert his
authority over Jesus and, by trying to do so, lost his
authority, because God had tricked him into losing it.
Again it is an odd idea—that God should conquer the devil
by a stratagem and trick. Another two hundred years
passed and Gregory the Great took up the idea. He used
a fantastic metaphor. The incarnation was a divine
stratagem to catch the great leviathan. The deity of
Christ was the hook, but His flesh was the bait. When the
bait was dangled before Leviathan, the devil, he swallowed
it, and tried to swallow the hook too and so was overcome
forever. Finally Peter, the Lombard, brings this idea to
its most grotesque and repulsive. " The Cross," he said,

" was a mousetrap to catch the devil, baited with the blood of Christ." All this simply shows what happens when men take a lovely and a precious picture and try to make a cold theology out of it.

Suppose we say, " Sorrow is the *price* of love," we mean that love cannot exist without the possibility of sorrow, but we never even think of trying to explain to whom that *price* is paid. Suppose we say that freedom can only be obtained at the *price* of blood, sweat and tears, we never think of investigating to whom that *price* is paid. This saying of Jesus is a simple and pictorial way of saying that, whatever else is true, it cost the life of Jesus Himself to bring men back from their sin into the love of God. It means that the cost of our salvation was the Cross of Christ. Beyond that we cannot go, and beyond that we do not need to go. We only know that something happened on the Cross which opened for us the way to God.

A MIRACLE BY THE WAYSIDE

Mark 10 : 46-52

They went to Jericho. As Jesus was passing through Jericho, on His way out of the city—His disciples and a great crowd were with Him—Bartimaeus, the son of Timaeus, a blind beggar, was sitting by the roadside. When he heard that Jesus of Nazareth was there he began to shout. " Son of David ! " he cried, " Jesus ! Have pity on me ! " Many rebuked him and told him to be quiet. But he shouted all the more, " Son of David ! Have pity on me ! " Jesus came to a stop. " Call him here ! " He said. They called the blind man. " Courage ! " they said to him. " Get up ! He is calling you ! " He threw off his cloak and leapt up and came to Jesus. Jesus said to him, " What do you want me to do for you? " The blind man said to Him, " Master teacher ! My prayer is that I might see again." Jesus said to him, " Go ! Your faith has cured you." Immediately he saw again, and he followed Him upon the road.

FOR Jesus the end of the road was not far away now. Jericho was only about 15 miles from Jerusalem. We must try to visualize this scene. The main road ran right through Jericho. Jesus was on His way to the Passover. When a distinguished Rabbi or teacher was on such a journey it was the custom that he was surrounded by a crowd of people, disciples and learners, who listened to him as he discoursed while he walked. That was one of the commonest ways of teaching. It was the law that every male Jew over twelve years of age who lived within 15 miles of Jerusalem must attend the Passover. It was clearly impossible that such a law should be fulfilled and that everyone should go. Those who were unable to go were in the habit of lining the streets of town and villages through which groups of Passover pilgrims must pass to bid them godspeed on their way. So then the streets of Jericho would be lined with people, and there would be even more than usual, for there would be many eager and curious to catch a glimpse of this audacious young Galilaean who had pitted Himself against the assembled might of orthodoxy. It is worth noting that Jericho had one special characteristic. There were attached to the Temple as many as over 20,000 priests, and as many levites. Obviously they could not all serve at the one time. They were therefore divided into twenty-six courses which served in rotation. Very many of these priests and levites resided in Jericho when they were not on actual temple duty. There must have been many of them in that crowd that day. At the Passover all were on duty for all were needed. It was one of the rare occasions when all did serve. But many would not have started yet. They would be doubly eager to see this rebel who was about to invade Jerusalem. And there would be many cold and bleak and hostile eyes in that crowd that day, because it was clear that if Jesus was right the whole Temple worship was one vast irrelevancy.

At the northern gate there sat a beggar, Bartimaeus by name. He heard the tramp of feet. He asked what was happening and who was passing. He was told that it was Jesus. And there and then he set up an uproar to attract Jesus' attention to him. To those who were listening to Jesus' teaching as He walked the uproar was an offence. They tried to silence Bartimaeus, but no one was going to take from him his one chance to escape from his world of darkness, and he cried with such violence and importunity that the procession stopped, and he was brought to Jesus. This is a most illuminating story. In it we can see many of the things which we might call the conditions of a miracle.

(i) There is the sheer persistence of Bartimaeus. Nothing would stop his clamour to come face to face with Jesus. He was utterly determined to meet the one person whom he longed to confront with his trouble. In the mind of Bartimaeus there was not just a vague, nebulous, wistful, sentimental wish to see Jesus. It was a desperate desire, and it is that desperate desire that gets things done.

(ii) His response to the call of Jesus was immediate and eager, so eager that he cast off his hindering cloak to run to Jesus the more quickly. Many a man hears the call of Jesus, but says in effect, " Wait until I have done this," or " Wait until I have finished that," but Bartimaeus came like a shot when Jesus called. There are certain chances which only happen once. Bartimaeus instinctively knew that. Sometimes we have a wave of longing to abandon some habit, to purify life of some wrong thing, to give ourselves more completely to Jesus. So very often we do not act on it on the moment—and the chance is gone, it may be never to come back.

(iii) He knew precisely what he wanted. It was sight he wanted. Too often our admiration for Jesus is a vague and sentimental attraction. When we go to a doctor we go wanting him to cure some definite ache or pain, asking him to deal with some definite situation. When we go to a dentist we do not ask him to extract *any* tooth, but the one tooth that is diseased. It should be so with us and Jesus. And that involves the one thing that so few people wish to face—*self-examination*. When we go to Jesus, if we are as desperately definite as Bartimaeus, things will happen.

(iv) Bartimaeus had a quite inadequate conception of Jesus. *Son of David* he insisted on calling Him. Now that was a Messianic title, but it has in it all the thought of a conquering Messiah, a king of David's line who would lead Israel to national greatness. That was a very inadequate idea of Jesus. But in spite of that Bartimaeus had *faith*, and faith made up a hundredfold for the inadequacy of his theology. The demand is not that we should fully understand Jesus. That, in any event, we can never do. The demand is for *faith*. A wise writer has said, " We must ask people to think, but we should not expect them to become theologians before they are Christians." Christianity begins with a personal reaction to Jesus, a reaction of love, an instinctive feeling that here is the one person who can meet our need. Even if we are never able to think things out theologically, that instinctive response and cry of the human heart is enough.

(v) In the end there is one precious touch. Bartimaeus may have been a beggar by the wayside, but Bartimaeus was a man of gratitude. Having received his sight, he followed Jesus. He did not selfishly go his way when his need was met. He began with need, went on to gratitude, and finished with loyalty—and that is a perfect summary of the stages of discipleship.

THE COMING OF THE KING

Mark II : 1-6

> When they were coming near to Jerusalem, to Bethphage and to Bethany, Jesus despatched two of His disciples, and said to them, " Go into the village opposite you, and as soon as you come into it, you will find tethered there a colt, on which no man has ever yet sat. Loose it and bring it to me. And if anyone says

to you, ' Why are you doing this? ' say, ' The Lord needs it,' and immediately he will send it." And they went away and they found the colt tethered, outside a door, on the open street, and they loosed it. And some of those who were standing by said to them, " What are you doing loosing this colt? " They said to them what Jesus had told them to say, and they let them go.

Now we have come to the last stage of the journey. There had been the time of withdrawal around Caesarea Philippi in the far north. There had been the time in Galilee. There had been the stay in the hill-country of Judaea and in the regions beyond Jordan. There had been the road through Jericho, and now there comes Jerusalem. Here we have to note something without which the story is almost unintelligible. When we read the first three gospels we get the idea that this was actually Jesus' first visit to Jerusalem. They are concerned to tell the story of Jesus' work in Galilee. We must always remember that the gospels are very short. Into their short compass is crammed the work of three years, and the writers were bound to select the things in which they were interested and of which they had special knowledge. But when we read the Fourth Gospel we find a very different story, for, in it, we find that Jesus was frequently in Jerusalem. (John 2 : 13, 5 : 1, 7 : 10.) We find in fact that Jesus regularly went up to Jerusalem for the great feasts. There is no real contradiction here. The first three gospels are specially interested in the Galilaean ministry, and the fourth is specially interested in the Judaean ministry. It is in fact true that even the first three have indications that Jesus was not infrequently in Jerusalem. There is the close friendship with Martha and Mary and Lazarus at Bethany, a friendship which speaks of many visits. There is the fact that Joseph of Arimathaea was a secret friend of Jesus. And above all there is Jesus' saying in Matthew 23 : 37 when He says that often He would have gathered together the people of Jerusalem as a hen gathers her chickens under her wings but they would not. Jesus could not have said that unless prior to it there had been more than one appeal which had met with a cold response. Now this in fact explains the incident of the colt. Jesus did not leave things until the last moment. He knew what He was going to do. Long ago He had arranged with a friend what He was going to do, and when He sent forward His disciples, He sent them with a pass-word that had been pre-arranged— " The Lord needs it now." This was not a sudden, reckless decision of Jesus. It was something to which all His life had been building up.

Bethphage and Bethany were villages near Jerusalem. Very probably *Bethphage* means *House of Figs*, and *Bethany* means *House of Dates*. They must have been very close because we know from the Jewish law that Bethphage was one of the circle of villages which marked the limit of a Sabbath day's journey, that is, less than a mile, while Bethany was one of the recognized lodging-places for pilgrims to the Passover when Jerusalem was full.

The prophets of Israel had always had a very distinctive method of getting their message across. When words had failed to move people they did something dramatic, as if to say, " If you will not hear, you must be compelled to see." (cp. specially I Kings II : 30-32.) These dramatic actions were what we might call acted warnings or dramatic sermons. That is what Jesus was doing here. Jesus' action was a deliberate dramatic claim to be Messiah. But we must be careful to note what He was doing. There was a saying of the prophet Zechariah (Zechariah 9 : 9), " Rejoice greatly, O daughter of Zion. Shout, O daughter of Jerusalem. Behold, thy king cometh unto thee. He is just and having salvation, lowly, and riding upon an ass, and upon a colt the foal of an ass." Now the whole impact of that is that *the King was coming in peace*. In Palestine the ass was not a despised beast. The ass was a noble beast. When a king went to war he rode on a horse, when he came

in peace he rode on an ass. G. K. Chesterton has a poem
in which he makes the modern donkey speak :

> " When fishes flew and forests walk'd
> And figs grew upon thorn,
> Some moment when the moon was blood
> Then surely I was born.

> " With monstrous head and sickening cry
> And ears like errant wings,
> The devil's walking parody
> Of all four-footed things.

> " The tatter'd outlaw of the earth
> Of ancient crooked will ;
> Starve, scourge, deride me, I am dumb,
> I keep my secret still.

> " Fools !   For I also had my hour,
> One far fierce hour and sweet ;
> There was a shout about my ears,
> And palms before my feet."

It is a wonderful poem. Nowadays the ass is a beast of
amused contempt, but in the time of Jesus it was the beast
of kings. But we must note *what kind of a king Jesus was
claiming to be.* He came meek and lowly. He came in peace
and for peace. They greeted Him as the Son of David,
but they did not understand. It was just at this time that
the Hebrew poems, *The Psalms of Solomon*, were written.
They represent the kind of Son of David whom people
expected. Here is their description of him :

> " Behold, O Lord, and raise up unto them their king,
> the son of David,
> At the time, in the which Thou seest, O God, that
>   he may reign over Israel, Thy servant.
> And gird him with strength that he may shatter
> unrighteous rulers,
> And that he may purge Jerusalem from nations
>   that trample her down to destruction.
> Wisely, righteously he shall thrust out sinners from
> the inheritance,
> He shall destroy the pride of sinners as a potter's
>   vessel.

With a rod of iron he shall break in pieces all their
  substance.
    He shall destroy the godless nations with the
      word of his mouth.
At his rebuke nations shall flee before him,
    And he shall reprove sinners for the thoughts of
      their hearts.
  .   .   .   .

" All nations shall be in fear before him,
  For he will smite the earth with the word of his mouth
    forever."
                                    (Psalms of Solomon 17 : 21-25, 39.)

That was the kind of king the people were looking for.
That was the kind of poem on which they nourished their
hearts. They were looking for a king who would shatter
and smash and break. And Jesus knew it—and He came
meek and lowly, riding upon an ass.

When Jesus rode into Jerusalem that day, He claimed
to be king, but He claimed to be King of peace. His very
action was a contradiction of all that men hoped for and
expected.

HE THAT COMETH

Mark 11 : 7-10

They brought the colt to Jesus, and they put their
garments on it, and mounted him on it. Many of them
spread their garments on the road. Others cut branches
from the fields and spread them on the road. And
those who were going before and those who were
following kept shouting, " Save now ! Blessed is he
who cometh in the name of the Lord ! Blessed is the
coming kingdom of our father David ! Send Thy
salvation from the heights of heaven ! "

THE colt they brought had never been ridden upon. That
was fitting, for a beast to be used for a sacred purpose
must never have been used for any other purpose. It was
so with the red heifer whose ashes cleansed from pollution
(Numbers 19 : 2, Deuteronomy 21 : 3).

The whole picture is the picture of a populace who mis-understood. It shows us a crowd of people thinking of kingship in the terms of conquest in which they had thought of it for so long. The very picture itself is oddly reminiscent of the picture of how Simon Maccabaeus entered Jerusalem a hundred and fifty years before after he had blasted Israel's enemies in battle. "And he entered into it the three and twentieth day of the seventh month, in the hundred, seventy and first year, with thanksgiving and branches of palm trees, and with harps, and cymbals, and viols, and hymns and songs, because there was destroyed a great enemy out of Israel." (I Maccabees 13 : 51.) It was a conqueror's welcome that they sought to give to Jesus, but they never dreamed of the kind of conqueror that He wished to be.

The very shouts which the crowd raised to Jesus show how their thoughts were running. When they spread their garments on the ground before Jesus, they did exactly what the crowd did when that man of blood Jehu was anointed king. (2 Kings 9 : 13.) They shouted, "Blessed is he that cometh in the name of the Lord!" That is a quotation from Psalm 118 : 26, and should really read a little differently, "Blessed in the name of the Lord is he that cometh!" There are three things to note about that shout. (i) It was the regular greeting with which pilgrims were addressed when they reached the Temple on the occasion of the great feasts. (ii) "He that cometh" was another name for the Messiah. When the Jews spoke about the Messiah, they talked of Him as *The One who is Coming*. (iii) But it is the whole origin of the Psalm from which the words come that makes them supremely suggestive. In 167 B.C. there had arisen an extraordinary king in Syria called Antiocheius. He had conceived it his duty to be a missionary of Hellenism and to introduce Greek ways of life, Greek thought and Greek religion wherever he could, even, if necessary, by force. He tried to do so in Palestine. For a time he conquered Palestine. To possess a copy of the law or to circumcise a child was a crime punishable by death. He desecrated the Temple Courts. He actually instituted the worship of Zeus where Jehovah had been worshipped. With a deliberate insult he offered swine's flesh on the great altar of the burnt-offering. He made the chambers round the Temple Court into brothels. He did everything he could to wipe out the Jewish faith. It was then that Judas Maccabaeus arose, and after an amazing career of conquest in 163 B.C. he drove Antiocheius out and he re-purified and re-consecrated the temple, an event which the Feast of the Dedication, or the Feast of Hanukah, still commemorates. And in all probability Psalm 118 was written and composed to commemorate that great day of purification and the battle which Judas Maccabaeus won. Once again, *it is a conqueror's psalm.*

Again and again we see the same thing happening in this whole incident. Jesus had claimed to be the Messiah, but He had done it in such a way as to try to show that the popular ideas of the Messiah were misguided and wrong. But the people did not see it. Their whole welcome was the welcome which befitted, not the King of love, but the conqueror who would shatter the enemies of Israel.

In verses 9 and 10 there is the word *Hosanna.* The word is consistently misunderstood. It is quoted and used as if it meant *Praise.* It is a simple transliteration of the Hebrew for *Save now!* It occurs in exactly the same form in 2 Samuel 14 : 4 and 2 Kings 6 : 26, where it is used by people seeking for help and protection at the hands of the king. When the people shouted *Hosanna* it was not in the least a cry of praise to Jesus, as it so often sounds like when we quote it. It was a cry to God to break in and to save His people now that the Messiah had come.

There is no incident which so shows the sheer courage of Jesus as this does. In the circumstances one might have expected Him to enter Jerusalem secretly and to keep hidden from the authorities who were out to destroy Him. Instead He entered in such a way that the attention of every eye was focussed upon Him. One of the most dangerous things a man can do is to go to people and tell them that all their accepted ideas and notions are wrong. Any man who tries to tear up by the roots a people's nationalistic dreams is in for trouble. But that is what Jesus deliberately was doing. Here we see Jesus making the last appeal of love and making it with a courage that is heroic.

THE QUIET BEFORE THE STORM

Mark 11 : 11

> And He came into Jerusalem into the Temple. After He had looked round everything, when it was now late, He went out to Bethany with The Twelve.

THIS simple verse shows us two things about Jesus which were typical of Him.

(i) It shows us Jesus deliberately summing up His task. The whole atmosphere of the last days is an atmosphere of deliberation. Jesus was not recklessly plunging into unknown dangers. He was doing everything with His eyes wide open. When He looked round everything He was like a commander who was summing up the strength of the opposition and his own resources preparatory to the decisive battle.

(ii) It shows us where Jesus got His strength. He went back to the peace of Bethany. Before He joined battle with men He sought the company and the presence of God. It was only because each day He faced God that He could face men with such courage and such gallantry.

(iii) This brief passage shows us something about The Twelve. They were still with Him. By this time it must have been quite plain to them that, as they saw it, Jesus was committing suicide. Sometimes we criticize them for their lack of loyalty in the last days, but it says something for them, that, little as they understood what was happening, they were still standing by Him.

THE FRUITLESS FIG-TREE

Mark 11 : 12-14, 20-21

> When, on the next day, they were coming out from Bethany, Jesus was hungry. From a distance He saw a fig-tree in leaf, and He went to it to see if He would find anything on it. When He came to it He found nothing except leaves, for it was not yet the season of figs. He said to it, " Let no one eat fruit from you for ever." And the disciples heard Him say it. . . . When they were going along the road early in the morning, they saw the fig-tree withered from the roots. Peter remembered what Jesus had said the day before and said, " Teacher ! Look ! The fig-tree which you cursed has withered away ! "

ALTHOUGH the story of the fig-tree is in Mark's gospel divided into two we take it as one. The first part of the story happened on the morning of one day, and the second part on the morning of the next day, and, chronologically, the cleansing of the Temple comes in between. But, when we are trying to see the meaning of the story we are better to take it as one.

There can be no doubt that this, without exception, is the most difficult story in the gospel narrative. To take it as literal, factual history presents difficulties which are well-nigh insuperable.

(i) The story does not ring true. To be frank, the whole incident does not seem worthy of Jesus. There seems a certain petulance in it. It is just the kind of story that is told of other wonder-workers but which is never told of Jesus. Still further, we have this basic difficulty. Jesus had always refused to use His miraculous powers for His own sake. He would not turn the stones into bread in the desert to satisfy His own hunger. Later He would not use His own miraculous powers to escape from His enemies. He *never* used His power for His own sake. And yet here He uses His power to blast a tree which had disappointed Him when He was hungry.

(ii) Still worse, the whole action was unreasonable. This was the Passover Season, that is the middle of April. The fig-tree in a sheltered spot may bear leaves as early as March, but never did a fig-tree bear figs until late May or June. Mark says that it was not the season for figs. Why blast the tree for failing to do that which it was not possible for it to do? It is both unreasonable and unjust. Some commentators, to save the situation, say that what Jesus was looking for was green figs, half-ripe figs, in their early stages, but those who have resided in Palestine assure us that such unripe fruit was unpleasant and was never eaten.

The whole story does not seem to fit Jesus at all. What are we to say about it?

If we are to take this as the story of something which actually and literally happened, we must take it as *an enacted parable*. We must in fact take it as one of these prophetic, symbolic, dramatic actions. If we take it that way it can be interpreted as the condemnation of two things.

(i) It is the condemnation of *promise without fulfilment*. The leaves on the tree might be taken as the promise of fruit, but there was no fruit there. It would be the condemnation especially of the people of Israel. All their history was a preparation for the coming of God's Chosen One. The whole promise of their national record was that when the Chosen One came they would be eager to receive Him, and, when He did come, the whole promise of their history was tragically contradicted and unfulfilled. Charles Lamb tells of a certain man called Samuel le Grice. In his life there were three stages. When he was young, people said of him, " He will do something." As he grew older and did nothing, they said of him, " He could do something if he tried." Towards the end they said of him, " He might have done something if he had tried." His whole life was the tale of a promise that was never fulfilled. If then this incident is an enacted parable it is the condemnation of unfulfilled promise.

(ii) It is the condemnation of *profession with practice*.
It might be taken that the tree with its leaves professed
to offer something and did not. The whole cry of the New
Testament is that a man can only be known by the fruits
of his life. "Ye shall know them by their fruits."
(Matthew 7 : 16.) "Bring forth fruits worthy of repentance." (Luke 3 : 8.) It is not the man who piously says,
"Lord, Lord," who will enter into the Kingdom but the
man who does God's will. (Matthew 7 : 21.) Unless a
man's religion makes himself a better and more useful man,
unless it makes his home happier, unless it makes life
better and easier for those with whom he is brought into
contact, it is not religion at all. No man can claim to be a
follower of Jesus Christ and remain entirely unlike the
Master whom he claims to love.

If this incident is to be taken literally and is an enacted
parable, that must be the meaning. But, relevant as these
lessons may be to life, it seems very difficult to extract
them from the incident, because it was quite unreasonable
to expect the fig-tree to bear figs when the time for figs
was still six weeks away.

What then are we to say? Luke does not relate this
incident at all, but Luke has the parable of the fruitless
fig-tree (Luke 12 : 6-9). Now that parable ends indecis-
ively. The master of the vineyard had wished to root up
the tree. The gardener had pled for another chance. The
last chance was given, and it was agreed that if the tree
bore fruit it should be spared, and if not it should be
destroyed. May it not be that this incident is a kind of
continuation of that parable? The people of Israel had
had their chance. They had failed to bear fruit. And now
was the time for their destruction. It has been suggested—
and it is quite possible—that on the road from Bethany
to Jerusalem there was a lonely blasted fig-tree, one of
these gaunt trees that sometimes appear stark on a land-
scape. It may well be that Jesus said to His disciples,
"You remember the parable I told you about the fruitless

fig-tree? Israel is still fruitless and will be blasted as that tree." It may well be that that lonely tree became associated in story and in men's minds with a saying of Jesus about the fate of fruitlessness, and so the story may have arisen.

Let the reader take ·it as he will. To us there seem insuperable difficulties in taking it literally. It seems to us to be in some way connected with the Parable of the Fruitless Tree. But in any event the whole lesson of the incident is that uselessness invited disaster.

THE WRATH OF JESUS

Mark II : I5-I9

> They came into Jerusalem, and when Jesus had come into the sacred precincts, He began to cast out those who sold and bought in the sacred place, and He overturned the tables of the money-changers and the seats of those who sold doves, and He would not allow that anyone should carry their gear through the sacred precincts. The burden of His teaching and speaking was, " Is it not written, My house shall be called a house of prayer for all nations, but you have made it a brigands' cave ? " The chief priests and the experts in the law heard Him, and they sought a way to destroy Him, for they were araid of Him, for the whole crowd was astonished at His teaching.
>
> And when evening came He went out of the city.

WE will visualize this far better if we have in our mind's eye a picture of the lay-out of the Temple precincts. There are two closely connected words used in the New Testament. The first word is *hieron*, which means *the sacred place*. This included the whole temple area. The temple area covered the top of Mount Zion and was about thirty acres in extent. It was surrounded by great walls which varied on each side, I,300 to I,000 feet in length. There was a wide outer space which was called *The Court of the Gentiles*. Into it anyone, Jew or Gentile, might come. At the inner edge of the Court of the Gentiles there was a low wall with tablets set into it which said that if a Gentile passed that point the penalty was death. Beyond the Court of the Gentiles a Gentile might not go. The next court was called the *Court of the Women*. It was so called because unless women had come actually to offer sacrifice they might not proceed farther. The next court was called the *Court of the Israelites*. It was in it that the congregation gathered on great occasions, and it was from it that the offerings were handed by the worshipper to the priests. The inmost court was called *The Court of the Priests*. The other important word is *naos*, which means *the Temple proper*, and it was in the Court of the Priests that the Temple itself stood. The whole area, including all the different Courts, was the sacred precincts (*hieron*). The special building itself within the Court of the Priests was the Temple (*naos*).

This incident took place in the Court of the Gentiles. Bit by bit the Court of the Gentiles had become almost entirely secularised. It had been meant to be a place of prayer and preparation, but there was in the time of Jesus a commercialised atmosphere of buying and selling which would have made prayer and devotion and meditation quite impossible. What made it worse was that the business which went on there was sheer exploitation of the pilgrims. Every Jew had to pay a temple tax of one half shekel a year. That was a sum of 1s. 2d. It does not seem much but it has to be evaluated against the fact that the standard day's wage for a working man was 8d. That tax had to be paid in one particular kind of coinage. For ordinary purposes Greek, Roman, Syrian, Egyptian, Phoenician, Tyrian coinages were all equally valid. But this had to be paid in shekels of the sanctuary. It was paid at the Passover time. Jews came from all over the world to the Passover and with all kinds of currencies. When they went to have their money changed they had to pay a fee of 2d., and should their coin exceed the tax, they had to pay another 2d. before they got their change. Most pilgrims had to pay this extra 4d. before they could pay their tax at all. We must remember that that was half a day's wage, which for them was a great deal of money. As for the sellers of doves—doves entered largely into the sacrificial system (Leviticus 12 : 8, 14 : 22, 15 : 14). A sacrificial victim had to be without blemish. Doves could be bought cheaply enough outside, but the temple inspectors would be sure to find something wrong with them, and would advise worshippers to buy them at the temple stalls. Outside doves cost as little as 9d. a pair, inside they cost as much as 15s. Again it was sheer imposition, and what made matters worse was that this business of buying and selling belonged to the family of Annas who had been High Priest. The Jews themselves were well aware of this abuse. The Talmud tells us that Rabbi Simon ben Gamaliel, on hearing that a pair of doves inside the temple cost a gold piece, insisted that the price be reduced to a silver piece. It was the fact that poor, humble pilgrims were being fleeced and swindled and imposed upon which moved Jesus to wrath. Lagrange, the great scholar, who knew the East so well, tells us that precisely the same situation obtains in Mecca to-day. The pilgrim, seeking the divine presence, finds himself in the middle of a noisy uproar, where the one aim of the sellers is to exact as high a price as possible and where the pilgrims argue and defend themselves with equal fierceness. Jesus used a vivid metaphor to describe the temple court. The road from Jerusalem to Jericho was notorious for its robbers. It was a narrow winding road, passing between rocky defiles. Amidst the rocks were the caves where the brigands lay in wait, and Jesus said, " There are worse brigands in the temple courts than ever there are in the caves of the Jericho road."

Verse 16 has the odd statement that Jesus would not allow anyone to carry his gear through the temple court. In point of fact the temple court provided a short cut from the eastern part of the city to the Mount of Olives. The Mishnah itself lays it down, "A man may not enter into the temple mount with his staff or his sandal or his wallet, or with the dust upon his feet, *nor may he make of it a short by-path.*" When Jesus did this He was reminding the Jews of their own laws. In His time the Jews thought so little of the sanctity of the outer court of the temple that they used it as a thoroughfare on their business errands. It was to their own laws that Jesus directed the attention of the Jews, and it was their own prophets that He quoted to them, for His condemnation consists of two quotations from the Old Testament, one from Isaiah 56 : 7 and one from Jeremiah 7 : 11.

What then was it that moved Jesus to such wrath?

(i) He was angry at the exploitation of the pilgrims. The Temple authorities were treating these pilgrims not as worshippers, not even as human beings, but simply as things to be exploited for their own ends. Man's exploitation of man always provokes the wrath of God, and doubly so when that exploitation is made under the cloak of religion.

(ii) He was angry at the desecration of God's Holy Place. Men had lost the sense of the presence of God in the house of God. They were commercialising the sacred and thereby violating it.

(iii) Is it possible that Jesus had an even deeper anger? He quoted Isaiah 56 : 7, " My house shall be a house of prayer *for all nations.*" And yet in that very same house there was a wall beyond which to pass was for the Gentile death. It may well be that Jesus was moved to anger by the exclusiveness and the separation of Jewish worship, and that He wished to remind them that God so loved, not the Jews, but *the world.*

THE LAWS OF PRAYER

Mark 11 : 22-26

> Jesus answered, " Have faith in God. This is the truth
> I tell you—whoever will say to this mountain, ' Be
> lifted up and be cast into the sea,' and who in his heart
> does not doubt, but believes that what he says is
> happening, it will be done for him. So then I tell you,
> believe that you have received everything for which
> you pray and ask, and it will be done for you. And
> whenever you stand praying, if you have anything
> against anyone, forgive it, so that your Father who is
> in heaven may forgive you your trespasses."

We return now to certain sayings which Mark attaches to
the story of the blasting of the fig-tree. We have noticed
more than once how certain sayings of Jesus stuck in men's
minds although the occasion on which He said them had
been forgotten. It is so here. The saying about the faith
which can remove mountains occurs in Matthew 17 : 20
and in Luke 17 : 6, and in each of the gospels it occurs in
a quite different context. The reason is that Jesus said it
far more than once, but that the real context of it had
often been forgotten. The saying about the necessity of
forgiving our fellow-men occurs in Matthew 6 : 12 and 14
again in a quite different context. We must approach these
sayings as not so much having to do with any particular
incidents, but as general rules which Jesus repeatedly laid
down.

This passage then gives us three rules for prayer.

(i) Prayer must be the prayer of faith. The phrase about
removing mountains was a quite common Jewish phrase.
It was a regular, vivid phrase for *removing difficulties*. It
was specially used of wise teachers. A good teacher who
could remove the difficulties which the minds of his
scholars encountered was called *a mountain-remover*. One
who heard a famous Rabbi teach said that " he saw Resh
Lachish as if he were *plucking up mountains*." So the
phrase means this, that if we have real faith, prayer is a

power which can solve any problem and make us able to deal with any difficulty. That sounds very simple, but it involves two things. First, it involves that we should be willing to take our problems and our difficulties to God. That in itself is a very real test. Sometimes our problems are that we wish to obtain something we should not desire at all, that we wish to achieve something which is actually a forbidden thing, that we wish to find a way to do something we should not even think of doing, that we wish to justify ourselves for doing or for having done something to which we should never lay our hands or apply our minds. One of the greatest tests of any problem is the simple test, " Can I take it to God and can I ask His help? " Second, it involves that we should be ready to accept God's guidance when He gives it to us. It is the commonest thing in the world for a person to ask for advice when all he really wants is approval for some action that he is already determined to take. It is useless to go to God and to ask for His guidance unless we are also willing to be humbly obedient enough to accept it. But if we do take our problems to God and if we are humble enough and brave enough to accept His guidance there does come the power which can conquer the difficulties of thought and of action.

(ii) Prayer must be the prayer of expectation. It is the universal fact that anything done or tried in the spirit of hope and confident expectation has a more than double chance of success. The patient who goes to a doctor and who has no confidence in the prescribed remedies has far less chance of recovery than the patient who goes confident that the doctor can cure him. When we pray, it must never be a mere formality. It must never be a ritual with no hope. James Burns quotes a scene from Leonard Merrick's book, *Conrad in Quest of His Youth.* " Do you think prayers are ever answered? " inquired Conrad. " In my life I have sent up many prayers, and always with the attempt to persuade myself that some former prayer had been fulfilled. But I knew. I knew in my heart none ever had been. Things that I wanted have come to me, but—I say it with all reverence—too late. . . ." Mr. Irquetson's fine hand wandered across his brow. "Once," he began conversationally, "I was passing with a friend through Grosvenor Street. It was when in the spring the tenant's fancy lightly turns to coats of paint, and we came to a ladder leaning against a house that was being redecorated. In stepping to the outer side of it my friend lifted his hat to it. You may know the superstition. He was a 'Varsity man, a man of considerable attainments. I said, ' Is it possible you believe in that nonsense? ' He said, ' N-no, I don't exactly believe in it, but I never throw away a chance '." On a sudden the Vicar's inflexion changed, his utterance was solemn, stirring, devout, " I think, sir, that most people pray on my friend's principle— they don't believe in it, but they never throw away a chance." There is much truth in that. For so many people prayer is either a pious ritual or a forlorn hope. It should be a thing of burning expectation. Maybe our trouble is that what we want from God is *our* answer, and when we do not get it we do not recognize *God's* answer which always comes.

(iii) Prayer must be the prayer of charity. The prayer of a bitter man cannot penetrate the wall of his own bitterness. Why? If we are to speak with God there must be some bond between us and God. There can never be any intimacy between two people who have nothing in common. The principle of God is love, for God is love. And if the ruling principle of a man's heart is bitterness and the unforgiving spirit, he has erected a barrier between himself and God. If ever the prayer of such a man is to be answered he must first pray that God would cleanse his heart from the bitter spirit and put into his heart the spirit of love. Then he can speak to God and God can speak to him.

A CUNNING QUESTION AND A PIERCING ANSWER

Mark 11 : 27-33.

> Once again they came to Jerusalem, and, when Jesus was walking in the Temple, the chief priests and the experts in the law and the elders came to Him, and said to Him, " By what kind of authority do you do these things? Or, who gave you authority to do these things?" Jesus said, " I will put one point to you, and, if you answer me, I will tell you by what kind of authority I do these things. Was the baptism of John from heaven? or was it from men? Answer me!" They discussed the matter among themselves. " If," they said, " we say, ' From heaven,' He will say, ' Why did you not believe in it? ' But, are we to say, ' From men '? "—for they were afraid of the people, for all truly held that John was a prophet. So they answered Jesus, " We do not know." So Jesus said to them, " Neither do I tell you by what kind of authority I do these things."

IN the sacred precincts there were two famous cloisters, one on the east and one on the south side of the Court of the Gentiles. The one on the east was called Solomon's Porch. It was a magnificent arcade made by Corinthian columns 35 feet high. The one on the south was even more splendid. It was called the Royal Cloister. It was formed by four rows of white marble columns, each 6 feet in diameter and 30 feet high. There were 162 of them. It was common for Rabbis and teachers to stroll in these columns and to teach as they walked. Most of the great cities of ancient times had these cloisters and arcades. They gave shelter from the sun and the wind and the rain, and, in point of fact, it was in these places that most of the religious and philosophic teaching was done. One of the most famous schools of all ancient thought was that of the Stoics. They received their name from the fact that Zeno, their founder, taught as he walked in the *Stoa Poikilē*, *The Painted Porch*, in Athens. The word *stoa* means *porch* or *arcade* and the Stoics were the school of the porch. It was in these cloisters in the Temple that Jesus was walking and teaching.

To Him there came a deputation of the chief priests the experts in the law, that is the scribes and the rabbis, and the elders. This deputation was in reality a deputation from the Sanhedrin, for these three groups formed the component parts of the Sanhedrin. They asked a most natural question. For a private individual, all on his own, to clear the Court of the Gentiles of its accustomed and official traders was a staggering thing. So they asked Jesus, " By what kind of authority do you act like that?" They hoped to put Jesus into a dilemma. If He said He was acting under His own authority they might well arrest Him as a megalomaniac before He did any further damage. If He said that He was acting on the authority of God they might well arrest Him on an obvious charge of blasphemy, on the grounds that God would never give any man authority to create a disturbance in the courts of His own house. Jesus saw quite clearly the dilemma in which they sought to involve Him, and His reply was to put them into a dilemma which was still worse. He said that He would answer on condition that they would answer one question for Him. His question was, " Was John the Baptist's work, in your opinion, human or divine? " This impaled them on the horns of an insoluble dilemma. If they said that it was divine they knew that Jesus would ask why they had stood out against it. Worse than that—if they said it was divine, Jesus could reply that John had in fact pointed all men to Him, and that therefore He was divinely attested and needed no further authority. If these members of the Sanhedrin agreed that John's work was divine, they would be compelled to accept Jesus as the Messiah. On the other hand, if they said that John's work was merely human, now that John had the added distinction of being a martyr, they knew quite well that the listening people would cause a riot. And so they were compelled to say weakly that they did not know, and thereby Jesus escaped the need to give them any answer to their question.

The whole story is a vivid example of what happens to

men who will not face the truth. To avoid facing the truth they have to twist and wriggle and in the end get themselves into a position in which they are so helplessly involved that they have nothing to say. The man who faces the truth may have the humiliation of saying that he was wrong, or the peril of standing by the truth, but at least the future for him is strong and bright. The man who will not face the truth has nothing but the prospect of deeper and deeper involvement in a situation which renders him helpless and ineffective.

REJECTION AND RETRIBUTION

Mark 12 : 1-12

Jesus began to speak to them in parables. A man planted a vineyard. He put a hedge round about it, and dug a wine vat, and built a tower. He let it out to cultivators and went abroad. At the right time he sent a servant to the cultivators that he might receive from the cultivators his share of the fruits of the vineyard. They took him and beat him and sent him away empty-handed. Again he sent another servant to them. They wounded him in the head, and treated him shamefully. He sent yet another. They killed him. So they treated many others, beating some and killing others. He had still one person left to send, his beloved son. Last of all he sent him to them. " They will respect my son," he said. But these cultivators said to each other, " This is the heir. Come, let us kill him, and the inheritance will be ours." So they took him and killed him and threw him out of the vineyard. What, then will the owner of the vineyard do? He will come and he will destroy the cultivators and he will give the vineyard to others. Have you not read this passage of scripture, " The stone which the builders rejected, this has become the headstone of the corner. This came from God, and it is in our eyes an amazing thing? " They tried to find a way to get hold of Him, for they feared the crowd, for they were well aware that He spoke this parable against them. So they let Him alone and went away.

WHEN we were dealing with the general principles of the interpretation of parables we said that a parable must never be treated as an allegory, and that a meaning must not be sought for every detail. We reminded ourselves that originally Jesus' parables were not meant to be read but to be spoken and the meaning of them was the meaning which flashed out when first they were heard. But to some extent this parable is an exception. It is a kind of hybrid, a cross between an allegory and a parable. Not all the details in it have an inner meaning, but more than usual have. And this is possible because Jesus was talking in pictures which were part and parcel of Jewish thought and imagery.

The owner of the vineyard is God. The *vineyard* itself is the people of Israel. This was a picture with which the Jews were perfectly familiar. In the Old Testament it is vividly used in Isaiah 5 : 1-7, a passage from which some of the details and the language of this passage are taken. The vineyard was given every equipment. There was a wall to mark out its boundaries, to keep out robbers and to defend it from the assaults of the wild boars. There was a wine vat. In a vineyard there was a wine press in which the grapes were trodden down with the feet. Beneath the wine press there was a wine vat into which the pressed out juice flowed. There was a tower. In this the wine was stored, the cultivators had their lodging, and from this watch was kept for robbers at the harvest time. *The cultivators* stand for *the rulers of Israel* throughout the history of the nation. The *servants* whom the owner sent stand for the *prophets*. *Servant* or *slave* of God is a regular title. So Moses was called (Joshua 14 : 7). So Aaron was called (Joshua 24 : 9). So David was called (2 Samuel 3 : 18). And the title occurs regularly in the books of the prophets (Amos 3 : 7, Jeremiah 7 : 25, Zechariah 1 : 6). *The son* is *Jesus Himself*. Even on the spur of the moment the hearers could have made these identifications because the thoughts and the pictures were all so familiar to them.

The story itself is a story of what might well happen in Palestine in the time of Jesus. Palestine had much labour unrest and many absentee landlords. The owner of such a vineyard might be a Jew who had sought a more comfortable land than Palestine, or he might be a Roman who regarded the vineyard as an investment for his money. If the owner followed the law, the first time for collecting the rental would be five years after the planting of the vineyard (Leviticus 19 : 23-25). In such a case the rental was paid in kind. It might be a fixed and agreed percentage of the crop, or it might be a stated amount, irrespective of what the crop came to. The story is by no means improbable and tells of the kind of thing which did actually happen.

The parable is so full of truths that we can only note them in the briefest way.

It tells us certain things about God.

(i) It tells us of *the generosity* of God. The vineyard was equipped with everything that was necessary to make the work of the cultivators easy and profitable. God is generous in the life and in the world that He gives to men.

(ii) It tells us of *the trust* of God. The owner went away and left the cultivators to run the vineyard themselves. God trusts us enough to give us freedom to run life as we choose. As someone has said, " The lovely thing about God is that He allows us to do so much for ourselves."

(iii) It tells us of *the patience* of God. Not once or twice but many times, the master gave the cultivators the chance to pay the debt they owed. He treated them with a courtesy and a patience which they little deserved.

(iv) It tells us of the triumph of the ultimate *justice* of God. Men might take advantage of the patience of God, but in the end there comes judgment and justice. God may bear long with disobedience and rebellion but in the end He acts.

This parable tells us something about Jesus.

(i) It tells us that He regarded Himself *not as a servant but as a son*. He deliberately removes Himself from the succession of the prophets. They were servants. He was son. In Him God's last and final word was being spoken. This parable was a deliberate challenge to the Jewish authorities because it contains the unmistakable claim of Jesus to be Messiah.

(ii) It tells us that *He knew that He was to die.* The Cross did not come to Jesus as a surprise. He knew that the way He had chosen could have no other ending. It is the greatness of His courage that He knew that and went inflexibly on.

(iii) It tells us that *He was sure of His ultimate triumph and vindication.* He knew that He would be maltreated and killed, but He also knew that that was not the end, that after the rejection would come the glory.

This parable tells us something about man.

(i) There could only be one reason why the cultivators thought that they could kill the son and then enter into possession of the vineyard. They must have thought that the owner was too far away to act, or that he was dead and out of the reckoning. Men still think that they can act against God and get away with it. But God is very much alive. Men seek to trade on their own freedom and His patience, but the day of reckoning comes.

(ii) If a man refuses his privileges and his responsibilities these privileges and responsibilities pass on to someone else. The parable has in it the whole germ of what was to come—the rejection of the Jews and the passing of their privileges and responsibilities to the Gentiles.

The parable closes with an Old Testament quotation which became very dear to the Church. The quotation about the stone that was rejected is from Psalm 118 : 22, 23. The stone that was rejected had become the stone that bound the corners of the building together, the stone that was the keystone of the arch, the most important stone of all. This passage fascinated the early Christian writers. It is quoted or referred to in Acts 4 : 11, I Peter 2 : 4, 7, Romans 9 : 32, 33, Ephesians 2 : 20. Originally, in the

Psalm, the reference was to the people of Israel. The great nations which had thought of themselves as architects of the structure of the world had regarded the people of Israel as unimportant and unhonoured. But, as the Psalmist saw it, the nation which had been regarded as of no importance would, some day, in God's economy become the greatest nation in the world. The Christian writers saw in the Psalmist's dream something which was perfectly fulfilled in the Death and Resurrection of Jesus.

CAESAR AND GOD

Mark 12 : 13-17

> They sent to Jesus some of the Pharisees and Herodians to try to trap Him in His speech. They came to Him and said, " Teacher, we know that you are genuine, and that you do not allow yourself to be influenced by anyone, for you are no respecter of persons, and you teach the way of God in truth. Is it right to pay tax to Caesar? Or not? Are we to pay? Or, are we not to pay? " Jesus knew well that they were acting a part. " Why are you trying to test me? " He said. " Bring me a denarius and let me see it." So they brought Him one. He said to them, " Whose portrait is this, and whose inscription is on it? " " Caesar's," they said to Him. Jesus said to them, " Render to Caesar the things which belong to Caesar, and to God the things that belong to God." And they were completely astonished at Him.

THERE is history behind this shrewd question, and bitter history too. When Herod the Great died in 4 B.C. he had ruled all Palestine, as a Roman tributary king. He had been loyal to the Romans and they had respected him and given him a great deal of freedom. When he died he divided his kingdom into three. To Herod Antipas he gave Galilee and Peraea. To Herod Philip he gave the wild district up in the north-east round Trachonitis and Ituraea and Abilene. To Archelaus he gave the south country including Judaea and Samaria. Antipas and Philip soon settled in and on the whole ruled wisely and well. But Archelaus was a complete failure as a king. The result was that in A.D. 6 the Romans had to step in and take over directly. Things were so unsatisfactory that southern Palestine could no longer be left as a semi-independent tributary kingdom. It had to become a province. It was governed by a procurator. Roman provinces fell into two classes. Those which were peaceful and which required no troops were governed by the senate and were ruled by proconsuls. Those which were trouble-centres and which required troops were the direct sphere of the Emperor and were governed by procurators. Southern Palestine fell naturally into the second category and tribute was in fact paid direct to the Emperor.

The first act of the governor, Cyrenius, was to take a census of the country, in order that he might make proper provision for fair taxation and general administration. The calmer section of the people accepted this as an inevitable necessity. But one Judas the Gaulonite raised violent opposition. He thundered that " taxation was no better than an introduction to slavery." He called on the people to rise, and said that God would only favour them, if they resorted to all the violence they could muster. He took the high ground that for the Jews God was the only Ruler and Lord. Rather than call any man Lord they would gladly die. The Romans dealt with Judas with their customary efficiency, but the battle-cry of Judas never died out. " No tribute to the Romans," became a rallying cry of the more fanatical Jewish patriots.

The actual taxes which were imposed were three.

(i) A ground tax, which consisted of one-tenth of all the grain and one-fifth of the wine and fruit produced. This was paid partly in kind and partly in money.

(ii) An income tax which amounted to one per cent. of a man's income.

(iii) A poll tax, which was levied on all men from fourteen to sixty-five and on all women from twelve to sixty-five. This poll tax was one *denarius*, roughly one shilling per head. It was the tax which hit everyone, and which everyone had to pay simply for the privilege of existing.

The approach of the Pharisees and Herodians was very subtle. They began with flattery. That flattery was designed to do two things. It was designed to disarm the suspicions that Jesus might have had. And when it stressed His courage and His honesty it was designed to make it impossible for Him to avoid giving an answer, without losing His reputation completely.

In view of all the circumstances the question which the Pharisees and Herodians put to Jesus was a masterpiece of shrewdness and cunning. They must have thought that they had Him impaled on the horns of a completely inescapable dilemma. If He said that it was lawful to pay tribute His influence with the populace would be gone forever, and He would be regarded as a traitor and a coward. If He said that it was not lawful to pay tribute then they could report Him to the Romans and have Him arrested as a revolutionary. They must have been sure that they had Jesus in a trap from which there was no escape.

Jesus said, " Show me a *denarius*." We may note in the passing that He Himself did not possess even one shilling piece. He asked whose image was on it. The image would be that of Tiberius, the reigning Emperor. All the Emperors were called Caesar. Round the coin there would be the title which declared that this was the coin " of Tiberius Caesar, the divine Augustus, son of Augustus," and on the reverse there would be the title " pontifex maximus," " the high priest of the Roman nation." Now we must understand the ancient view of coinage or this whole incident is not intelligible. In regard to coinage the ancient peoples held three consistent principles.

(i) Coinage is the sign of power. When anyone conquered a nation, or, if anyone was a successful rebel, the first thing he did was to issue his own coinage. That and that alone was the final guarantee of kingship and power.

(ii) Where the coin was valid the king's power held good. A king's sway was held to be measurable by the area in which his coins were valid currency.

(iii) Because a coin had the king's head and inscription on it, it was held, at least in some sense, to be the property of the king, and to be his personal property. Jesus' answer therefore was this, " By using the coinage of Tiberius you in any event recognize his political power in Palestine. Apart altogether from that, the coinage is his own anyway because it has his name on it. By giving it to him you give him what is in any event his own. Give it to him but remember that there is a sphere in life which belongs to God and not to Caesar."

Never did any man lay down a more influential principle than this. It was a principle which conserved at one and the same time the civil and the religious power. Rawlinson reminds us that Lord Acton, the great historian, said of this saying of Jesus, " Those words . . . gave to the civil power, under the protection of conscience, a sacredness it had never enjoyed and bounds it had never acknowledged, and they were the repudiation of absolutism and the inauguration of freedom." At one and the same time these words asserted the rights of the state and the liberty of conscience.

On the whole the New Testament lays down three great principles with regard to the individual Christian and the state.

(i) The state is ordained by God. Without the laws of the state life would be a chaos. Men cannot live together unless they agree to obey the laws of living together. Without the state there is many a valuable service no man could enjoy. No individual man could have his own water supply, his own sewage system, his own transport system, his own social security organisation. The state is the origin of many of the things which make life livable.

(ii) No man can accept all the benefits which the state gives him and then opt out of all the responsibilities. It is beyond question that the Roman government brought to the ancient world a sense of security it never had before. For the most part, except in certain notorious areas, the seas were cleared of pirates and the roads of brigands, civil wars were changed for peace and unpredictable and capricious tyranny for Roman impartial justice. As E. J. Goodspeed wrote, " It was the glory of the Roman Empire that it brought peace to a troubled world. Under its sway the regions of Asia Minor and the East enjoyed tranquillity and security to an extent and for a length of time unknown before and probably since. This was the *pax Romana*. The provincial, under Roman sway, found himself in a position to conduct his business, provide for his family, send his letters, and make his journeys in security, thanks to the strong hand of Rome." It is still true that no man can honourably receive all the benefits which living in a state confer upon him and then opt out of all the responsibilities of citizenship.

(iii) But there is a limit. E. A. Abbott has a suggestive thought. The coin had Caesar's *image* upon it, and therefore belonged to Caesar. Man has God's *image* upon him— God created man in His own image (Genesis I : 26, 27)— and therefore belongs to God. The inevitable conclusion is that, if the state remains within its proper boundaries and makes its proper demands, then the individual must give to it his loyalty and his service, but in the last analysis both state and man belong to God, and therefore, should the claims of state and God conflict, loyalty to God comes first. But it remains true, that, in all ordinary circumstances, a man's Christianity should make him a better citizen than any other man.

THE WRONG IDEA OF THE LIFE TO COME

Mark 12 : 18-27

There came to Jesus Sadducees, who are a party who say that the resurrection of the dead does not exist. They put the following problem to Him. " Teacher," they said, " Moses wrote the law for us, that, if a man's brother dies and leaves behind him a wife, and does not leave a family, the law is that the brother should take his wife, and should raise up a family to his brother. There were seven brothers. The first took a wife, and died, and left no family. The second took her, and he died, and left behind no family. The third did the same. The seven left no family. Last of all, the woman died. At the resurrection whose wife will she be? For the seven had her as wife." Jesus said to them, "Are you not in error and for this reason—because you do not know the scriptures, nor do you know the power of God? When people rise from the dead, they neither marry, nor are they given in marriage, but they are like the angels in heaven. With regard to the dead, and the fact that they do rise, have you not read in the Book of Moses, in the passage about The Bush, how God said to him, ' I am the God of Abraham, and the God of Isaac, and the God of Jacob.' God is not the God of the dead, but the God of the living. You are far wrong."

THIS is the only time in Mark's gospel when the Sadducees appear, and their appearance is entirely characteristic of them. The Sadducees were not a large Jewish party. They were aristocratic and wealthy. They included most of the priests. The office of high priest was regularly held by a Sadducee. Being the wealthy and aristocratic party, they were not unnaturally collaborationist, for they wished to retain their comforts and their privileges. It was from them that the governing classes came, those who were prepared to collaborate with the Romans in the government of the country. They differed very widely from the Pharisees in certain matters. First, the Sadducees accepted only the written scriptures and they attached more importance to the Pentateuch, the first five books of the Old Testament, than to all the rest. They did not accept the mass of oral law and tradition, the rules and regulations which were so dear to the Pharisees. It was on the written Mosaic Law that they took their stand. Second, the Sadducees did not believe in immortality, nor in spirits and angels. They said that in the early books of the Bible there was no evidence for immortality, and they did not accept it.

So the Sadducees came to Jesus with a test question, a question which was designed to make the whole belief in the individual resurrection look ridiculous. The Jewish Law had an institution called Levirate Marriage. Its regulations are laid down in Deuteronomy 25 : 5-10. If a group of brothers lived together—that is a point that is omitted in the Sadducees' quotation of the law—and if one of them died and left no issue, it was the duty of the next to take his brother's widow as wife and to raise up issue to his brother. Theoretically this would go on so long as there were brothers left and so long as no child was born. When a child was born, the child was held to be the offspring of the *original* husband. Now it is clear that the whole point of this law was to ensure two things—first, that the family name continued, and second, that the family property remained within the family. As a matter of fact, strange as the whole matter seems to us, there were certain not unsimilar regulations in Greek law. If a Greek father had a considerable estate and had only a daughter, the daughter, being a woman, could not inherit direct. Either her husband or her son would be the direct heir. But if the daughter was unmarried the father could leave his property *and his daughter* to anyone he chose. Such a person, in order to inherit the property, had to marry the heiress, even if he had to divorce an already existing wife to do so. And, if in such circumstances, a father died without making a will, the nearest relation could claim the heiress daughter as his wife. It is the same principle again. The whole thing is designed to maintain the family and to retain the property within the family to which it belonged.

The question that the Sadducees asked, therefore, may have presented an exaggerated case, with the story of the *seven* brothers, but it was a question founded on a well-known Jewish law.

The questions of the Sadducees was simply this—if, in accordance with the regulations governing Levirate Marriage, one woman has been married in turn to seven brothers, if there is a resurrection of the dead, whose wife is she when that resurrection comes? The Sadducees thought that by asking that question they had rendered the whole idea of a resurrection completely ridiculous.

Jesus' answer really falls into two parts.

First, He deals with what we might call *the manner* of the resurrection. He lays it down that when the resurrection comes and a person rises again, the old laws of physical life no longer obtain, that the risen are like the angels, and that physical things like marrying and being married no longer enter into the case. In point of fact, Jesus was saying nothing new. In Enoch the promise is, " Ye shall have great joy as the angels of heaven." In the Apocalypse of Baruch it is said that the righteous shall be made " like unto the angels." And the rabbinic writings themselves said that in the life to come " there is no eating and drinking, no begetting of children, no bargaining, jealousy, hatred and strife, but that the righteous sit with crowns on their heads, and are satisfied with the glory of God." It is Jesus' point that the life to come cannot be thought of in terms of this life at all.

Second, He deals with *the fact* of the resurrection. Here He meets the Sadducees on their own ground. They insisted that in the Pentateuch, by which they set so much store, there was no evidence for immortality. From the Pentateuch Jesus draws His proof. In Exodus 3 : 6, God calls Himself the God of Abraham, the God of Isaac and the God of Jacob. If God is the God of these patriarchs even yet it means that they must still be alive, for the living God must be the God of living people, and not of those who are extinguished and dead. And if the patriarchs are alive then the resurrection is proved. On their own grounds, and with an argument to which they could find no answer, Jesus had defeated the Sadducees.

This passage may seem to deal with a matter which is very recondite and remote. It is an argument on terms which are quite out of the orbit of our experience. But in spite of that two eternally valid truths emerge.

(i) The Sadducees had made the mistake of creating heaven in the image of earth. They thought of heaven in terms of the things of this earth. Men have always done so. The Red Indians, who were by nature hunters, conceived of a heaven which was a happy hunting ground. The Vikings, who were by nature warriors, thought of a Valhalla where they would fight all day, where at night the dead would be raised and the wounded made whole again, and where they would spend the evening in banquets, drinking wine from cups made from the skulls of their conquered foes. The Mohammedans were a desert people living in circumstances where luxury was unknown. They therefore conceived of heaven as a place where men would live a life which was replete with every sensual and bodily pleasure. The Jews hated the sea and thought of heaven as a place where there would be no more sea. All men shrink from sorrow and from pain, and heaven would be a place where the tears are wiped from every eye and where there would be no more pain. Always men create in thought a heaven to suit themselves. Sometimes that idea can be even poignantly beautiful. During the 1914-18 War *The Westminster Gazette* printed a lovely little poem about those who had died in war for their country :

" They left the fury of the fight,
    And they were tired.
The gates of heaven were open quite,
    Unguarded and unwired.
There was no sound of any gun,
    The land was still and green,
Wide hills lay silent in the sun,
    Blue valleys slept between.

> " They saw far off a little wood
>   Stand up against the sky.
>   Knee deep in grass a great tree stood,
>   Some lazy cows went by.
>   There were some rooks sailed overhead,
>   And once a church bell pealed.
>   ' God, but it's England ! ' someone said,
>   'And there's a cricket field '."

There is a wistful beauty there, and there is real truth. But we will do well to remember that Paul was right (I Corinthians 2 : 9) when he took the words of the prophet (Isaiah 64 : 4) and made them his own, " Eye hath not seen, nor ear heard, neither have entered into the heart of man, the things which God hath prepared for them that love Him." The life of the heavenly places will be greater than any conception that this life can supply.

(ii) In the end Jesus based his conviction of the resurrection on the fact that the relationship between God and a good man is a relationship that nothing can break. Once a man has entered into a personal relationship with the eternal God that relationship is eternal. God was the friend of Abraham, Isaac and Jacob when they lived. That friendship cannot cease with death. " God," as Loisy said, " cannot cease to be the God of those who served Him and loved Him." As the Psalmist said, " I am continually with Thee. Thou hast holden me by my right hand. Thou shalt guide me with Thy countenance and afterward receive me into glory." (Psalm 73 : 23, 24.) He cannot conceive of his relationship with God ever being broken. In a word, there is only one immortal thing—and that is love.

LOVE FOR GOD AND LOVE FOR MEN

Mark 12 : 28-34

One of the experts in the law, who had listened to the discussion, and who realized that Jesus had answered them well, approached Him and asked Him, " What is the first commandment of all? " Jesus answered,

" ' The Lord Thy God is one Lord, and you must love the Lord your God with your whole heart, and your whole soul, and your whole mind, and your whole strength.' This is the second, ' You must love your neighbour as yourself.' There is no other commandment which is greater than these." The expert in the law said to Him, " Teacher, you have in truth spoken well, because God is one, and there is no other except Him, and to love Him with your whole heart, and your whole understanding, and your whole strength, and to love your neighbour as yourself is better than all burnt-offerings of whole victims and sacrifices." When Jesus saw that he had answered wisely, He said to him, " You are not far from the Kingdom of God." And no one any longer dared to ask Him any questions.

THERE would be no love lost between the expert in the law and the Sadducees. The whole profession of the scribes was to interpret the law and to be an expert in all its many rules and regulations. The trade of the expert in the law was to know and to apply the oral law, while, as we have seen, the Sadducee did not accept the oral law at all. The expert in the law would no doubt be well satisfied with the discomfiture of the Sadducees.

This scribe came to Jesus with a question which was often a matter of debate in the rabbinic schools. In Judaism there was a kind of double tendency. There was the tendency to expand the law limitlessly into hundreds and thousands of rules and regulations. But there was also a tendency to try to gather up the law into one sentence, one general statement which would be a compendium of its whole message. Hillel was once asked by a proselyte to instruct him in the whole law while he stood on one leg. Hillel's answer was, " What thou hatest for thyself, do not to thy neighbour. This is the whole law, the rest is commentary. Go and learn." Akiba had already said, " ' Thou shalt love thy neighbour as thyself '—this is the greatest, general principle in the law." Simon the Righteous had said, " On three things stands the world—on the law, on the worship, and on works of love."

Sammlai had taught that Moses received 613 precepts on Mount Sinai, 355 according to the days of the sun year, and 248 according to the generations of men. David came and reduced the 613 to 11 in Psalm 15.

> Lord, who shall abide in Thy tabernacle,
> who shall dwell in Thy holy hill?

1. He that walketh uprightly.
2. And worketh righteousness.
3. And speaketh truth in his heart.
4. He that backbiteth not with his tongue.
5. Nor doeth evil to his neighbour.
6. Nor taketh up a reproach against his neighbour.
7. In whose eyes a vile person is condemned.
8. But he honoureth them that fear the Lord.
9. He that sweareth to his own hurt and changeth not.
10. He that putteth not out his money to usury.
11. Nor taketh reward against the innocent.

Isaiah came and reduced them all to 6. (Isaiah 33 : 15.)

1. He that walketh righteously.
2. And walketh uprightly.
3. He that despiseth the gain of oppressions.
4. That shaketh his hand from holding bribes.
5. That stoppeth his ears from hearing blood.
6. And shutteth his eyes from seeing evil.

> He shall dwell on high.

Micah came and reduced the 6 to 3. (Micah 6 : 8.)

> He hath showed thee, O man, what is good, and what doth the Lord require of thee?

1. To do justly.
2. To love mercy.
3. To walk humbly before thy God.

Once again Isaiah brought the 3 down to 2. (Isaiah 66 : 1.)

1. Keep ye judgment.
2. And do justice.

And finally Habbakuk reduced them all to one. (Habbakuk 2: 4.)

> The just shall live by faith.

It can be seen that rabbinic ingenuity did try to contract as well as to expand the law. There were really two schools of thought. There were those who did believe that there were lighter and weightier matters of the law, that there were great principles which were all important to grasp. As Augustine later said, " Love God—and do what you like." But there were others who were much against this, who held that every smallest principle was equally binding, and to try to distinguish between their relative importances was highly dangerous. The expert who asked Jesus this question was asking Jesus about something which was a very living issue in Jewish thought and discussion.

For answer Jesus took two great commandments and put them together.

(i) " Hear, O Israel, the Lord Thy God is one Lord." That single sentence is the real creed of Judaism (Deuteronomy 6 : 4). It had three uses. It is called *The Shema*. *Shema* is the imperative of the Hebrew verb *to hear*, and it is so called from the first word in it. (*a*) It was the sentence with which the service of the synagogue always began and still begins. The full Shema is Deuteronomy 6 : 4-9, 11 : 13-21, Numbers 15 : 37-41. It is the declaration that God is the only God and there is no other, the foundation of Jewish monotheism. (*b*) The three passages of the Shema were contained in the *phylacteries* (Matthew 23 : 5), which were little leather boxes which the devout Jew wore on his forehead and on his wrist when he was at prayer. As he prayed he reminded himself of his creed. His warrant for wearing *phylacteries* he found in Deuteronomy 6 : 8. (*c*) The Shema was contained in a little cylindrical box called the *Mezuzah* which was and still is affixed to the door of every Jewish house and the door of every room within it, to remind the Jew of God in his going out and his coming in. When Jesus quoted this sentence as the first commandment, every devout Jew would agree with Him.

(ii) " Thou shalt love thy neighbour as thyself." That
is a quotation from Leviticus 19 : 18. Jesus did one thing
with it. In its original context it has to do with a man's
fellow Jew. It would not have included the Gentile, whom
it was quite permissible to hate. But Jesus quoted it
without qualification and without limiting boundaries. He
took an old law and filled it with a new meaning.

The new thing that Jesus did was to put these two
commandments together. No rabbi had ever done that
before. There is only one suggestion of connection before.
Round about 100 B.C. there was composed a series of
tractates called *The Testaments of the Twelve Patriarchs*,
in which some unknown writer put into the mouths of the
patriarchs very fine teaching. In The Testament of
Issachar (5 : 2) we read :

> " Love the Lord and love your neighbour,
> Have compassion on the poor and weak."

In the same testament (7 : 6) we read :
> " I loved the Lord,
> Likewise also every man with my whole heart."

In *The Testament of Dan* (5 : 3) we read :
> " Love the Lord through all your life,
> And one another with a true heart."

But no one until Jesus came took and put the two commandments together and made them one. Religion to
Jesus was loving God and loving men. He would have said
that the only way in which a man can prove that he loves
God is by showing that he loves men.

The scribe willingly accepted this, and went on to say
that such a love was better than all sacrifices. In that he
was in line with the highest thought of his people. Long,
long ago Samuel had said, " Hath the Lord as great delight
in burnt-offerings and sacrifices, as in obeying the voice
of the Lord? Behold, to obey is better than sacrifice, and
to hearken than the fat of rams." (I Samuel 15 : 22.)
Hosea had heard God say, " I desired mercy and not
sacrifice." (Hosea 6 : 6.) But it is always easy to let

ritual take the place of charity. It is always easy to let
worship become a thing of the Church building instead of a
thing of the whole life. The priest and the levite could
pass by the wounded traveller because they were eager to
get on with the ritual of the temple. This scribe had risen
beyond his contemporaries and that is why he found himself in sympathy with Jesus.

There must have been a look of love in Jesus' eyes, and
a look of appeal, as He said to him, " You have gone so far.
Will you not come the whole way, and accept my way of
things, and then you will be a true citizen of the Kingdom?"

THE SON OF DAVID

Mark 12 : 35-37a

> While Jesus was teaching in the sacred precincts, He
> said, " How can the experts in the law say that God's
> Anointed One is the Son of David? David himself,
> moved by the Holy Spirit, said, ' The Lord said to
> my Lord, Sit at my right hand until I make your
> enemies a footstool for your feet.' David himself calls
> Him Lord. And how then can He be his son?"

FOR us this a difficult passage to understand, because it
uses thoughts and methods of argument which are strange
to us. But it would not be at all difficult for the crowd who
heard it in the Temple precincts in Jerusalem, for they
were well accustomed to just such ways of arguing and of
using scripture.

We may begin by noting one thing which helps to make
the passage clearer. The Authorised Version translates
verse 35, " How say the scribes that Christ is the Son of
David." In the early parts of the New Testament Christ
is never a proper name, as nowadays it has come to be.
It has in fact in this passage the definite article before it and
should be translated *The Christ. Christos* is the Greek for
anointed, and *Messiah* is the Hebrew for *anointed*. *Christos*
and *Messiah* are in fact the Greek and the Hebrew for the

same word, and both mean *The Anointed One*. The reason
for the use of the title is that in ancient times a man was
made king by being anointed with oil, which is still a part
of our own coronation ceremony. *Christos* and *Messiah*
then both mean *God's Anointed King*, the great one who is
to come from God to save His people. So when Jesus asks,
" How say the scribes that Christ is the Son of David?"
He is not directly referring to Himself. He is posing the
questions, " How can the scribes say that God's Anointed
King who is to come is the Son of David."

The argument which Jesus puts forward to support His
question is this. He quotes Psalm 110 : 1—" The Lord
said to my Lord sit thou at my right hand." The Jews at
this time assumed that all the Psalms came from the hand
of David. They therefore believed that this Psalm was
composed by David. They also held that this Psalm
referred to the coming Messiah, the coming Anointed One
of God. Now in this verse David refers to this coming one
as *his Lord*. How, asks Jesus, if He be his son can David
address him by the title of Lord?

What is Jesus seeking to teach here? Of all titles for the
coming Messiah the commonest was Son of David. At all
times the Jews looked forward to a God-sent deliverer who
would be of David's line. (Isaiah 9 : 2-7, 11 : 1-9,
Jeremiah 23 : 5 ff, 33 : 14-18, Ezekiel 34 : 23 ff, 37 : 24,
Psalm 89 : 20 ff.) It was by that title that Jesus Himself
was often addressed, especially by the crowds (Mark 10: 47ff,
Matthew 9 : 27, 12 : 23, 15 : 22, 21 : 9, 15). All through
the New Testament the conviction that Jesus was in fact
the Son of David, in His physical descent, occur
(Romans 1 : 3, 2 Timothy 2 : 8, Matthew 1 : 1-17,
Luke 3 : 23-38). The genealogies of Jesus which are given
in the passages from Matthew and Luke which we have
cited are to show that Jesus was in fact of the lineage of
David. What Jesus is doing is this—He is not denying
that the Messiah is the Son of David, nor is He saying that
He is not the Son of David. What He is saying is that

He is the Son of David—*and far more*. The Coming One was not only David's son—*He was David's Lord*.

The trouble was that the title Son of David had got itself inextricably entangled with the idea of a conquering Messiah. It had got involved in political and nationalistic hopes and dreams, and aims and ambitions. It was used for the hoped for founder of an earthly kingdom. What Jesus is doing is that He is saying that the title *Son of David*, as it was popularly used, is a quite inadequate description of Himself. He was *Lord*. Now this word *Lord* (in the Greek *kurios*) is the regular translation of Jahweh (Jehovah) in the Greek version of the Hebrew scriptures. Always its use would turn men's thoughts to God. What Jesus is saying is that He came not to found any earthly kingdom. He came *to bring men God*.

Jesus is doing here what He so constantly tried to do. He is trying to take from men's minds their idea of a conquering warrior Messiah who would found an earthly Empire, and seeking to put into them the idea of a Messiah who would be the servant of God, and who would bring to men the love of God.

THE WRONG KIND OF RELIGION

Mark 12 : 37b-40

> The mass of the people listened to Him with pleasure. And in His teaching He said, " Beware of the experts in the law, who like to walk about in flowing robes, and who like greetings in the market-places, and the front seats in the synagogue, and the places of highest honour at meals, men who devour widows' houses, and who, in pretence, pray at great length. These will receive a more abundant condemnation."

THE first sentence of this passage most probably goes with this section and not, as in the Authorised Version, with the passage which goes before. The verse divisions of the New Testament were first inserted by Stephanus in the sixteenth century. It was said that he put them in while riding from his house to his printing factory. They are by no means always where the most suitable divisions, and this seems to be one where the divisions ought to be changed. It is far more likely that the mass of the people listened with pleasure to a denunciation of the scribes than they did to a theological argument. There are certain minds to whom invective is always attractive.

In this passage Jesus makes a series of charges against the scribes. They like to walk about in flowing robes. In the East a long robe which swept the ground was the sign of a notable. It was the kind of robe in which no one could either hurry or work, and was the sign of the leisured man of honour. It may be that the phrase has another meaning. Matthew 23 : 5 says that " they loved to enlarge the borders of their garments." In obedience to Numbers 15 : 38 the Jews wore tassels at the edge of their outer robe. These tassels were to remind them that they were the people of God. Quite possibly these legal experts wore outsize tassels for special prominence. At all events they liked to dress in such a way that it drew attention to themselves and to the honour they enjoyed.

They liked greetings in the market-place. The scribes loved to be greeted with honour and with respect. The very title *Rabbi* means " My great one." To be so addressed was agreeable to their vanity.

They liked the front seats in the synagogue. In the synagogue, in front of the ark where the sacred volumes were kept, and facing the congregation, there was a bench where the specially distinguished sat. It had the advantage that no one who sat there could possibly be missed. It was in full view of the admiring congregation.

They liked the highest places at feasts. At feasts precedence was strictly fixed. The first place was that on the right of the host, the second that on the left of the host, and so on, alternating right and left, round the table. It was easy to tell the honour in which a man was held by the place at which he sat.

They devoured widows' houses. This is a savage charge. Josephus, who was himself a Pharisee, says of certain times of intrigue in Jewish history, that " the Pharisees valued themselves highly upon their exact skill in the law of their fathers, and made men believe that they (the Pharisees) were highly favoured by God," and that " they inveigled " certain women into their schemes and plottings. The idea behind this seems to be this. An expert in the law could take no pay for his teaching. He had to teach for nothing. He was supposed to have a trade by which, with his hands, he earned his daily bread. But these legal experts had managed to convey to people that there was no higher duty and privilege than to support a rabbi in comfort, that, in fact such a support would undoubtedly entitle him or her who gave it to a high place in the heavenly academy. In religious matters it is a sad fact that women have always been imposed upon by religious charlatans, and it would seem that these scribes and Pharisees imposed on simple people who could ill afford to support them. They would never lack for dupes.

The long prayers of the Scribes and Pharisees were notorious. It has been said that the prayers were not so much offered to God as they were offered to men. They were offered in such a place and in such a way that no one could fail to see how pious they were.

This passage, as stern a passage as Jesus ever spoke, warns against three things.

(i) It warns against the desire for prominence. It is still true that many a man accepts an office in the Church because he thinks that he has earned and deserved it, rather than because he desires to render still more selfless service to the house and the people of God. Men still regard office in the Church as a privilege and not as a responsibility.

(ii) It warns against the desire for deference. Almost

everyone likes to be treated with respect. And yet the basic fact of Christianity is that it ought to make a man wish to obliterate self rather than to exalt self. There is a story of a monk in the old days, a very holy man, who was sent to take up office as abbot in a monastery. He looked so humble a person that, when he arrived, he was sent to work in the kitchen as a scullion, because no one recognized him. Without a word of protest, and with no attempt to take his position, he went and washed the dishes and did the most menial tasks. And it was only when the bishop arrived a considerable time later that the mistake was discovered and that the humble monk took up his true position. The man who enters upon office for the respect which will be given to him has begun in the wrong way, and cannot, unless he changes, ever be in any sense *the servant* of Christ and of his fellow-men.

(iii) It warns against the attempt to make a traffic of religion. It is still possible to use religious connections for self-gain and self-advancement. But this is a warning to all who are in the Church for what they can get out of it, and not for what they can put into it.

THE GREATEST GIFT

Mark 12 : 41-44

> When Jesus had sat down opposite the treasury, He was watching how the crowd threw their money into the treasury, and many rich people threw in large sums. A poor widow woman came and threw in two mites which make up half a farthing. He called His disciples and said to them, " This is the truth I tell you—this poor widow woman has thrown in more than all the people who threw money into the treasury, for all of them threw their contributions in out of their abundance, but she out of her lack has thrown in everything that she had, all she had to live on."

BETWEEN the Court of the Gentiles and the Court of the Women there was the Gate Beautiful. It may well be that

Jesus had gone to sit quietly there after the argument and the tension of the Court of the Gentiles and the discussions in the cloisters. In the Court of the Women there were thirteen collecting boxes called " The Trumpets," because they were so shaped. Each of them was for a special purpose, for instance to buy corn or wine or oil for the sacrifices. They were for contributions for the daily sacrifices and expenses of the Temple. Many people threw in quite considerable contributions. Then there came a widow. She flung in two mites. The coin so called was a *lepton,* which literally means *a thin one.* It was the smallest of all coins and was worth one sixteenth of a penny. And yet Jesus said that that tiny contributions was greater than all the others, for the others had thrown in what they could spare easily enough, and still have plenty left, while the widow had flung in everything that she had.

Here is a lesson in giving :

(i) Giving to be real giving must be sacrificial. It is never the amount of the gift that matters, but the cost of the gift to the giver. It is not the size, but the sacrifice of the gift. Real generosity gives until it hurts. For many of us it is a real question if ever our giving to God's work was any sacrifice at all. There are few people who will do without their pleasures to give a little more to the work of God. It may well be a sign of the decadence of the Church and the failure of our Christianity that gifts have to be coaxed out of Church people, and that often they will not give at all unless they get something for their money in the way of entertainment or of goods. There can be few of us who can read this story without shame.

(ii) Giving which is real giving has a certain recklessness in it. The woman might have kept one coin. It would not have been much but it would have been something, but she gave everything she had. There is a great symbolic truth here. It is our tragedy that there is so often some part of our lives, some part of our activities, some part of ourselves which we do not give to Christ. Somehow there is always something which we hold back. We rarely make the final sacrifice and the final surrender.

(iii) It is a strange and a lovely thing that the person whom the New Testament and Jesus hand down to history as a pattern of generosity was a person who gave a gift of half a farthing. We may feel that we have not much in the way of material gifts or personal gifts to give to Christ, but if we put all that we have and are at His disposal He can do things with it and with us that are beyond our imaginings.

THE THINGS TO COME

MARK 13 is one of the most difficult chapters in the New Testament for a modern reader to understand. That is so because Mark 13 is one of the most Jewish chapters in the Bible. From beginning to end it is thinking in terms of Jewish history and Jewish ideas. All through it Jesus is using terms and pictures which were very familiar to the Jews of His day, but which are very strange, and indeed, unknown, to many modern readers. Even so, it is not possible to disregard this chapter and simply to slip over it, because this chapter is the source of many ideas about the Second Coming of Jesus. The difficulty about the Doctrine of the Second Coming is that nowadays people are apt either completely to disregard it, and never even to think about it, or they are apt to become so completely unbalanced about it that it becomes for them practically the only doctrine of the Christian faith. It may be that if we study this chapter with some care we may come to a wise and sane and correct view about this doctrine.

We shall first of all glance at the Jewish background against which this chapter must be read. We shall then try to make an analysis of the various elements which go to make it up. We will then study it section by section in the usual way. And, finally, we shall try to extract from it the great truths which are permanently valid and which must always be remembered.

The Day of the Lord

This whole chapter must be read with one thing in mind. Again and again we have to return to this matter because there is so much of the New Testament which is not intelligible without it. The Jews never doubted that they were the Chosen People, and they never doubted that one day they would occupy the place in the world which the Chosen People, as they saw it, deserved and were bound to have in the end. They had long since abandoned the idea that they could ever win that place by human means, and they were confident that in the end God would directly intervene in history and win it for them. The day of God's intervention was *The Day of the Lord*. Before that Day of the Lord there would be a time of terror and trouble. It itself would be a shattering time when the world would be shaken to its foundations, and when judgment would come. But it would be followed by the new world and the new age and the new glory. In one sense this idea is the product of unconquerable *optimism*. The Jew was quite certain that God would break in. In another sense it was the product of bleak *pessimism*, because it was based on the idea that this world was utterly bad and only its complete destruction and the emergence of a new world would suffice. They did not look for reformation. They looked for a complete remoulding and re-creating of the entire scheme of things.

Let us look at some of the Old Testament passages about the Day of the Lord. Amos writes (5 : 16-20) :

" Wailing shall be in all the broad ways, and they shall say in all the streets, Alas ! Alas ! and they shall call the husbandman to mourning, and such as are skilful of lamentation to wailing. And in all the vineyards shall be wailing, for I will pass through the midst of thee saith the Lord. Woe unto you that desire the Day of the Lord ! Wherefore would ye have the Day of the Lord? It is darkness and not light . . . even very dark and no brightness in it."

Isaiah (13 : 6-16) has a terrible passage about the Day of
the Lord :

> " Howl ye ! for the Day of the Lord is at hand. As
> destruction from the Almighty shall it come. . . .
> Behold the Day of the Lord cometh, cruel with
> wrath and fierce anger, to make the land a desola-
> tion, and to destroy the sinners thereof out of it.
> For the stars of heaven and the constellations thereof
> shall not give their light. The sun shall be darkened
> in his going forth, and the moon shall not cause her
> light to shine. . . . Therefore I will make the heavens
> to tremble, and the earth shall be shaken out of her
> place, in the wrath of the Lord of Hosts, and in the
> Day of His fierce anger. . . . "

The second and third chapters of Joel are full of terrible
descriptions of the Day of the Lord :

> " The Day of the Lord cometh . . . a day of darkness and
> gloominess, a day of clouds and thick darkness. . . .
> I will show wonders in the heaven and in the earth,
> blood and fire, and pillars of smoke. The sun shall be
> turned into darkness and the moon into blood,
> before the great and terrible Day of the Lord come."

Again and again such passages of terror meet us in the Old
Testament. The Day of the Lord will be sudden, shattering,
terrifying. The world will reel with the destruction of it.
The very course of nature will be uprooted, and God, the
judge, will come.

Between the Old and the New Testaments there was a
time when the Jews knew no freedom. It was therefore
only natural that their hopes and dreams of the Day of the
Lord would become even more vivid. In that time a kind
of popular religious literature grew up. Jesus would know
it. All the Jews would be familiar with its picture. The
writings of which this literature consisted are called
Apocalypses. *Apokalupsis* means *an unveiling*. These books
are dreams and visions of what will happen when the Day
of the Lord comes and in the terrible time immediately
before it. They continue to use the Old Testament imagery,

and to supplement it with new details. But, it must be noted, that all these books are dreams and visions. They are attempts to paint the unpaintable and to speak the unspeakable. They are poetry, not prose. They are visions, not science. They are dreams, not history. They were never meant to be taken prosaically as maps of the future and timetables of events to come.

We will see that every single detail in this chapter can be parallelled in the visions of the Old Testament and of the literature between the Testaments. All through this chapter Jesus was taking the language, the imagery, the apparatus of apocalyptic literature, and using it to try to make people understand. He was working with the only ideas that people knew. But He knew, and they knew, that these things were only pictures, for no man knew what God would do when God broke in.

The different Strands

Further we must note this. In this chapter there are various strands of thought. The gospel writers had a way of collecting Jesus' sayings on any subject. It was a wise way to write, and excellent for teaching purposes. Here Mark, as it were, collects, *Jesus' sayings about the future.* Now even a cursory reading, with no special knowledge, shows that, though all these sayings were about the future, they were not all about the same things. There are in fact in this chapter *five* different strands.

(i) *There are prophecies of the destruction of Jerusalem.* We get them in verses 1 and 2, 14-20. Jesus foresaw the end of the holy city. As we shall see, Jesus was right. Jerusalem fell in A.D. 70. The Temple was destroyed, and the most terrible things happened, as Jesus foresaw.

(ii) *There is warning of persecution to come.* We get that in verses 9-13. Jesus foresaw that His followers would have to go through the most heart-breaking and soul-searing experiences, and He warned them in advance.

(iii) *There are warnings of the dangers of the last days.* We get them in verses 3 to 6 and 21 and 22. Jesus saw quite clearly that men would come who would twist and adulterate the Christian faith. It was bound to be so, for men listen always to their own proud minds rather than to the voice of God. He wished to defend His own people in advance from the heresies and the lies which would invade the Church.

(iv) *There are warnings of the Second Coming.* Now, here is the important point—these warnings of the Second Coming are dressed in the language which has to do with the Day of the Lord. We get them in verses 7 and 8 and 24 to 27. The imagery of the Day of the Lord and of the Second Coming are inextricably mixed up. It had to be so, because no man could possibly literally know what would happen in either case. It is visions and dreams in which we have to deal. The only pictures which Jesus could use about His own Second Coming were the pictures which prophets and apocalyptists had already used about the Day of the Lord. Here again is the warning. These are not meant to be taken literally. They are meant as impressionistic pictures, as seer's visions, designed to impress upon men the greatness of that event when it should come.

(v) *There are warnings of the necessity to be on the watch.* We get them in verses 28-37. If men live in the shadow of eternity, if men live with the constant possibility of the intervention of God, if men live with the prospect of the consummation of the coming of Christ ever before them, if the times and the seasons are known to none but God, then there is the necessity ever to be ready.

This chapter will make far more sense if we remember these various strands which are in it, and if we remember that every strand is unfolded in language and imagery which goes back to the Old Testament and apocalyptic pictures of the Day of the Lord.

Because that is so, we will study the chapter in detail, not in consecutive verses, but in the various passages of which the various strands consist.

A CITY'S DOOM

Mark 13 : 1, 2

> As they were going out of the sacred precincts, one
> of His disciples said to Jesus, "Teacher, see! What
> stones and what buildings!" Jesus said to him, "You
> see this great building? Not one stone will be left
> on another which will not be thrown down!"

WE begin with the prophecies of Jesus which foretold the
doom of Jerusalem. The Temple which Herod built was
one of the wonders of the world. It was begun in 20-19 B.C.
and in the time of Jesus it was not yet completely finished.
It was built on the top of Mount Moriah. Instead of
levelling off the summit of the mountain a kind of vast
platform had been formed by raising up walls of massive
masonry and so enclosing the whole area. On these walls
a platform was laid, strengthened by piers which
distributed the weight of the superstructure. Josephus
tells us that some of these stones were forty feet long, by
twelve feet high, by eighteen feet wide. It would be some
of these vast stones that moved the Galilaean disciples to
such wondering amazement. The most magnificent entrance
to the Temple was at the south-west angle. Here between
the city and the Temple hill there stretched the Tyropoeon
Valley. A marvellous bridge spanned the valley. Each arch
was forty-one and a half feet and there were stones used
in the building of it which measured twenty-four feet long.
The Tyropoeon valley was no less than two hundred and
twenty-five feet below. The breadth of the cleft that the
bridge spanned was three hundred and fifty-four feet, and
the bridge itself was fifty feet in breadth. The bridge led
straight into the Royal Porch. The porch consisted of a
double row of Corinthian pillars all thirty-seven and a half
feet high and each one of them cut out of one solid block
of marble. Of the actual Temple building itself, the Holy
Place, Josephus writes, "Now the outward face of the
Temple in its front wanted nothing that was likely to
surprise men's minds or their eyes, for it was covered

all over with plates of gold of great weight, and, at the first rising of the sun, reflected back a very fiery splendour, and made those who forced themselves to look upon it to turn their eyes away, just as they would have done at the sun's own rays. But this Temple appeared to strangers, when they were at a distance, like a mountain covered with snow, for, as to those parts of it which were not gilt, they were exceeding white. . . . Of its stones, some of them were forty-five cubits in length, five in height and six in breadth." A cubit is eighteen inches.

It was all this splendour that so impressed the disciples. The Temple seemed the summit of human art and achievement, and it seemed so vast and solid that it would stand for ever. And Jesus made the astonishing statement that the day was coming when not one of these stones would stand upon another. In less than fifty years the prophecy of Jesus came tragically true.

> " Pride of man and earthly glory,
>   Sword and crown betray his trust ;
> What with care and toil he buildeth,
>   Tower and temple, fall to dust.
>   But God's power,
>   Hour by hour,
>   Is my temple and my tower."

A CITY'S AGONY

Mark 13 : 14-20

When you see the abomination of desolation standing where he ought not (let him who reads understand), then let those who are in Judaea flee to the mountains. Let him who is on the house-top not come down, nor let him go in to take anything out of his house. And let him who is working in the field not turn back to pick up his cloak. Woe to women who are with child and to those whose babes are at their breasts in these days! Pray that it may not happen in the stormy weather. These days will be a tribulation such as has never happened from the beginning of the

THE GOSPEL OF MARK

creation which God has created until now, and such
as will never happen again. Unless the Lord had
shortened the days no living creature could have
survived. But, for the sake of the chosen ones whom
He chose, He shortened the days.

HERE Jesus forecasts some of the awful terror of the siege
and the final fall of Jerusalem. It was His warning that
when the first signs of it came people ought to flee in time,
not even waiting to pick up their clothes or to try to save
their goods. In point of fact the people did precisely the
opposite. They crowded into Jerusalem, and death came
in ways that are almost too terrible to think about.

The phrase *the abomination of desolation* has its origin
in the Book of Daniel (Daniel 9 : 27 ; 11 : 31 ; 12 : 11).
The Hebrew expression literally means *the profanation
that appals*. The origin of the phrase was in connection
with Antiocheius. We have already seen that he tried to
stamp out the Jewish religion and introduce Greek thought
and Greek ways. We saw how he desecrated the Temple
by offering swine's flesh on the great altar, and by setting
up public brothels in the sacred courts. Before the very
Holy Place itself he set up a great statue of Olympian Zeus
and ordered the Jews to worship it. In connection with
that the writer of First Maccabees says (1 : 54) " Now the
fifteenth day of the month Casleu, in the hundred and
forty-fifth year, they set up the abomination of desolation
upon the altar and builded idol altars throughout the cities
of Juda on every side." The phrase *the abomination of
desolation, the profanation that appals*, originally described
the heathen image and all that accompanied it with which
Antiocheius desecrated the Temple. It is Jesus' prophecy
that the same kind of thing was going to happen again.
It very nearly happened literally in the year A.D. 40.
Caligula was then Roman Emperor. He was an epileptic
and he was mad. But he insisted that he was a god. He
heard of the imageless worship of the Temple of Jerusalem
and planned to set up his own statue in the Holy Place.

His advisers besought him not to do so, for they knew that, if he did so, a bloody civil war would result in Palestine. He was obstinate, but fortunately he died in A.D. 41 before he could carry out his plan of desecration.

What does Jesus mean when He speaks about *the abomination of desolation*? In the time of Jesus men expected not only a Messiah, they also expected the emergence of a power who would be the very incarnation of evil, a power who would gather up into himself everything that was against God. Paul called that power *The Man of Sin* (2 Thessalonians 2 : 3). John of the *Revelation* saw that power in Rome (Revelation 17). What Jesus was saying was, " Some day, quite soon, you will see the very incarnate power of evil, rise up in a deliberate attempt to destroy the people and the Holy Place of God." He takes the old phrase and uses it to describe the terrible things that are about to happen.

It was in A.D. 70 that Jerusalem finally fell to the besieging army of Titus, who was to be Emperor of Rome. The horrors of that siege form one of the grimmest pages in history. The people crowded into Jerusalem from the countryside. Titus had no alternative but to starve the city into subjection. The matter was complicated by the fact that even at that terrible time there were sects and factions inside the city itself, and Jerusalem was torn without and within. Josephus tells the story of that terrible siege on the fifth book of *The Wars of the Jews*. He tells us that 97,000 were taken captive and 1,100,000 perished by slow starvation and the sword. He tells us that, " Then did the famine widen its progress and devoured the people by whole houses and families. The upper rooms were full of women and children, dying of starvation. The lanes of the city were full of the dead bodies of the aged. The children and the young men wandered about the market places like shadows, all swelled with famine, and fell down dead wheresoever their misery seized them. As for burying them, those that were sick themselves were not able to do it. And those that were hearty and well were deterred by the great multitude of the dead, and the uncertainty when they would die themselves, for many died as they were burying others, and many went to their own coffins before the fatal hour. There was no lamentation made under these calamities . . . the famine confounded all natural passions. . . . A deep silence and a kind of deadly night had seized upon the city." To make it still grimmer there were the inevitable ghouls who plundered the dead bodies. Josephus tells grimly how when not even any herbs were available " some persons were driven to such terrible distress as to search the common sewers and old dung-hills of cattle, and to eat the dung which they got there, and what they could not endure so much as to see, they now used for food." He paints a grim picture of men gnawing the leather of straps and shoes, and tells a terrible story of a woman who killed and roasted her child, and offered a share of that terrible meal to those who came seeking food.

The prophecy that Jesus made of terrible days ahead for Jerusalem came most abundantly true. Those who crowded into the city for safety died by the hundred thousand, and only those who took His advice and fled to the hills were saved.

THE HARD WAY

Mark 13 : 9-13

> Take heed to yourselves, for they will hand you over to councils, and they will scourge you in synagogues, and you will stand before governors and kings for my sake, and it will be your opportunity to bear your witness to them. The gospel must first be preached to all nations. And when they hand you over and bring you before authorities, do not worry beforehand about what you will say, but speak whatever is given you in that hour, for it is not you who speak but the Holy Spirit. Brother shall hand over brother to

death, and father child. And children will rise up
against parents, and will kill them. And you will be
hated of all for the sake of my name. But the man
who has endured to the end, he will be saved.

Now we come to the warnings of persecution to come.
Jesus never left His followers in any doubt that they had
chosen a hard way. No man could say that he had not
known the conditions of Christ's service in advance.

The handing over to councils and the scourging in
synagogues refer to Jewish persecution. In Jerusalem
there was the great Sanhedrin, the supreme court of the
Jews, but every town and village had its local Sanhedrin.
Before such local Sanhedrins the self-confessed heretics
would be tried, and in the synagogue they would be publicly
scourged. The governors and kings refer to trials before
the Roman courts, such trials as Paul faced before Felix
and Festus and Agrippa.

It was a fact that the Christians were wonderfully
strengthened in their trials. When we read of the trials
of the martyrs, even though they were often ignorant and
unlettered men, the impression that we often get is that
it was the judges and not the Christians who were on trial.
The Christian faith enabled the simplest folk to fear God
so much that they never feared the face of any man.

It was true that even those of a man's own family
sometimes betrayed him. In the early Roman Empire
one of the curses of the times was the informer (*delator*).
There were those who, in their attempts to curry favour
with the authorities, would not hesitate to betray their
own kith and kin. That must have been the sorest blow
of all. It is told that in Hitler Germany a man was arrested
because he stood for freedom. He stood imprisonment
and torture with stoic and uncomplaining fortitude.
Finally, with spirit still unbroken, he was released. Some
short time afterwards he committed suicide. Others
wondered why he had committed suicide after his release.
Those who knew him well knew the reason—he had

discovered that his own son was the person who had informed against him. The treachery of his own broke him in a way that the cruelty of his enemies was unable to achieve.

We must note that this family and domestic hostility was one of the regular items in the catalogue of terror of the last and terrible days, as the Jews say them, " Friends shall attack one another suddenly " (4 Esdras 5 : 9). "And they shall hate one another and provoke one another to fight " (2 Baruch 70 : 3). " And they shall strive with one another, the young with the old, and the old with the young, the poor with the rich, the lowly with the great, the beggar with the prince " (Jubilees 23 : 19). " Children shall shame the elders, and the elders shall rise up before the children " (The Mishnah, Sotah 9 : 15). " For the son dishonoureth the father, the daughter riseth up against her mother, the daughter-in-law against her mother-in-law. A man's enemies are the men of his own house " (Micah 7 : 6). It is always true that life becomes a hell upon earth when personal loyalties are destroyed, and when there is no love which a man may trust.

It was true that the Christians were hated. Tacitus talks of Christianity as an accursed superstition. Suetonius called it a new and evil superstition. The main reason for the hatred was the way in which Christianity cut across family ties. It was true that in those days a man or a woman had to love Christ more than father or mother, or son or daughter. But the matter was complicated by the fact that the Christians were much slandered. It is beyond doubt that the Jews did much to encourage these slanders. The most serious slander was the charge that the Christians were cannibals, a charge that was supported by the words of the sacrament which speak of eating Christ's body and drinking his blood.

In this, as in all other things, it is the man who endures to the end who is saved. Life is not a short, sharp sprint. It is a marathon race. Life is not a single battle. It is a long campaign. Dr. G. J. Jeffrey tells of a famous man who refused to have his biography written in the days of his fame and when he was still alive. " I have seen too many men fall out on the last lap of the race," he said. Life is never safe until it reaches journey's end. It was Bunyan who, in his dream, saw that from the very gates of heaven there was a way to hell. It is the man who endures *to the end* who will be saved.

THE DANGERS OF THE LAST DAYS

Mark 13 : 3-6 and 21-23

> As He was sitting on the Mount of Olives, opposite the sacred precincts of the Temple, Peter and James and John and Andrew privately asked Jesus, " Tell us, when shall these things be? And what sign will there be when these things are going to be completed? " Jesus began to say to them, " See that no one misleads you. Many will come in my name, and say, ' I am he,' and they will lead many astray."

> " And if some one then says to you, ' See! Here is the Messiah! ' or, ' See! There he is! ' do not believe them. For false Messiahs and false prophets will arise, and they will produce signs and wonders to lead the elect astray, if it is possible. But do you look to yourselves! See! I have told you beforehand all that will happen."

JESUS was well aware that, before the end would come, heretics and twisters of the truth would arise. It was not long before the Church had its heretics. Heresy arises from three main causes.

(i) Heresy arises from constructing doctrine to suit oneself. The human mind has an infinite capacity for wishful thinking. In a famous sentence, the Psalmist said, " The fool hath said in his heart, ' There is no God.' " Now the fool about whom the Psalmist was speaking was not a fool in the sense that he had no intelligence. He was a *moral* fool. He was, as we say, *playing the fool.*

329

His statement that there was no God was made because he did not wish there to be a God. If there was a God so much the worse for him. Therefore he eliminated God from his doctrine and from his universe. One particular kind of heresy has always been with us. That is the heresy of *antinomianism*. The antinomian begins with the principle that law has been abolished—and in a sense he is right. He goes on to say that there is nothing but *grace*—and again in a sense he is right. He then goes on to argue— as Paul shows us in Romans 6—on lines like these. " You say that God's grace is wide enough to cover every sin? " " Yes." " You say that God's grace can forgive any sin? " " Yes." " You say that God's grace is the greatest and the most wonderful thing in the universe? " " Yes." " Then," the antinomian concludes, " let us go on sinning to our hearts' content, for the more we sin, the more chances we give to this amazing grace of God to operate. Sin is a good thing for sin gives grace a chance to work. Therefore, let us do whatever we like." The grace of God has been twisted to suit the man who wants to sin. The same kind of argument is used by the man who declares that the only important thing in life is the soul, and that a man's body is quite unimportant. If that is so, the argument runs, then a man can do what he likes with his body. If he is so inclined he can sate and glut its desires, for the body does not matter. The man has twisted to suit his own lusts. One of the commonest ways to arrive in heresy is to mould Christian truth to suit ourselves. Can it be that the doctrine of hell and the doctrine of the Second Coming have both dropped out of much religious thought because they are both uncomfortable doctrines? No one would wish to bring either back in their crude forms, but it can be that they have dropped *too far* out of Christian thought because it does not suit us to believe in them?

(ii) Heresy arises from overstressing one part of the truth. It is, for instance, always wrong to overstress one attribute of God. If we think only of God's *holiness*, we can never attain to any intimacy with God, and we tend to a deism in which God is entirely remote and separate from the world. If we think only of God's *justice*, we can never be free of the fear of God. We become haunted and not helped by our religion. If we think only of God's *love*, religion can become a very easy-going sentimental thing. There is more in the New Testament than Luke 15. Always there is a paradox in Christianity. God is love, yet God is justice. Man is free, yet God is in control. Man is a creature of time, yet also he is a creature of eternity. G. K. Chesterton said that orthodoxy was like a man walking along a ridge like a knife-edge with a yawning chasm on either side. One step too much to right or left and disaster follows. We must, as the Greeks insisted, see life steady and see it *whole*.

(iii) Heresy arises from trying to produce a religion which will suit people, a religion which will be popular and attractive. To do that religion has to be watered down. The sting, the condemnation, the humiliation, the moral demand, have to be taken out of it. It is not our job to alter Christianity to suit people, but to alter people to suit Christianity.

(iv) Heresy arises from divorcing oneself from the Christian fellowship. When a man thinks alone he runs a grave danger of thinking astray. There is such a thing as the tradition of the Church. There is such a conception as the Church as the guardian of truth. If a man finds that his thinking separates himself from the fellowship of men, the chances are that there is something wrong with his thinking. It is the Roman Catholic principle that a man cannot have God for his Father unless he has the Church for his mother—and there is truth there.

(v) Heresy arises from the attempt to be completely intelligible. Here is one of the great paradoxes. We are under the bounden duty of trying to understand our faith. But it is also true that because we are finite creatures and because God is infinite we can never fully understand.

For that very reason a faith that can be neatly stated in a series of propositions and neatly proved in a series of logical steps like a geometrical theorem is an impossibility and a contradiction in terms. As G. K. Chesterton said, " It is only the fool who tries to get the heavens inside his head, and not unnaturally his head bursts. The wise man is content to get his head inside the heavens." Even at our most intellectual we must remember that there is a place for the ultimate mystery before which we can only worship, wonder and adore.

> " How could I praise,
> If such as I could understand? "

" I believe," as Tertullian said, " because it is impossible."

HIS COMING AGAIN

Mark 13 : 7, 8 and 24-27

> Jesus said, " When you hear of wars and reports of wars, do not be disturbed. These things must happen. But the end is not yet. Nation shall rise against nation, and kingdom against kingdom. In certain places there will be earthquakes. There will be famines. These things are the beginning of the birth-pangs of the new age."

> " And in those days, after that tribulation, the sun will be darkened, and the moon will not give its light, and the stars will be falling from heaven, and the powers in the heavens will be shaken. And then they will see the Son of Man coming in the clouds with much power and glory. And then he will send his angels and they will gather the chosen ones from the four winds, from the edge of the earth to the edge of the heaven."

HERE Jesus unmistakably speaks of His coming again. But—and this is important—He clothes the idea in three pictures which are part and parcel of the apparatus connected with the Day of the Lord.

(i) **The Day of the Lord was to be preceded by a time of wars.** 4 Ezra declares that before the day of the Lord there will be,

> " Quakings of places
> Tumult of peoples,
> Scheming of nations,
> Confusion of leaders,
> Disquietude of princes." (9 : 3).

The same book says,

> " And there shall come astonishment of mind upon the dwellers on earth. And they shall plan to war one against another, city against city, place against place, people against people, and kingdom against kingdom." (13 : 31).

The Sibylline Oracles foresee that,

> " King captures king and takes his land, and nations ravage nations and potentates people, and rulers all flee to another land, and the land is changed in men and a barbarian empire ravages Hellas and drains the rich land of its wealth, and men come face to face in strife." (3 : 633-647).

Second Baruch has the same ideas. In 27 : 5-13 this book singles out twelve things which will precede the new age.

> " In the first part there will be the beginning of commotions. In the second part there shall be the slayings of great ones. In the third part the fall of many by death. In the fourth part the sending of the sword. In the fifth part famine and with-holding of rain. In the sixth part earthquakes and terrors . . . (there is a blank in the manuscript here). . . . In the eighth part a multitude of spectres and attacks of the evil spirits. In the ninth part the fall of fire. In the tenth part rapine and much oppression. In the eleventh part wickedness and unchastity. In the twelfth part confusion from the mingling together of all those things aforesaid."

> " All the inhabitants of the earth shall be moved against one another." (48 : 32.)

> " And they shall hate one another,
> And provoke one another to fight.

• • • • • • • • • • •

> And it shall come to pass that whosoever comes safe
> out of the war shall die in the earthquake,
> And whosoever gets safe out of the earthquake
> shall be burned by the fire,
> And whosoever gets safe out of the fire shall be
> destroyed by famine."

It is abundantly clear that when Jesus spoke of wars and
rumours of wars He was using pictures which were part
and parcel of Jewish dreams of the future.

(ii) The Day of the Lord was to be preceded by the
darkening of sun and moon. The Old Testament itself is
full of that (Amos 8 : 9, Joel 2 : 10, 3 : 15, Ezekiel 32 :
7, 8, Isaiah 13 : 10, 34 : 4). Again the popular literature
of Jesus' day is full of this :

> " Then shall the sun suddenly shine forth by night,
> And the moon by day.
>
> .   .   .   .
>
> The outgoings of the stars shall change."
>
> (4 Ezra 5 : 4-7.)

2 Baruch 32 : 1 speaks of " the time in which the mighty
one is to shake the whole creation." The Sibylline Oracles
(3 : 796-806) talks of a time when " swords in the star-lit
heaven appear by night towards dusk and towards dawn
. . . and all the brightness of the sun fails at midday from
the heaven, and the moon's rays shine forth and come back
to earth, and a sign comes from the rocks with dripping
streams of blood." The Assumption of Moses foresees a
time when :

> " The horns of the sun shall be broken and he shall be
> turned into darkness,
> And the moon shall not give her light, and be
> turned wholly into blood,
> And the circle of the stars shall be disturbed." (10:5.)

Once again it is clear that Jesus is using the popular
language which everyone knew.

(iii) It was a regular part of the imagery that the Jews
were to be gathered back to Palestine from the four corners of
the earth. The Old Testament itself is full of that idea

(Isaiah 27 : 13, 35 : 8-10, Micah 7 : 12, Zechariah 10 : 6-11). Again the popular literature loves the idea :

> " Blow ye in Zion on the trumpet to summon the saints,
> Cause ye to be heard in Jerusalem the voice of him that bringeth good tidings,
> For God hath had pity on Israel in visiting them.
> Stand on the height, O Jerusalem, and behold thy children,
> From the East and the West gathered together by the Lord." (Psalms of Solomon 11 : 1-3.)

> " The Lord will gather you together in faith through His tender mercy, and for the sake of Abraham and Isaac and Jacob."
>
> (The Testament of Asher 7 : 5-7.)

This is something we have to note. When we read the pictorial words of Jesus about the Second Coming we must remember that he is giving us neither a map of eternity nor a timetable to the future, but that He is simply using the language and the pictures that many a Jew knew and used for centuries before Him.

But it is extremely interesting to note that the things that Jesus prophesied were in fact happening. He prophesied wars and the dreaded Parthians were in fact pressing in on the Roman frontiers. He prophesied earthquakes and within forty years the Roman world was aghast at the earthquake which devastated Laodicaea, and fascinated by the eruption of Vesuvius which buried Pompeii in lava, so that she lay lost for centuries. He prophesied famines, and in fact there was famine in Rome in the days of Claudius. It was in fact such a time of terror in the near future that when Tacitus began his histories he said that everything that was happening seemed to prove that the gods were seeking, not for salvation, but for vengeance on the Roman Empire.

In this passage the one thing that we must retain is the fact that Jesus did foretell that He would come again. The imagery we can disregard.

BE ON THE WATCH

Mark 13 : 28-37

> Jesus said, " Learn the lesson the fig-tree offers you.
> As soon as its branches become tender, and it puts
> forth its leaves, you know that summer is near. So
> must you too know, when you see these things
> happening, that the end is near at the doors. This is
> the truth I tell you—this generation will not pass
> away until these things happen. Heaven and earth
> will pass away but my words will never pass away.
> But no man knows about that day and that hour, not
> even the angels in heaven, not even the Son, no one
> except the Father. Be watchful, be wakeful, be
> praying, for you do not know when the time is. It is
> like when a man goes abroad, and leaves his home, and
> puts his servants in charge, and orders the door-keeper
> to be on the watch. So then be watchful ! For you
> do not know when the master of the house comes, late
> in the evening, at midnight, at cockrow, or in the early
> day. Watch ! in case he comes suddenly and finds you
> sleeping. What I say to you, I say to all—be on the
> watch ! "

THERE are two special things to note in this passage.

(i) It is sometimes held that when Jesus said that these
things were to happen within this generation He was in
error. But it is clear that Jesus was right, for this sentence
does not refer to the Second Coming. It could not when
the next sentence says He does not know when that day
will be. It refers to Jesus' prophecies about the fall of
Jerusalem and the destruction of the Temple which were
abundantly fulfilled.

(ii) Jesus says that He does not know the day or the
hour when He will come again. There were things which
even He left without questioning in the hand of God.
There can be no greater warning and rebuke to those who
work out dates and timetables as to when He will come
again. Surely it is nothing less than blasphemy for us to
enquire into that of which our Lord consented to be
ignorant.

(iii) So Jesus draws one practical conclusion. We are like men who know that their master will come, but who do not know when. We live in the shadow of eternity. That is no reason for fearful and hysterical expectation. But it does mean that day by day our work must be completed and done. It does mean that we must so live that it does not matter when He comes. It gives us the great task in life of making every day fit for Him to see, and being at any moment ready to meet Him face to face. All life becomes a preparation to meet the King.

———————

We began by saying that this was a very difficult chapter, but that in the end it had permanent truth to tell us. What is some of that truth?

(i) It tells us that only the man of God can see into the secrets of history. Jesus saw the fate of Jerusalem. Others were blind to it, but He saw it. To be a real statesman a man must be a man of God. To guide his country a man must be himself God-guided. It is only the man who knows God who can enter into something of the plan of God.

(ii) It tells us two things about the Doctrine of the Second Coming. (*a*) It tells us that that doctrine contains a fact which we forget or disregard at our peril. (*b*) It tells us that we must remember that the imagery in which it is clothed is the imagery of Jesus' own time, and that to speculate on it is useless, when Jesus Himself was content not to know. The one thing of which we can be sure is that history is going somewhere. There is a consummation to come.

(iii) It tells us that of all things to forget God and to become immersed in earth is most foolish. The wise man is the man who never forgets that he must be ready when the summons comes. If he lives in that memory for him, the end will not be terror, but eternal joy.

THE LAST ACT BEGINS

Mark 14 : 1, 2

> The Feast of the Passover and of Unleavened Bread
> was due in two days' time. And the chief priests and
> experts in the law were trying to find some way to
> seize Jesus by some stratagem and to kill Him, for they
> said, "This must not be done at the Feast itself in
> case there should be a disturbance of the people."

THE last crowded act of Jesus' life was now about to open.
The Feast of the Passover and the Feast of Unleavened
Bread were really two different things. The Feast of the
Passover fell on 14th Nisan, that is, about 14th April.
The Feast of Unleavened Bread consisted of the seven
days following the Passover. The Passover itself was a
major Feast and was kept like a Sabbath. The Feast of
Unleavened Bread was called a minor festival, and,
although no new work could be begun during it, such
work as was "necessary for public interest or to provide
against private loss " was allowable. The really great day
was the Passover Day.

The Passover was one of the three compulsory feasts.
The other two were The Feast of Pentecost and the Feast
of Tabernacles. To these feasts every male adult Jew who
lived within 15 miles of Jerusalem was bound to come.

The Passover had a double significance. (*a*) It had an
historical significance. (Exodus 12.) It commemorated the
deliverance of the children of Israel from their bondage
in Egypt. The old story was that God had sent plague after
plague on Egypt, and, as each plague came, Pharaoh
promised to let the people go. But, when each plague
abated, he hardened his heart and went back on his word.
Finally there came that terrible night when the Angel of
Death was to walk through the land of Egypt and slay
every first-born son in every home. The Israelites were to
slay a lamb. With a bunch of hyssop they were to smear
the lintel of the door-post with the blood of the lamb, and
when the Angel of Death saw the door-post so marked, he

would *pass over* that house and its occupants would be safe. Before they went upon their way the Israelites were to eat a meal of a roasted lamb and unleavened bread. It was that " passover," that deliverance, and that meal that the Feast of the Passover commemorated. (*b*) It had an *agricultural significance*. It marked the ingathering of the barley harvest. On that day a sheaf of barley had to be waved before the Lord (Leviticus 23 : 10, 11). And not till after that had been done could the barley of the new crop be sold in the shops, or bread made with the new flour be eaten.

Every possible preparation was made for the Passover. For a month beforehand the meaning of the Passover was expounded in the Synagogue, and the lesson of the Passover was taught daily in the schools. It was the aim to see that no one should come ignorant and unprepared to the feast. The roads were all put in order, the bridges were repaired. One special thing was done. It was very common to bury people beside the road. Now if any pilgrim had touched one of these wayside tombs he would technically have been in contact with a dead body, and would have been thus rendered unclean and so would have been unable to take part in the feast. So then before the Passover all the wayside tombs were white-washed, in order to make them stand out, so that the pilgrims could avoid them. Psalms 120-134 are entitled *Psalms of Degree*, and it may well be that these were the psalms which the pilgrims sang on their way to the feast, as they sought to lighten the road with their music. It is said that Psalm 122 was the psalm which they actually sang as they climbed the hill to the Temple on the last lap of their journey.

As we have already seen, it was compulsory for every adult male Jew who lived within 15 miles of Jerusalem to come to the Passover, but far more than these came. It was the one ambition of every Jew to eat at least one Passover in Jerusalem before he died. And therefore from every country in the world pilgrims came flocking to

Jerusalem for the Passover Feast. During the Passover all lodging was free. The city could not hold the crowds, and Bethany and Bethphage were two of the outlying villages where the pilgrims lodged. There is a passage in Josephus which gives us an idea of how many pilgrims actually came. Joseph tells that Cestius who was the Governor of Palestine round about A.D. 65 had some difficulty in persuading Nero of the great importance of the Jewish religion. To impress Nero, he asked the then High Priest to take a census of the lambs slain at the Passover in one year. The number, according to Josephus, was 256,500. Now the law was that there must be a minimum party of ten people to one lamb, which means that there must have been close on 3,000,000 pilgrims in Jerusalem.

It was just there that the problem of the Jewish authorities lay. During the Passover feeling ran very high. The remembrance of the old deliverance from Egypt made them long for a new deliverance from Rome. At no time was nationalist feeling so intense. Jerusalem was not the Roman headquarters in Judaea. The governor had his residence and the soldiers were stationed in Caesarea. During the Passover time special detachments of troops were drafted into Jerusalem and quartered in the Tower of Antonia which overlooked the Temple. The Romans knew that at a Passover time anything might happen and they were taking no chances. The Jewish authorities well knew that in an inflammable atmosphere like that, the arrest of Jesus might well provoke a riot. That is why they sought some secret stratagem whereby they might arrest Him, and have Him in their power before the populace knew anything about it.

The last act of Jesus' life was to be played out in a city crammed with Jews who had come from the ends of the earth. They had come to commemorate the event whereby their nation was delivered from slavery in Egypt long ago. And at that very time, God's deliverer of mankind was crucified upon His Cross.

LOVE'S EXTRAVAGANCE

Mark 14 : 3-9

> While Jesus was in Bethany, while He was reclining
> at a table in the house of Simon the leper, there came
> a woman who had a phial of ointment of pure nard.
> She broke the phial and poured it over his head.
> Some of them said indignantly to each other, " To
> what purpose is the waste of this ointment? This
> ointment could have been sold for more than ten
> pounds, and the money could have been given to the
> poor." And they were angry at her. Jesus said,
> " Let her be ! Why do you trouble her? It is a lovely
> thing that she has done to me. You have always got
> the poor with you, and you can do something for them
> any time you like, but you have not got me always.
> She has done what she could. She has taken my body
> and anointed it beforehand against my burial. This
> is the truth I tell you—wherever the good news shall
> be proclaimed throughout the whole world, the story
> of what she has done will be told, so that she will
> always be remembered."

THE poignancy of this story lies in the fact that it tells us
of almost the last kindness that Jesus had done to Him.

He was in the house of a man called Simon the leper, in
the village of Bethany. In Palestine people did not sit to
eat. They reclined on low couches. They lay on the couch
resting on the left elbow and using the right hand to take
their food. So then anyone coming up to someone lying
like this would stand well above them. To Jesus there
came a woman with an alabaster phial of ointment. It was
the custom to pour a few drops of perfume on a guest when
he arrived at a house or when he sat down to a meal. This
phial held nard which was a very precious ointment made
from a rare plant that came from far-off India. But it was
not a few drops that this woman poured on the head of
Jesus. She broke the flask and anointed him with the
whole contents.

There may be more than one reason why she broke the
flask. Maybe she broke it as a sign that all was to be used.

341

There was a custom in the East that if a glass was used by a distinguished guest or stranger, after he had used it, it was broken so that it would never again be touched by the hand of any lesser person. Maybe there was something of that in the woman's mind. But there was one thing which was not in her mind, but which we see now. Jesus saw it. It was the custom in the East, first to bathe, then to anoint the bodies of the dead. After the body had been anointed, the flask in which the perfume had been contained was broken and the fragments were laid with the dead body in the tomb. Although she did not mean it so, that was the very thing that that woman was doing.

Her action provoked the grudging criticism of some of the bystanders. The flask was worth more than 300 *denarii*. A *denarius* was a Roman coin worth about a shilling. We have to remember that, in those days, a working man's wage was one shilling a day. It would have cost an ordinary man almost a year's pay to buy that flask of ointment. To some of them it seemed a shameful waste. The money might have been given to the poor. But Jesus understood. He quoted their own scriptures to them. " The poor shall never cease out of the land." (Deuteronomy 15 : 11.) " You can help the poor any time," Jesus said, " but you have not long to do anything for me now." " This," He said, " is like anointing my body beforehand for its burial."

This whole story shows the action of love.

(i) Jesus said that it was a *lovely* thing that the woman had done. In Greek there are two words for *good*. There is *agathos* which describes a thing which is morally good. And there is *kalos* which describes a thing which is not only good but *lovely*. A thing might be *agathos*, and yet be hard, stern, austere, unattractive. But a thing which is *kalos* is winsome and lovely, with a certain bloom of charm upon it. Struthers of Greenock used to say that it would do the Church more good than anything else if Christians would sometimes " *do a bonnie thing*." That is exactly what *kalos* means, and that is exactly what this woman did. Love does not only do good things. Love does lovely things.

(ii) If love is true love there must always be a certain extravagance in it. It does not nicely calculate the less or more. It is not concerned to see how little it can decently give. If it gave all it had, if indeed it gave all the world, the gift would still be too little. There is a recklessness in love which refuses to count the cost.

(iii) Love can see that there are things the chance to do which only comes once. It is one of the tragedies of life that often we are moved to do something fine, and we do not do it. It may be that we are too shy to do it and that we feel awkward about it. It may be that second thoughts suggest a more prudent and commonsense course. It comes in the simplest things—the impulse to send a letter to someone to thank them for something that they have done, the impulse to tell someone how much we love them and how grateful we are to them, the impulse to give some special gift or speak some special word. And the tragedy is that the impulse is so often strangled at birth. This would be a so much lovelier world if there were more people like this woman, who acted on her impulse of love, because she knew in her heart of hearts that if she did not do it then she would never do it at all. How that last extravagant, impulsive kindness must have uplifted Jesus' heart.

(iv) We may note one thing more. Once again we see the invincible confidence of Jesus. The Cross loomed close ahead now, but He never believed that the Cross would be the end. He knew that the good news would go all round the world. And with the good news there went the story of this lovely thing, done with love's reckless extravagance, done on the impulse of the moment, done out of a heart of love.

THE TRAITOR

Mark 14 : 10, 11

> Judas Iscariot, the man who was one of The Twelve, went away to the chief priests to betray Jesus to them. When they had listened to his offer, they were delighted, and they promised to give him money. So he began to search for a convenient method of betraying Him.

It is with consummate artistry that Mark sets side by side the anointing at Bethany and the betrayal by Judas. Without comment Mark sets side by side the act of generous love, and the act of terrible treachery.

There is always a shudder of the heart as we think of Judas. Dante sets him in the lowest of all hells, which was a hell of cold and ice, a hell designed for those who were not hot sinners swept away by angry passions, but who were cold, calculating, deliberate sinners against the love of God.

Mark tells the story with such economy of words that he leaves us no material for speculation. But at the back of Judas' action we can distinguish certain things.

(i) There was *covetousness*. Matthew 26 : 15 actually tells us that Judas went to the authorities and asked what price they were prepared to pay and drove a bargain with them for thirty pieces of silver. John 11 : 27 drops a hint. That verse tells us that the authorities had asked for information as to where Jesus could be found that they might arrest Him. It may well be that by this time Jesus was to all intents and purposes an outlaw with a price upon His head, and that Judas knew it, and wished to acquire the offered reward. John is quite definite about it. He tells us that Judas was the treasurer of the apostolic band and used his position to pilfer from the common purse (John 13 : 6). It may be so. The desire for money can be a terrible thing. It can make a man blind to decency and honesty and honour. It can make him care not how he gets so long as he gets. Judas discovered too late that some things cost too much.

(ii) Undoubtedly there must have been *jealousy*. Klopstock, the German poet, thought that Judas, when he joined The Twelve, had every gift and every virtue which might have made him great, but that bit by bit he became consumed with jealousy of John, the Beloved Disciple, and that this jealousy drove him to his terrible act. It is easy to see that there were tensions in The Twelve. The rest were able to overcome them, and it may well be that Judas was the one man who had an unconquerable and uncontrollable demon of jealousy within his heart. There are few things which can wreck life for ourselves and for others as jealousy can.

(iii) Undoubtedly there was *ambition*. Again and again we see how The Twelve thought of the Kingdom in earthly terms, and how they dreamed of high position in it. Judas must have been like that. It may well be that, while the others still clung to their dreams, he was the first to see how far wrong these dreams were, how little chance they ever had of any earthly fulfilment. And it may well be that in his disillusionment the love he once bore to Jesus turned to hate. In *Henry the Eighth* Shakespeare makes Wolsey say to Thomas Cromwell :

> " Cromwell, I charge thee, fling away ambition ;
> By that sin fell the angels ; how can man then,
> The image of his Maker, hope to win by it?
> Love thyself last."

There is an ambition which will trample on love and honour and all lovely things to gain the end it has set its heart upon.

(iv) Men's minds have always been fascinated by the idea that it may be that Judas did not want Jesus to die at all. It is almost certain that Judas was a fanatical nationalist and that he had seen in Jesus the one person who could make his dreams of national power and glory come true. But now he saw Jesus drifting to death on a cross. So, it may be, in one last attempt to make his dream come true, he betrayed Jesus *in order to force Jesus' hand.* He delivered Him to the authorities with the idea that now Jesus would be compelled to act in order to save Himself, and that that action would be the beginning of the victorious campaign he dreamed of. It may be that that idea of Judas is supported by the fact that when he saw what he had done he went and flung the accursed money at the feet of the Jewish authorities and went out and hung himself and so committed suicide (Matthew 27 : 3-5). If that is so the tragedy of Judas is the greatest tragedy in history.

(v) Both Luke and John say the same thing. They say quite simply, that the devil entered into Judas (Luke 22 : 3, John 13 : 27). In the last analysis that is what happened. Judas wanted Jesus to be what he wanted Him to be, and not what Jesus wanted to be. In reality Judas attached himself to Jesus, not so much to become a follower of Jesus, as to use Jesus to work out the plans and desires and schemes of his own ambitious heart. So far from surrendering to Jesus, he wanted Jesus to surrender to him, and when Jesus took His own way, the way of the Cross, Judas was so incensed that he betrayed Him. The very essence of sin is pride. The very core of sin is independence. The very heart of sin is the desire to do what we like and not what God likes. That is what the Devil, Satan, the Evil One stands for. He stands for everything which is against God and which will not bow to God. That is the very spirit which was incarnate in Judas.

We shudder at Judas. But let us think again—covetousness, jealousy, ambition, the dominant desire to have our own way of things. Are we so very different? These are the things which made Judas betray Jesus, and these are the things which still make men betray Him in every age.

PREPARING FOR THE FEAST

Mark 14 : 12-16

On the first day of The Feast of Unleavened Bread,
when they were sacrificing the Passover Lamb, Jesus'
disciples said to Him, " Where do you wish us to go
and to make the necessary preparations for you to
eat the Passover?" He despatched two of His
disciples, and said to them. " Go into the city, and
there will meet you a man carrying an earthen pitcher
of water. Follow him, and wherever he enters in, say
to the householder, ' The teacher says, " Where is my
room, where I may eat the Passover with my disciples?"' He will show you a large upper room,
furnished and prepared. There get things ready for
us." So the disciples went away, and they came into
the city, and found everything just as He had told
them. And they got everything ready for the
Passover Feast.

IT may seem an unusual word to use in connection with
Jesus, but, as we read the narrative of the last week of
Jesus' life, we cannot help being struck with what we can
only call His efficiency of arrangement. Again and again
we see that Jesus did not leave things until the last moment.
Long before He had arranged that the colt should be ready
for His ride into Jerusalem, and here again we see that all
His arrangements had been made long beforehand. Jesus'
disciples wished to know where they would eat the
Passover. Jesus sent them into Jerusalem with instructions to look for a man carrying an earthen pitcher of water.
That was a pre-arranged signal. To carry a water-pot was
a woman's duty. It was a thing that no man would ever
do. A man with a water-pot on his shoulder would stand
out in any crowd as much as, say, a man on a wet day with
a lady's umbrella. Jesus did not leave things until the
last minute. Long ago He had arranged a last meeting-
place for Himself and for His disciples, and had arranged
just how it was to be found.

The larger Jewish houses had upper rooms. Such houses
looked exactly like a smaller box placed on the top of a

bigger box. The smaller box was the upper room, and it was approached by an outside stair, which made it unnecessary to go through the main room in order to get to it. The upper room had many uses. It was a store-room, it was a place for quiet and meditation, it was a guest-room when visitors arrived. But in particular it was the place where a Rabbi taught his chosen band of intimate disciples. Jesus was following the custom that any Jewish Rabbi might follow.

We must remember one thing about the Jewish way of reckoning days. In Jewish reckoning the new day begins at 6 p.m. in the evening. Up until 6 p.m. it was 13th Nisan, the day of the preparation for the Passover. But 14th Nisan, the Passover day itself, began at 6 p.m. To put it in English terms, to the Jew *Friday* begins at 6 p.m. on Thursday.

What were the preparations that a Jew made for The Passover?

The first ceremony was *the ceremonial search for leaven.* Before the Passover every particle of leaven must be banished from the house. That was so because the first Passover in Egypt (Exodus 12) had been eaten with unleavened bread. Unleavened bread is not like bread at all. It is like a water-biscuit. It had been used in Egypt because it can be baked very much more quickly than a loaf baked with leaven, and the first Passover, the Passover of escape from Egypt, had been eaten in haste, with everyone ready for the road. In addition to that, leaven was the symbol of corruption. Leaven is fermented dough, and the Jew identified fermentation with putrefaction, and so leaven stood for rottenness and corruption. The day before the Passover the master of the house took a lighted candle and ceremonially searched the house for leaven. Before the search he prayed,

> "Blessed art Thou, Jehovah, our God, King of the Universe, who hast sanctified us by Thy command-ments, and commanded us to remove the leaven."

At the end of the search the householder said,

> " All the leaven that is in my possession, that which
> I have seen and that which I have not seen, be it
> null, be it accounted as the dust of the earth."

Next, on the afternoon before the Passover evening,
there came *the sacrifice of the Passover Lamb*. All the people
came to the Temple. The worshipper must slay his own
lamb, thereby, as it were, making his own sacrifice. But
in Jewish eyes all blood is sacred to God, because the Jew
equated the blood and the life. It was quite natural that
he should do so because, if a person or an animal is wounded,
as the blood flows away, so does the life. So in the Temple
the worshipper slew his own lamb. Between the worshippers
and the altar there were two long lines of priests, each with
a gold or silver bowl. As the lamb's throat was slit the
blood was caught in one of these bowls, and passed up the
line, until the priest at the end of the line dashed the bowl
of blood upon the altar. The carcase was then flayed, the
entrails and the fat were extracted, because they were part
of the necessary sacrifice, and then the carcase was handed
back to the worshipper. If the figures of Josephus are
anywhere nearly correct, and there were more than a
quarter of a million lambs slain, the scene in the Temple
courts and the blood-stained condition of the altar can
hardly be imagined. The lamb was carried home to be
roasted. It must not be boiled. Nothing must touch it,
not even the sides of a pot. It had to be roasted over an
open fire on a spit made of pomegranate wood. The spit
went right through the lamb from mouth to vent, and the
lamb had to be roasted entire with head and legs and tail
still attached to the body.

The table itself was shaped like a square with one side
open. It was low and the guests reclined at it on couches,
resting on their left arms and having their right arms free
to use for eating.

There were certain things which were necessary, and

these are the things which the disciples would have to prepare and get ready.

(i) There was the *lamb*, and the lamb was to remind them of how their houses had been protected by the badge of blood when the Angel of Death passed through Egypt.

(ii) There was the *unleavened bread* which was to remind them of the bread they had eaten in haste when they escaped from slavery.

(iii) There was a *bowl of salt water*, to remind them of the tears they had shed in Egypt and of the waters of the Red Sea through which they had miraculously passed to safety.

(iv) There was a collection of *bitter herbs*—horse radish, chicory, endive, lettuce, horehound—to remind them of the bitterness of slavery in Egypt.

(v) There was a paste called *Charosheth*, which was a mixture of apples, dates, pomegranates and nuts, and which was to remind them of the clay of which they had made bricks in Egypt. Through it there were sticks of cinnamon to remind them of the straw with which the bricks had been made.

(vi) There were *four cups of wine*. The cups contained a little more than half a pint of wine, but three parts of wine were mixed with two of water. The four cups, which were drunk at different stages of the meal, were to remind them of the four promises in Exodus 6 : 6, 7,

> " I will bring you out from under the burdens of the Egyptians.
> I will rid you of their bondage.
> I will redeem you with an outstretched arm.
> I will take you to me for a people, and I will be your God."

Such were the preparations which had to be made for the Passover. Every detail spoke of that great day of deliverance when God liberated His people from their bondage in Egypt. It was at that feast that He who liberated the world from sin was to sit at His last meal with His disciples.

LOVE'S LAST APPEAL

Mark 14 : 17-21

When it was evening, Jesus came with The Twelve. As they were reclining at table and eating, Jesus said, " This is the truth I tell you—one of you will betray me, one who is eating with me," They began to be grieved, and to say to Him, one by one, " Surely it cannot be I ? " He said to them, " One of The Twelve, one who dips his hand with me into the dish. The Son of Man goes as it stands written about Him, but woe to that man through whom the Son of Man is betrayed. It had been good for him, if that man had not been born."

As we have seen, the new day began at 6 p.m., and when the Passover evening had come Jesus came and sat down with The Twelve. There was only one change in the old ritual which had been observed so many centuries ago in Egypt. At the first Passover Feast in Egypt, the meal had been eaten standing (Exodus 12 : 11). But that had been a sign of haste, a sign that they were slaves escaping from slavery. In the time of Jesus the regulation was that the meal should be eaten reclining, for that was the sign of a free man, with a home and a country of his own.

This is a poignant passage. All the time there was a text running in Jesus' mind. " Yea, mine own familiar friend, in whom I trusted, which did eat of my bread, hath lifted up his heel against me." (Psalm 41 : 9.) These words were in Jesus' mind all the time. We can see certain great things here.

(i) Jesus knew what was going to happen. That is the supreme courage of Jesus, especially in the last days. It would have been easy for Him to escape, and yet inflexibly He went on. Homer tells how the great warrior Achilles was told that if he went out to his last battle he would surely be killed. His answer was, " Nevertheless I am for going on." With a full knowledge of what lay ahead, Jesus was for going on.

(ii) Jesus could see into the heart of Judas. The curious thing is that the other disciples seem to have had no suspicions. If they had known what Judas was engaged in doing, it is very certain that they would have attacked him and stopped him even by violence. Here is something to remember. There may be things which we seek to hide from our fellow men. There may even be things which we succeed in hiding from our fellow men. But we cannot succeed in hiding them from Jesus Christ. He is the searcher of the hearts of men. He knew what was in man.

" Our thoughts lie open to Thy sight ;
And naked to Thy glance.
Our secret sins are in the light
Of Thy pure countenance."

Blessed indeed are the pure in heart.

(iii) In this passage we see Jesus offering two things to Judas. (a) He is making love's last appeal. It is as if He was saying to Judas, " I know what you are going to do. Will you not stop even yet? " (b) He is offering Judas a last warning. He is telling him in advance of the consequences of the thing that it is in his heart to do. But we must note this, for it is of the essence of the way in which God deals with us—*there is no compulsion*. Without a doubt Jesus could forcibly have stopped Judas. All He had to do was to tell the other eleven what Judas was meditating and planning, and Judas would never have left that room alive that night, for the others would have murdered him rather than let him go. Here is the whole human situation. God has given us wills that are free. His love appeals to us. His truth warns us. But there is no compulsion. It is the awful responsibility of man that he can spurn the appeal of God's love, and disregard the warning of God's voice. In the end there is no one but ourselves responsible for our sins.

In Greek legend two famous travellers passed the rocks where the Sirens sang. The Sirens sat on these rocks and sang with such sweetness that they lured mariners irresistibly to their doom. Ulysses sailed past these rocks. His method was to stop the sailors ears so that they could not hear, and to order them to bind himself to the mast with ropes so that, however much he struggled, he would not be able to answer to that seductive sweetness. He resisted by compulsion. The other traveller was Orpheus, the sweetest musician of all. His method was to play and sing with such surpassing sweetness as his ship passed the rocks where the Sirens were, that the attraction of the song of the Sirens was never even heard because of the attraction of the song he sang. His method was to answer the appeal of seduction with a still greater appeal. God's way is the second way. He does not by forcible compulsion stop us whether we like it or not from sin. God seeks to make us love Him so much that His voice is more sweetly insistent to us than all the voices which call us away from Him.

THE SYMBOL OF SALVATION

Mark 14 : 22-26

> As they were eating, Jesus took a loaf and gave thanks for it, and broke it and gave it to them and said, " Take this. This is my body." And, after He had given thanks, He took a cup and gave it to them, and they all drank from it. And He said to them, " This is the blood of the new covenant which is being shed for many. Truly I tell you, I will no longer drink of the fruit of the vine, until that day when I drink it new in the Kingdom of God." And, after they had sung the Psalm, they went out to the Mount of Olives.

WE must first set out the various steps of the Passover Feast, so that in our mind's eye we can follow what Jesus and His disciples were doing. The steps came in this order.

(i) *The Cup of the Kiddush. Kiddush* means *sanctification* or *separation.* This was the act which, as it were, separated this meal from all other common meals. The head of the family took the cup and prayed over it, and then all drank of it.

(ii) *The first hand washing.* This was carried out only by the person who was to celebrate the feast. Three times he had to wash his hands in the prescribed way which we have already described when we were studying chapter 7.

(iii) A piece of parsley or lettuce was then taken and dipped in the bowl of salt water and eaten. This was an appetizer to the meal, but the parsley stood for the hyssop with which the lintel had been smeared with blood, and the salt stood for the tears of Egypt and for the waters of the Red Sea through which Israel had been brought in safety.

(iv) *The Breaking of Bread.* Two blessings were used at the breaking of bread. " Blessed be Thou, O Lord, our God, King of the Universe, who bringest forth from the earth." Or, " Blessed art Thou, our Father in heaven, who givest us to-day the bread necessary for us." On the table there lay three circles of unleavened bread. The middle one was taken and broken. At this point only a little was eaten. It was to remind the Jews of the bread of affliction that they ate in Egypt and it was broken to remind them that slaves had never a whole loaf, but only broken crusts to eat. As it was broken the head of the family said, " This is the bread of affliction which our forefathers ate in the land of Egypt. Whosoever is hungry let him come and eat. Whosoever is in need let him come and keep the Passover with us." (In the modern celebration in strange lands, here is added the famous prayer, " This year we keep it here, next year in the land of Israel. This year as slaves, next year as free.")

(v) Next comes the *Relating* of the story of Deliverance. The youngest person present has to ask what makes this day different from all other days, and why all this is being done. And the head of the house has thereupon to tell the whole story of the history of Israel down to the great deliverance which the Passover commemorates. To the Jew the Passover can never become a ritual. It is always a commemoration of the power and the mercy of God.

(vi) Psalms 113, 114 are sung. Psalms 113-118 are known as *The Hallel*, which means The Praise of God. All these psalms are praising psalms. They were part of the very earliest material which a Jewish boy had to commit to memory when he was very young.

(vii) The Second Cup is drunk. It is called *The Cup of Haggadah*, which means The Cup of Explaining or Proclaiming.

(viii) All those who are present now wash their hands in preparation for the meal.

(ix) A grace is said. " Blessed art Thou, O Lord, our God, who bringest forth fruit from the earth. Blessed art Thou, O God, who has sanctified us with Thy commandment and enjoined us to eat unleavened cakes." Thereafter small pieces of the unleavened bread are distributed.

(x) Some of the *bitter herbs* are placed between two pieces of unleavened bread and then dipped in the *Charosheth* and eaten. This is what is called *The Sop*. It was the reminder of slavery and of the bricks that once they had been compelled to make.

(xi) Then follows the meal proper. The whole lamb must be eaten. Anything left over must be destroyed and must not be used for any common meal.

(xii) The hands are cleansed again.

(xiii) The remainder of the unleavened bread is eaten.

(xiv) There is a prayer of thanksgiving, which contains a petition for the coming of Elijah to herald the Messiah. Then the third cup is drunk, which is called *The Cup of Thanksgiving*. The blessing over the cup is, " Blessed art Thou, O Lord, our God, King of the Universe, who hast created the fruit of the vine."

(xv) The second part of *The Hallel*—Psalms 115-118— is sung.

(xvi) The fourth cup is drunk, and Psalm 136, which is known as *The Great Hallel*, is sung.

(xvii) Two short prayers are said :

355

" All Thy works shall praise Thee, O Lord, our God. And Thy saints, the righteous, who do Thy good pleasure, and all Thy people, the house of Israel, with joyous song, let them praise and bless and magnify and glorify and exalt and reverence and sanctify and scribe the Kingdom to Thy name, O God, our King. For it is good to praise Thee, and pleasure to sing praises to Thy name, for from everlasting unto everlasting Thou art God."

" The breath of all that lives shall praise Thy name, O Lord, our God. And the spirit of all flesh shall continually glorify and exalt Thy memorial, O God, our King. For from everlasting unto everlasting Thou art God, and beside Thee we have no king, redeemer or saviour."

Thus ended the Passover Feast. If the feast that Jesus and His disciples sat at was the Passover Feast it must have been the two items (xiii) and (xiv) that Jesus took and made His own, and (xvi) must have been the hymn they sang before they went out to the Mount of Olives.

Now let us see what Jesus was doing, and what He was seeking to impress upon His men. More than once we have seen that the prophets of Israel resorted to symbolic, dramatic actions when they felt that words were not enough. That is what Ahijah did when he rent the robe into twelve pieces and gave ten to Jeroboam in token that ten of the tribes would make him king (I Kings II : 29-32). That is what Jeremiah did, when he made bonds and yokes and wore them in token of the coming servitude (Jeremiah 27). And that is what the prophet Hananiah did when he broke the yokes that Jeremiah wore (Jeremiah 28 : 10, 11). That is the kind of thing that Ezekiel was continually doing (Ezekiel 4 : 1-8, 5 : 1-4). It was as if words were easily forgotten, but a dramatic action would print itself on the memory. That is what Jesus did, and He allied this dramatic action with the ancient feast of His people so that it would be the more imprinted on the minds of His men. He said, " Look ! Just as this bread is broken my body is broken for you ! Just as this cup of red wine is poured out my blood is shed for you."

What did He mean when He said that the cup stood for a new covenant? The word *covenant* is a common word in Jewish religion. The basis of Jewish religion was that God had entered into a *covenant* with Israel. The word means something like an arrangement, a bargain, a relationship. Now the acceptance of *the old covenant* is set out in Exodus 24 : 3-8. And from that passage we see that the covenant was entirely dependent on Israel keeping the law. If the law was broken the covenant was broken and the relationship between God and the nation was shattered. *It was a relationship which was entirely dependent on law and on obedience to the law.* God was judge. And since no man can keep the law the people were ever in default. But Jesus says, " I am introducing and ratifying *a new covenant,* a new kind of relationship between God and man. And it is not dependent on *law,* it is dependent on *the blood that I will shed."* That is to say, it is dependent solely on *love.* The new covenant was a relationship between man and God which was not dependent on law but on love. In other words Jesus says, " I am doing what I am doing to show you how much God loves you." Men were no longer simply *under the law of God.* Because of what Jesus did and came to tell, they were forever *within the love of God.* That is the very essence of what the Sacrament says to us.

We may note one thing more. In the last sentence we see again the two things that we have so often seen. Jesus was sure of two things. He knew He was to die, and He knew His Kingdom would come. He was certain of the Cross, but He was just as certain of the glory. And the reason for the two certainties is, that He was certain of the love of God as He was of the sin of man, and He knew that in the end that love would conquer that sin.

THE FAILURE OF FRIENDS

Mark 14 : 27-31

> Jesus said to them, " You will all fall away from me,
> for it stands written, ' I will smite the shepherd and
> the sheep will be scattered.' But after I have been
> raised to life again, I will go before you into Galilee."
> Peter said to Him, " All the others may fall away
> from you, but I will not." Jesus said to him, " This
> is the truth I tell you—to-day, this night, before the
> cock crows twice you will deny me three times."
> Peter began to insist vehemently, " If I must die with
> you I will not deny you." So, too, they all said.

IT is the tremendous thing about Jesus that there was
nothing for which He was not prepared. The opposition,
the misunderstanding, the enmity of the orthodox religious
people of His day, the betrayal by one of His own inner
circle, the pain and the agony of the Cross—He was prepared for them all. But, maybe, that which hurt Him
most was the failure of His friends. It is when a man is up
against it that a man needs his friends most, and that was
exactly when Jesus' friends left Him all alone and let Him
down. There was nothing in the whole gamut of physical
pain and mental torture that Jesus did not pass through.
Sir Hugh Walpole wrote a great novel called *Fortitude*.
It is the story of one also called Peter, whose creed was,
" It isn't life that matters, but the courage you bring to
it." Life did everything that it possibly could to Peter.
At the end, on his own mountain top, Peter heard a voice,
" Blessed be pain and torment and every torture of the
body. Blessed be all loss and the failure of friends and the
sacrifice of love. Blessed be all failure and the ruin of every
earthly hope. Blessed be all sorrow and torment, hardships,
and endurances that demand courage. Blessed be these
things—for of these things cometh the making of a man."
And Peter fell to praying, " Make of me a man . . . to be
afraid of nothing, to be ready for everything. Love,
friendship, success . . . to take it if it comes, to care nothing

if these things are not for me. Make me brave. Make me brave." Jesus had supremely, more than anyone who ever lived, this quality of fortitude, this ability to remain erect no matter with what blows life assaulted Him, this serenity when there was nothing but heartbreak behind and torture in front. Inevitably every now and then we find ourselves catching our breath at the sheer heroism of Jesus.

When Jesus foretold this tragic failure of loyalty, Peter could not believe that it would happen. In the days of the Stewart troubles they captured the Cock of the North, the Marquis of Huntly. They told him to abandon his loyalty. They pointed at the block and the axe and told him that unless he abandoned his loyalty he would be executed then and there. His answer was, " You can take my head from my shoulders but you will never take my heart from my king." That is what Peter said that night. Now there is a lesson in the word that Jesus used for " fall away." The Authorised Version translates it " be offended." The Greek verb is *skandalizein*. It comes from the word *skandalon* or *skandalēthron* which means the bait in a trap, the stick on to which the animal was lured, and which snapped the trap when the animal stepped on it. So the word *skandalizein* came to mean to entrap, or to trip up by some trick or guile. Peter was too sure. He had forgotten the traps that life can lay for the best of men. He had forgotten that the best of men can step on a slippery place and fall. He had forgotten his own human weakness and the strength of the devil's temptations. But there is one thing to be remembered about Peter—*his heart was in the right place*. Better be a Peter with a flaming heart of love, even if that love did for a moment fail and fail most shamefully, than a Judas with a cold heart of hate. Let the man who never broke a promise, let the man who never in his life was disloyal in thought or action to a pledge, condemn Peter. Peter loved Jesus, and even if love failed, love rose again.

359

THY WILL BE DONE

Mark 14 : 32-42

> They came to a place the name of which is Gethsemane. Jesus said to His disciples, " Sit here while I pray." He took Peter and James and John with Him, and began to be in great distress and trouble of mind. He said to them, " My soul is sore grieved even to death. Stay here and watch." He went on a little farther and fell on the ground and prayed that, if it was possible, this hour might pass from Him. He said, " Abba, Father, everything is possible to you. Take this cup from me—but not what I wish, but what you wish." He came and He found them sleeping and He said to Peter, " Simon, are you sleeping? Could you not stay awake for one hour? Watch and pray lest you enter into some testing time. The spirit is willing but the flesh is weak." And again He went away and prayed in the same words. And again He came and found them sleeping, for their eyes were weighed down with sleep. And they did not know how to answer Him. And He came the third time and said to them, " Sleep on now. Take your rest. It is enough. The hour has come. See ! The Son of Man is betrayed into the hands of sinners. Rise ! Let us be going ! He who betrays me has come ! "

THIS is a passage which we almost fear to read, for to read it seems to be to intrude into the private agony of Jesus.

To have stayed in the upper room would have been dangerous. With the authorities on the watch for Him, and with Judas bent on treachery, the upper room might have been raided at any time. But Jesus had another place to which to go. The fact that Judas knew to look for Him in Gethsemane shows that Jesus was in the habit of going there. In Jerusalem itself there were no gardens. The city was too crowded, and there was a strange law that the city's sacred soil might not be polluted with manure for the gardens. But some of the rich and well-to-do people possessed private gardens out on the Mount of Olives where they took their rest. Jesus must have had some wealthy friend who gave Him the privilege of using his garden at night.

When Jesus went to Gethsemane there were two things He sorely desired. He wanted *human fellowship* and He wanted *God's fellowship*. "It is not good that the man should be alone," God said in the beginning. (Genesis 2 : 18.) In time of trouble we want someone with us. We do not necessarily want them to do anything. We do not necessarily even want to talk to them or them to talk to us. We only want them there. Jesus was like that. And it was so strange that men who so short a time before had been protesting that they would die for Him, could not stay awake for Him one single hour. But none can blame them, for the excitement and the tensity had drained their strength and their resistance power.

Certain things are clear about Jesus in this passage.

(i) He did not want to die. He was thirty-three and no one wants to die with life just opening on to the best of the years. He had done so little and there was a world waiting to be saved. He knew what crucifixion was like, and He shuddered away from it. The Cross would lose all its value if it had been easy for Jesus. He had to compel Himself to go on—just as we have so often to do.

(ii) He did not fully understand why this had to be. He only knew beyond a doubt that this was the will of God, and that He must go on. Jesus, too, had to make that great venture of faith, He had to accept—as we so often have to do—what He could not understand.

(iii) He submitted to the will of God. *Abba* is the Aramaic for *My Father*. And it is that one word which made all the difference. Jesus was not submitting to a God who made a cynical sport of men. Hardy finishes his novel *Tess*, after telling of Tess's tragic life, with the terrible sentence, " The President of the Immortals had finished His sport with Tess." God was not like that. Jesus was not submitting to a God who was an iron fate.

> " But helpless pieces of the game he plays,
>   Upon this chequer board of nights and days,
>   Hither and thither moves and mates and slays—
> And one by one back in the closet lays."

God was not like that. Even in this terrible hour, when God was making this terrible demand, God was *Father*. When Richard Cameron, the covenanter, was killed, his head and hands were cut off by one Murray and taken to Edinburgh. " His father being in prison for the same cause, the enemy carried them to him, to add grief unto his former sorrow, and inquired if he knew them. Taking his sons head and hands, which were very fair (being a man of a fair complexion like himself) he kissed them and said, ' I know them—I know them. They are my son's—my own dear son's. It is the Lord. Good is the will of the Lord, who cannot wrong me nor mine, but hath made goodness and mercy to follow us all our days.'" If we can call God *Father* everything becomes bearable. Time and again we will not understand, but always we will be certain that " The Father's hand will never cause His child a needless tear." That is what Jesus knew. That is why He could go on—and it can be so with us.

We must note how the passage ends. The traitor and his gang had arrived. What was Jesus' reaction? Not to run away, and even yet, in the night it would have been easy to escape. His reaction was *to face them*. To the end He would neither turn aside nor turn back.

THE ARREST

Mark 14 : 43-50

And immediately, while He was still speaking, Judas, one of The Twelve arrived, and with him a crowd with swords and cudgels from the chief priests, and the experts in the law, and the elders. The betrayer had given them this sign. " Whom I shall kiss," he said, " that is He. Seize Him and take Him away

securely." So when he had come, immediately he
stepped forward. " Rabbi ! " he said—and kissed Him
as a lover would. They laid hands on Him and seized
Him. One of those standing by drew his sword and
struck the High Priest's servant and cut off his ear.
Jesus said to them, " Have you come out with swords
and cudgels to arrest me as you would come against a
brigand? Daily I was with you teaching in the Temple
precincts, and you did not seize me—but, let it be,
that the scriptures may be fulfilled." And they all
left Him and fled.

THERE is sheer drama here, and, even in Mark's economy
of words, the characters stand out before us.

(i) There is Judas, the traitor. He knew that the people
knew Jesus well enough by sight. But he felt that in the
dim light of the garden, with the darkness of the trees lit
in pools of light, by the flare of the torches, they needed a
definite indication of who they were to arrest. And so he
chose that most terrible of signs—a kiss. It was customary
to greet a Rabbi with a kiss. It was a sign of respect and
affection for a well-loved teacher. But there is a terrible
thing here. When Judas says, "Whom I shall kiss, that is
He," he used the word *philein* which is the ordinary word.
But when it is said that he came forward and kissed Jesus
the word is *kataphilein*. Now the *kata-* is intensive and
kataphilein is the word for to kiss as *a lover kisses his
beloved*. The sign of the betrayal was not a mere formal
kiss of respectful greeting. It was a lover's kiss. That is
the grimmest and most terrible thing in all the gospel story.

(ii) There is the arresting mob. They came from the
chief priests, the scribes and the elders. These were the
three sections of the Sanhedrin, the supreme court of the
Jews, and Mark means that they came from the Sanhedrin.
Even under Roman jurisdiction the Sanhedrin had certain
police rights and duties in Jerusalem and had its own
police force. No doubt an assorted rabble had attached
themselves to them on the way. Somehow Mark manages
to convey the wrought up excitement of those who came to

make the arrest. Maybe they had come prepared for bloodshed with nerves taut and tense. It is they who emanate terror—not Jesus.

(iii) There is the man of the forlorn hope who drew his sword and struck one blow. John (18 : 10) tells us that it was Peter. It sounds like Peter, and Mark very likely omits the name because it was not yet safe to write it down. In the scuffle no one saw who struck the blow. It was better that no one should know. But when John wrote another forty years later it was quite safe to write it down. It may be wrong to draw a sword and hack at a man, but somehow we are glad that there was one man there who, at least on the impulse of the moment, was prepared to strike a blow for Jesus.

(iv) There were the disciples. Their nerve cracked. They could not face this. Frankly they were afraid that they too would share the fate of Jesus, and they fled.

(v) There was Jesus Himself. And the strange thing is that in all this disordered scene Jesus is the one oasis of serenity. As we read the story it reads as if He, not the Sanhedrin police, was directing affairs. For Him the struggle in the Garden was over, and now there was the peace of the man who knows that He is following the will of God.

A CERTAIN YOUNG MAN

Mark 14 : 51, 52

> And a certain young man was following Him, clothed in a linen sheet over his naked body. And they tried to seize him, but he left the linen sheet and escaped naked.

THESE are two strange and fascinating verses. At first sight they seem so completely irrelevant. They seem to add nothing to the narrative and yet there must be some reason for them being there. We saw in the introduction

that Matthew and Luke used Mark as the basis of their
work and that they include in their gospels practically
everything that is in Mark. But they do not include these
two verses. That would seem to show us that this incident
was interesting to Mark and not really interesting to
anyone else. Why then are they there? And why was this
incident so interesting to Mark that he felt that he must
include it? By far the most probable answer is that the
young man was no other than Mark himself, and that this
is his way of saying, " I was there," without mentioning
his own name at all.

When we read Acts we find that the meeting place and
head-quarters of the Jerusalem Church was apparently in
the house of Mary, the mother of John Mark (Acts 12 : 12).
Now, if that be so, it is at least probable that the upper
room in which the Last Supper was eaten was that same
room, the room in Mark's mother's house. There could be
no more natural place than that room to be the centre of
the Church. If we can assume that there are two possibilities. (i) It may be that Mark was actually present at
the Last Supper. He was young, just a boy, and maybe
no one really noticed him. But he was fascinated with
Jesus, and when the company went out into the dark he
slipped out after them when he ought to have been in bed,
with only the linen sheet over his naked body. It may be
that all the time Mark was there in the shadows listening
and watching. That in fact would explain one thing.
Where did the Gethsemane narrative come from? If the
disciples were all asleep how did anyone know about the
struggle of soul that Jesus had there? It may be that the
one witness was none other than Mark as he stood silent
in the shadows, watching with a boy's reverence the greatest
hero he had ever known. (ii) The alternative theory is this.
It also begins from the supposition that the Last Supper
was eaten in Mark's mother's house. From John's narrative
we know that Judas left the company before the meal was
fully ended (John 13 : 30). It may be that it was to the

upper room that Judas meant to lead the Temple police so that they might secretly arrest Jesus. But when Judas came back with the police, Jesus and His disciples were gone. Naturally there was recrimination and argument. The uproar wakened Mark. He heard Judas propose that they should go on and try the Garden of Gethsemane. Quickly Mark wrapped his bed-sheet about him and sped through the night to the Garden to warn Jesus. But he arrived too late, and in the scuffle that followed was very nearly arrested himself.

Whatever may be true, we may take it as fairly certain that Mark put in these two verses because they were about himself. He could never forget that night. He was too humble to put his own name in, but in this way he wrote his signature, and said, to him who could read between the lines, " I, too, when I was a boy, was there."

THE TRIAL

Mark 14 : 53, 55-65

They took Jesus away to the High Priest, and all the chief priests and experts in the law and elders assembled with Him. . . . The chief priests and the whole Sanhedrin were trying to find some evidence against Jesus, in order to put Him to death, and they could not find any, for there were many who bore false witness against Him, but their evidence did not agree. Some stood up and bore false witness against Him. " We heard Him saying," they said, " 'I will destroy this Temple made with hands and in three days' time I will build another not made with hands '." But not even so did their evidence agree. So the High Priest stood up in the midst and questioned Jesus. " Do you give no answer? " he said. " What is the evidence that these men are alleging against you? " Jesus remained silent and gave no answer. Again the High Priest questioned Him, and said to Him, "Are you God's Anointed One, the Son of the Blessed One? " Jesus said, " I am, and you will see the Son of Man seated on the right hand of power, and coming with the clouds of heaven." The High Priest rent his garments. "What need," he said, "have we of witnesses? You have listened to blasphemy. How does it seem to you?" And they all adjudged Him to be liable to death. And some began to spit upon Him, and to cover His face, and to buffet Him, and to say to Him, "Prophesy!" And the servants received Him with blows.

THINGS were moving quickly now to their inevitable end.

At this time the powers of the Sanhedrin were limited because the Romans were the rulers of the country. The Sanhedrin had full power over religious matters and questions. It seems also to have had a certain amount of police court power. But it had no power to inflict the death penalty. If this that Mark describes was a meeting of the Sanhedrin it must be compared to a Grand Jury. Its function was not to condemn, but to prepare a charge on which the criminal could be tried before the Roman governor.

There is no doubt that in the trial of Jesus the Sanhedrin broke all its own laws. The regulations for the procedure of the Sanhedrin are in one of the tractates of the *Mishnah*. Naturally enough some of these regulations are rather ideals than actual practices which were carried out, but, even allowing for that, the whole procedure of this night was composed of a series of flagrant injustices.

The Sanhedrin was the supreme court of the Jews. It was composed of seventy-one members. Within its membership there were Sadducees—the priestly classes were all Sadducees—Pharisees and Scribes, who were experts in the law, and respected men who were elders. It appears that any vacancies in the court were filled by co-option. The High Priest presided over the court. The court sat in a semi-circle in such a way that any member could see any other member. Facing it there sat the students of the Rabbis. They were allowed to speak on behalf of the person on trial but not against him. The official meeting place of the Sanhedrin was The Hall of

Hewn Stone which was within the Temple precincts, and the decisions of the Sanhedrin were not valid unless arrived at at a meeting held in that place. The court could not meet at night, nor could it meet at any of the great feasts. When evidence was taken, witnesses were examined separately and their evidence to be valid must agree in every detail. Each individual member of the Sanhedrin must give his verdict separately, beginning from the youngest and going on to the eldest. If the verdict was a verdict of death, a night must elapse before it was carried out so that the court might have a chance to change its mind and its decision towards mercy. It can be seen that on point after point the Sanhedrin broke its own rules. It was not meeting in its own building. It was meeting at night. There is no word of individually given verdicts. A night was not allowed to elapse before the penalty of death was inflicted. In their eagerness to eliminate Jesus, the Jewish authorities did not hesitate to stoop to breaking their own laws.

At first the court could not get even false witnesses to agree. The false witnesses accused Jesus of having said that He would destroy the Temple. It may well be that someone had overheard Jesus speaking as He did in Mark 13 : 2, and saying that not one of these stones would be left upon another, and had maliciously twisted the saying into a threat to destroy the Temple. There is an old legend which tells how the Sanhedrin could get plenty of the kind of evidence that they did not want, for man after man came forward saying, " I was a leper and He cleansed me. I was blind and He made me able to see. I was deaf and He made me able to hear. I was lame and He made me able to walk. I was paralysed and He gave me back my strength." But that was not the evidence that the Sanhedrin desired.

At last the High Priest took the matter into his own hands. And when he did so, he asked the very kind of question that the law completely forbade. He asked a leading question. It was naturally forbidden to ask questions by answering which the person on trial might incriminate himself. No man could be asked to condemn himself, but that was the very question that the High Priest asked. Bluntly He asked Jesus if He was the Messiah. Clearly Jesus felt that it was time that the whole wretched business was ended. Without hesitation He answered that He was. It was a charge of blasphemy, insult against God. The Sanhedrin had what it wanted, a charge which merited the death penalty, and they were savagely content.

Once again we see the two great characteristics of Jesus emerge.

(i) We see His *courage*. He knew that to make that answer was to die, and yet unhesitatingly He made it. Had He denied the charges they would have been powerless to touch Him.

(ii) We see His *confidence*. Even with the Cross now a certainty He still continued to speak with complete confidence of His ultimate triumph.

Surely it is the most terrible of tragedies to see Him who came to offer men love denied even bare justice, and humiliated by the crude and cruel horse-play of the Sanhedrin servants and guards.

COURAGE AND COWARDICE

Mark 14 : 54, 66-72

And Peter followed Him at a distance, right into the courtyard of the High Priest's house, and he was sitting there with the servants, warming himself at the fire. . . . When Peter was below in the courtyard, one of the maidservants of the High Priest came up, and when she saw Peter warming himself, she looked closely at him. "You, too," she said, "were with the Nazarene, with Jesus." He denied it. "I do not know," he said, "or understand what you are saying." He went out into the porch, and the cock crew. The maidservant saw him and again began to say to the bystanders, " This man was one of them." But he again denied it. Soon afterwards the bystanders said to Peter, " In truth you are one of them, for you are a Galilaean." He began to curse and to swear, " I do not know the man you are talking about." And immediately cockcrow sounded. And Peter remembered the word, how Jesus had said to him, " Before the cock crow twice you will deny me three times." And he flung his cloak about his head and wept.

SOMETIMES we tell this story in such a way as to do Peter far far less than justice. The thing that we so often fail to recognize is that up to the very last Peter's career this night had been a career of fantastically reckless courage. He had begun by drawing his sword in the Garden with the reckless courage of a man who would take on a whole mob all by himself. In that scuffle he had wounded the servant of the High Priest. Now common prudence would have urged that Peter should lie very low. The last place that anyone would have dreamed that Peter would go to would have been the courtyard of the High Priest's house—and yet that is precisely where he did go. That in itself was sheer audacity. It may be that the others had fled, but Peter was keeping his word. Even if the others had gone he would stick to Jesus. And then the queer mixture of human nature emerged. He was sitting by the fire for the night was cold. No doubt he was huddled in his cloak. Maybe someone poked the fire or flung a fresh log upon it, and it flared up with a fitful flame and Peter was recognized. Straightway he denied all connection with Jesus. *But*—and here is the forgotten point—any prudent man would have left that courtyard as fast as his legs could carry him—but not Peter. He would not go. The same thing happened again, and again Peter denied Jesus, but again he could not go. The same thing happened again. Again Peter denied Jesus, Peter did not curse Jesus' name. What he did was that he swore he did not know Jesus, and called down curses on himself if he was not telling the truth. Still it seems

370

that Peter did not mean to move. And then something happened. Very probably what happened was this. The Roman night was divided into four watches from 6 p.m. to 6 a.m. At the end of the third watch, at three o'clock in the morning, the guard was changed. When the guard was changed there was a bugle call which was called the *gallicinium*, which is the Latin for the *cockcrow*. Most likely what happened was that as Peter spoke his third denial, the clear note of the bugle call rang out throughout the silent city and smote on the ear of Peter, and Peter remembered and his heart broke. Make no mistake— Peter fell to a temptation which would only have come to a man of fantastic courage. It ill becomes prudent and safety-seeking little men to criticize Peter for falling to a temptation which would never, in the same circumstances, have come to them at all. Every man has his breaking-point. Peter had reached his, but nine hundred and ninety-nine men out of every thousand would have reached their breaking-point long ago. We would do well to be amazed at Peter's courage rather than to be shocked at his fall.

But there is another thing. There is only one source from which this story could have come—and that source is Peter himself. Remember we saw in the introduction that Mark's gospel is the preaching material of Peter. That is to say, over and over again, Peter must have told the story of his own denial. " That is what I did," he must have said, " and this amazing Jesus never stopped loving me." There was an evangelist called Brownlow North. He was a man of God, but in his youth he had lived a wild life. One Sunday he was to preach in Aberdeen. Before he entered the pulpit a letter was handed to him. The writer of the letter recounted a shameful incident in Brownlow North's life before he became a Christian and stated that if Brownlow North dared to preach he would rise in the Church and publicly proclaim what once he had done. Brownlow North took the letter into the pulpit with him. He read it to the congregation. He told them that it was

371

perfectly true. Then he told them how, through Christ, he had been forgiven, how he had been enabled to overcome himself and put the past behind him, how, through Christ, he was a new creature. He used his own shame as a magnet to draw men to Christ. That is what Peter did. He told men, " I hurt Him and I let Him down like that, and still He loved and forgave me—and He can do the same for you."

When we read this passage with understanding the story of Peter's cowardice becomes the epic of his courage and the story of his shame becomes the tale of his glory.

THE SILENCE OF JESUS

Mark 15 : 1-5

> Immediately, early in the morning, the chief priests, together with the elders and the experts in the law— that is to say, the whole Sanhedrin—held a consulta- tion. They bound Jesus and took Him away and handed Him over to Pilate. Pilate asked Him, "Are you the King of the Jews?" Jesus answered, " It is you who say so." The chief priests made many accusations against Him. Pilate again questioned Him, " Have you no answer to make?" he said. " See how many accusations they have made against you." Jesus answered nothing further, and Pilate was amazed.

As soon as it was light the Sanhedrin met to confirm the conclusions they had arrived at during their meeting in the night. They themselves had no power to carry out the death penalty. That had to be imposed by the Roman governor and carried out by the Roman authorities. It is from Luke that we learn how deep and determined the bitter malice of the Jews was. As we have seen, the charge at which they had arrived was a charge of blasphemy, of insulting God. But that was not the charge on which they brought Jesus before Pilate. They knew well that Pilate would have had nothing to do with a charge which he would have considered a Jewish religious argument. When they brought Jesus to Pilate they charged Him with perverting the people, and forbidding them to give tribute to Caesar, and calling Himself a king. (Luke 23 : 1, 2.) They had to evolve a political charge or Pilate would not have listened. They knew that the charge was a lie—and so did Pilate. Pilate asked Jesus, "Are you the King of the Jews?" Jesus gave him a strange answer. He said, "It is you who say so." Jesus did not say yes or no. What He did say was this, "I may have claimed to be the King of the Jews, but you know very well that the interpretation that my accusers are putting on that claim is not my interpretation. I am no political revolutionary. My kingdom is a kingdom of love." Pilate knew that perfectly well. Then Pilate went on to question Jesus more, and the Jewish authorities went on to multiply their charges—and Jesus answered nothing and remained completely silent.

There is a time when silence is more eloquent than words, for silence can say things that words can never say.

(i) There is the silence of *wondering admiration*. It is a compliment for any performance or oration to be greeted with thunderous applause, but it is a still greater compliment for it to be greeted with a hushed silence which knows that applause would be quite out of place. It is a compliment to be praised or thanked in words, but it is a still greater compliment to receive a look of the eyes which plainly says that there are no words to be found.

(ii) There is the silence of *contempt*. It is possible to greet someone's statements or arguments or excuses with silence which shows that they are not worth answering, with a silence eloquent of contempt. Instead of answering someone's protestation the listener may turn on his heel and contemptuously leave them unanswered.

(iii) There is a silence of *fear*. A man may remain silent for no other reason than that he is afraid to speak. The cowardice of his soul may stop him saying the things he knows he ought to say. Fear may gag him into a shameful silence.

(iv) There is the silence of *the heart that is hurt*. When a person has been really hurt and wounded he does not break into protests and recriminations and angry words. The deepest sorrow is a dumb sorrow, which is past anger and past rebuke and past anything that speech can say, and which can only silently look its sorrow.

(v) There is the silence of *tragedy*, and that is the silence which is silent because there is nothing to be said. That was why Jesus was silent. He knew that there could be no bridge between Himself and the Jewish leaders. He knew that there was nothing in Pilate to which He could ultimately appeal. He knew that the lines of communication were broken. The hatred of the Jews was an iron curtain which no words could penetrate. The cowardice of Pilate in face of the mob was a barrier no words could pierce. It is a terrible thing when a man's heart is such that even Jesus knows it is hopeless to speak. God save us from that !

THE CHOICE OF THE MOB

Mark 15 : 6-15

At the time of the Feast, it was the custom for the governor to release to the people a prisoner, whom they were accustomed to choose. There was a man called Barabbas, confined with the revolutionaries, who had committed murder during the insurrection. The crowd approached Pilate's judgment seat and began to request that he should carry out the customary procedure for them. Pilate answered, " Do you wish me to release to you the King of the Jews? " For he knew that the chief priests had handed Him over to him through sheer malice. The chief priests stirred up the mob to demand the release of Barabbas all the more. Pilate again asked them, " What shall I do to the man you call the King of the Jews? " Again they shrieked, " Crucify Him ! " Pilate said to them,

" What harm has He done? " They shrieked the more vehemently, " Crucify Him ! " Pilate wished to please the mob, and he released Barabbas for them, and, when he had scourged Jesus, he handed Him over to them to be crucified.

OF Barabbas we know nothing other than what we read in the gospel story. He was not a thief, he was a brigand. He was no petty pilferer or sneak thief. He was a bandit, and there must have been a rough audacity about him that would appeal to the crowd. Perhaps we may guess what he was. Palestine was filled with insurrections. It was an inflammable land. In particular there was one group of Jews called the *Sicarii*, which means the dagger-bearers. They were violent, fanatical nationalists. They were pledged to murder and assassination by any possible means. They carried their daggers beneath their cloaks and used them as they could. It is very likely that Barabbas was a man like that, and, thug though he was, he was a brave man, a patriot according to his lights, and it is understandable that he was popular with the mob.

People have always felt it a mystery that less than a week before the crowd were shouting a welcome when Jesus rode into Jerusalem and that now they were shrieking for his crucifixion. There is no real mystery. The reason is quite simply that this was a different crowd. Think of the arrest. It was deliberately secret. True, the disciples fled and must have spread the news, but they could not have known that the Sanhedrin was going to violate its own laws and carry out a travesty of a trial by night. There can have been very few of Jesus' supporters in that crowd. Who then were the crowd? Think again. The crowd knew that there was this custom whereby a prisoner was released at the Passover time. It may well be that this was a crowd which had assembled with the deliberate intention of demanding the release of Barabbas. They were in fact *a mob of Barabbas' supporters*. When they saw the possibility that Jesus might be released and not Barabbas they went mad. To the chief priests this was a heaven-sent opportunity. Circumstances had played into their hands. They fanned the popular clamour for Barabbas and it was easy, for it was the release of Barabbas that that crowd had come to claim. It was not that the crowd was fickle. It was that it was necessarily a different crowd.

Nonetheless, here is the choice of the crowd. Confronted with the choice between Jesus and Barabbas, they chose Barabbas without hesitation.

(i) They chose *lawlessness instead of law*. They chose the law-breaker instead of Jesus. One of the New Testament words for sin is *anomia*, which means lawlessness. In the human heart there is a streak which resents law, which desires to do as it likes, which wants to smash the confining barriers and kick over the traces and refuse all discipline. There is something of that in every man. Kipling makes the old soldier say in *Mandalay* :

" Ship me somewheres east of Suez, where the best is
    like the worst,
  Where there aren't no Ten Commandments an' a
    man can raise a thirst."

There are times when most of us wish there were no Ten Commandments. The mob was the representative of men when it chose lawlessness instead of law.

(ii) They chose *war instead of peace*. They chose the man of blood instead of the Prince of Peace. In almost three thousand years of history there has been less than one hundred and thirty years where there has not been a war raging somewhere. Men in their incredible folly have sought to settle things by war which settles nothing. The mob were doing what men have so often done when they chose the warrior and rejected the man of peace.

(iii) They chose *hatred and violence instead of love.* Barabbas and Jesus stood for two different ways. Barabbas stood for the heart of hate, the stab of the dagger, the violence of bitterness. Jesus stood for the way of love. As so often has happened, hate reigned supreme in the hearts of men, and love was rejected. Men insisted on taking their own way to conquest, and refused to see that the only conquest is the conquest of love.

There can be hidden tragedy in a word. " When he had scourged Him "—it is one word in the Greek. The Roman scourge was a terrible thing. The criminal was bent and bound in such a way that his back was exposed. The scourge was a long leathern thong, studded here and there with sharpened pieces of lead and bits of bone. It literally tore a man's back to ribbons. Sometimes it tore a man's eye out. Some men died under it. Some men emerged from the ordeal raving mad. Few retained consciousness through it. It was that that they did to Jesus.

THE SOLDIERS' MOCKERY

Mark 15 : 16-20

The soldiers led Jesus away into the hall, which is the Praetorium, and they called together the whole company. They clad Him in a purple robe, and they plaited a crown of thorns and put it on Him, and they began to salute Him, " Hail ! King of the Jews ! " And they struck His head with a reed, and they spat on Him, and they knelt down before Him and worshipped Him. And after they had made sport of Him, they took off the purple robe, and clad Him in His own clothes. And they led Him away to crucify Him.

THE Roman ritual of condemnation was fixed and settled. The judge said *Illum duci ad crucem placet*, " The sentence is that this man should be taken to a cross." And then he turned to the guard and said, I, *miles*, *expedi crucem*, " Go, soldier, and prepare the cross." It was when the cross was being prepared that Jesus was in the hands of the soldiers. The Praetorium was the residence of the governor, his headquarters, and the soldiers involved would be the headquarters cohort of the guard. We would do well to remember that Jesus had already undergone the agony of scourging before this horse-play of the soldiers began.

It may well be that of all that happened to Him this hurt Jesus least. The actions of the Jews had been venomous with hatred. The consent of Pilate had been a cowardly evasion of responsibility. There was cruelty in the action of the soldiers, but there was no malice. To them Jesus was only another man for a cross, and they carried out their barrack-room pantomime of royalty and worship, not with any malice, but as a coarse jest.

It was the beginning of much mockery to come. Always the Christian was liable to be regarded as a jest. Scribbled on the walls of Pompeii, just as the walls are still chalked with coarse jests to-day, there is a picture of a man, a Christian kneeling before an ass, and below it, there is scrawled the words, "Anaximenes worships his God." If ever people make a jest of our Christianity, it will help us to remember that they did it to Jesus in a way that is worse than anything that is likely to happen to us.

THE CROSS

Mark 15 : 21-28

> And they impressed into service a man called Simon of Cyrene, who was passing by, on his way in from the country, the father of Alexander and Rufus, and they made him carry His Cross. So they brought Him to the place Golgotha, which means the place of a skull. They offered Him wine mingled with myrrh, but He would not take it. They crucified Him. And they divided out His garments, throwing dice for them to decide who should take what. It was nine o'clock in the morning when they crucified Him. And the inscription of the charge against Him was written on the Cross—"The King of the Jews." With Him they crucified two brigands, one on His right hand and one on His left.

THE routine of crucifixion did not alter. When the cross was prepared the criminal had himself to carry it to the place of execution. He was placed in the middle of a hollow square of four soldiers. In front there marched a soldier carrying a board on which was the crime of which the prisoner was guilty. The board was afterwards affixed to the cross. They took not the shortest but the longest way to the place of execution. They followed every possible street and lane so that as many as possible should see and take warning. When they reached the place of crucifixion, the cross was laid flat on the ground. The prisoner was stretched upon it, and his hands were nailed to it. The feet were not nailed but only loosely bound. Between the prisoner's legs there projected a ledge of wood called the saddle, which was to take his weight when the cross was raised upright or the nails would have torn through the flesh of the hands. The cross was then lifted upright and set in its socket—and the criminal was left to die. The cross was not tall. It was shaped like the letter T, and had no top piece at all. Sometimes prisoners hung for as long as a week, dying of hunger and of thirst, suffering until they went mad.

This must have been a grim day for Simon of Cyrene. Palestine was an occupied country and any man might be impressed into the Roman service for any task. The sign of impressment was a tap of the shoulder with the flat of a Roman spear. Simon was from Cyrene in Africa. No doubt he had come from that far off land for the Passover. No doubt he had scraped and saved for half a lifetime in order to come. No doubt he was gratifying the ambition of a lifetime to eat one Passover in Jerusalem—and then this happened to him. At the moment Simon must have bitterly resented it. He must have hated the Romans, and hated this criminal whose cross he was being forced to carry. But we may legitimately speculate what happened to Simon. It may be that it was his intention when he got to Golgotha to fling the cross down on the ground and hasten as quickly as he could from the scene. And it may be that he did not. It may be that he lingered on because something about Jesus fascinated him. He is described as *the father of Alexander and Rufus.* Now such a description must have been meant to identify him. The people for whom the gospel was written must have been meant to recognize him by this description. It is most likely that Mark's gospel was first written for the Church at Rome. Now let us turn to Paul's letter to Rome and read 16 : 13. " Salute Rufus, chosen in the Lord, and his mother and mine." Rufus was so choice a Christian that he was *chosen in the Lord.* The mother of Rufus was so dear to Paul that he could call her his own mother. Things must have happened to Simon on Golgotha. Now turn to Acts 13 : 1. There is a list of the men of Antioch who sent Paul and Barnabas out on that epoch-making first mission to the Gentiles. The name of one is *Simeon that was called Niger. Simeon* is another form of *Simon. Niger* was the regular name for a man of swarthy skin who came from Africa, and Cyrene is in Africa. Here it may well be that we are meeting Simon again. Maybe it is true that Simon's experience on the way to Golgotha bound his heart forever and forever to Jesus. Maybe it made him a Christian. Maybe in the after days he was a leader in Antioch and was instrumental in the first mission to the Gentiles. Maybe because Simon was compelled to carry the Cross of Jesus the first mission to the Gentiles took place. And that means that maybe *we* are Christians because one day a Passover pilgrim from Cyrene, to his bitter resentment at the moment, was impressed by a nameless Roman officer to carry the Cross of Christ.

They offered Jesus drugged wine and He would not drink it. There was a company of pious and merciful women in Jerusalem who came to every crucifixion and who gave the criminals a drink of drugged wine to ease the terrible pain. They offered it to Jesus—and He refused it. When Dr. Johnson was ill with his last illness he asked his doctor to tell him honestly if he could recover. The doctor said he could not recover without a miracle.

" Then," said Johnson, " I will take no more physic, not even opiates, for I have prayed that I may render up my soul to God unclouded." Jesus was resolved to taste death at its bitterest and to go to God with open eyes.

The soldiers diced for His clothes. We have seen how the prisoner was marched to the place of crucifixion amid the four soldiers. These soldiers had as their perquisite the clothes of the criminal. Now a Jew wore *five* articles of clothing—the inner robe, the outer robe, the sandals, the girdle and the turban. When the four lesser things had been assigned that left the great outer robe. It would have been useless to cut it up, and so the soldiers gambled for it in the shadow of the Cross.

Jesus was crucified between two thieves. It was the symbol of His whole life that to the end He companied with sinners.

THE LIMITLESS LOVE

Mark 15 : 29-32

> Those who were passing by hurled their insults at Him, wagging their heads at Him. "Aha !" they said, " you who are going to pull down the Temple and build it in three days, come down from the Cross and save yourself ! " Even so the chief priests jested with each other, with the experts in the law. " He saved others," they said, " He cannot save Himself. Let this Anointed One of God, This King of Israel, come down from the Cross, so that we may see it and believe." And those who were crucified with Him flung their taunts at Him.

THE Jewish leaders flung one last challenge at Jesus. " Come down from the Cross," they said, " and we will believe in you." It was precisely the wrong challenge. As General Booth said long ago, " It is because Jesus did *not* come down from the Cross that we believe in Him." The death of Jesus was absolutely necessary. The great reason of its necessity was this. Jesus came to tell men of the love of God. More, He was Himself the incarnate love of God.

And if Jesus had refused the Cross, if in the end He had come down from the Cross, it would have meant that there was a limit to the love of God, that there was something which the love of God was not prepared to suffer for men, that there was a line beyond which the love of God would not go. But, because Jesus went the whole way and died on the Cross, it means that there is literally no limit to the love of God, that there is nothing in all the universe which the love of God is not prepared to suffer for men, that there is nothing, not even death on a cross, which the love of God will refuse to bear for man. When we look at the Cross, Jesus is saying to us, " God loves you like that, with a love that is limitless, a love that will bear every suffering earth has to offer for you." If Jesus had come down we could not have believed that, but because He refused to come down we believe and we rest our souls in the limitless love of God.

TRAGEDY AND TRIUMPH

Mark 15 : 33-41

When it was twelve o'clock midday, there came a darkness over the whole earth, and it lasted until three o'clock in the afternoon. And at three o'clock Jesus cried with a great voice, " Eloi, Eloi lama sabachthani? " which means, " My God ! My God ! Why have you abandoned me? " When certain of the bystanders heard it, they said, " See ! He is calling for Elijah ! " Someone ran and soaked a sponge in vinegar and gave Him a drink. " Let be ! " he said, " till we see if Elijah is going to come and take Him down." Jesus uttered a great shout—and died. And the veil of the Temple was rent in two from top to bottom. When the centurion who was standing opposite Him saw that He died like this, he said, " Truly this man was the Son of God." There were some women watching from a distance, amongst whom were Mary of Magdala, and Mary the mother of James the little and of Joses, and Salome. They had accompanied Him in Galilee and had attended to His needs. And there were many others who had come up with Him to Jerusalem.

So there comes the last scene of all, a scene so terrible that the sky was unnaturally darkened so that it seemed that even nature could not bear to look upon what was happening. Let us look at the various people in this scene.

(i) There was Jesus. Two things Jesus said (a) He uttered the terrible cry, " My God ! My God ! Why have you abandoned me? " There is a mystery behind that cry which we cannot penetrate. Maybe it was like this. Jesus had taken this life of ours upon Him. He had done our work and faced our temptations and borne our trials. He had suffered all that life could bring to Him. He had known the failure of friends, the hatred of foes, the malice of enemies. He had known the most searing pain that life can offer. Up to this moment Jesus had gone through every experience of life, *except one—He had never known the consequence of sin.* Now if there is one thing sin does, it is that it separates us from God. It puts up between us and God a barrier like an unscalable wall. That was the one human experience through which Jesus had never passed because He was without sin. It may be that at this moment that experience came upon Him. It did not come because He had sinned, but it came because before He could completely identify Himself with our humanity He had to go through it. In this terrible, grim, bleak moment Jesus really and truly identified Himself with the sin of man. Here we have the divine paradox—Jesus knew what it was to be a sinner. No man can understand an experience unless he goes through it. And this experience must have been doubly agonizing for Jesus, because He had never known what it was to be separated by this barrier from God. That is why He can understand so well. That is why we need never fear to go to Him when sin cuts us off from God. Because He has gone through it He can help others who are going through it. There is no depth of human experience which Christ has not shared and plumbed. (b) There was the great shout. Both Matthew (27 : 50) and Luke (23 : 46) tell of that great shout. John does not mention the shout but he tells us that Jesus died, having said, " It is finished." (John 19 : 30.) Now in the original that would be one word. *And that one word was the great shout.* " Finished ! " Jesus died with the cry of triumph on His lips, His task accomplished, His work completed, His victory won. After the terrible dark there came the light again, and He went home to God a victor triumphant.

(ii) There was the bystander who wished to see if Elijah would come. He had a kind of morbid curiosity in the face of the Cross. The whole terrible scene did not move him to awe or reverence or even pity. He wanted to experiment while Jesus died.

(iii) There was the centurion. The centurion was a hard-bitten Roman soldier. He was the equivalent of a regimental sergeant-major. He had fought in many a campaign and he had seen many a man die, but he had never seen a man die like this, and he was sure that Jesus was the Son of God. If Jesus had only lived and taught and healed He might have attracted many, but it is the Cross which speaks straight to the heart of men.

(iv) There were the women in the distance. They were bewildered, heart-broken, drenched in sorrow—*but they were there.* They loved so much that they could not leave Him. Love clings to Christ even when the intellect cannot understand. It is only love which can give us a hold on Christ that not even the most bewildering experiences can break.

There is one other thing to note. " The temple veil was rent in twain from top to bottom." That was the curtain which shut off the Holy of Holies, into which no man might go. Symbolically that tells us two things. (*a*) The way to God was now wide open. Into the Holy of Holies only the High Priest could go, and he only once a year on the Day of Atonement. But now, the veil was rent, and the way to God was wide open to every man. (*b*) Within the Holy of Holies dwelt the very essence of God. But now with

384

the death of Jesus the veil which hid God was rent and men could see God face to face. No longer was God hidden. No longer need men guess and grope. Men could look at Jesus and say, " That is what God is like. God loves me like that."

THE MAN WHO GAVE JESUS A TOMB

Mark 15 : 42-47

> When it was now evening, since it was the Day of Preparation, that is, the day before the Sabbath, Joseph of Arimathaea, a respected member of the council, and a man who was himself waiting for the Kingdom of God, ventured to go to Pilate and asked for the body of Jesus. Pilate was amazed that He was already dead. He summoned the centurion, and asked if He had been long dead. And when he had learned the facts from the centurion, he granted the body to Joseph. And Joseph bought fine linen, and he took Him down from the Cross and wrapped Him in the linen, and put Him in a tomb which had been hewn out of rock, and he rolled a stone against the door of the tomb. And Mary of Magdala and Mary the mother of Joses saw where He had been laid.

JESUS died at three o'clock in the afternoon. He died on the Friday afternoon, and the next day was the Sabbath. Now we have already seen that the next day started at 6 p.m. Therefore when Jesus died it was already the time of preparation for the Sabbath, and there was very little time to waste, for after 6 p.m. the Sabbath law would operate and no work could be done. Joseph of Arimathaea acted quickly. It frequently happened that the bodies of criminals were never buried at all, but were simply taken down and left for the vultures and the scavenging wild dogs to deal with. In fact it has been suggested that Golgotha may have been called the Place of a Skull because it was littered with skulls left lying from previous cruci-fixions. Joseph went to Pilate. It often happened that criminals hung for days on their crosses before they died, and Pilate was amazed that Jesus was dead only six hours after He had been crucified, but, when he had checked the facts with the centurion, he gave the body to Joseph.

Joseph is a curious study.

(i) It may well be that it is from Joseph that all the information about the trial before the Sanhedrin came. Certainly none of the disciples were there. The information must have come from some member of the Sanhedrin, and it is very probable that it was from Joseph that it came. If that is so Joseph had a very real share in the writing of the gospel story.

(ii) There is a certain tragedy about Joseph. He was a member of the Sanhedrin and yet we hear no word that he in any way spoke one word in Jesus' favour or intervened on His behalf. Joseph is the man who gave Jesus a tomb when He was dead, but who was silent when He was alive. It is one of the commonest tragedies of life that we keep our wreaths for people's graves and orations and praises until they are dead. It would be infinitely better to give them some of these flowers and some of these words of gratitude when they are still alive.

(iii) But we cannot blame Joseph overmuch, for Joseph was another of these people for whom the Cross of Jesus did what not even the life of Jesus could do. When he had seen Jesus alive he had felt His attraction, but had gone no further. But when he saw Jesus die—and he must have been present at the crucifixion—his heart was broken in love. First the centurion, then Joseph—it is an amazing thing how soon Jesus' words came true that when He was lifted up from the earth He would draw all men unto Him. (John 12 : 32.)

TELL PETER

Mark 16 : 1-8

When the Sabbath had passed, Mary of Magdala and Mary the mother of James and Salome bought spices to go and anoint His body. Very early in the morning on the first day of the week, when the sun was rising, they went to the tomb. They kept saying to each other, " Who will roll away the stone from the door of the tomb for us? " They looked up and they saw that the stone had been rolled away, for it was very large. And they went into the tomb, and they saw a young man sitting on the right side, clothed in a long, white robe. They were utterly amazed. He said to them, " Do not be amazed. You are looking for Jesus of Nazareth who was crucified. He is risen. He is not here. See ! There is the place where they laid Him. But go ! Tell His disciples and Peter, ' He goes before you into Galilee. There you will see Him as He told you '." And they went out and fled from the tomb, for fear and astonishment gripped them. And they told no one anything for they were afraid.

THERE had not been time to render the last services to the body of Jesus. The Sabbath had intervened and the women who wished to anoint the body had not been able to do so. Immediately the Sabbath had passed, as early as possible, they set out on their sad task. They were worried about one thing. Tombs had no doors. When the word door is mentioned it really means *opening*. In front of the opening there ran a groove, and in the groove a circular stone as big as a cart-wheel, and the women knew that it was quite beyond their strength to move a stone like that. But when they reached the tomb the stone was rolled away, and in it there was the messenger who gave them the unbelievable news that Jesus had risen from the dead.

One thing is certain—if Jesus had not risen from the dead we would never have heard of Him. The attitude of the women was that they had come to pay the last tribute to a dead body. The attitude of the disciples was that everything had finished in tragedy. By far the best proof of the Resurrection is the existence of the Christian Church. Nothing else could have changed sad and despairing men and women into people radiant with joy and flaming with courage. The Resurrection is the central fact of the whole

Christian faith. Because we believe in the Resurrection certain things follow.

(i) Jesus is not a figure in a book, He is a living presence. It is not enough to study the story of Jesus as we study the life of any other great historical figure. It may be that we begin that way but we must end by meeting Him.

(ii) Jesus is not a memory, He is a presence. The dearest memory fades. The Greeks had a word by which they described time which means *time which wipes all things out.* Long since, time would have wiped out the memory of Jesus unless He had been a living presence forever with us.

> " And warm, sweet, tender, even yet
>   A present help is He;
>   And faith has still its Oliver,
>   And love its Galilee."

Jesus is not someone whom we discuss, He is someone whom we meet.

(iii) That means that the Christian life is not the life of the man who *knows about* Jesus, but of the man who *knows* Jesus. There is all the difference in the world between *knowing about* a person and *knowing* a person. We *know about* Queen Elizabeth or Sir Winston Churchill or President Eisenhower, but very few of us *know* them. The greatest scholar in the world, the man who knows everything about Jesus, is less than the humblest Christian who knows Him every day.

(iv) It also means that there is an endless quality about the Christian faith. The Christian faith should never stand still. Just because our Lord is a living Lord there are new wonders and new truths waiting to be discovered all the time.

But the most precious thing in this passage is in two words which are in no other gospel. " Go," said the messenger. " Tell His disciples *and Peter*." How that message must have cheered Peter's heart when he got it! He must have been tortured with the memory of his disloyalty, and suddenly there comes a message, a special message for him. He of all the disciples is specially picked out. It is characteristic of Jesus that He thought, not at all of the wrong Peter had done Him, but altogether of the remorse that Peter was undergoing. Jesus was far more eager to comfort the penitent sinner than to punish the sin. Someone has said, " The most precious thing about Jesus is the way in which He trusts us on the field of our defeat."

THE COMMISSION OF THE CHURCH

Mark 16 : 9-20

When He had risen early on the first day of the week, He appeared first to Mary of Magdala, out of whom He had cast seven devils. She went and told the news to those who had been with Him, who were mourning and weeping. When they heard that He was alive and had been seen by her, they did not believe.

After that He appeared in another form to two of them as they walked, as they were on their way to the country. And they went away and told the news to the rest, but they did not believe it.

Later He appeared to the eleven as they were sitting at meat and rebuked them for their disbelief and the obtuseness of their minds, because they had not believed those who saw Him after He had risen. He said to them, " Go into the whole world and preach the goodness. He who believes and is baptized will be saved. He who does not believe will be condemned. These signs will accompany those who believe. By my name they will cast out devils. They will speak with new tongues. They will lift serpents, and even if they drink any deadly thing it will not hurt them. They will place their hands on the infirm and they will be well."

So the Lord Jesus, after He had spoken to them, was taken up into heaven, and sat down at the right hand of God.

They went out and preached everywhere, while the Lord worked with them, and confirmed their message by the signs that accompanied it.

As we saw in the introduction Mark's gospel really stops at verse 8. We have only to read this passage to see how different it is from the rest of the gospels, and it is in none of the great manuscripts of the gospels. This is a later summary which replaces the ending which either Mark did not live to write, or which at some time went lost.

Its great interest is the picture of the duty of the Church that it gives to us. The man who wrote this concluding section obviously believed that the Church had certain tasks committed to it by Jesus.

(i) The Church has a preaching task. It is the duty of the Church, and that means that it is the duty of every Christian, to tell the story of the good news of Jesus to those who have never heard it. The Christian duty is to be the herald of Jesus Christ.

(ii) The Church has a healing task. Here is the fact that we have seen again and again. Christianity is concerned with men's bodies as well as men's minds. Jesus wished to bring health to the body and health to the soul.

(iii) The Church was a Church of power. We need not take everything literally. We need not think that the Christian is literally to have the power to lift venomous snakes and drink poisonous liquids and take no harm. But at the back of this picturesque language there is the conviction that the Christian is filled with a power to cope with life and deal with life that others do not and cannot possess.

(iv) The Church would never be left alone to do its work. Always Christ works with it and in it and through it. The Lord of the Church is still in the Church and He is still the Lord of power.

And so the gospel finishes with the message that the Christian life is the life lived in the presence and the power of Him who was crucified and rose again.